Hossein Shahbazi

# Teaching Social Studies in Middle and Secondary Schools

# Teaching Social Studies in Middle and Secondary Schools

*Second Edition*

**PETER H. MARTORELLA**
*North Carolina State University*

Merrill,
an imprint of Prentice Hall
Upper Saddle River, New Jersey     Columbus, Ohio

**Library of Congress Cataloging-in-Publication Data**
Martorella, Peter H.
Teaching social studies in middle and secondary schools / Peter H. Martorella.—2nd ed.
p. cm.
Includes bibliographical references and index.
ISBN 0-13-442070-5
1. Social sciences—Study and teaching (Secondary)—United States.
H62.5.U5M38 1996
300'.71'273—dc20 95-31925
CIP

Editor: Bradley J. Potthoff
Production Editor: Mary Harlan
Copy Editor: Lucinda Peck
Photo Editor: Anne Vega
Design Coordinator: Julia Zonneveld Van Hook
Text Designer: Donna Chernin
Cover Designer: Proof Positive/Farrowlyne Associates, Inc.
Cover art: Don Weller/The Image Bank
Production Manager: Pamela D. Bennett
Electronic Text Management: Marilyn Wilson Phelps, Matthew Williams, Karen L. Bretz, Tracey Ward
Illustrations: Kurt Wendling

This book was set in Bookman by Prentice Hall/Merrill and was printed and bound by R.R. Donnelley & Sons Company. The cover was printed by Phoenix Color Corp.



Photo credits: Scott Cunningham/Merrill/Prentice Hall: pp. 2, 28, 51, 162, 189, 200, 252, 324, 345, 408; Barb Schwartz/Merrill/Prentice Hall: p. 71; Anne Vega/Merrill/Prentice Hall: pp. 21, 60, 90, 99, 130, 136, 232, 268, 274, 298, 308, 358, 373; Tom Watson/Merrill/Prentice Hall: pp. 217, 390.

Printed in the United States of America

10 9 8 7 6 5 4 3 2 1

ISBN: 0-13-022553-3

Prentice-Hall International (UK) Limited, *London*
Prentice-Hall of Australia Pty. Limited, *Sydney*
Prentice-Hall Canada Inc., *Toronto*
Prentice-Hall Hispanoamericana, S.A., *Mexico*
Prentice-Hall of India Private Limited, *New Delhi*
Prentice-Hall of Japan, Inc., *Tokyo*
Pearson Education Asia Pte. Ltd., *Singapore*
Editoria Prentice-Hall do Brasil, Ltda., *Rio De Janeiro*

# Preface

Many revised editions of a text are like a house with a new coat of paint. They seek to refurbish a structure with a solid foundation that has given good service but weathered a bit over time. Such revisions largely avoid structural changes and concentrate on cosmetic improvements.

Other textbook revisions include varying degrees of structural remodeling. These processes may include additions to accommodate rapid development of a field, emerging trends, or examples of effective practice. Like relocations of furniture and lighting, such revisions attempt to highlight a new focus or better accentuate salient ideas and issues.

The second edition of *Teaching Social Studies in Middle and Secondary Schools* falls within the second tradition of revisions. As with many home remodeling projects, this revision has been guided in part by the suggestions and comments of several generations of reader visitors. As part of the remodeling, a new chapter has been added to address the urgent issues surrounding how to prepare students to live in a global and culturally diverse world. Additionally, the revision has attempted to keep pace with rapid developments in emerging microprocessor-based technologies—especially multimedia applications, distance learning, cable television, and telecommunications. To this end, the chapter on technology has undergone major changes.

In addition to the earlier emphasis on constructivist themes in Chapters 5 through 8, related discussions now have been woven more extensively throughout the text. Similarly, discussions of developmental issues and implications, which formerly were organized in a single chapter, have been interspersed throughout the text at points where they have the greatest relevancy.

While discussions of enduring salient topics such as cooperative learning have been retained, others that have become prominent in recent educational discourse have been added. These include integrated curriculum, block scheduling, and authentic assessments. Included also is consideration of the emerging national standards in the areas of geography, history, civics, economics, and social studies, and the issues that surround them. Likewise, the chapter on comprehending, communicating, and remembering subject matter has been updated and expanded to incorporate recent insights from the field of reading.

In the face of many social changes over the past five years, the book has maintained its core theme: Preparing a new generation of young citizens for the world of the future is a major responsibility of social studies educators. Citizenship ends have guided and shaped the social studies curriculum since its inception. The struggle among contending ideologies over the direction of the social studies curriculum typically has occurred within the framework of competing notions of the good citizen.

Within the tradition of citizenship education, I contend that the fundamental purpose of the social studies curriculum should be to *develop reflective, competent, and concerned citizens.* In pursuit of this purpose, I argue the social studies curriculum should include a balance of matters of the *head*, the *hand*, and the *heart*.

These premises undergird all the chapters within the book. As the text unfolds, it illustrates the implications of the premises for daily social studies instruction in the middle and secondary grades.

The book is divided into three major parts. In Part I, we examine the origins and evolving state of the social studies and citizenship education across the United States. This segment provides a window into the dynamics of the profession and a feel for the ferment, controversies, and challenges that characterize social studies teaching in the middle and secondary grades. It also includes a discussion of ways to move the walls of the classroom beyond the school and incorporate the community into the social studies curriculum. This part of the book also offers ideas on how to advance the professional growth of social studies teachers.

Part II focuses on the art, science, and craft of social studies teaching against the backdrop of engaging students in knowledge construction. This part of the text draws heavily upon grounded theory, research, and practitioner wisdom in formulating instructional models, applications, and examples. Illustrations and strategies from a wide range of different social studies projects and materials developed over the past several decades are provided.

The final segment, Part III, examines approaches to analyzing and improving social studies instruction, while incorporating emerging technologies. These approaches include ways to create a positive classroom environment and provide for students with special needs through individualizing instruction. In addition, this section of the text addresses the implications of global realities and the increasing cultural diversity within our nation.

Several special features are included in the text to enhance readability and facilitate learning. Each chapter opens with a detailed outline to serve as an advance organizer. Correspondingly, at the end of each chapter, two types of activities are suggested to extend discussions: those to be done in groups and those to be done alone. In addition, a number of field-tested lessons and activities from a variety of sources have been included throughout the text. For easy reference, a list of these lessons and activities appears at the end of the Contents.

Ideally, readers will find there are many layers to the book. The initial and thickest one is designed for preservice teachers, those who are new to the field. Our primary goal is to help prepare them for their first teaching experience and a career as a professional social studies educator in either a middle or a secondary school.

Further layers of the book can be uncovered by inservice teachers through an examination of the many references embedded throughout the text. The references are a pathway to the issues, debates, and controversies that engage scholars and practitioners alike.

Although the text points to the frontiers of scholarship in my attempt to reflect the most recent insights of researchers, veteran classroom teachers, curriculum specialists, students, and critics, it does not ignore the rich legacy which the field of social studies education has inherited. It incorporates significant developments within the profession that have emerged over the past seven decades, including those from the dynamic era of the "new social studies."

As I launch this second edition, I wish to acknowledge the many and varied contributions of those who reviewed the manuscript:

- Thomas B. Goodkind, University of Connecticut
- Carl L. Harris, Sam Houston State University
- John H. Litcher, Wake Forest University

In addition, I find it necessary once more to acknowledge what the careful observer will quickly note: the imprints of John Dewey are especially heavy upon the text. Further, the seminal contributions of Alan Griffin, one of the giants within the field of social studies education, were a continual source of inspiration.

*Peter H. Martorella*

# Brief Contents

# Contents

## CHAPTER 6
## Promoting Reflective Inquiry: Developing and Applying Concepts, Generalizations, and Hypotheses 162



## CHAPTER 7
## Fostering Citizenship Competency: Developing and Applying Social, Research and Analysis, Chronology, and Spatial Skills 200

## LESSONS AND ACTIVITIES

### Middle Grades



### Secondary Grades

PART I

# The State of the Social Studies and Citizenship Education

CHAPTER 1

# Alternative Perspectives on the Social Studies and Citizenship Education

**The Contemporary Social Studies Teacher**

Certification of Social Studies Teachers
Teaching Portfolios
Teacher Performance Assessment Centers

**The Origins and Evolution of the Social Studies**

The 1916 Report of the Committee on the Social Studies
The New Social Studies
Social Studies in the 1980s and 1990s

**Alternative Definitions of the Social Studies**

A Working Definition of the Social Studies

**Citizenship Education as the Purpose of the Social Studies**

The Context of Citizenship Education

**Alternative Perspectives on a Curriculum for Effective Citizenship Education**

Examination of the Closed Areas of Society
Respect for Individual Human Dignity
Socialization and Countersocialization
Acquiring Basic Competencies
Classifying Alternative Perspectives on Citizenship Education

**The Enduring Goal of the Social Studies Curriculum: Reflective, Competent, and Concerned Citizens**

The Nature of the Effective Citizen
Social Studies as a Matter of the Head, the Hand, and the Heart
Balance in the Curriculum

*Willie Gatlin, a bear of a man-child, ambled into ninth-grade civics class and heaved into a seat at the back. Then he curled his tree-trunk legs around the front of his desk, and scowled from beneath a neon Oakland Raider's cap.*

*"Outta my face," he snarled at the student who tried to pass by in the aisle. Challenges briefly were exchanged and quickly forgotten as the room rapidly began to fill with the buzz and blur of adolescent voices and shapes.*

*Willie pulled the brim of his cap down further and closed his eyes; the questions tumbled out: Why am I here? What good will this course do me? What is social studies and civics? What does all this have to do with my life?*

*Meanwhile, at the other end of the classroom, Regina, animated and smiling, positioned herself near the front door and chalkboard. At the sound of the period bell, she opened her notebook to the section with the tab, "civics."*

*"I wonder how this course will be different from American history?" she thought. "Maybe a geography or sociology elective would be more useful. On the other hand," she wondered, "doesn't civics include current events and almost everything that is part of our lives?"*

*A new school year was underway.*

Throughout the twentieth century, social studies educators have waged a vigorous debate over the answers to Willie's and Regina's questions. Three key dimensions of the debate concern:

1. The *nature* of the social studies;
2. The *purpose* of the social studies; and
3. The *sources* of subject matter for the field.

We will examine, in turn, the context of each of these and related issues as they have been analyzed by social studies educators for over 75 years. First, however, we briefly consider what it means to be a teacher of social studies in middle and secondary schools—those that typically include grades 5 through 12—on the edge of the twenty-first century.

## THE CONTEMPORARY SOCIAL STUDIES TEACHER

Each state sets its own requirements for social studies teachers in the middle or secondary grades. Among all other subject-area teachers, social studies teachers potentially have the most diverse responsibilities in their assignments. Certification as a social studies teacher in most states permits one to teach courses in history, geography, sociology, anthropology, and psychology. It also typically authorizes one to teach economics, political science, civics, government, philosophy, consumer education, and numerous other courses with combinations of these titles.

In practice, of course, social studies teachers typically are called on to teach a small number of the possible options. For example, two teaching schedules, one from a first-year middle-school teacher and the other from an experienced secondary-school teacher are shown in Figure 1.1 (see Chapter 4 for alternative patterns of scheduling classes).

History and political science are the two disciplines that primarily are represented in the middle and secondary social studies curriculum. The social studies staff in a typical middle or secondary school likely will contain a mix of teachers who have a primary core of course work in one or more of the areas we have mentioned.

**Figure 1.1**
**Schedules of Social Studies Teachers in Middle and Secondary Schools**

**Teacher:** Susan Albright **School:** Turner Middle School

| *Period* | *Teaching Assignment* |
|---|---|
| 1 | 8th-grade American History (Team) |
| 2 | 8th-grade American History (Team) |
| 3 | Planning Period |
| 4 | 9th-grade Civics |
| 5 | Lunch Period |
| 6 | 9th-grade Civics |
| 7 | 9th-grade Civics |

**Other Assignments:** Hall duty one week each month during half of lunch period; advisor for Student Council.

**Teacher:** Jerry Koslowski **School:** Cady High School

| *Period* | *Teaching Assignment* |
|---|---|
| 1 | 10th-grade World History |
| 2 | 10th-grade World History |
| 3 | 10th-grade World History |
| 4 | Lunch Period |
| 5 | 12th-grade Problems of Democracy |
| 6 | 12th-grade Problems of Democracy |
| 7 | Planning Period |

**Other Assignments:** Bus duty in the morning one month during year; advisor for yearbook.

## Certification of Social Studies Teachers

In addition to completing a required number of courses in the social sciences and professional education, certified social studies teachers typically complete a supervised *student teaching* or *internship* experience in a middle or secondary school. States provide an *initial* or *provisional* certification upon successful completion of course work and the internship. Some states now offer separate certification authorizations for teaching in the middle grades (typically covering grades 5 or 6 though grade 9) or the secondary grades (typically grades 9 through 12). The traditional certification pattern has covered authorization for teaching in grades 7 through 12.

In recent years, educators have emphasized assessment of the quality as well as the quantity of professional training and competencies that both preservice (beginning) and inservice (experienced) teachers have acquired.

These assessment efforts typically involve some combination of standardized paper-and-pencil measures of relevant teaching and subject-matter knowledge.

## Teaching Portfolios

As part of the certification and assessment process, teachers sometimes are asked to create *portfolios* of items such as sample lesson plans, examples of student work, and videotapes of teaching. They also may include observation notes by supervisors, mentors, and cooperating teachers.

## Teacher Performance Assessment Centers

Qualitative assessments of social studies teachers may occur in a special facility known as a *teacher performance assessment center.* An example of such a center is the Assessment Development Laboratory, currently under development by the National Board for Professional Teaching Standards. Assessment centers include components such as written assessments, direct observation of practice by trained observers, documentation of performance during supervised field experiences, and assessment center exercises (Shulman, 1987).

Assessment centers represent a departure from the conventional ways of assessing teaching competency. They require candidates to come to a center where they are asked to demonstrate in simulated environments competencies related to teaching in their subject area.

For example, a social studies teacher might be given the task of planning and teaching a new lesson within a specified block of time. The teacher then would teach the lesson to a small group of students who might have been coached to play certain roles during the lesson. The same teacher also might be asked to critique a social studies textbook according to criteria provided. Whatever new models the states adopt to assess the teaching ability of social studies teachers in the future, they increasingly will focus on the quality of candidates' experiences and look to more realistic settings in which to measure competencies.

# THE ORIGINS AND EVOLUTION OF THE SOCIAL STUDIES

What are the origins of social studies? In the early history of our nation, the social studies curriculum drew heavily on the areas of history, geography, and civics. The term *social studies,* Saxe (1991, 1992) has reported, became the official term used to designate the curriculum in the late nineteenth and early twentieth century. He contended it came into use as an outgrowth of the writings of Sarah Bolton, Lady Jane Wilde, Heber Newton, and later, Thomas Jesse Jones. Saxe (1991) noted further: "From Newton and Jones we find that the initial use and sharpening of the term 'social studies' was directly tied to the utilization of social science data as a force in the improvement of human welfare" (p. 17).

Jones later served as a member of a group known as the Committee on the Social Studies. The Committee, comprised of 21 members representing different social science disciplines and different levels of professional education, had been appointed by the National Education Association in 1912. Its charge was to make recommendations concerning the reorganization of the secondary curriculum.

## The 1916 Report of the Committee on the Social Studies

The final report of the Committee, issued in 1916, has been called by Hertzberg (1981) "probably the most influential in the history of the social studies" (p. 2). One social studies educator, Engle (1976), has credited the Committee's report with setting the general direction of the field from that time forward.

The 1916 report defined the social studies as "those whose subject matter relates directly to the organization and development of human society, and to man as a member of social groups" (U.S. Bureau of Education, 1916, p. 9). It also laid out the broad aims or goals for the social studies, the cultivation of the "good citizen," a theme I will examine in detail in later chapters. In addition, the report sketched some guidelines for the curriculum and touched on a variety of other issues, including the preparation of teachers and text materials.

Although the report looked to the social sciences as the primary sources of enlightenment for the preparation of good citizens, the high ideals the report embodied clearly required a broader base of subject matter. For example, it asserted, "The social studies should cultivate a sense of membership in the 'world community,' with all the sympathies and sense of justice that this involves among the different divisions of human society" (U.S. Bureau of Education, 1916, p. 9).

**Legacy of the 1916 Report.** Among other features, the 1916 report reflected the diversity of disciplines that individuals on the Committee represented, the dominant perspective being that of history. It also reflected the emergence of the behavioral sciences and the growth of professional associations. Additionally, it represented the flowering of progressivism and the apprehension of a nation on the brink of a world war (Hertzberg, 1981). The report became the touchstone for conceptions of what the social studies curriculum should be for the next eight decades, transcending the dramatic shifts in the nation and the world over that period.

The report also gave impetus to the rise, in 1921, of the first professional organization devoted to the concerns of social studies teachers, the National Council for the Social Studies (NCSS). Sixteen years later, the NCSS would publish the first professional journal for social studies teachers, *Social Education*. More than half a century later, in 1988, it would publish a second journal devoted to the elementary grades, *Social Studies and the Young Learner*.

A major legacy of the 1916 report has been a festering debate that continues to the present concerning both the nature of the social studies and the subject's relationship to the social sciences. The first sentence of the book *Defining the Social Studies*, written in 1977, captures the flavor of contemporary debates and analyses: "The field of social studies is so caught up in ambiguity, inconsistency, and contradiction that it represents a complex educational enigma. It has also defied any final definition acceptable to all factions of the field" (Barr, Barth, & Shermis, 1977, p. 1). In exasperation, Barr, Barth, and Shermis (1977) concluded, "If the social studies is what the scholars in the field say it is, it is a schizophrenic bastard child" (p. 1).

## The New Social Studies

During the Cold War era, the Soviet Union ushered in the era of space exploration with its launching of *Sputnik* in 1957. It also initiated an intense and extensive reassessment of the American educational system. If the Soviets, then our Cold War adversaries, had beaten the United States into space, conventional wisdom said, something must be wrong with our schools and their curricula.

First, the science and mathematics, and later the foreign language curricula came under intense scrutiny. In response, the federal government sponsored a wave of reforms aimed at improving the curriculum of the schools. By the mid 1960s, the social studies also were drawn under the umbrella of reform. From that point forward through the early years of the 1970s, the social studies would witness an unprecedented period of innovation with respect to both the development of curricular materials and related teacher education efforts.

The fruits of this period became known as the "new social studies." The efforts at innovation were fueled primarily with funds from the federal government and private foundations. Ultimately, commercial publishers would underwrite the final stages of development and publication of some of the curricular products. Haas (1977), who was directly involved in the evolution of the new social studies, has written of the period, "If measured by sheer output of materials, the period 1964 to 1972 is unequaled in the history of social studies education in this country" (p. 61).

Driving the new social studies were over 50 major projects (Fenton, 1967) and scores of minor ones touching every grade level (Haas, 1977).

The projects were scattered throughout the nation in different centers. A firsthand observer of many of these projects and the director of a history project at Carnegie Mellon University, Fenton (1967), wrote of them:

> They are organized in a variety of ways: one or two professors in a university run most of them; organizations of scholars such as the American Anthropological Association administer a few; others are run by school systems, groups of schools or universities, or independent non-profit corporations . . . some projects aim to turn out a single course for a single dicipline [sic], such as a course in tenth-grade geography; others are preparing units of material—anthropology, sociology, economics—which can fit into existing course structures; still others propose to develop entire curriculum sequences or to isolate the principles upon which curricula can be built. (p. 4)

Included in the new social studies were projects for the middle and secondary grades such as:

- Man: A Course of Study (MACOS)
- The University of Minnesota Project Social Studies, K–12
- The Anthropology Curriculum Study Project
- Sociological Resources for the Social Studies
- The High School Geography Project

A sample lesson from *Sociological Resources for the Social Studies* relating to poverty is shown in Figure 1.2. The excerpted lesson is the first of a series of 12 that form a unit entitled *The Incidence and Effects of Poverty in the United States.*

Many of the projects were based on the seminal ideas in psychologist Jerome Bruner's *The Process of Education* (1960). Particularly appealing to social studies educators were Bruner's ideas concerning the structure of the disciplines and discovery modes of learning. Bruner himself was extensively involved in *MACOS*, a middle grades curriculum that integrated the disciplines of anthropology and biology to help students discover the similarities and differences between humans and animals.

**Legacy of the New Social Studies.** Despite all the concerted efforts at curricular reform, the new social studies projects collectively failed to affect significantly the scope (list of topics and courses) and sequence (order of topics and courses) patterns of the social studies curriculum across the United States (Fancett & Hawke, 1982; Haas, 1977, 1986; Massialas, 1992). By some accounts, the projects did not have any significant impact on teaching practices either (Shaver, Davis, & Hepburn, 1979; Superka, Hawke, & Morrissett, 1980).

How can we account for this? Lockwood (1985) has suggested three basic reasons why the new social studies had limited lasting effects. One

**Figure 1.2**
**Excerpt From Lesson on Poverty from the "Episodes in Social Inquiry Series"**

**Lesson 1**

DISCUSSION OF MOTIVATIONAL PICTURES AND REPORT ON QUESTIONNAIRE ABOUT POVERTY

**OBJECTIVES**

1. To stimulate interest in the subject of poverty.
2. To find out how much the class knows about poverty and what their attitudes toward the poor are.
3. To give concrete meaning to the word *poverty* and to show the diversity of its symptoms and effects.

**SUGGESTED TEACHING PROCEDURE**

At the start of this lesson, distribute the student texts and have students examine the six pictures in the text showing people in poverty.

(1) *Common elements in poverty.* After the pictures have been examined, ask the students what all the pictures have in common. Some will probably say, "They are all pictures of poor people," or "They are about poverty." But what makes them think these people are poor? What sorts of things do the poor have in common? This discussion should elicit some of the characteristics of poor people: powerlessness (e.g., children and the aged lack political and economic power), despair, hopelessness, apathy, low level of living as reflected in poor and crowded housing, inadequate diet, shabby clothes, and worn and broken furniture. It is not necessary to spend much time discussing the characteristics of poverty since these are dealt with in more detail later in the episode.

(2) *Diversity among the poor.* A more important question to ask is: How do these pictures *differ* from each other? Students will see that there is great diversity

*Note.* From Sociological Resources for the Social Studies, *Instructor's Guide for the Incidence and Effects of Poverty in the United States* (pp. 16–17), 1969, Boston: Allyn & Bacon.

reason he offered was that teachers perceived that adoption of the innovations would have required major changes in the scope and sequence of existing curricula and teaching practices. Another reason was that the reading levels of the new social studies materials were too advanced. A third reason he advanced was that students lacked the intellectual capacities required to use the materials. Massialas (1992) also has argued that the new social studies lacked a research base and that projects failed to adequately address issues such as gender and ethnicity (see also Fenton, 1991; Rossi, 1992).

**Figure 1.2 continued**

among the poor. The poor include the young and the old, people of all ethnic groups (whites, blacks, Indians, etc.), urban and rural dwellers, and people who are healthy as well as those who are disabled. One of the objectives of this lesson is to give concrete meaning to the word *poverty* and to show the diversity of its symptoms and effects.

(3) *Using pictures as data suggesting the nature of poverty.* Following the opening discussion of similarities and differences in the pictures, you may want to have the students respond to the questions asked about each picture. These questions are designed to encourage students to think about areas of poverty touched on later in the episode. Students should begin to see that poverty is more than just a shabby, run-down physical environment or unemployment or lack of money. They should be on the way to discovering that poverty is a condition that allows us to make predictions about a poor person's relationships with other people and his connection with the institutions of society. They should begin to see that income or property is a clue that tells us where we stand in relationship to other people. Students should also start to see that although we often see poverty in psychological terms (frustration, despair, apathy), these states of mind are generated by conditions in the social order.*

You will notice that there are no answers given to the questions. The questions are to develop interest in the study of poverty and to encourage student thinking about areas to be covered later. As discussion leader, you should strive to elicit as many and as full responses as possible from the students. (You will have a similar role in many of the lessons that follow.) Permit students to challenge each other's statements. But be sure to leave enough time for the tally committee chairman to report on the questionnaire administered earlier.

* None of these things should be explicitly stated (at least by the instructor) at this time. They point to an enlarged conception of poverty and its meaning that should emerge throughout the study of this episode.

There is evidence, however, that the new social studies did have some significant sporadic effects. The new social studies, for example, gave rise to a larger role for the emerging social sciences. Similarly, although the new social studies failed to shake the dominance of the textbook as the primary instrument of instruction, it did stimulate the use of commercial and teacher-made supplementary materials. Similarly, it encouraged the use of media in teaching.

Although the new social studies did not substantially loosen the grip of teacher-centered approaches, it opened the door for a more active role for students and for greater consideration of their concerns in the curriculum. It also increased the use of instructional strategies that emphasized students' inquiry in the learning process, presaging later constructivist arguments for greater engagement of students in the learning process. The new social studies also helped establish the principle that affective concerns relating to significant beliefs, attitudes, and values should have a place in social studies classes.

## Social Studies in the 1980s and 1990s

In contrast to the excitement of the new social studies era, the 1980s were a period of reaction and soul searching for the social studies. One author summed up the decade with the following metaphor:

> It can be argued that the 1980's must be the adolescent period for social studies as social studies educators, through their journals and in dialogue at national and regional meetings, are diligently seeking consensus on definition and purpose, as well as agreement on scope and sequence. At this point it is unclear how long the adolescent period will last for social studies. (Atwood, 1982, p. 10)

At the beginning of the 1990s, the social studies were awash with alternative scope and sequence curriculum proposals. These offered new options for social studies educators and text publishers to consider in modifying programs and materials. In a later chapter, we will examine in detail a cross-section of these initiatives and the forces that gave rise to them.

**National Standards for the Social Studies Curriculum.** By 1995, in addition to alternative scope and sequence models, several groups, including the NCSS, had either advanced proposals for national standards for the social studies or had projects in progress (see Chapter 13). Standards set out voluntary guidelines for what students in kindergarten through grade 12 should know and be able to do in subject areas such as civics, history, geography, and economics (U.S. Department of Education, 1994).

An illustrative standard for grades 9 through 12, related to civic ideals and practices, is provided in Figure 1.3. Chapter 13 also includes a discussion of how national standards can be related to evaluation and assessment.

As we approach the last half of the 1990s, the future is still largely uncharted for the social studies. In part, this phenomenon reflects the historic economic, political, and social upheavals the world has experienced in recent years. It also represents the shifts in our society from a national to a global perspective and the emergence of new notions of what will be required of effective citizens in an increasingly interdependent and culturally diverse world.

# ALTERNATIVE DEFINITIONS OF THE SOCIAL STUDIES

Since the term *social studies* came into use as an outgrowth of the report of the Committee on the Social Studies in 1916 (U.S. Bureau of Education,

**Figure 1.3**
**An Illustrative Performance Standard (Grades 9–12)**

**CONTENT STANDARD**—Students should be able to explain the essential characteristics of limited and unlimited governments.
**PERFORMANCE STANDARD: BASIC LEVEL**—To demonstrate a basic level of proficiency, a student's response should include the following essential characteristics of limited and unlimited government and provide at least one historical and contemporary example of each type of government.

| LIMITED GOVERNMENTS | UNLIMITED GOVERNMENTS |
|---|---|
| MAJOR CHARACTERISTICS | |
| • powers effectively restricted by constitutions and other laws, e.g.,<br>• goals of government and means used to attain them do not violate the constitution<br>• effective limits on police/court powers<br>• limits on powers of executive and legislatures<br>• laws apply to governors as well as the governed<br>• no taxation without consent of the governed | • constitutional restraints, if any, not effective, e.g.,<br>• police power not effectively limited<br>• courts controlled by executive<br>• executive not restricted by a legislature or the courts |
| HISTORICAL EXAMPLES | |
| • the United States<br>• Great Britain | • Italy under Mussolini<br>• Spain under Franco |
| CONTEMPORARY EXAMPLES | |
| • Israel<br>• Japan | • Iraq<br>• Libya |

*Note.* From *National Standards for Civics and Government* (p. 140) by Center for Civic Education, 1994, Calabasas, CA.

1916), through the era of the new social studies, and into the 1990s, many social studies educators have attempted, without success, to set out a definition of the field that would embrace all of the disparate views. Consider the following examples:

> The social studies are the social sciences simplified for pedagogical purposes. (Wesley, 1950, p. 34)

> Social studies is the integrated study of the social sciences and humanities to promote civic competence. (National Council for the Social Studies, 1993, p.3)

> The social studies are concerned exclusively with the education of citizens. In a democracy, citizenship education consists of two related but somewhat disparate parts: the first socialization, the second countersocialization. (Engle & Ochoa, 1988, p. 13)
>
> The social studies is an integration of experience and knowledge concerning human relations for the purpose of citizenship education. (Barr, Barth & Shermis, 1977, p. 69)
>
> Social studies is a basic subject of the K–12 curriculum that (1) derives its goals from the nature of citizenship in a democratic society that is closely linked to other nations and peoples of the world; (2) draws its content primarily from history, the social sciences, and, in some respects, from the humanities and science; and (3) is taught in ways that reflect an awareness of the personal, social, and cultural experiences and developmental levels of learners. (Task Force on Scope and Sequence, 1984, p. 251)

None of these definitions, nor any others proposed, have yet attracted a consensus. The diversity reflected in the definitions that have been proposed reveals that the field reflects a lively and healthy controversy about what the social studies curriculum in middle and secondary schools should be. As Lybarger (1991) has underscored: "One of the most remarkable aspects of the history of the social studies has been the ongoing debates over the nature, scope, and definition of the field" (p. 9).

### A Working Definition of the Social Studies

As a point of reference, we will use throughout the text a working definition of the social studies. It is consistent with the purpose of the social studies curriculum that we will consider later in the chapter.

The **social studies** are:

> Selected information and modes of investigation from the social sciences,
>
> Selected information from any area that relates directly to an understanding of individuals, groups, and societies and
>
> Applications of the selected information to citizenship education.

## CITIZENSHIP EDUCATION AS THE PURPOSE OF THE SOCIAL STUDIES

Many of the definitions that have been proposed over the years point toward citizenship education. To function, even nominally, all societies must engage in some form of citizenship education. Those entrusted with the formal responsibilities for the maintenance, defense, and improvement of the society depend on some degree of citizen participation so that social, political, and economic institutions can operate.

Citizenship provides individuals with a sense of identity and belonging. It also may bestow such benefits as the promise of a high standard of living, educational and health-care benefits, opportunities for self fulfillment, and a sense of belonging to a larger social group.

Early in the history of our nation, long before the rise of public schools and the social studies curriculum, citizenship education was a societal concern. During its infancy, our nation, in fashioning and maintaining a political revolution, required a new breed of citizen to guide it along the path to democracy. The historian Cremin (1980) has noted of the period:

> The goal was nothing less than a new republican individual of virtuous character, abiding patriotism, and prudent wisdom, fashioned by education into an independent yet loyal citizen. Without such individuals, the test in liberty would be short-lived at best. (p. 5)

### The Context of Citizenship Education

Citizenship education in our society occurs in many forms, both outside and inside of schools. Institutions external to the school, including those of the mass media, increasingly have assumed a larger role in the process. Advertisements, for example, on billboards and book covers urge students to serve their country in the military, to use condoms to prevent social epidemics, and to protect the environment. Political action groups, representing every shade of the political spectrum and fueled by tax exemptions, now loom as a major force in the political process.

Citizenship education within the schools also takes place in many ways, both within the formal and the "hidden" curriculum, the policies, mores, activities, rules, norms, and models that the school provides outside of the classroom. Within the classroom, civic education has several dimensions, as Oppenheim and Torney (1974) have reminded us:

> Civic education does not merely consist in the transmission of a body of *knowledge*, . . . it aims at inculcating certain shared *attitudes* and values, such as a democratic outlook, political responsibility, the ideals of tolerance and social justice, respect for authority, and so on. . . . Indeed, the cognitive content of the curriculum is frequently used in order to highlight the underlying principles and ideology; thus, information about electoral systems could be utilized in order to bring out fundamental ideas about equality and majority rule." (p. 13)

## ALTERNATIVE PERSPECTIVES ON A CURRICULUM FOR EFFECTIVE CITIZENSHIP EDUCATION

As we have noted, social studies educators generally agree that citizenship education should be the major focus of the social studies curriculum. Beyond this basic statement of agreement, however, there are disagreements regarding which specific purpose the curriculum should serve in promoting citizenship education. We will characterize these different views as alternative perspectives on citizenship education.

A related debate continues over the characteristics of the ideal or "good" citizen, who is the object of the social studies curriculum. In our discussions, we will use the term, **effective citizen,** to refer to this idealized type.

Over the past quarter century, a number of social studies educators have attempted to delineate the characteristics of effective citizenship in relation to our democratic society and the social studies curriculum. A cross section of these views shows that citizenship education should consist of these elements:

1. Examination of the closed areas of society,
2. Respect for individual human dignity,
3. Socialization and countersocialization, and
4. Acquiring basic competencies.

## Examination of the Closed Areas of Society

Perhaps one of the most influential social studies methods texts ever published is *Teaching High School Social Studies,* by Hunt and Metcalf (1955). It laid the groundwork for future social studies educators to forge links between three forces:

1. The tensions inherent in a pluralistic, democratic society,
2. The requirements of effective citizenship in such a society, and
3. The nature of the social studies curriculum.

Hunt and Metcalf (1955, 1968) asserted that the primary role of education in a democracy was to examine the competing cultural traditions that exist in our society. They argued that students should be asked to examine reflectively those areas in our culture that traditionally have been closed to scrutiny, which they called the **closed areas of society.**

Closed areas, they maintained, embraced issues related to sex, religion, race and ethnicity, economics, and politics. Closed areas vary from one period to another, Hunt and Metcalf observed, noting, for example, that sexual topics were less open to discussion at the turn of the century than they are now. Other subjects, they noted, remain constant as closed areas, such as criticism of American foreign policy in time of war.

## Respect for Individual Human Dignity

Arguing in the tradition of Hunt and Metcalf, Oliver, Shaver, and Newmann (Newmann with Oliver, 1970; Oliver & Shaver, 1966) have asserted that adherence to a fundamental criterion, respect for individual human dignity, undergirds effective citizenship. Newmann with Oliver (1970) also observed that,

> A sense of individual worth might be defined as a composite of several criteria: the ability to make choices that affect one's life (e.g., in career, religion, politics, or family relations); guarantees of physical protection of life and property; equal treatment under the law; ability to defend oneself against prosecution by the state; and others. (p. 15)

Oliver, Shaver, and Newmann advocated that students examine enduring *public issues* organized into narrative case studies. **Public issues** are problems or dilemmas about values that persist over time, for example: Should those in the northern states in the years preceding the Civil War have obeyed the fugitive slave laws?

When conflicts arose about the value of respect for human dignity, Oliver, Shaver, and Newmann urged rational consent (i.e., reflective, open discussion) as the method of conflict resolution. Where, for example, two values, such as honesty and loyalty, clashed, the conflict could be resolved by an appeal to the value of respect for human dignity.

As Oliver and Shaver (1966) have noted, arguments that favor respect for individual human dignity as a root value rest on faith rather than reason: "There is no final proof of such a value; when one pushes to the heart of human values, he must invariably end up accepting some tenet on faith. . . . We frankly accept the value of human dignity as a societal goal in a society in which the commitment is central" (p. 10).

## Socialization and Countersocialization

Engle and Ochoa (1988) also linked citizenship education to the basic ideals of democracy. They have argued that a citizenship education program should include four core components: basic knowledge, commitment to the democratic ideal, basic intellectual skills, and political skills. They consider commitment to the democratic ideal to be the most basic of the four, asserting the value judgment: "Democracy is best among social systems if one accepts the idea that respect for the worth of the individual human being is the most highly valued of all human attributes" (Engle & Ochoa, 1988, p. 23).

Specifically, Engle and Ochoa highlighted five basic dimensions of a commitment to the democratic ideal:

1. Respect for the dignity of the individual,
2. The right of individuals and groups to participate in decisions within the society as a whole,
3. The right of all citizens to be informed,

4. The existence of an open society in the sense that change and improvement are taken for granted, and
5. The exercise of individual independence from the group.

They also advocated a mix of socialization and countersocialization in the social studies curriculum. **Socialization** relates to the process of learning the customs, traditions, rules, and practices of a society. **Countersocialization,** in turn, refers to the process of learning how to be a reflective, independent, and responsible social critic of society.

## Acquiring Basic Competencies

Some proponents of citizenship education have argued that it should consist of a core of basic civic competencies that all citizens acquire. For example, the Basic Citizenship Competencies Project (Remy, 1979), took a different approach than the preceding authors to identifying the effective citizen. The project members—who had input from a national panel of political scientists, educators, and citizens—identified seven basic competencies that all Americans should have:

1. *Acquiring and Using Information:* Competence in acquiring and processing information about political situations.
2. *Assessing Involvement:* Competence in assessing one's involvement and stake in political situations, issues, decisions, and policies.
3. *Making Decisions:* Competence in making thoughtful decisions regarding group governance and problems of citizenship.
4. *Making Judgments:* Competence in developing and using standards such as justice, ethics, morality and practicality to make judgments about people, institutions, policies, and decisions.
5. *Communicating:* Competence in communicating ideas to other citizens, decision makers, leaders and officials.
6. *Cooperating:* Competence in cooperating and working with others in groups and organizations to achieve mutual goals.
7. *Promoting Interests:* Competence in working with bureaucratically organized institutions in order to promote and protect one's interests and values. (Remy, 1979, pp. 3–4)

Taking a similar approach, Hartoonian (1985) outlined a 15-point set of guidelines for developing what he characterized as **the enlightened citizen.** He defined the enlightened citizen as one "who understands his or her own political and economic responsibilities within a democratic society, who can function in the American economic system, who can relate positively with fellow citizens, and who can pursue further knowledge" (Hartoonian, 1985, p. 6).

Hartoonian's 15 points consist of helping students to:

1. Recognize the importance of their own worth.
2. Accept responsibility for their own actions.

3. Demonstrate respect for the welfare of others.
4. Place restraints on personal behavior.
5. Demonstrate respect for authority.
6. Accept responsibility for effective group activities.
7. Demonstrate receptivity to examining conflicting viewpoints.
8. Acknowledge the importance of analyzing one's views.
9. Acquire facility in rational analysis.
10. Demonstrate a commitment to the rights of each individual.
11. Use the rules and procedures for decision making.
12. Compare and contrast fundamental beliefs of our nation and those of others.
13. Appreciate the importance of working with others to solve problems.
14. Accept both leadership roles and others' leadership.
15. Accept contributions of others in groups. (p. 6)

Other advocates for civic education have incorporated citizenship competencies within a broader skeleton of goals. As an illustration, *Civitas* is a project that provides a K–12 framework for citizenship education that integrates the development of knowledge, skills, and social service (Center for Civic Education, 1991).

## Classifying Alternative Perspectives on Citizenship Education

Arguments such as those advanced by authors in the preceding section and by other social studies educators may be regarded as alternative views concerning how the social studies curriculum should contribute to citizenship education.

For over a decade, investigators Barr, Barth, and Shermis (1977) analyzed and attempted to categorize the various statements of purposes related to citizenship education that various social studies educators have advanced in the twentieth century. The authors created three categories into which they grouped all approaches to citizenship education—social studies taught as (a) *transmission of the cultural heritage*, (b) *the social sciences*, and (c) *reflective inquiry*.

I have extended their set of categories by drawing on the further analyses of Engle (1977) and Nelson and Michaelis (1980) to create two additional categories, social studies taught as *informed social criticism* and *personal development*. These five major perspectives on citizenship education and their respective emphases are summarized briefly in Figure 1.4.

These five perspectives certainly do not exhaust all of the possible classifications. Furthermore, none of the alternative categories that have been outlined completely avoids overlap among the others. Often one category, when analyzed and discussed, appears to include all other categories of purposes. Teaching social studies as social criticism, for example, may at times include teaching for reflective inquiry.

**Figure 1.4**
**Alternate Perspectives on Citizenship Education**

| *Perspective* Social studies should be taught as: | *Description* Citizenship education should consist of: |
|---|---|
| Transmission of the Cultural Heritage | Transmitting traditional knowledge and values as a framework for making decisions |
| Social Science | Mastering social science concepts, generalizations, and processes to build a knowledge base for later learning |
| Reflective Inquiry | Employing a process of thinking and learning in which knowledge is derived from what citizens need to know in order to make decisions and solve problems |
| Informed Social Criticism | Providing opportunities for an examination, critique, and revision of past traditions, existing social practices, and modes of problem solving |
| Personal Development | Developing a positive self-concept, and a strong sense of personal efficacy |

Nevertheless, it may be helpful to clarify your own views by considering some of the different emphases or dominant perspectives that each statement of purpose reflects. As you do this, you may wish to borrow elements of several categories to create a new composite category of your own.

## THE ENDURING GOAL OF THE SOCIAL STUDIES CURRICULUM: REFLECTIVE, COMPETENT, AND CONCERNED CITIZENS

Frequently, arguments over the purpose of the social studies cannot be easily categorized into one of the five perspectives shown in Figure 1.4. For example, in 1992 the NCSS (National Council, 1993) endorsed the view: "The primary purpose of social studies is to help young people develop the ability to make informed and reasoned decisions for the public good as citizens of a culturally diverse, democratic society in an interdependent world" (p. 2).

Similarly, my position does not match neatly with any one of the five perspectives, although it draws on several of them. My perspective borrows heavily from the tradition of *reflective inquiry,* as developed in the works of Dewey (1933), Engle (1977), Griffin (1992), Hullfish and Smith (1961), and Hunt and Metcalf (1968).

**The enduring goal of the social studies curriculum is to develop refective, competent, and concerned citizens.**

It also includes an emphasis on learning to be an informed and responsible social critic of society, as described by Engle and Ochoa (1988). Additionally, the perspective reflects the influence of recent research in the field of cognitive psychology that addresses how individuals construct, integrate, retrieve, and apply knowledge.

## The Nature of the Effective Citizen

The effective young citizens that such a perspective seeks to develop require a three-dimensional social studies program, one that emphasizes rationality, skillful behavior, and social consciousness. Further, such a program must cast citizen roles within the framework of a democratic society and its corresponding continuing needs for maintenance, nurturance, and renewal.

Effective citizens in this vision have an informed view of their societal birthrights and the constitutional and legal bedrock that undergird them. They also accept a corresponding commitment to contribute to the sustenance and improvement of their society and the preservation of other citizens' rights.

Such citizens are *nationalistic* because nationalism engenders a strong sense of community and identification with others who have similar characteristics, experiences, commitments, and aspirations. At the same time, effective citizens also are *global minded* because all peoples of the world are passengers on the same spaceship earth. Their destinies are inextricably intertwined.

**Reflective, Competent, and Concerned Citizens.** The young citizens who emerge from such a program, I will characterize as **reflective, competent,** and **concerned.** I propose that reflection, competence, and concern, in some form, can be nurtured at all levels, from the primary through the intermediate, middle, and secondary grades. Correspondingly, throughout the text I will argue that the basic purpose of the social studies curriculum across the grades is to develop reflective, competent, and concerned citizens.

*Reflective* individuals are critical thinkers who make decisions and solve problems on the basis of the best evidence available. *Competent* citizens possess a repertoire of skills to aid them in decision making and problem solving. *Concerned* citizens investigate their social world, address issues they identify as significant, exercise their rights, and carry out their responsibilities as members of a social community.

## Social Studies as a Matter of the Head, the Hand, and the Heart

I characterize social studies programs that seek to develop the three dimensions of the reflective, competent, and concerned citizen by way of a simple metaphor, **social studies as a matter of the head, the hand, and the heart.** The head represents reflection, the hand denotes competencies, and the heart symbolizes concern. The characteristics of the reflective, competent, and concerned citizen are summarized in Figure 1.5. Subsequent

**Figure 1.5**
**The Reflective, Competent, and Concerned Citizen**

**Social Studies as a Matter of the Head: Reflection**

The *reflective* citizen has knowledge of a body of concepts, facts, and generalizations concerning the organization, understanding, and development of individuals, groups, and societies. Also the reflective citizen can engage in hypothesis formation and testing, problem solving, and decision making.

**Social Studies as a Matter of the Hand: Competence**

The *competent* citizen has a repertoire of skills. These include social, research and analysis, chronology, and spatial skills.

**Social Studies as a Matter of the Heart: Concern**

The *concerned* citizen has an awareness of his or her rights and responsibilities in a democracy, a sense of social consciousness, and a well-grounded framework for deciding what is right and what is wrong and for acting on decisions. Additionally the concerned citizen has learned how to identify and analyze issues and to suspend judgment concerning alternative beliefs, attitudes, values, customs, and cultures.

Fred Murphy is a legend in Williamsville. Murphy taught history, but not the way most people remember it. He told stories. He brought historical figures to life, with anecdotes that revealed their foibles as well as their strengths. History is people, his students learned, and that is a lesson they will remember much longer than any date or historical fact.

Along the way—and rather painlessly—Murphy's students also learned an awful lot of history.

"There can't be many people in the country who do what Mr. Murphy does for high school students," Williamsville South parent Marjorie McNabb said. "He makes history come alive for these students, not only dramatically, but also accurately."

"I'm live and in color," Murphy explained. "I'm in show business. I've got to keep my audience. If I play to an empty house, (the students) may be here, but they're not with me...."

Murphy leaves on top. "I'd have to say he's the best teacher I've ever had," 1983 graduate Marah Searle said. "The one word for him is dynamic. He's so interested in the material, he makes it interesting for us, and we get interested in it."

Murphy's favorite historical figure is Franklin D. Roosevelt: an FDR bust in his classroom is nicknamed St. Francis I. His favorite teaching topic is the Depression, which he taught partly through personal anecdotes...

Murphy gave his students insights into the characters of historical figures such as Hamilton, Jackson, Marshall and FDR, with colorful and memorable anecdotes.

"I wanted them to know the truth about America," he said. "I know that sounds corny. I didn't make these people out to be saints. They weren't, but they were good people."

He hopes his students learned that no country was perfect. America's treatment of the Indians and slavery proved that here. "But there is no other country quite like ours," he added.

Murphy's recipe for teaching success is simple. He loves his subject—U.S. and European history and sociology—and he loves children...

His advice for would-be teachers? "If you don't like kids, don't get into the profession... The beauty of teaching is that you stay young. Young people are enthusiastic. They're not cynical yet."

From "Murphy Taught History 30 Years, Became a Legend in Williamsville," by G. Warner, in *Buffalo News* (June 12, 1985, "second front page").

chapters will provide more detailed analyses about what each of these three dimensions of the effective citizen entails and will describe how they may be developed through social studies instruction.

**The Interrelationship of the Head, the Hand, and the Heart.** Thinking, skillful action, and feeling are intertwined. No one of the three dimensions operates in isolation from the others. The head, the hand, and the heart are interrelated and work in concert.

The relationship between head, hand, and heart often is not systematic or linear. Tina, an 11th grader, may read an article about an issue—abortion on demand, for example. As a result, she begins to examine its dimensions rationally and systematically by employing her research skills. Her level of social consciousness and concern then is aroused, and she is driven to investigate further. Finally, she may be moved to social protest and action to support her position on the issue. This cycle of events, however, just as easily might have begun more dramatically as a matter of the heart had Tina experienced an unwanted pregnancy.

## Balance in the Curriculum

Social studies programs designed within this framework should offer students a balance of activities and subject matter for growth in the areas of reflection, competence, and concern. The relative amounts of attention or proportions of time paid to matters of the head or the hand or the heart may vary according to the grade level, the abilities and needs of students, and the current needs of society. The "hand," for example, may receive more weight in the social studies curriculum in the lower grades and less in later years. Some attention to all three dimensions, however, is necessary for a balanced social studies program.

## GROUP ACTIVITIES

1. Discuss your recollections of social studies when you were in the middle and secondary grades. Are they pleasant or unpleasant?
2. Refer to the issues of the last two years of the following professional journals: *The Social Studies*, *Social Education*, and *The Journal of Geography*. Read two articles that interest you from each of the journals. Be prepared to discuss the essence of the articles and the reasons they interested you.
3. Select five different individuals for an interview. Ask them to answer the question: "What are the characteristics of a good citizen?" Summarize the similarities and differences in the answers. Then, state your own answer in a sentence or two.
4. Consider the various perspectives on citizenship education discussed in this chapter and try to formulate your own position. Also, defend the position that you have taken by explaining the reasons behind your choices.
5. Discuss which of the three dimensions—the head, the heart, or the hand—should receive the most emphasis in the middle grades. Which in the secondary grades? Why?
6. Identify a specific topic that you think is likely to be a "closed area" in a 12th-grade social studies class. Why?

## INDIVIDUAL ACTIVITIES

1. After consulting the References at the end of this chapter, locate a copy or a description of a curriculum project for the middle or secondary grades that was developed during the period of the "new social studies." Note which characteristics of the project you find especially appealing and which you regard as weaknesses.

2. Locate a copy of your state's guidelines for the teaching of social studies in the middle and secondary grades. Indicate which are specific and which are general.
3. Examine two other social studies methods texts for the middle and secondary grades. What do they describe as the primary purpose of the social studies curriculum? How do they define the social studies?

## REFERENCES


Atwood, V. (1982). A historical perspective of social studies. *Journal of Thought, 17,* 7–11.

Barr, R. D., Barth, J. L., & Shermis, S. S. (1977). *Defining the social studies,* Bulletin 51. Washington, DC: National Council for the Social Studies.

Bruner, J. (1960). *The process of education.* Cambridge, MA: Harvard University Press.

Center for Civic Education. (1991). *CIVITAS: A framework for civic education.* Calabassas, CA: Author.

Cremin, L. A. (1980). *American education: The national experience, 1783–1876.* New York: Harper & Row.

Dewey, J. (1933). *How we think.* Boston: D. C. Heath.

Engle, S. H. (1976). Exploring the meaning of the social studies. In P. H. Martorella (Ed.), *Social studies strategies: Theory into practice.* New York: Harper & Row.

Engle, S. H. (1977). Comments of Shirley H. Engle. In R. D. Barr, J. L. Barth, & S. S. Shermis. *Defining the social studies,* Bulletin 51. Washington, DC: National Council for the Social Studies.

Engle, S. H., & Ochoa, A. (1988). *Education for democratic citizenship: Decision making in the social studies.* New York: Teachers College Press.

Fancett, V., & Hawke, S. (1982). Instructional practices in social studies. *The current state of social studies: A report of project SPAN.* Boulder, CO: Social Science Education Consortium.

Fenton, E. (1967). *The new social studies.* New York: Holt, Rinehart, and Winston.

Fenton, E. (1991). Reflections on the "new social studies." *The Social Studies, 82,* 84–90.

Griffin, A. F. (1992). *A philosophical approach to the subject matter preparation of teachers of history.* Dubuque, IA: National Council for the Social Studies/ Kendall Hunt.

Haas, J. D. (1977). *The era of the new social studies.* Boulder, CO: Social Science Education Consortium.

Haas, J. D. (1986). Is the social studies curriculum impervious to change? *The Social Studies, 77,* 61–65.

Hartoonian, H. M. (1985). The social studies: Foundation for citizenship education in our democratic republic. *The Social Studies, 49,* 5–8.

Hertzberg, H. (1981). *Social studies reform: 1880–1980.* Boulder, CO: Social Science Education Consortium.

Hullfish, H. G., & Smith, P. G. (1961). *Reflective thinking: The method of education.* New York: Dodd, Mead.

Hunt, M. P., & Metcalf, L. E. (1955). *Teaching high school social studies: Problems in reflective thinking and social understanding.* New York: Harper & Row.

Hunt, M. P., & Metcalf, L. E. (1968). *Teaching high school social studies: Problems in reflective thinking and social understanding* (2nd ed.). New York: Harper & Row.

Lockwood, A. L. (1985). A place for ethical reasoning in the social studies curriculum. *The Social Studies, 76,* 264–268.

Lybarger, M. B. (1991). The historiography of social studies: Retrospect, circumspect, and prospect. In J. P. Shaver (Ed.), *Handbook of research on social studies teaching and learning.* New York: Macmillan.

Massialas, B. G. (1992). The "new social studies"—retrospect and prospect. *The Social Studies, 83,* 120–124.

National Council for the Social Studies. (1993, January/February). *The social studies professional.* Washington, DC: Author.

Nelson, J. L., & Michaelis, J. V. (1980). *Secondary social studies.* Englewood Cliffs, NJ: Prentice Hall.

Newmann, F. M., with Oliver, D. W. (1970). *Clarifying public controversy: An approach to teaching social studies.* Boston: Little, Brown.

Oliver, D. W., & Shaver, J. P. (1966). *Teaching public issues in the high school.* Boston: Houghton Mifflin.

Oppenheim, A. N., & Torney, J. (1974). *The measurement of children's civic attitudes in different nations.* New York: Halsted Press.

Remy, R. C. (1979). *Handbook of basic citizenship competencies.* Alexandria, VA: Association for Supervision and Curriculum Development.

Rossi, J. A. (1992). Uniformity, diversity, and the "new social studies. *The Social Studies, 83,* 41–45.

Saxe, D. W. (1991). *Social studies in schools: A history of the early years.* Albany, NY: State University of New York Press.

Saxe, D. W. (1992). Social studies foundations. *Review of Educational Research, 62,* 259–277.

Shaver, J. P., Davis, O. L., Jr., & Hepburn, S. W. (1979). The status of social studies education: Impressions from three NSF studies. *Social Education, 39,* 150–153.

Shulman, L. S. (1987). Assessment for teaching: An initiative for the profession. *Phi Delta Kappan, 69,* 38–44.

Superka, D. P., Hawke, S., & Morrissett, I. (1980). The current and future status of the social studies. *Social Education, 40,* 362–369.

Task Force on Scope and Sequence. (1984). In search of a scope and sequence for social studies. *Social Education, 48,* 249–262.

U.S. Bureau of Education. (1916). *Report of the committee on social studies.* Washington, DC: Government Printing Office.

U.S. Department of Education. (1994). *High standards for all.* Washington, DC: Author.

Wesley, E. B. (1950). *Teaching social studies in high schools* (3rd ed.). Boston: D. C. Heath.

CHAPTER 2

# Teaching and Learning Social Studies

**Engaging Students in Constructing Knowledge**

Schemata and Prior Knowledge in Social Studies Instruction
Sources of Subject Matter for the Social Studies

**The Social Sciences as Sources of Subject Matter for the Social Studies**

Geography
History
Economics
Political Science
Anthropology
Sociology
Psychology

**Other Sources of Subject Matter for the Social Studies**

Multidisciplinary, Thematic and Interdisciplinary, and Area Studies Approaches

**The School and Community as Sources of Social Data**

Using Community Resource Persons Effectively
Field Work in the Community
Collecting Oral Histories
Conducting Surveys and Interviews
Communicating with the Community About the Social Studies Program
Alerting the Community to School Activities

**Professional Resources for the Developing Social Studies Teacher**

Organizational Resources
Professional Journals
Effective Citizenship as Professional Development

*In the fifth-period social studies class at Maple Glen Middle School, five groups of seventh graders are busily constructing large poster charts. When completed, each group's charts will be used to compare quality-of-life indicators across sets of selected Asian, African, and European nations.*

*The students are clustered around tables analyzing data and consulting reference works the teacher, Ms. Argonne, has identified. They also are examining their textbooks and recent articles culled from the library.*

*Additionally, some students periodically refer to the large wall maps at the front of the class. To gather up-to-date unpublished information, several youngsters have exchanged e-mail communications over the Internet with their peers in the various nations under investigation.*

*Ms. Argonne circulates among the groups, monitoring student activities, offering additional information, and suggesting new sources to pursue to ensure accuracy and balance. Before the students use the classroom computer to go online to collect data, she critiques the questions that students will relay over the Internet. Ms. Argonne also illustrates how to document and summarize the information gathered from various sources.*

*When the groups complete the charts, Ms. Argonne will provide them with a set of questions to use in processing the data they have collected, summarized, and recorded. She also will help the students develop generalizations concerning the social, political, and economic conditions in the nations.*

*Eventually, the groups will have an opportunity to compare and discuss their respective findings and any new questions they may have generated. They also will be able to suggest further indicators of quality of life that may be relevant to examine in the various countries.*

## ENGAGING STUDENTS IN CONSTRUCTING KNOWLEDGE

From reflective encounters with social data, such as in the activity just outlined, students construct knowledge. "In the social studies, what is presented by the teacher or in the textbook as public and agreed-upon knowledge or beliefs, is received by the student and given meaning in terms of his or her past experience and cognitive capabilities or structures" (Torney-Purta, 1991, p. 190). In this sense, knowledge does not exist independent of learning. It arises from students' interactions with texts, images, other people, and the larger culture in which they reside.

Knowledge is the fabric of social studies instruction. Woven into it are the facts, generalizations, skills, hypotheses, beliefs, attitudes, values, and theories that students and teachers construct in social studies programs. The threads from which the rich and intricate patterns are spun are concepts.

During knowledge construction, students activate both cognitive and affective processes. *Cognitive processes* refer generally to how individuals confront, encode, reflect on, transform, and store information. In turn, *affective processes* relate to the beliefs, attitudes, values, and ethical positions we bring to and derive from analyses. Both of these processes also shape the meanings we extract from information.

### Schemata and Prior Knowledge in Social Studies Instruction

Our knowledge is organized into **schemata,** which are mental structures that represent a set of related information (Howard, 1987). Schemata provide the basis for comprehending, remembering, and learning information. Schema theory posits that the form and content of all new knowledge is in some way shaped by our **prior knowledge** (i.e., existing knowledge).

We apply our individual collections of schemata to each new knowledge acquisition task. Students, for example, bring their map schemata to the study of spatial issues. They have certain expectations concerning the kinds of information a map contains and the types of questions a map can answer.

Schemata are activated when our experiences elicit them. Perkins (1986) cited the example of how the date 1492 can serve as an important cognitive peg for analysis of parallel historical events. He suggested that such key dates in American history provide a structure for placing intermediate events. In this way, dates become not merely facts but tools for collecting and remembering information.

When our prior knowledge conflicts with new data, restructuring of schemata may occur. New schemata are formed when we make comparisons with prior ones and modify them to reflect our current experiences. For example, a boy may acquire some new information relating to Indians who lived in caves. From this encounter, he then shapes a revised schema that accommodates earlier information about different Indian habitats. On the other hand, firmly embedded prior knowledge may be resistant to transformation and require skillful challenging by a teacher (Marzano, Brandt, Hughes, Jones, Presseisen, Rankin, & Suhor, 1988).

## Sources of Subject Matter for the Social Studies

The process of knowledge acquisition transcends the disciplinary boundaries established by social scientists and other scholars. Further, disciplines themselves are in a constant state of flux, with shifting parameters.

In solving a problem, a student is less likely to be concerned about whether the relevant data are drawn, let us say, from the discipline of history, than whether they contribute to a solution, whatever the source. Note, for example, the middle grades activity in Figure 2.1, which involves students in problem-solving activities that draw on geography, history, math, English, art, and current events.

In unusually harsh and strident terms, over a half century ago John Dewey (1933) attacked the dualism that isolates the concerns of scholars for their disciplines from the cognitive and affective needs of learners:

> The gullibility of specialized scholars when out of their own lines, their extravagant habits of inference and speech, their ineptness in reaching conclusions in practical matters, their egotistical engrossments in their own subjects, are extreme examples of the bad effects of severing studies completely from their ordinary connections in life. (p. 62)

Hunt and Metcalf (1968) also have argued: "Content assumes an emergent character. From the standpoint of the learner, it comes into existence

**Figure 2.1**
**Middle Grades Activity with Multidisciplinary Emphasis**

**Lesson Plan**

**Chunnel Vision**

by Jody Smothers Marcello

This lesson plan is designed for use with the May 1994 *National Geographic* article "The Light at the End of the Chunnel," by Cathy Newman. The article focuses on the social and historical implications of connecting France and Great Britain via the English Channel Tunnel—or Chunnel. For the first time in their history, the British have a "land" link to the Continent. This lesson explores the importance of the Chunnel—a name coined from "channel" and "tunnel"—through geographic and historical perspectives.

**Connection with the Curriculum**
Geography, history, math, English, current events, social studies, art

**Teaching Level:** Grades 6–8; adaptable for higher and lower grades

**Geographic Themes:** Human/Environment Interaction, Movement, Region, Location, Place

**Materials:**
May 1994 *National Geographic*
Paper and pencil for creating sketch maps
Atlases or pull-down maps of the United Kingdom, France, and Europe
Set of encyclopedias
Art supplies (see alternative activity)

**Introducing the Lesson**
To launch the lesson, have students formulate mental maps of the English Channel region. Before the students read the article, ask them to sketch a map of the region based on their mental maps, and make a list of what they know about the Channel, including its size. Then distribute photocopies of the maps in this lesson. Have students compare their sketch maps with the photocopied maps. Acquaint the students with the Channel's true location and dimensions [approximately 350 miles long and 21 to 100 miles wide]. How wide is the English Channel at the point of the Chunnel?

Now ask the students to read the *National Geographic* article. You may wish to read the article to younger students and review the illustrations with them.

**Mapping the English Channel and Its Environs**
On the inset map, ask students to identify and label the North Sea, Atlantic Ocean, English Channel, France, and Great Britain. (Great Britain is the portion of the United Kingdom that comprises England, Scotland, and Wales.) On the larger map, have them use an atlas as a reference to label the countries, the capitals, the cities and towns marked with a dot, and the Seine and Thames Rivers.

Cities and towns shown on the map:
*In Belgium:* Antwerp, Brussels, Ostend.
*In France:* Amiens, Caen, Calais, Cherbourg, Coquelles, Dieppe, Le Havre, Paris, Rouen.
*In the Netherlands:* Hoek van Holland, Rotterdam.
*In the United Kingdom:* Dover, Folkestone, Harwich, London, Newhaven, Portland, Portsmouth, Reading, Southampton.

*Note.* From "Chunnel Vision." This lesson plan, by Jody Smothers Marcello, is reprinted courtesy of the National Geographic Society. 

**Figure 2.1 continued**

Present an overview of the area, highlighting the significant regions and place-names on both sides of the Channel. As you present place-names, ask students to identify the names familiar to them from history, drama, literature, and music. In addition, ask the students to refer to an atlas to see which names from this region have been given to cars (e.g., Plymouth, Calais), cows (e.g., Jersey, Guernsey), and other objects in our culture. Discuss—or ask the students to research—the etymology of some of the place-names. Would a "Plymouth" or "Portsmouth" be found inland? Why or why not? What do the suffixes "-ton," "-ham," "-ford," "-chester," and "-shire" mean?

**English Channel History**

The English Channel has long played an integral part in England's, and subsequently Great Britain's, history. Discuss with the students why Great Britain has been called an "island fortress" and the English Channel a "moat."

Divide students into eight groups. Ask each group to research one of the events in the numbered list below. (School encyclopedias will work well for this assignment.) Each group should prepare a report for the class that focuses on the questions listed below. As part of each report, a map should be prepared and used as a visual aid when groups report orally to the class.

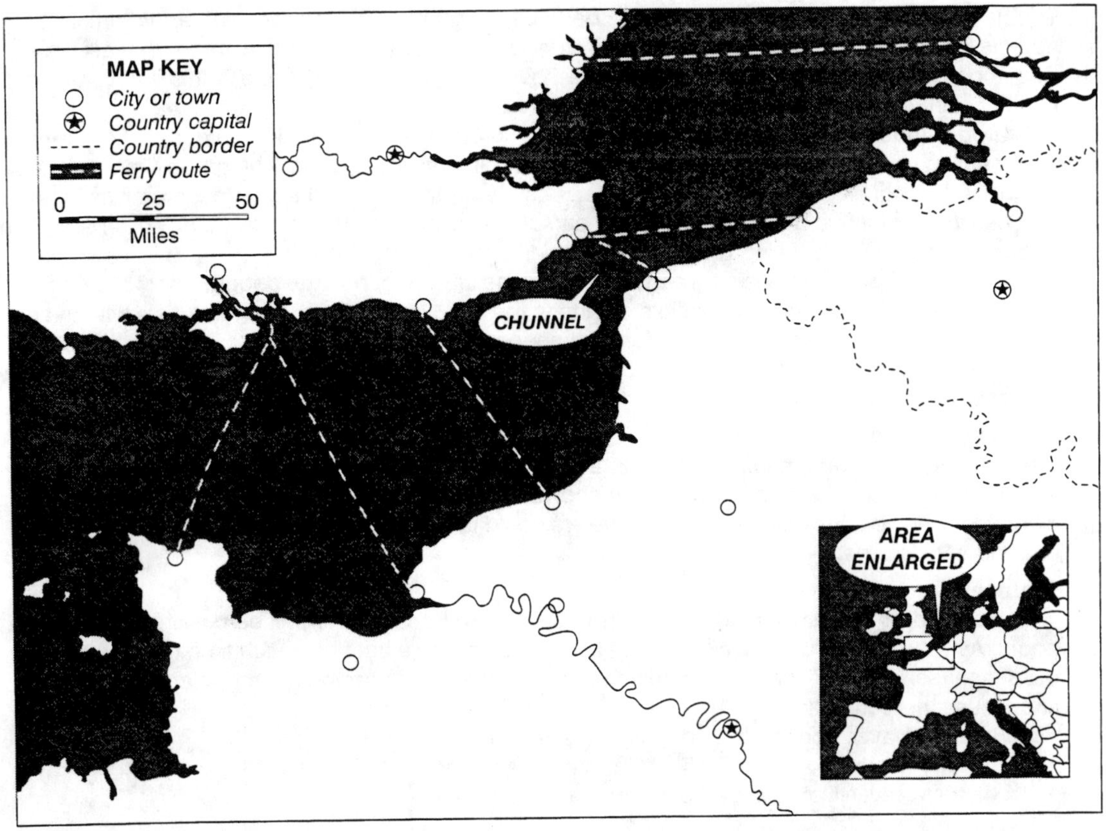

**Figure 2.1 continued**

**Historic Events**

1. First Invasion of England by the Celts: 500 B.C.
2. Roman Conquest of England: 55 B.C.–A.D. 80s
3. Germanic Invasions of England: mid–400s
4. Norman Conquest of England (Battle of Hastings): 1066
5. Hundred Years War: 1337–1453
6. Defeat of the Spanish Armada: 1588
7. D Day Invasion of Normandy: June 6, 1944
8. Completion of Chunnel: May 1994

***Research Questions***

- Who have been foes of the English?
- Did the Channel protect England? If so, how?
- What groups have been able to invade England?
- In what cases did the Channel aid an invasion, either of England or of France?
- How did this event change England, and the course of English, European, or world events?

**Alternate Activity: Chunnel Masterwork (Tapestry of Events)**

The Bayeux Tapestry, illustrated and described in an August 1966 *National Geographic* article, depicts the story of William the Conqueror's Norman Conquest of England in 1066, the last time England was invaded by an enemy. The English Channel played a large role in this event, as it did in other events both earlier and later in England's history.

Divide students into eight groups. Assign each group the task of making a panel of a "tapestry" representing one of the significant events in English history listed above. The groups may use a rectangle or a square of canvas to embroider a scene, or they may sketch onto the canvas in pencil and use tubes of fabric paint for color. They can also use large construction or craft paper and paints or computer software drawing programs.

At the heart of each panel, they should depict the important role the geography of the English Channel played in the event. If possible, examine the 1966 *National Geographic* article with the class to see the tapestry. (A picture of a portion of the tapestry appears in the *World Book Encyclopedia* entries about England and the Norman Conquest.) Discuss how this tapestry is a record of both history and geography, "a picture story for an illiterate public," and yet a masterwork of artistry.

**Chunnel Routing**

Have students use road maps of Great Britain, London, France, Paris, Belgium, and Brussels and the map included with this lesson that shows ferry crossings and the Chunnel to generate their own maps showing the specific routes travelers could take on a trip from London to Paris or London to Brussels.

**Chunnel Savings**

With the building of the Chunnel, the trip from London to Paris by train will be possible in just three hours. Ask students to use the map, with their labels, to figure out how much time the new three-hour passenger service will save over a traditional train-and-ferry trip between London and Paris. They should use this schedule:

- The train leaves London at 8:33 A.M. and arrives in Dover at 10:16 A.M.
- The ferry leaves Dover at 10:45 A.M. and arrives in Calais at 12:20 P.M.
- The train leaves Calais at 12:40 P.M. and arrives in Paris at 2:32 P.M.

**Figure 2.1 continued**

**Chunnel Flow**

The article "The Light at the End of the Chunnel" notes that only 30 percent of the round-trips through the Chunnel are expected to originate in France. Ask students to speculate on the factors that might create this uneven flow, with many more of the round-trips starting at Great Britain.

**Chunnel Math**

- The Chunnel passageway is 31 miles long. What is the average speed of a train that travels through the tunnel in the 35 minutes scheduled for the passage?
- About two years after it opens, the Chunnel is expected to carry eight million passengers a year. Given that total, how many riders will the trains carry each day?

$$\frac{8{,}000{,}000 \text{ riders}}{12 \text{ months}} = \frac{666{,}666 \text{ riders}}{1 \text{ month}}$$

$$\frac{666{,}666 \text{ riders}}{1 \text{ month}} \times \frac{1 \text{ month}}{30 \text{ days}} = \frac{22{,}222 \text{ riders}}{1 \text{ day}}$$

- Have students calculate the volume of traffic in a local area in or near the school. For example, how many students per day travel up and down your school's busiest hallway or stairwell? Ask students to study different intersections in town and count the number of cars that go by at several times during the day—as well as the number of passengers per car—and then make an estimate of the number of people passing through the intersections each day. (Students may want to compare their results with those of students in neighboring communities that may be larger or smaller than theirs). Compare the findings with the number of passengers they calculated to be traveling through the Chunnel each day.

**Chunnel Power**

The shuttle trains using the Chunnel will require 160 megawatts of electricity, equal to the peak load of a city of 250,000. Have students investigate the amount of power used by trains in the United States or by the Shinkasen, Japan's Bullet Train. Ask them to find out from their local power company the peak megawatt load of their community. (For example, 20 to 21 megawatts of power is the maximum electrical power load in the author's hometown of 8,500 people, in Alaska. This peak results from many homes being electrically heated; the peak occurs in midwinter, when heat demands are high. The maximum megawatt load may be different in other towns of similar population where a majority of homes are heated by gas, for example.)

**Chunnel Plans**

Define and discuss the concept of infrastructure. Then have students make a list of harbors, subway systems, airports, rail systems, major roads, tunnels, bridges, and ferry terminals—as well as utility facilities (for telephones, water, gas, electricity, steam, and wind or solar power)—in their local area or surrounding region. What is the importance of infrastructure?

What are some considerations for public works projects of the scope and nature of the Chunnel? Have teams of students devise a plan for the infrastructure that would support the Chunnel or a local proposed public works project. Then have the teams compare their plans and check to see whether each team has given consideration to all necessary factors.

**Figure 2.1 continued**

**Chunnel Discussion Questions**

- What factors need to be considered in building a bridge between two land masses? In digging a tunnel?
- Why did the Seikan Tunnel of Japan take 18 years to build, whereas the Chunnel took less than 7 years?
- How is the completion of the Chunnel likely to affect the ferry service lines between England and France? (See the map.)
- The English Channel is known as the world's busiest sea passage. Will the opening of the Chunnel affect this status? Why, or why not?
- Why is the Battle of Hastings (October 14, 1066) considered a battle that changed the course of history?
- How did the Battle of Hastings make England once more a part of Europe?
- How did the 1805 Battle of Trafalgar keep Great Britain safe from Napoleon, who had been planning an invasion of Great Britain since 1803?
- It has been said that the English Channel "helped shape the independent character of the British people." How might that be so?
- How has the building of the Chunnel changed the English and French landscapes, and how has it changed the human/environment interaction in the Channel region?
- Why did the French and English finally agree to the Chunnel? What specifically did former Prime Minister Thatcher and President Mitterrand see as the benefits of this project?
- How does the Chunnel serve as a symbol of the European Union?

**Extension Activities**

- Research the Channel Islands and have students make an illustrated map that characterizes the uniqueness of the islands, their political ties to Great Britain, and their location near France.
- Map other transportation links of the world, including canals (e.g., Suez Canal, Panama Canal, Main-Danube Canal) and other busy water passageways (e.g., Strait of Gilbraltar, Strait of Malacca, Strait of Hormuz, the Bosporus, Korea Strait). Have students research and discuss who controls these passageways, why they may be called choke points, and how they have played important roles in world events.
- It has taken expert swimmers an average of 12 hours to cross the English Channel. Have students make a time line of the swimmers who have crossed the Channel and record the crossing time of each one.

**References**

Allen, Bryan, "Winged Victory of *Gossamer Albatross," National Geographic*, Nov. 1979, 640–651.

Guterl, F. V., and R. Ruthen, "Chunnel Vision: An Undersea Link Between Great Britain and France," *Scientific American,* Jan. 1991, 22–26.

*National Geographic Atlas of the World,* National Geographic Society, Washington, D.C., revised sixth edition, 1992.

*National Geographic Picture Atlas of Our World,* National Geographic Society, Washington, D.C., revised 1993.

Setton, Kenneth M. "900 Years Ago: the Norman Conquest," *National Geographic,* Aug. 1966, 206–251 [out of print].

as it is needed, it does not have a life independent of his own" (pp. 281–282). In identifying subject matter for the social studies curriculum, teachers must search for information that will enable students to construct knowledge that will be useful in their current and future roles as citizens.

The subject matter that fuels functional knowledge in social studies classes must be drawn from a number of sources, including the social sciences, other disciplines, and interdisciplinary areas. It also must embrace the school and the community. Together these resources constitute a vast reservoir of information for the social studies curriculum.

## THE SOCIAL SCIENCES AS SOURCES OF SUBJECT MATTER FOR THE SOCIAL STUDIES

The academic disciplines of the social sciences are the touchstones of the social studies (Gross & Dynneson, 1991). Most social studies educators would concede that the field of social studies gains a significant portion of its identity from the disciplines of the social sciences: history, political science, geography, economics, sociology, anthropology, and psychology (see Figure 2.2). We will consider history, which arguably may be regarded as a discipline from either the humanities or the social sciences or both, as one of the social sciences throughout our discussion. Among all the social sciences, history and geography particularly have nourished the social studies curriculum throughout its history.

**Figure 2.2**
**Contributions of the Social Sciences to the Social Studies Curriculum**

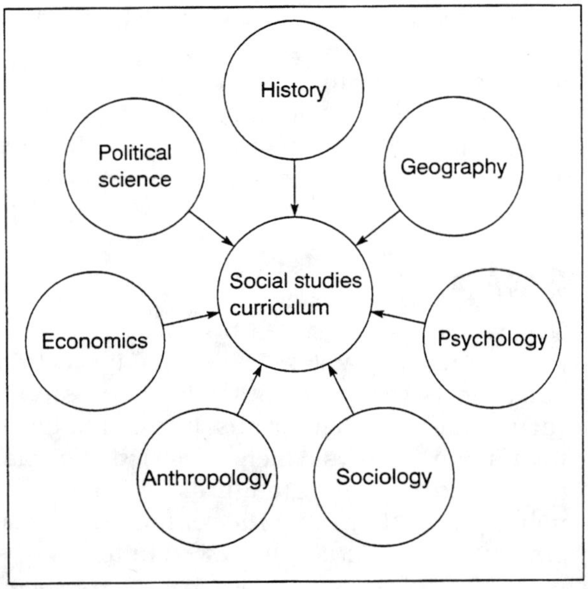

The *methods of inquiry* used in the social sciences, such as the formulation and testing of hypotheses, also are important sources of social studies subject matter. To function effectively in their daily lives, citizens often need the same skills as social scientists. Citizens, for example, must frequently locate data or verify information.

The social sciences all share many commonalities—their use of the scientific method, focus on understanding and explaining human behavior, and systematic collection and application of data. Their methods are both quantitative and qualitative. Social scientists measure phenomena and draw inferences from observations. They also share an interest in predicting patterns of behavior, a concern for verification of information, and a desire for objectivity.

Hartoonian (1994) has observed:

> Like students and citizens, scholars attempt to find out not only what happened but also why it happened, what trends can be suggested, and how humans behave in certain social settings. Some of the most important questions they consider include:
>
> - How can a topic, issue, theme, or event best be conceptualized?
> - What defines a historical period? What defines a theme? What defines an issue? What is a symbol system?
> - What constitutes primary and secondary evidence? How can evidence be evaluated and used?
> - How are cause and effect relationships handled in narrative and discourse? (pp. 2–3)

Each social science discipline, however, claims special insights and characteristics that provide its distinct identification. In the sections that follow, the nature and scope of each of the social sciences are outlined.

To examine the social science disciplines in more depth, you may wish to consult a comprehensive reference source such as the *International Encyclopedia of the Social Sciences* (17 vols.)(New York: Macmillan, 1968). Also, dictionaries such as the *Dictionary of Human Geography* can identify and define the major concepts for each of the social science disciplines.

## Geography

Geographers sometimes organize their discipline in terms of five central themes: location, place, relationships within place, movement, and region. *Location* is the description of the positions of people and places on the earth's surface in either absolute or relative terms. *Place* is seen as detailing the human or physical characteristics of places on the earth. *Relationships within place* refer to cultural and physical relationships of human settlements. The theme of *movement* describes relationships between and among places. *Region* is viewed in terms of the various ways that areas may be identified, such as governmental units, language, religious or ethnic groups, and landform characteristics.

The concept of place is central to the discipline of geography. Geographers are concerned with the location and character of places on the earth's surface. They have an abiding interest in how places affect the people who live there. Foremost is their interest in why people and things are located in particular places. They attempt to relate these places to events and explain how goods, events, and people pass from place to place. They also try to ascertain the factors that have shaped these places.

Geographers attempt to accurately describe, from many perspectives, locations on the earth's surface. They examine, for example, what is below ground in the form of rocks and mineral deposits and what is above in the form of climate.

Maps and globes of all types are geographers' basic tools. They also use census counts and data from surveys and field work. Aerial photos and remote sensing images also are tools of the geographer.

Other major concepts that are addressed by geographers include *population distribution, spatial interaction, environment,* and *boundaries.*

## History

History includes chronicles, interpretations, syntheses, explanations, and cause-effect relationships. In essence, history is always a selective representation of reality. It is one or more individual's chronicles or recollections of what occurred using his or her frame of reference. Such chronicles may be oral, visual, or written, and they may relate to oneself, others, events, nations, social groups, and the like. As chroniclers, historians are concerned with constructing a coherent, accurate, and representative narrative of phenomena over time.

Although absolute objectivity—the search for truth regardless of personal preferences or objectives—is unachievable, some historians in the tradition of Otto von Ranke regard it as their methodological goal. Others, in the spirit of James Harvey Robinson and Carl Becker, consider such a goal "history without an objective" and urge historians to state explicitly the frames of reference that they bring to their analyses.

Since it is impossible to record everything about any event or individual, and since all records are colored to some extent by our attitudes and frame of reference, history is a selective *interpretation* of what occurred. Often the task of recording and interpreting an event also involves investigating and reconciling alternative accounts and incorporating documents into a pattern of verified evidence. Hence, history is also a synthesis and explanation of many different facts concerning the past.

Historians search for the *causes* of events, as well as the *effects*. Where the relationships between the two are ambiguous, historians construct hypotheses about causal relationships. Over time, as new evidence is uncovered, hypotheses are tested and determined, tentatively, to be facts or are rejected.

In addition to the ones mentioned, major concepts that are addressed by historians include *change, the past, nationalism,* and *conflict.*

## Economics

Economics is concerned with relationships that people form to satisfy material needs. More specifically, the discipline deals with production, consumption, and exchange. The objects of these three activities are some set of goods (e.g., cars) or services (e.g., lawn cutting).

Since countries often differ in their systems for organizing production, consumption, and exchange, economists compare their applications. Economists also examine comparatively specific economic institutions within a nation, such as banks and small businesses. Similarly, they examine the international patterns of exchange or currencies and how these affect economic behavior among countries.

Within the framework of production, consumption, and exchange, economists also study, document, and attempt to predict patterns of human behavior. Other issues that they consider include job specialization, incentives, markets and prices, productivity, and benefits to be derived in relation to the costs incurred. Economists also examine the surplus or scarcity of goods and services in relationship to peoples' needs and wants.

Since these issues arise at all levels and on all scales—an international conglomerate (macro-level) or a local lawn-cutter (micro-level)—economists often examine them according to the scope of their impact. They also consider patterns of interdependence among nations and the relative levels of their imports and exports.

In addition to the ones mentioned, major concepts that are addressed by economists include *cost, division of labor, standard of living,* and *balance of payments.*

## Political Science

The discipline of political science has its roots in philosophy and history. Works such as Plato's *Republic* and Aristotle's *Politics,* for example, are used today in college classes both in philosophy and political science. Broadly speaking, political science is concerned with an analysis of power and the processes by which individuals and groups control and manage one another. Power may be applied at the governmental level through the ballot box and political parties, but it also is exercised in many social settings. Power, in some form, is exercised by all individuals throughout society.

Above all, political science is concerned with the organization and governance of nations and other social units. Political scientists, for example, are interested in political interaction among institutions and the competing demands of various groups in our society as they affect governmental institutions. They analyze how different constituencies or interest groups influence and shape public policy. Such analyses include polls of public opinion and investigations of the impact of the mass media.

At the international level, political scientists are concerned with the relationships among nations, including the ways in which cooperation and ties develop and the ways in which conflicts emerge and are resolved. Political scientists trace patterns of interdependence and compare and contrast political systems. They also examine national and international legal systems and agreements between nations.

Other major concepts that are addressed by political scientists include *rules, citizenship, justice,* and *political systems.*

## Anthropology

Closely aligned with the discipline of sociology is anthropology. Anthropologists, speaking broadly, like to say that their discipline is the study of humankind. They are interested in both the biological and the environmental determinants of human behavior. Since its scope is far ranging and the discipline has a number of major subdivisions, anthropology is perhaps the most difficult subject to define.

*Culture* is a central concept in anthropology, much like the concept of *place* in geography. Culture refers to the entire way of life of a society, especially shared ideas and language. Culture is unique to humans, and it is learned rather than inherited. The totality of how individuals use their genetic inheritance to adapt to and shape their environment makes up the major framework of what most anthropologists consider culture.

*Cultural anthropologists* are interested in how cultures evolve, change over time, and are modified through interaction with other cultures. These scholars study cultural or subcultural groups to ascertain common patterns of behavior. They live among the groups, functioning as participant observers (recording observational data). Another group of anthropologists, *archaeologists,* unearth the past through excavations (digs) of artifacts from past generations and carbon-dating techniques. *Physical anthropologists* share many interests with natural scientists such as biologists, including the study of nonhuman primates and animal fossils.

Other major concepts that are addressed by anthropologists include *enculturation, cultural diffusion, cultural change,* and *traditions.*

## Sociology

Sociology is the study of human interactions within groups. Sociologists study people in social settings, sometimes called *social systems.* They exercise wide latitude in their fields of investigation. For example, within various community settings, they examine behavior in basic social units such as the family, ethnic groupings, social classes, organizations, and clubs.

Sociologists are interested in how the basic types of institutions—for example, social, religious, economic, political, and legal institutions—affect our daily lives. Other areas that sociologists examine include how the actions of individuals in groups preserve or change social systems, such as worker behavior in plants or teacher activities in schools.

Sociologists attempt to abstract patterns from cumulative individual studies. From the study of different cases of specific social systems, such as the various families within a small community, sociologists try to derive general principles that can be applied to all similar groups.

Since the scope of sociology includes some analysis of behavior in every major institution within society, it often overlaps with the other social sciences. For example, the work of a sociologist studying the political behavior of various groups during a national election and that of a political scientist analyzing voting patterns may intersect.

Other major concepts that are addressed by sociologists include *norms, status, socialization,* and *roles.*

### Psychology

A discipline with many subdivisions, psychology focuses on understanding individual mental processes and behaviors. Modern psychology derives from earlier religious and philosophical studies into the nature of humans and the reasons for their behavior. The question of whether an individual has a free will, for example, was merely shifted into a scientific arena as psychology developed.

The boundaries of psychology are often difficult to determine, since its investigations spill over into the areas of biology, medicine, and physics, as well as into the other social sciences. Psychologists study animal as well as human behavior. Like anthropologists, they are interested in both the genetic and learned aspects of behavior. The major branches of the discipline concentrate on investigating the learning process, which psychologists regard as a major determinant of human behavior.

Psychology has both an applied and an experimental side. Some branches, such as counseling psychology, apply knowledge directly to the solution of human problems in clinical settings similar to a doctor-patient relationship. Other psychologists function in laboratory environments conducting controlled experiments, which may not have any short-term applications to human behavior.

In addition to the ones mentioned, major concepts that are addressed by psychologists include *values, self, motivation,* and *learning.*

## OTHER SOURCES OF SUBJECT MATTER FOR THE SOCIAL STUDIES

Besides the findings and methods of inquiry of the social sciences, the social studies curriculum has and will continue to draw on many other areas for data. The social studies are concerned with the application of

**Figure 2.3**
**Other Sources of the Social Studies Curriculum**

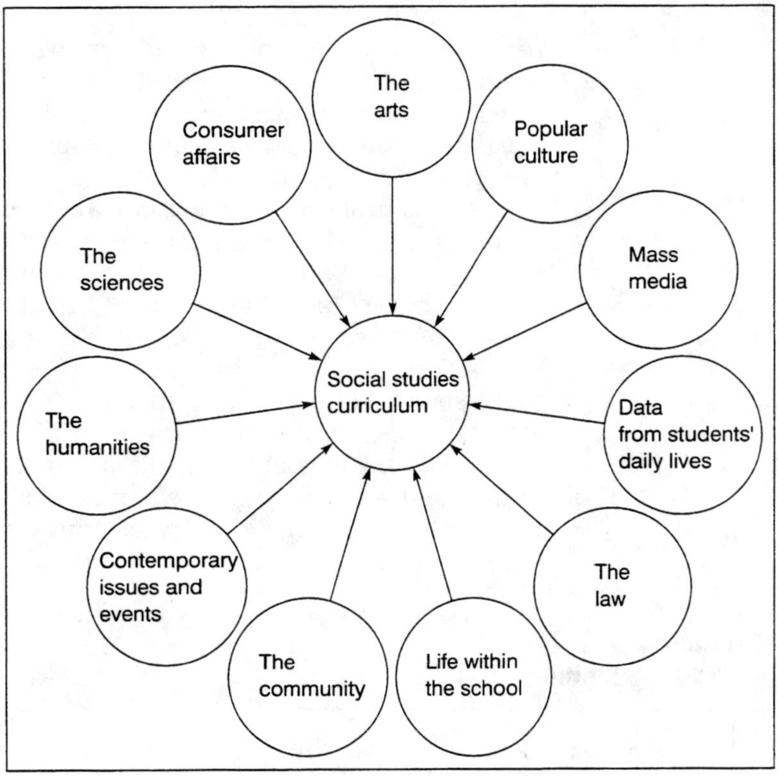


social knowledge to citizenship education. Many sources of information beyond the social sciences can aid in this task.

The arts and sciences, the law, religion, popular culture and music, data from students' daily lives, the social life within the school, and the mass media are but a sample of the possible sources of subject matter that are outside the framework of the social sciences, but which bear on the human condition (see Figure 2.3). Subject matter within these areas that relates to the organization, understanding, and development of individuals, groups, and societies has considerable relevancy for the social studies curriculum.

## Multidisciplinary, Thematic and Interdisciplinary, and Area Studies Approaches

In teaching social studies, we may draw primarily on the subject matter of a particular social science discipline, such as when we look to history for an account of the Vietnam War. On other occasions, we may wish to link the perspectives of multiple disciplines, wherein several of the social sciences are tapped to solve a problem or analyze an issue. This would be the case when we used the combined insights of economists, sociologists, anthropologists, and geographers to help explain why some areas of the United States are growing more rapidly than others.

An example of interrelating the perspectives of disciplines in media occurs in the video series for secondary students, *Geography in U.S. History* (Backler, Patrick, & Stoltman, 1992). The programs link key geographic themes (see Chapter 3) with historic contexts in addressing issues. Figure 2.4 illustrates the linkages in a sample of five of the video programs.

Although the traditional social science disciplines are important structured sources of systematically analyzed data for students' knowledge construction, insightful and creative contributions of scholars do not always fit neatly into any existing or single discipline. Many areas of study within the middle and secondary grades can be enriched by combining subject matter that is drawn from a variety of sources and related to a central theme (Jenkins & Tanner, 1992). Tackling issues such as poverty, the homeless,

**Figure 2.4**
**Program Outline**

| Program Outline | Historical Topic | Geographic Theme | Cognitive Skill |
|---|---|---|---|
| North vs. South in the Founding of the USA 1787–1796 | Establishing constitutional government; growth of political democracy | Regions | Interpreting geographic information |
| Jefferson Decides to Purchase Louisiana 1801–1813 | Territorial expansion/westward movement | Location | Organizing and presenting information |
| Clash of Cultures on the Great Plains 1865–1890 | Settlement of the frontier | Human/environment relationships | Formulating and testing generalizations |
| An Industrial Revolution in Pittsburgh 1865–1900 | Industrial development | Place | Making evaluations |
| A Nation of Immigrants: The Chinese-American Experience 1850–1990 | Immigration | Movement | Interpreting geographic information |

*Note.* From "Geography in U.S. History: A Video Project" by A. L. Backler, J. P. Patrick, and J. P. Stoltman, 1992, *The Social Studies,* p. 60.

the threat of AIDS, the destruction of the ozone layer, the imbalance of resources and wealth among nations of the world, and the nuclear arms race often involves the holistic application of disciplines such as mathematics, science, literature, and the arts.

Shapiro and Merryfield (1995) have described how one high school used interdisciplinary themes and teacher teams in a global conflict course. In addition to a social studies team member, English, science, and mathematics teachers were involved in planning units that had global connections and curricula from each discipline. For example, the biology teacher engaged students to consider genetic engineering and its global moral implications.

Similar to thematic approaches, area studies have emerged as a significant way to address important issues relating to ethnicity, peace, gender, race, and morality. An example is a program developed at Brown University organized around two questions: Why does world hunger persist in a world of plenty? and What can be done to reduce or prevent hunger now and in the future? (Kates, 1989). The program brought together, from many different disciplines in both the arts and sciences, scholars and professionals who were committed to the pursuit of answers to those questions.

## THE SCHOOL AND COMMUNITY AS SOURCES OF SOCIAL DATA

Middle and secondary level students also need to be guided in systematically using their schools and communities as laboratories for social data. To this end, they require assignments and activities that encourage them to view data from their daily life experiences as relevant and legitimate subject matter for analysis in the classroom. For example, a unit on crime might begin with students collecting objective data concerning the occurrence of crime in their own neighborhoods or communities. Similarly, the study of contemporary bureaucracies might begin with an analysis of the school as a bureaucratic system.

Beyond the classroom, every school has a rich environment at its doorstep—the community in which it resides. Probably one of the least tapped resources for social studies teaching is the wealth of material that generally is available within every community. Local organizations and businesses, for example, often will cooperate with teachers in arranging field trips, guest speakers, information, and assistance.

Also, public agencies such as police and fire departments sometimes have special programs and speakers that they will provide to schools. Other sources of speakers include colleges and universities, the Chamber of Commerce, the League of Women Voters, and museums. Individuals in the community are, likewise, generally eager to offer their assistance to local schools.

## Using Community Resource Persons Effectively

Typical uses of community resource persons include having individuals who represent different career areas report on what they do. It also includes having persons work with students as mentors (described in Chapter 12). Additionally, it may include drawing on community members who have specialized advice concerning selected topics.

The South Carolina Department of Education (1987) has prepared a useful set of general guidelines for using resource speakers. The agency's suggestions appear in Figure 2.5.

A number of practical suggestions for integrating resource speakers into the regular social studies curriculum are available (Cohen, 1988;

**Figure 2.5**
**Guide for Using Resource Speakers**

**Locating Resources**

Community/school contacts may be made through:

- Partnership coordinator in the school district
- Businesses (domestic or foreign owned)
- Local Chamber of Commerce
- College or university
- Technical education center
- Parent interest survey
- Identification of students for peer teaching
- Local speakers bureau
- School volunteer coordinator
- Clubs
- Museums

**Contacting Community Resources**

How?

- Personal contact
- Phone call
- Written request stating exact need
- Combination of the above

Through whom?

- Partnership coordinator in the school district
- Public relations or community relations executive (business)
- Survey information (parents)
- Local Chamber of Commerce

**Preparing Students**

Please remember: The purpose is to enrich and enhance, not to teach the unit!

Let the students help with preparations whenever possible. A feeling of responsibility helps ensure interest.

Students will profit from understanding of some kind of expected measurable results. They should know what will be expected from them prior to the visit. The results may take the form of one or more of the following:

- Quiz
- Puzzle or "Treasure Hunt"
- Identification list
- Report or summary
- Problem solving
- Model or project
- Interview results
- Letter

Secure materials and biographical information from the speaker in advance. These materials may include:

- Posters or brochures
- Background of speaker
- History of the company
- Photographs
- Audiovisual aids to be shown in advance

*Note.* From *Guide for Using Guest Speakers and Field Trips* (pp. 8–9) by South Carolina Department of Education, 1987, Columbia: South Carolina Department of Education. Copyright 1987 by South Carolina Department of Education.

Dunn, 1988; Fernekes, 1988; Glassman, 1988; Monti, 1988; Sapon-Shevin, 1988). Fernekes (1988) described how speakers were used in one social studies class dealing with the Vietnam War. Three veterans of the war were invited to the class and interviewed and taped separately by the whole class. Questions ranged from subjects such as daily schedules to specific duties that veterans were expected to fulfill. They also dealt with matters such as death, feelings, and fears.

Fernekes (1988) provided a model of how teachers could prepare their classes to use resource speakers effectively. He described 10 procedures that his secondary class was asked to follow before the speakers arrived:

1. In-class brainstorming of question topics.
2. Development of sample questions. . . .
3. Review of student questions by the instructor.
4. Sample interviews on a different topic with the instructor.
5. Debriefing of sample interview to assist in improvement of student questioning techniques.
6. Personal contact with informants [speakers] to explain purposes of visit and clarification of procedures for use of tape.
7. Visit of informant for taped interview.
8. Evaluation of completed interview in terms of course learning objectives.
9. Thank-you letter to the informant.
10. Copying of tape; depositing of original and copy in school library. (p. 53)

Lamm (1989) prepared her middle-school class for a speaker's visit by involving it in a related activity prior to the speaker's arrival. The speaker was a Children's Services Worker from a local social service agency who was to serve the class as a resource on the problem of child abuse. The day before the speaker arrived, the teacher gave each member of the class a card that contained one piece of information concerning a case of an abused child. Students were asked to seek out and form a group with other class members who had related information on the same child. Once the group was formed, students were to discuss what they believed would be an appropriate remedy to the case of abuse.

When the speaker arrived the following day, she spent the session comparing the group's recommendations with what the services bureau typically would do in cases similar to the ones the students considered. A follow-up discussion brought out the key issues involved in child abuse cases and detailed the scope of the problem nationally and locally.

## Field Work in the Community

In addition to bringing the community to the school to enrich lessons, students can go into the field, either independently or under teacher supervision. Armstrong and Savage (1976) have observed that the community can function as a laboratory for students that generates a "higher degree of personal commitment and enthusiasm for social studies than can be anticipated when books, films, and other simulators of reality are used" (p. 164). Some examples of community sites for field visits are museums, construction sites, factories, television studios, waterfronts, military bases, and archaeological excavations.

Social scientists refer to the process of gathering information on-site directly, rather than secondhand through texts and other such materials, as field work. **Field work** is often used to generate or test hypotheses in problem solving or to provide clear examples in concept learning.

Field work should be a pleasant change-of-pace activity for students but not merely a diversion. In field work, students act on what they observe or experience. They do this by relating their field experiences to other information they have studied or are studying, and then reflecting on the connections. It is important that a trip to the field be an *integral* part of school instruction. Excellent examples of how this can occur appear in *Ralph Nader Presents Civics for Democracy, A Journal for Teachers and Students* (Isaac, 1992). The book provides guidelines for community action projects, as well as case studies of successful student activities.

Often it may be appropriate to have individual students or small groups working in the field, either during or after school hours. These arrangements can involve mentorships, similar to the one described in Chapter 12, service activities, and a host of data collection projects.

When an entire class is to be engaged in field work during normal school hours, a great deal of teacher planning is involved to ensure a successful and productive experience. The planning process may be viewed in three stages—before the trip, during the trip, and after the trip—as the following guidelines suggest.

### *Before the Trip*

1. Establish clear and specific objectives for the trip. Plan to share these with the students either before or after the trip, as appropriate to your instructional strategy.
2. View the trip as a *means* rather than an end. Consider such issues as how time will be used and how variety in experiences will be provided.
3. Familiarize yourself with the major features of the site you will visit. Identify those features of the visit that will interest students and reflect *action* (i.e., people doing things).
4. Make a list of those features of the site you plan to discuss and emphasize during the trip. Then make some notes on the types of comments and questions you plan to raise concerning them.
5. If possible, obtain pictures, written information, slides, and the like to introduce the site to be visited. In preparing for the visit, focus on special features you wish students to notice.

6. If appropriate, provide students with a sheet of points to consider and data to collect during the visit. If students are to engage in an activity, be sure to indicate what they are expected to do and not to do.
7. Develop a checklist of all the procedural, administrative details that need to be arranged, such as confirmation of visitation date, bus plans, parental permissions, provisions for meals or snacks (if any), restroom facilities, safety precautions (if necessary), and special student dress (if needed).
8. Organize a simple file system for collecting all forms or funds required from students and parents.

*During the Trip*

9. Focus students' attention on those features of the trip that are most important. Have them observe and record, where appropriate, answers to questions such as (a) "What things did I see?" (b) "Which people did I see, and what were they doing?" (c) "How did ________ get done? (d) Which people were involved? (e) What materials were used?"
10. Where possible, engage students in some activity during the visit. Where this is not possible, raise related questions and provide relevant information.
11. Take pictures or slides or make a videotape to use in discussing important aspects of the trip during the follow-up.
12. Make brief notes on what seemed to interest and bore students and on the more important questions that were asked. Note also those points you would like to call attention to during the follow-up discussion.

*After the Trip*

13. Ask students to offer their open-ended impressions of what they learned from the trip and what they enjoyed most from it and why.
14. Review your notes from the trip and discuss important points, referring to the data students collected.
15. Review (or identify) the objectives for the trip and relate the experiences to previous learning.
16. Engage the students in additional related follow-up activities.
17. While the procedural and substantive features of the trip are still fresh in your mind, construct a file card of notes for future reference.

The activity described in Figure 2.6 offers an example of how field work can be harnessed to aid a community, as well as help students develop citizenship skills. It involves a group of high school students and the issue of deforestation in southern Florida (Isaac, 1992).

**Figure 2.6**
**Profiles of Students in Action**

**Saving What's Left of Florida**

It all started in 1987, when Charles DeVeney, a teacher at Coral Springs High School in Florida, was biking to work and saw that land near the school was slated to be cleared for development. He spoke to his outdoor education class about the rapid rate of deforestation in southern Florida and of his desire to preserve some of the area's nature for future generations. The students wanted to know what they could do.

So DeVeney and his students formed a club, called Save What's Left, to try to save the 68 acres of dense wetlands, including a large stand of cypress trees, that were to be cut down to build soccer fields. The students began by writing letters to anyone they could think of who might be able to stop the destruction of the trees.

At first, no one in the community listened. So Save What's Left students began to gather signatures on petitions to protest the development. Standing on the sidewalk in front of their school, they held signs asking drivers passing by in their cars to stop to sign the students' petition. The response was so overwhelming that on the second day of petitioning, the highway patrol had to direct traffic. Save What's Left eventually gathered 3,500 signatures from community residents concerned about the rapid rate of development....

The students spoke at city and county council meetings and gathered petitions to convince the City and County Commissions to ask residents to vote to buy the land. After two years, the issue was put on the ballot for the voters to decide. In March of 1989, Broward County voters approved a $75 million bond issue to buy the 68 acres of Coral Springs trees as well as 13 other sites in the county. The 68 acres turned out to be the largest cypress tree stand left in Broward County. County Commissioner John Hart said, "It was because of people like these kids in Save What's Left that this got done."

The city of Coral Springs and Save What's Left have since begun a project to completely restore the land over the next few years. Eventually it will be used as an outdoor classroom in which to teach environmental appreciation and to inspire other environmentalists to use their power to "save what's left."

*Note.* From *Ralph Nader Presents: Civics for Democracy: A Journey for Teachers and Students* by K. Isaac, 1992, Washington, D.C.: Essential Books.

## Collecting Oral Histories

A data collection project that lends itself well to individual and small group field work is recording oral histories (Mehaffy, Sitton, Davis, Jr., 1979). An **oral history** may be defined as any record of "reminiscences about which the narrator can speak from first-hand knowledge" (Baum, 1977, p. 1). Although, the emphasis in oral histories is on the spoken word, they may include both audio and video data. A videotape, "The Oral Historian's Work," by Edward Ives, available from the Southern Oral History Project at the University of North Carolina (919/962-8076), provides a model of how an oral history can be taken.

As field work, recording oral histories provides students with a sense of personal engagement in a stream of events (Totten, 1989). The activity

**Collecting oral histories is one way to extend social studies learning beyond the school.**

also helps to tie specific events and the larger sweep of history to a real person who was affected by them. Further, when the narrator is a local person, the history may help to tie the local community into the national history being examined in the classroom.

**Procedures for Collecting Oral Histories.** Numerous collections of rich oral histories already exist across the United States (see Smith, 1988). They cover a wide array of topics and themes, such as female homesteaders (see Jones-Eddy, 1992; Zimmerman, 1981). A particularly extensive collection can be found at the John F. Kennedy Library at the University of Massachusetts in Boston. *The Black Women Oral History Project* at Radcliffe College is an example of a smaller collection.

In field work, however, the emphasis is on students *recording* oral histories. Totten (1989) suggested that a teacher introduce students to the procedures involved in recording oral histories by having them observe the teacher conduct one in class. He recommended that prior to the recording, students be involved in developing the set of questions to be asked.

Foci for oral histories include themes, events, issues, recollections of individuals, periods and places, and biographies. Each focus requires different types of questions to bring out relevant data. Zimmerman (1981), for example, recommended detailed and open-ended questioning procedures for collecting oral biographies that included items such as:

- What have been the major accomplishments in your life?
- What have been the biggest problems, mistakes, or adversities in your life?

## Conducting Surveys and Interviews

Closely related to oral interviews are *surveys* and *interviews*. These techniques also allow students to transform the school and community into a laboratory for gathering social data. Surveys and interviews can help answer questions such as:

- What do you think is the most important invention of the past 100 years, and why? (Downs, 1993, p. 104; see Figure 2.7 for sample activity).
- How do people on my block feel about the idea of raising taxes to create a new park in the community?

## Communicating with the Community About the Social Studies Program

"Whatever happened to history and geography?" someone in the school community is likely to ask. "Why don't the kids know all of the names of the states and capitals anymore?" another may wonder.

Since many aspects of the social studies program that students in the middle and secondary grades study today will differ considerably from the programs their parents and other members of the community have experienced, teachers should anticipate community questions such as those mentioned in the preceding paragraph. When the school curriculum does not reflect people's recollections of their own school experiences, it is not unusual to find that they are puzzled or apprehensive about the changes.

One of the important roles that a contemporary social studies teacher plays is communicating with parents and parent surrogates about students' progress in class and the nature of the social studies program. As members of the school community as a whole have become increasingly involved with the schools, they too wish to be well informed.

The net effect is that teachers need to interact on an ongoing basis with various sectors of the community to better achieve their classroom objectives and promote the welfare of their students. This process often involves publicizing the activities and goals of the school and the social studies program and preparing informational materials and programs. It also may include engaging in public dialogue and inviting parents and others to aid and observe in classrooms and examine curriculum materials and policy statements of the school. Additionally, it may involve soliciting

**Figure 2.7**
**Using Survey and Interview Techniques**

**Student Surveys**
After a unit on the industrial revolution and inventions, I sent every student home with a neon yellow sheet of paper with the question: What do you think is the most important invention of the past 100 years, and why? Students had brainstormed aloud in class and had come up with inventions such as plastic, microwaves, vaccinations, rocket engines, television, and a few inventions such as the telephone, which is actually slightly older than one hundred years.

For this assignment, students asked the survey question of a parent, a teacher, and a friend who did not attend the school. Students were instructed to record and paraphrase respondents' answers and to return the survey within one week....

My seventh graders liked the assignment because it was easily achievable, involved outside interaction, and stimulated their thinking. We tabulated the results from all six of my classes and found that the most frequently given response was "vaccinations," followed closely by "the electric light bulb."

For a school-wide project, several teachers might poll their classes and compare responses across classes or grade levels. Other possible survey questions for students to field test include:

1. What would you most like to see invented that has not been invented yet, and why?
2. If you could travel back in time to any year or period in history, what would it be, and why?
3. Which historical figure would you like to be, and why?
4. If you could invite any historical figure to dinner, who would it be, and why?
5. If you could have been the first person to discover something or some place, what would it be, and why?

Teachers might also introduce students to the notion of Delphic polling, in which they show survey responses to participants, and then ask new questions incorporating the first survey responses. This involves the theory that people are usually influenced by others' responses. For example, students tell participants that in the first survey, 60 percent of respondents wanted to be George Washington, 30 percent Abe Lincoln, and 10 percent Betsy Ross. The participants then rank their choices, and a new perspective is added to the primary study. Even younger students can handle comparative data when the concept is clearly explained to them. Moreover, they are taking a hands-on approach to public opinion and survey methods.

*Note.* From "Getting Parents and Students Involved: Using Survey and Interview Techniques" by J.R. Downs, 1993, *The Social Studies,* p. 104.

parents and surrogates to cooperate in encouraging students to work toward program objectives and to maintain appropriate standards of conduct in the classroom.

## Alerting the Community to School Activities

Local school board meetings provide one forum to publicize school and classroom activities. In smaller communities where board agendas are not overfilled, there are often opportunities for students, as well as teachers, to participate in programs. At a minimum, it may be possible for a teacher to briefly publicize some special classroom activity or project in which community members might be interested.

Some social studies teachers use the local newspaper as a vehicle to reach out to the community. In some cases, students themselves have been encouraged to contribute articles, even on a regular basis, reporting on matters such as school life, student achievements, academic programs, emerging issues, and important events. In other cases, teachers and administrators regularly contact the local press to publicize school matters that they feel are important to share with the community.

Events such as "Back to School Night" are also an important way of both involving parents and surrogates in the life of the school and communicating the nature of their youngster's educational program. It is especially important that new teachers develop a well-thought-out program for such occasions, since it is rare that they will have an opportunity to communicate directly with parents and community members. The impressions of the teachers, classroom, and school that individuals receive during the event often stay with them throughout the year.

Some of the types of activities that teachers have used for such meetings are:

1. Showing slides of typical classroom scenes or activities or special class events.
2. Providing an overview through charts and transparencies of what the year's social studies work will be, along with a question-and-answer period.
3. Having members of one or more classes report on different phases of the social studies program.
4. Involving parents themselves in some sample activities similar to the ones that the students have done in class.
5. Collecting questions from parents in advance of the night and organizing discussions around them.
6. Introducing and explaining new programs, materials, units, activities, or procedures.

## PROFESSIONAL RESOURCES FOR THE DEVELOPING SOCIAL STUDIES TEACHER

Today's social studies teacher in the middle and secondary grades has access to a wealth of sources for professional development. Not the least of these is the extensive network across the United States of colleges and universities; teacher centers; local, state, and national professional organizations; and various governmental agencies.

Teachers should identify those resources that will enable them to grow as professionals and enrich their instruction. This process includes locating individuals, agencies, centers, and organizations that help keep teachers abreast of new developments, issues, and trends within their field.

## Organizational Resources

To aid them in their search, teachers can look especially to professional organizations that focus exclusively on the social studies. The following list identifies some major institutions that meet this criterion:

American Anthropological Association
1703 New Hampshire Avenue, NW
Washington, DC 20009

American Bar Association
750 N. Lake Shore Drive
Chicago, IL 60611

American Economic Association
1313 21st Avenue South, Suite 809
Nashville, TN 37212

American Historical Association
400 A Street, SE
Washington, DC 20003

American Political Science Association
1527 New Hampshire Avenue, NW
Washington, DC 20036

American Psychological Association
1200 17th Street, NW
Washington, DC 20036

American Sociological Association
1722 N Street, NW
Washington, DC 20036

Association of American Geographers
1700 Sixteenth Street, NW
Washington, DC 20009

Educational Resources Information Center (ERIC)
Clearinghouse for Social Studies/Social Science Education
Indiana University
2805 E. 10th Street
Bloomington, IN 47408-2698

Joint Council on Economic Education
432 Park Avenue South
New York, NY 10016

National Council for Geographic Education
Department of Geography and Regional Planning
Indiana University of Pennsylvania
Indiana, PA 15705

National Council for the Social Studies
3501 Newark Street, NW
Washington, DC 20016

Organization of American Historians
112 N. Bryan Street
Bloomington, IN 47408

These organizations produce a number of materials, including guidelines and policy statements, such as the ones that have been referenced through the text. Their periodical publications include newsletters and journals. They also sponsor annual regional and national conferences for teachers of social studies on topics covering a range of issues in the field.

Some of these organizations also represent the interests of social studies teachers before state and federal legislative bodies. The National Council for the Social Studies (NCSS) and the National Council for Geographic Education (NCGE) also elect representatives from their membership to serve as officers and committee members. This provides classroom teachers with an opportunity to participate in establishing policies and practices for the organizations.

In addition to these national organizations, affiliate units in many states provide similar services. There also are regional social studies organizations that cover several states. The national organizations listed can provide information on the affiliates.

## Professional Journals

A number of specialized professional periodicals are available for social studies teachers. Some of the periodicals are sponsored by the organizations cited. They include:

- *The History Teacher*
- *Journal of Economic Education*
- *Journal of Geography*
- *Social Education*
- *The Social Studies*

- *Teaching Political Science*
- *Teaching Sociology*

## Effective Citizenship as Professional Development

Due to the unique relationship of the social studies to citizenship education, social studies teachers carry a special professional responsibility. If they are to promote with any credibility the development of reflective, competent, and concerned citizens, they must reflect, in their own patterns of development, some of the same citizenship qualities that they espouse for students. In this arena, professional and personal development merge.

Each individual professional must determine what is required to fulfill this responsibility. However, Engle and Ochoa (1988) indirectly provided a starting point for introspection. They laid out six questions that they suggested might be used to survey students who had graduated as a way of inferring the impact of the social studies curriculum on their lives. Social studies teachers, by turning the questions on themselves, thus have a rudimentary initial instrument of self-analysis to gauge the stage of their citizenship development.

- Do you keep up with community and national issues?
- Are you active in community affairs?
- Do you subscribe to news magazines?
- Are you registered to vote?
- Did you vote in the last election?
- Have you followed current global and political issues such as protectionism, the national debt?
- Do you belong to any civic groups? (Engle & Ochoa, 1988, p. 191)

## GROUP ACTIVITIES

1. Which of the social sciences do you think should receive the most emphasis in the middle grades? In the secondary grades? What are the reasons for your answers?
2. In your own local community, make a list of the community resources on which a social studies teacher could draw. Compare your list with those of others in the group.
3. Refer to the discussion that illustrates how perspectives from each of the social sciences can be incorporated into the curriculum. Pick a grade level, 5 through 12, and a topic and discuss the various social science perspectives that you feel would be appropriate to include.
4. Compare the certification requirements for middle grades and secondary social studies teachers in your or another state. What changes, if any, would you recommend? Why?

## INDIVIDUAL ACTIVITIES

1. Consult the *International Encyclopedia of the Social Sciences* (17 vols.). (New York: Macmillan, 1968). Summarize the definition provided for each of the social sciences.
2. Besides those listed in the chapter, develop a list of 10 additional concepts related to each of the social sciences.
3. Obtain a copy of a brochure that explains the structure of a basal social studies program for the middle grades. Note the extent to which the series of texts incorporates elements of each of the social sciences. Also, identify any other disciplines that are represented in the texts.
4. Write to each of the organizations listed in this chapter to obtain information concerning their services, materials, and conferences.
5. In addition to those included in the chapter, identify professional journals that you think would be especially useful for middle grades and secondary teachers.
6. Identify some of the resources available in your local community that could be used in social studies classes for the middle and the secondary grades.

## REFERENCES

Armstrong, D. A., & Savage, Jr., T. V. (1976). A framework for utilizing the community for social learning in grades 4 to 6. *Social Education, 40,* 164–167.

Backler, A. L., Patrick, J. P., & Stoltman, J. P. (1992). Geography in U.S. history: A video project. *The Social Studies,* 58–63.

Baum, W. K. (1977). *Oral history for the local historical society.* Nashville, TN: American Association for State and Local History.

Cohen, S. (1988). Vietnam in the classroom. *Social Education, 52,* 47–48.

Dewey, J. (1933). *How we think.* Boston: D. C. Heath.

Downs, J. R. (1993). Getting parents and students involved: Using survey and interview techniques. *The Social Studies,* 104–106.

Dunn, J. P. (1988). Teaching teachers to teach the Vietnam War. *Social Education, 52,* 37–38.

Engle, S., & Ochoa, A. (1988). *Education for democratic citizenship: Decision making in the social studies.* New York: Teachers College Press.

Fernekes, W. R. (1988). Student inquiries about the Vietnam War. *Social Education, 52,* 53–54.

Glassman, J. (1988). Teaching students and ourselves about the Vietnam War. *Social Education, 52,* 35–36.

Gross, R. E., & Dynneson, T. (Eds.). (1991). *Social science perspectives on citizenship education.* New York: Teachers College Press.

Hartoonian, M. J. (1994). *The knowledge connection.* Madison, WI: Wisconsin Department of Public Instruction.

Howard, R. W. (1987). *Concepts and schemata: An introduction.* Philadelphia: Cassell.
Hunt, M. P., & Metcalf, L. E. (1968). *Teaching high school social studies: Problems in reflective thinking and social understanding* (2nd ed.). New York: Harper & Row.
Isaac, K. (1992). *Ralph Nader presents: Civics for democracy: A journey for teachers and students.* Washington, DC: Essential Books.
Jenkins, J. M., & Tanner, D. L. (Eds.). (1992). *Restructuring an interdisciplinary curriculum.* Reston, VA: National Association of Secondary School Principals.
Jones, E. J. (1992). *Homesteading women: An oral history of Colorado, 1890–1950.* New York: Twayne.
Kates, R. W. (1989, May 17). The great questions of science and society do not fit neatly into single disciplines. *The Chronicle of Higher Education,* p. B1, B3.
Lamm, L. (1989). *Facilitating learning through the effective use of resource persons in the classroom.* Unpublished manuscript. North Carolina State University, Department of Curriculum and Instruction, Raleigh.
Marzano, R. J., Brandt, R. S., Hughes, C. S., Jones, B. F., Presseisen, B. Z., Rankin, S. C., & Suhor, C. (1988). *Dimensions of thinking: A framework for curriculum and instruction.* Alexandria, VA: Association for Supervision and Curriculum Development.
Mehaffy, G. L., Sitton, T., & Davis, O. L., Jr. (1979). *Oral history in the classroom.* How to do it series. Washington, DC: National Council for the Social Studies.
Monti, J. (1988). Guest speaker programs bring community members to school. *NASSP Bulletin, 72,* 113.
Perkins, D. L. (1986). *Knowledge as design.* Hillsdale, NJ: Erlbaum.
Sapon-Shevin, M. (1988). A mini-course for junior high school students. *Social Education, 52,* 272–275.
Shapiro, S., & Merryfield, M. M. (1995). A case study of unit planning in the context of school reform. In M. M. Merryfield & R. C. Remy (Eds.), *Teaching about international conflict and peace* (pp. 41–124). Albany, NY: SUNY Press.
Smith, A. (1988). *Directory of oral history collections.* New York: Onyx Press.
South Carolina Department of Education. (1987). *Guide for using guest speakers and field trips.* Columbia, SC: Department of Education.
Torney-Purta, J. (1991). Schema theory and cognitive psychology: Implications for social studies. *Theory and Research in Social Education, 19,* 189–210.
Totten, S. (1989). Using oral histories to address social issues in the classroom. *Social Education, 53,* 114–116.
Zimmerman, W. (1981). *How to tape instant oral biographies.* New York: Guarionex Press.

CHAPTER 3

# Alternative Scope and Sequence Patterns in the Social Studies

*Suppose that you randomly chose 10 states from across the United States and then selected one city from each. From each city, you identified one school and one eighth-grade social studies class.*

*What would you expect the curriculum in each class to be?*

*What criteria would you surmise were used to establish the curriculum?*

*Who or which agency has the primary responsibility for determining what students in these classes will study?*

*The answers to these questions are rooted in our history and constitutional framework. Since the framers of the Constitution rejected a national system of education, the matter of schools and curriculum fell to the individual states. States, in turn, often granted considerable authority in these matters to local governments.*

*Consequently, we have no national control of curriculum. Rather there exists a collection of thousands of local school districts and governing boards, each with varying degrees of autonomy over its social studies curriculum.*

## EXISTING SOCIAL STUDIES SCOPE AND SEQUENCE PATTERNS

Each state varies with respect to the degree of control it exercises over the curriculum, including the **scope and sequence** patterns that local school districts may adopt. **Scope** refers to the topics that are included in the curriculum, and **sequence** to the order in which they appear (see Joyce, Little, & Wronski, 1991).

Even though local school districts are subject to general guidelines and standards for the social studies curriculum established by each state, the district often has considerable freedom in developing its social studies program. This means that the potential for variety in the social studies curriculum scope and sequence patterns across the United States is great.

However, although the principle of local control holds out the promise of diversity in curriculum offerings, the reality is that there is considerable homogeneity in the social studies programs in grades K through 12 across the 50 states. Typically, the pattern remains as follows (Superka, Hawke, & Morrissett, 1980):

| | |
|---|---|
| K–Grade 1 | Self, Family, School |
| Grade 2 | Neighborhoods |
| Grade 3 | Communities |
| Grade 4 | State history, geographic regions |
| Grade 5 | United States history, culture, and geography |
| Grade 6 | World cultures, history, and geography |
| Grade 7 | World cultures, history, and geography |
| Grade 8 | American history |
| Grade 9 | Civics |
| Grade 10 | World history |
| Grade 11 | American history |
| Grade 12 | American government |

## The Curriculum Pattern in the Elementary Grades

The existing organizational pattern of the social studies curriculum in grades K through 6 follows what has been characterized by Hanna (1963) as the **expanding communities approach.** This approach, which has dominated the elementary curriculum for several decades, is based on the notion that a student will be introduced each year of school to an increasingly expanding social environment, moving from examining the self and the family in grades K through 1 to the world at large in grade 6. Hanna's model also identified nine categories of basic human activities that should be addressed each year of the social studies curriculum: expressing, producing, transporting, communicating, educating, recreating, protecting, governing, and creating (Powers, 1986).

## The Curriculum Pattern in the Middle and Secondary Grades

The long-term impact of the 1916 report of the Committee on Social Studies (see Chapter 1) ironically proved to be pervasive and enduring, extending into the 1990s. Note the close similarities between the typical national pattern described in the preceding section and the general recommendations in the 1916 report of the Committee on Social Studies for grades 7 through 12.

*Recommendations of the Committee on Social Studies*

| | |
|---|---|
| Grades 7–9 | Geography, European history, American history, Civics |
| Grade 10 | European history |
| Grade 11 | American history |
| Grade 12 | Problems of democracy |

Contrary to the intent of the committee, its report became a paradigm of what the scope and sequence of courses in the curriculum should be. The committee itself had refrained from offering detailed outlines of courses. It believed that the selection of topics and the organization of subject matter should be determined by the needs of each community.

A further irony spawned by the report was that its recommendations were often viewed as being literal, timeless, and universal, applicable in all particulars to all generations and communities. The committee's intent, however, had been to sketch only general principles on which different schools could build their curricula in concert with the changing character of each time period, community, and group of students.

The 1916 Committee constructed its recommendations in the context of a vastly different school population than the one that exists today. It saw its immediate task as planning a social studies curriculum that emphasized citizenship education for a nation in which the majority of students completed their education without entering high school. Such a short period of education meant that all of the essential elements in the curriculum needed to be provided before the 10th grade.

## The Dominance of Traditional Scope and Sequence Patterns

Why has the dominant national scope and sequence pattern for the social studies curriculum endured so long? A major part of the answer lies perhaps in several factors that are interrelated: *tradition, accrediting agencies and professional organizations, preservice teacher education programs,* and *patterns of textbook selection and adoption.*

The weight of tradition bears down heavily on those who would challenge the conventional scope and sequence of the social studies curriculum. Parents and community members tend to encourage preservation of the status quo. Teachers themselves are often more comfortable with the known than the unknown.

Moreover, tradition influences the norms for accrediting agencies that examine the quality of school districts across the country. It is also an important consideration for national organizations, such as the National

Council for the Social Studies (NCSS) and the National Council for Geographic Education (NCGE), which provide curricular guidelines for programs. These organizations represent thousands of social studies teachers across the United States and Canada.

Tradition also establishes some of the basic goals for preservice teacher education programs that seek to prepare teachers for existing conditions in schools, as well as for the future. Often in such programs the emphasis is on socialization of new teachers into the present curriculum rather than on consideration of alternatives. Correspondingly, the subject matter background of middle and secondary grades preservice teachers frequently has been shaped to best prepare them for the dominant scope and sequence pattern rather than for the consideration and development of alternatives. This pattern of preparation also typically stresses traditional disciplines, such as history, and deemphasizes or ignores the newer social science disciplines and interdisciplinary studies.

## BASAL TEXTBOOKS AND THE SOCIAL STUDIES CURRICULUM

Perhaps the most significant factor that influences the standardization of the scope and sequence pattern of the social studies curriculum, however, is the system of selecting and adopting **basal textbooks** that schools employ. The impact of textbooks on perpetuating the scope and sequence of the curriculum has been profound. The best research evidence available suggests that, in social studies, basal texts are used extensively and more often than other types of curricular materials (Shaver, Davis, & Hepburn, 1979).

A basal textbook represents the major elements that the author or publisher regards as basic to provide an appropriate social studies curriculum for a particular grade or subject. Generally publishers of basal social studies texts build them around some model or notion of scope and sequence related to the grades for which the texts have been developed. Thus, adopting a basal text, in effect, means adopting the curricular pattern on which it is based.

### Use of Basal Texts in the Social Studies

Teachers and schools often build on a basal text, using commercially produced and teacher-made supplementary materials, newspapers, articles, and trade books. Some teachers use no textbook at all, instead creating their own programs by following general scope and sequence guidelines. Other teachers use texts primarily as reference books. Still other teachers use a *multitext* approach, picking those units or chapters from each textbook that best meet their specific curricular needs. As we will consider in

Chapter 10, textbook publishers may also offer supplementary books, such as adolescent literature, correlated to the basal text.

Surprisingly perhaps, basal textbook series available from major publishers display striking similarities with respect to the scope and sequence models they incorporate. Contrary to the canons of capitalism that we might expect to operate when major corporations are competing for large profits from widely distributed heterogeneous customers, basal texts reflect more homogeneity than diversity. Although individual basal texts differ considerably in the types of activities, pictorial content, and specific objectives they include, in the main they reflect the *dominant* curricular pattern that we considered earlier.

Mehlinger (1992, p. 149) has noted: "textbook publishers mainly reinforce the status quo. They exist to provide school customers with textbooks needed to teach the existing curriculum. Publishers rarely make money by launching ventures that deviate greatly from current practice." Typically, publishers provide few alternatives for educators who wish to experiment with different curriculum configurations or even vary the grade levels at which certain subjects—for example, world cultures—are studied (Parker, 1991).

## Selection and Adoption of Basal Textbooks

Textbook adoption for books that appear in elementary, middle, and secondary classrooms occurs in two basic ways. One is through **local selection** in which local districts are free to adopt any texts they wish. The other is through **state selection** in which the state in some fashion selects and prescribes the books that local districts may use.

Currently, a majority of states permit local selections of basals. However, 22 states use state adoption procedures. They are as follows: Alabama, Arkansas, California, Florida, Georgia, Hawaii, Idaho, Indiana, Kentucky, Louisiana, Mississippi, Nevada, New Mexico, North Carolina, Oklahoma, Oregon, South Carolina, Tennessee, Texas, Utah, Virginia, and West Virginia.

Texts typically are adopted for a 5- or 6-year cycle. Adoption committees at the state level often include parents, teachers, college and university faculty, civic leaders, and organizational representatives. A sample form that has been used by adoption committees to evaluate social studies texts is shown in Figure 3.1.

## Criticisms of Basal Textbooks

Both the process of selecting members of textbook adoption committees, as well as the selection criteria they use and the recommendations they make, often are politically sensitive and controversial issues (Keith, 1981). A number of reviews have charged that the textbooks that emerge from the state

**Figure 3.1**
**Sample of a Social Studies Textbook Evaluation Form**

AMERICAN HISTORY

**SOCIAL STUDIES**
**Grades 8, 11–12, and A.P. History**

TEXTBOOK EVALUATION FORM

DIVISION OF INSTRUCTIONAL MATERIALS & TECHNOLOGY
DEPARTMENT OF CURRICULUM & INSTRUCTION
MEMPHIS CITY SCHOOLS—MEMPHIS, TENNESSEE

copyright 1990

*LIST SECTION TOTALS BELOW*

| | |
|---|---|
| A. TEXTBOOK DEVELOPMENT | ______ |
| B. PUBLISHER | ______ |
| C. COST | ______ |
| D. PHYSICAL FEATURES | ______ |
| E. ORGANIZATION | ______ |
| F. INSTRUCTIONAL FEATURES | ______ |
| G. INSTRUCTIONAL CONTENT | ______ |
| H. TEACHER'S EDITION | ______ |
| I. ANCILLARY MATERIALS | ______ |
| *TOTALS - SECTIONS A–I* | ______ |

**Complete one form for each textbook evaluated for each grade level or course.**

Name of Textbook ______________________________

Name of Publisher ______________________________

Name of Series ______________________________

Name of Committee______________________________Evaluation Date____________________, 1990

**RESPOND TO ALL OF THE STATEMENTS LISTED BELOW BY USING THE FOLLOWING SCALE.**

STRONGLY DISAGREE 0 — 1 — 2 — 3 — 4 — 5 — 6 STRONGLY AGREE

AGREE

N - **Not Applicable**
**No Information**

**A. TEXTBOOK DEVELOPMENT**

1. There is evidence that the development team of authors, advisors, and consultants includes a wide range of people (Grades 1–12 and university teachers). ______
2. There is evidence that the text and ancillary materials were successfully field-tested. ______
3. The field-test data were used to refine and improve the text and ancillary materials. ______
4. The textbook reflects current thinking and knowledge (consider the publication date). ______
5. The textbook can be used successfully for the next six years. ______

**Textbook Development Total** ______

**B. PUBLISHER**

1. The publisher will provide, at no cost, sufficient professional consultants to help implement the program. ______
2. The publisher will provide, at no cost, continuous consultant services to meet school and classroom needs. ______
3. The publisher will correlate its program to the MCS's social studies objectives within a reasonable time period. ______
4. Reliable and quality service has been provided in the past by the publisher. ______
5. The consultants provided at the hearing were knowledgeable and competent. ______

**Publisher Total** ______

*Note.* From Division of Instructional Materials, Department of Curriculum & Instruction, Memphis City Schools, Memphis, Tennessee. Used with permission.

**Figure 3.1**
**continued**

**C. COST**

1. The cost of the textbook is comparable to the cost of other textbooks in the field. ______
2. The cost of ancillary materials is comparable to the cost of other ancillary materials in the field. ______

**Cost Total** ______

**D. PHYSICAL FEATURES OF THE TEXTBOOK**

1. The size and weight of the text are appropriate for the age of the student. ______
2. The type size and style are clear and appropriate for the age group. ______
3. The binding and cover are durable. ______
4. The paper quality is good. Non-glare paper is used. ______
5. The page layout is uncluttered and balanced. There is sufficient white space for easy reading. ______
6. Provisions for emphasis (heavy type, boxes, color, italics, etc.) are clear and appropriate. ______
7. The illustrations, tables, figures, graphs, charts, and maps are free from sexual and cultural bias. ______
8. The illustrations, tables, figures, graphs, charts, and maps are relevant and functional. ______
9. The cover is attractive, well designed, and appealing to students. ______

**Physical Features of Textbook Total** ______

**E. ORGANIZATION OF TEXTBOOK**

1. The table of contents shows a logical development of the subject. ______
2. The glossaries/appendices are clear and comprehensive. ______
3. There is uniformity in lesson format within a single text. ______
4. The unit/chapter introductions are clear and comprehensive. ______
5. The unit/chapter summaries suitably reinforce the content. ______
6. There are sufficient, relevant, and well-placed unit/chapter tests. ______
7. There are sufficient, relevant, and well-placed practice exercises. ______
8. The references, bibliographies, and resources are sufficient. ______

**Organization of Textbook Total** ______

**F. INSTRUCTIONAL FEATURES OF TEXTBOOK**

1. The text is written in clear, simple, and logical terms. ______
2. Sentence structure and grammar are correct. ______
3. The style of writing improves comprehension. ______
4. The text provides sufficiently for individual differences. There are suggestions and alternative resources/activities for enrichment as well as for remediation. ______
5. The reading level is appropriate. ______
6. Key vocabulary is made clear in context or in the glossary. ______
7. End-of-lesson questions review key ideas and vocabulary. ______
8. Atlas and gazetteer sections reinforce the lesson. ______
9. Skills are introduced, taught, and maintained throughout the text. ______
10. The activities appeal to a wide range of student abilities and interests. ______

(Instructional Features of Textbook continued on next page)

**Figure 3.1 continued**

**INSTRUCTIONAL FEATURES OF TEXTBOOK - CONTINUED**

11. The students are sufficiently encouraged to develop skills beyond literal comprehension. ______
12. New concepts are identified in an easily distinguishable manner (boldface type, etc.). ______
13. There are opportunities for students to apply their skills to interesting, real-world situations. ______
14. There are sufficient activities for independent research and reports.
15. Content is presented in chronological order. ______

**Instructional Features of Textbook Total** ______

**G. INSTRUCTIONAL CONTENT OF TEXTBOOK**

1. The objectives listed in the proposed curriculum guide under Strand I can be successfully taught using this textbook. ______
2. The objectives listed in the proposed curriculum guide under Strand II can be successfully taught using this textbook. ______
3. The objectives listed in the proposed curriculum guide under Strand III can be successfully taught using this textbook. ______
4. The objectives listed in the proposed curriculum guide under Strand IV can be successfully taught using this textbook. ______
5. The objectives listed in the proposed curriculum guide under Strand V can be successfully taught using this textbook. ______
6. The objectives listed in the proposed curriculum guide under Strand VI can be successfully taught using this textbook. ______
7. The objectives listed in the proposed curriculum guide under Strand VII can be successfully taught using this textbook. ______
8. The objectives listed in the proposed curriculum guide under Strand VIII can be successfully taught using this textbook. ______
9. The objectives listed in the proposed curriculum guide under Strand IX can be successfully taught using this textbook. ______
10. The objectives listed in the proposed curriculum guide under Strand X can be successfully taught using this textbook.
11. The objectives listed in the proposed curriculum guide under Strand XI can be successfully taught using this textbook. ______
12. Map/Globe skills are an integral part of the lesson. ______
13. Map/Globe skills are reinforced in content-related activities. ______
14. Critical thinking skill development is provided at the lesson, chapter, and/or unit level. ______
15. Coverage of the content is adequate and balanced. ______
16. Sufficient examples of relationships between past and present are provided. ______
17. Covers important historical events and people. ______
18. Biographies of famous people are highlighted. ______
19. The content is actual and factual. ______
20. Historical events are clearly presented and supported by quotations and examples from firsthand accounts. ______
21. Includes all social studies disciplines (history, geography, government, etc.). ______

**Figure 3.1 continued**

22. Emphasizes responsibilities of citizenship in a democratic society. ______
23. Controversial issues are treated factually and objectively. ______
24. The content is free of biases and prejudices. ______
25. The content is free of sexual and cultural stereotypes. ______
26. Contributions of the sexes and various cultural groups are reflected fairly. ______

**Instructional Content of Textbook Total** ______

**H. TEACHER'S EDITION/RESOURCE PACKAGE**

1. The teacher's edition is easy to use. ______
2. The teacher's edition is comprehensive, well organized, and contains sufficient information for even the inexperienced teacher. ______
3. Step-by-step plans are included on how to implement the student's text in the classroom. ______
4. Objectives are clearly stated. ______
5. Scope and sequence for each level is provided. ______
6. Sufficient, complementary assessment tools are included. ______
7. Supplementary components are referenced in the teaching plans at the appropriate place. ______
8. Teaching techniques are suggested that improve instructional effectiveness. ______
9. Includes provision for reteaching skills and concepts related to objectives. ______
10. Sufficient activities and optional strategies are provided for enrichment and remediation. ______
11. Answers to exercises and tests are provided on the facsimiles of the student pages. ______
12. Lists of key vocabulary are included for each unit. ______
13. Includes a variety of strategies for teaching skills and alternative strategies for reteaching. ______
14. The size of type is suitable. ______

**Teacher's Edition Total** ______

**I. ANCILLARY MATERIALS**

1. Duplicating/blackline masters are of high quality. ______
2. Printed and/or audiovisual materials being provided are no charge are of high quality and enhance instruction. ______
3. Quality printed and/or audiovisual materials are available at no charge to conduct independent inservice and to aid the individual teacher. ______
4. Transparencies that are being provided at no charge enhance instruction. ______
5. Software components are available to aid the individual teacher to enhance instruction, meet individual needs, and for remediation. ______

**Testing and Management System**

6. Tests are provided for assessment of facts, vocabulary, main ideas, and skills. ______
7. Sufficient, relevant, and well-placed unit/chapter tests are provided. ______
8. End of level tests (end-of-book) are provided. ______
9. Placement, diagnostic, and assessment tests provided are reliable and valid. ______

(Ancillary Materials continued on next page)

**Figure 3.1 continued**

**ANCILLARY MATERIALS – CONTINUED**

10. Reproduction rights to placement, diagnostic, and assessment tests are provided to the Memphis City Schools at no charge. ______

**Workbooks**

11. Workbooks are clear and well organized. ______
12. Practice relates to previously taught skills, vocabulary, and concepts. ______
13. Material extends understanding—not merely "busy work." ______
14. Include a variety of activities and response formats. ______
15. Workbooks are simple enough for independent work. ______
16. Workbooks are appealing to a wide range of students. ______
17. Sufficient amount of writing space is given. ______

**Ancillary Materials Total** ______

We, the duly constituted members of the Textbook Adoption Committee, do hereby certify that the information contained in this document represents a consensus opinion that is supported by the undersigned.

1.______________________________________________
(Name, School, Date)

2.______________________________________________
(Name, School, Date)

3.______________________________________________
(Name, School, Date)

adoption process are, among other things, bland, overburdened with factual context, overly sensitive to pressure groups, distorted, and watered down (e.g., Brophy, 1991; Nelson, 1992; People for the American Way, 1986, 1987; Sewall, 1987; Tyson-Bernstein, 1988).

Textbooks also have been charged with ignoring critical analyses of significant social issues. One social studies teacher characterized the adoption choices in her school district in this fashion: "We had to choose between a brain-dead textbook, with no controversy and therefore no content, and one that didn't cover all the topics in the curriculum" (Needham, 1989, p. 4).

Also, social studies textbooks often have been found to be riddled with inaccuracies. In 1992, for example, the State Board of Education in Texas fined publishers $647,000 after more than 3,700 errors were discovered in U.S. history textbooks (Viadero, 1992).

**Critics have argued that social studies texts ignore important social issues.**

## Implications of State Adoption Policies

The implications of state adoption policies for the 28 states and the District of Columbia that do *not* have them and permit local selection are considerable. Since the costs of developing and producing major texts are extensive, publishers have been reluctant to produce more than one for each grade level. Their objective was to design their products for the greatest possible sales. This involved attending carefully to the adoption criteria formulated by the states with the largest student populations among the group of 22 having state adoption policies. The net effect of state adoption policies has been that a small minority of states have had a major impact on the textbooks that are available to all states.

However, in the wake of controversies over the nature of state adoption processes and the quality of the textbooks they provide for our classrooms, there are signs of changes within the publishing industry. These should have major implications for the curricular choices schools have. In 1992, the *Social Studies Review* reported that:

> The actual number of mass-market social studies textbooks has been gradually diminishing. Some publishers are concluding that it is no longer economic to develop and sell "one-size-fits-all" products. Educators more than ever insist on radically different themes and interpretations in their history books.

> Increasingly, the position of mass-market textbook publishers seems threatened, and among the headaches are the controversies that attend social studies texts. . . .
>
> The evident movement away from mass-market history textbooks surely creates opportunities for niche textbooks that seek particular audiences. The trend may benefit publishers who produce supplementary and specialized products, including collections of stories, biographies, documents, and other non-traditional source materials. CD-ROMs and video formats will undoubtedly continue to make inroads as teaching devices. ("Textbooks Today," 1992, p. 2)

State adoption processes also are undergoing changes. Utah and Texas, for example, now permit adoptions of newer technology resources such as videodiscs (see Chapter 11) in lieu of textbooks.

## ALTERNATIVE SOCIAL STUDIES SCOPE AND SEQUENCE PATTERNS

As noted, the social studies texts that are found in our social studies classes mirror the dominant K through 12 scope and sequence pattern that was outlined earlier. Surprisingly, although this pattern prevails across the United States, there is no explicit national consensus among social studies educators concerning what the scope and sequence of the social studies curriculum *should* be. Nor is there agreement on whether it would even be desirable to adopt a single scope and sequence model for all the nation's classrooms.

To the contrary, since the 1916 report of the Committee on Social Studies, many social studies educators and various groups have proposed and encouraged the development of alternative patterns for organizing the curriculum (e.g., Joyce, 1972; Welton & Mallan, 1992). In recent years especially, states and national groups dissatisfied with the dominant pattern of the social studies have advocated detailed alternatives. Also, some have worked through the political process to implement their recommendations. We will consider briefly several such alternatives, one proposed by a *state board* (California), one by a *foundation* (Bradley Commission), one by a *national commission* (The National Commission on Social Studies in the Schools), and several others by *national professional organizations* (NCGE and NCSS).

### The California Model

In 1990, the state of California adopted its own framework for the social studies curriculum entitled *History-Social Science Framework for California Public Schools, Kindergarten Through Grade 12* (History-Social Science Framework, 1988). Among other differences with the dominant national pattern, the California model places heavy emphasis on the discipline of history. The organizational plan established new social studies guidelines for each school within the state. A summary of the scope and sequence framework for grades K through 12 is shown in Figure 3.2.

Although the California model directly affects only one state, it ultimately may impact on other states. Through its influence as our largest state and the major state purchaser of textbooks, California in the past often set the standards for what publishers include in social studies text-

**Figure 3.2**
**California History-Social Science Framework: Scope and Sequence**

K **Learning and Working, Now and Long Ago**
Helping children learn their way in new school role by analyzing problems, considering alternatives and appreciating democratic values. Readings: *Jack and the Beanstalk, Goldilocks, Aesop's Fables.*

1 **A Child's Place in Time and Space**
Developing social skills, expanding geographic and economic awareness, building a three-dimensional floor map, neighborhood studies. Readings: *Little Toot, Little Red Lighthouse, Mulligan's Steam Shovel.*

2 **People Who Make a Difference**
Studying people who supply our needs, farmers and laborers on wheat and vegetable farms, effect of climate on crops, urban development. Readings: *Johnny Appleseed,* folk tales, myths, legends.

3 **Understanding Continuity and Change**
Constructing history of region, California geography, terrain model of locality, Native Americans, classroom time line. Readings: *White Stallion, Wagon Wheels, The Drinking Gourd.*

4 **California: A Changing State**
Pre-Columbian times, Spanish conquest, colonial Mexico, Gold Rush, rapid population growth, new Immigrants, physical and cultural geography, modern California urban growth and technology.

5 **U.S. History and Geography: Making a New Nation, to 1850.**
The land before Columbus, Age of Exploration, settling colonies, settling Trans-Appalachian West, War of Independence, Young Republic, Westward Ho! Readings: *Immigrant Kids, Waiting for Mama.*

*Note.* From *History-Social Science Framework,* copyright 1988, California State Department of Education.

**Figure 3.2 continued**

**6 World History and Geography: Ancient Civilizations**

Ancient Civilizations to AD 500: Stone Age, Mesopotamia, Egypt, Hebrews and Greeks, Early Civilizations of India and China, Rome. Readings: Greek and Roman literature, Bible.

**7 World History and Geography: Medieval and Early Modern Times**

Medieval AD 500 to 1789: Fall of Rome, Islam, China and Japan, Medieval society, European Reformation and Renaissance, Enlightenment. Readings: *Pillow Book, Song of Roland, Tale of Genji, Koju-ki.*

**8 United States History and Geography: Growth and Conflict**

Course covers 1783 to 1914: New Nation, Constitution, launching the ship of state, the West, the Northeast, the South, Civil War, Industrial Age. Readings: *Huckleberry Finn, My Antonia.*

**9 Elective Courses in History-Social Science**

Semester courses: Our State, Physical Geography, Cultural Geography, Humanities, Anthropology, Psychology, Sociology, Women's History, Ethnic Studies, Area Studies-Culture, Law-related Education.

**10 World History and Geography: The Modern World, 1789 to Present**

Unresolved world problems, Enlightenment, Industrial Revolution, Imperialism, WWI, WWII, Nationalism, Soviet Union, China, Africa, Mexico. Readings: *We, Darkness at Noon, Krystallnacht.*

**11 U.S. History and Geography: Continuity and Change in 20th Century**

Progressive Era, Jazz Age, Great Depression, WWII, Cold War, American post-war society, recent times. Readings: *Grapes of Wrath.*

**12 Principles of American Democracy/Economics**

One semester deals with Constitution, Bill of Rights, court system, Federalism, and comparative governments. Another semester is economic systems, micro/macroeconomics, international economics.

books. This meant, for example, that a sparsely populated state with a relatively small student population such as Vermont had to select its social studies texts from those designed to fit California's scope and sequence.

## The Bradley Commission on History Model

In 1988, an independent foundation, *The Bradley Commission on History in Schools,* issued its recommendations for alternative scope and sequence guidelines. These covered all grades and emphasized the role of history in the curriculum (Bradley Commission on History in Schools, 1988). The commission included some of the same members who worked on the California model.

The recommendations included three alternative patterns for grades K through 6 and four alternatives for grades 7 through 12 (see Figure 3.3). As a comparison of Figures 3.2 and 3.3 reveals, the sets of recommendations by the State of California and the Bradley Commission have several points in common.

## The National Council for Geographic Education/Association of American Geographers Model

At the same time that advocates for the study of history asserted its claim for supremacy in the curriculum (e.g., Ravitch & Finn, 1987), a strong base of support for the systematic study of geography also developed. As surveys of student knowledge of geography revealed major deficiencies, there was growing national alarm over the prevalence of geographic illiteracy. It was argued, for example, that students were ill prepared for an era of increasing global interdependence.

Providing leadership for this issue, the NCGE and the Association of American Geographers (AAG) in 1984 issued a set of scope and sequence guidelines that emphasized the study of geography, K through 12 (Joint Committee on Geographic Education, 1984; see also Petersen, Natoli, & Boehm, 1994). The organizations recommended specific courses for grades 7 through 12 but only general guidelines for geographic topics to be included in the elementary school curriculum. Their general recommendations for grades 7 through 12 are summarized in Figure 3.4.

## The National Commission on Social Studies in the Schools Model

A joint project of the American Historical Association, the Organization of American Historians, the Carnegie Foundation for the Advancement of Teaching, and the NCSS, the National Commission on Social Studies in the Schools in 1989 offered its recommendations for a K through 12 social studies curriculum (National Commission, 1989). Its proposal avoided specifying particular subject matter for each grade level. At the same time, the commission's recommendations included a strong emphasis on history and geography across all the grades. This is illustrated in the summary of the curriculum for grades 4 through 12 in Figure 3.5.

## The National Council for the Social Studies Scope and Sequence Initiatives

As the national organization representing social studies teachers, the NCSS has searched over the years for a consensus set of scope and sequence pat-

**Figure 3.3**
**The Bradley Commission on History Scope and Sequence for Grades 7–12**

**Pattern A**

| Grade | Course |
|---|---|
| 7 | Regional and neighborhood history and geography |
| 8 | U.S. history and geography |
| 9 | History of Western civilization |
| 10 | World history and geography |
| 11 | U.S. history and geography |
| 12 | American government; social studies elective |

**Pattern B**

| Grade | Course |
|---|---|
| 7 | Social studies elective; local history |
| 8 | U.S. history and geography |
| 9 | World and Western history to 1789 |
| 10 | World and Western history since 1789 |
| 11 | U.S. history and geography |
| 12 | American government; social studies elective |

**Pattern C**

| Grade | Course |
|---|---|
| 7 | World history geography to 1789 |
| 8 | U.S. history and geography to 1914 |
| 9 | Social studies electives |
| 10 | World history, culture, and geography since 1789 |
| 11 | U.S. history and geography, 20th century |
| 12 | American government; social studies elective |

**Pattern D**

| Grade | Course |
|---|---|
| 7 | Social studies electives; local history |
| 8 | History of European civilization |
| 9 | History of non-European civilizations |
| 10 | U.S. history and geography to 1865 |
| 11 | U.S. history and geography since 1865 |
| 12 | American government; social studies elective |

*Note.* From Bradley Commission on History in Schools (1988, pp. 20–21).

**Figure 3.4**
**The Joint Committee on Geographic Education Scope and Sequence for Grades 7–12**

| Grade level | Courses | Course length | |
|---|---|---|---|
| 7–9 | State or Regional Geography | one semester | |
| 7–9 | World Geography (human/physical/regional) | two semesters | |
| 8–10 | Earth Sciences (contains a substantial component of physical geography) | two semesters | |
| 8–10 | Geography of the United States | one semester | |
| 9–12 | a. Environmental Geography | | |
| | b. Urban Geography | | |
| | c. Political Geography/Global Geographic Issues | at least one semester each of two of these courses | two semesters |
| | d. Historical/Cultural Geography | | |
| | e. Economic Geography | | |
| | f. Problems in Local Geography | | |
| 11–12 | Honors Courses in Geography | one to four semesters | |

From Joint Committee on Geographic Education (1984, p. 18).

terns that it could adopt on behalf of its membership and recommend to schools. Early in the 1980s, the NCSS House of Delegates called for the appointment of a committee to develop a series of scope and sequence options for the K through 12 curriculum in social studies. As an outgrowth, the NCSS formed a Task Force on Scope and Sequence, which completed and published its report in 1983–1984 (Task Force on Scope and Sequence, 1984).

The Task Force recommendations generated considerable discussion but little consensus among social studies educators. As a result of the debate, the council invited five additional sets of authors to develop further scope and sequence alternatives (Bragaw, 1986). These were reported in a special issue of *Social Education* that appeared in November/December, 1986.

**The National Council for the Social Studies Alternatives.** In an attempt to resolve the scope and sequence issue, the NCSS in 1988 appointed an ad hoc committee to make recommendations among the alternatives for the council's endorsement. Specifically the ad hoc committee was charged with reviewing all NCSS position statements and guidelines and other pertinent materials, including reviews of relevant research. Further, it was to derive basic principles, criteria, and guidelines that should be reflected in any

**Figure 3.5**
**The National Commission on Social Studies in the Schools for Social Studies Curriculum in Grades 4–12**

| Grade | Scope |
|---|---|
| 4–6 | Three social studies courses should be taught during these grades: (a) United States history, (b) world history, and (c) geography, both physical and cultural. These courses draw much of their content from concepts of the social sciences, especially political science, economics, and anthropology. The order in which these courses are taught is less important than that each course receives the equivalent of a full year's attention.... By the end of grade 6, pupils should know much factual information from the disciplines of history, geography, government, and economics and have an elementary sense of how that information relates to national and global understanding. |
| 7–8 | At these grades, students ought to concentrate their attention on local and national social, political, and economic relationships and patterns of behavior. Two courses are recommended: a study of the local community and a study of the nation.<br>A course focusing on the local community is of particular importance for citizens of a highly mobile society.... The second major course to be taught in grades 7 and 8 addresses the economic and political development of the United States and its changing socio-economic-political relationships with the rest of the world.... By studying the community and the nation in consecutive years, students will be better able to grasp the relationships to new locales and to take responsibility for participation in community affairs. |
| 9–11 | An extension of the study of United States history and geography and of world history and geography is appropriate in these grades when students are more mature and analytical. The best arrangement would be to actually combine study of the United States with study of the world by teaching our nation's history as part of the general story of humanity — including cultural, economic, and political systems — in recent centuries. To achieve this end, a three-year sequence is needed....<br>**1. World and American History and Geography to 1750** This course should emphasize major civilizations with some attention to other societies as well....<br>**2. World and American History and Geography, 1750–1900** Three transformations of modern times should be emphasized in this course: the democratic revolution, the industrial and technological revolution, and the modern growth and mobility of population and the impact that has had....<br>**3. World and American History and Geography Since 1900** The theme of this course ought to be the study of how the three dominant movements of the 19th century worked themselves out in the 20th.... |
| 12 | Schools should require two semester-length courses at grade 12....<br>**1. Government/Economics** Government and economics may be taught separately or in combination....<br>**2. Other Twelfth-Grade Course Options** Students should have the opportunity to choose other courses: (a) courses in anthropology, sociology, psychology... ; (b) a well-conceived multidisciplinary study of contemporary or recurrent issues, which is always hard to design but which has been done well in many schools over the years; or (c) a supervised experience in community service. |

*Note.* The National Commission on Social Studies in the Schools (1989, pp. 9–20).

**Figure 3.6**
**Scope and Sequence Criteria**

**A social studies scope and sequence should:**

1. State the purpose and rationale of the program.
2. Be internally consistent with its stated purposes and rationale.
3. Designate content at every grade level, K–12.
4. Recognize that learning is cumulative.
5. Reflect a balance of local, national, and global content.
6. Reflect a balance of past, present, and future content.
7. Provide for students' understanding of the structure and function of social, economic, and political institutions.
8. Emphasize concepts and generalizations from history and the social sciences.
9. Promote the integration of skills and knowledge.
10. Promote the integration of content across subject areas.
11. Promote the use of a variety of teaching methods and instructional materials.
12. Foster active learning and social interaction.
13. Reflect a clear commitment to democratic beliefs and values.
14. Reflect a global perspective.
15. Foster the knowledge and appreciation of cultural heritage.
16. Foster the knowledge and appreciation of diversity.
17. Foster the building of self-esteem.
18. Be consistent with current research pertaining to how children learn.
19. Be consistent with current scholarship in the disciplines.
20. Incorporate thinking skills and interpersonal skills at all levels.
21. Stress the identification, understanding, and solution of local, national, and global problems.
22. Provide many opportunities for students to learn and practice the basic skills of participation, from observation to advocacy.
23. Promote the transfer of knowledge and skills to life.
24. Have the potential to challenge and excite students.

*Note.* From *Social Studies Curriculum Planning Resources* (p. 16) by National Council for the Social Studies, 1990, Washington, DC: Author.

social studies curriculum scope and sequence design. Additionally, the committee was to identify three scope and sequence models that most nearly met the criteria it established.

In carrying out its charge and looking to official NCSS policy statements and guidelines, the committee developed 24 general criteria for evaluating a scope and sequence model. These, shown in Figure 3.6, were used to assess the various alternative models that already had been published.

The committee also recognized that, with varying degrees of modifications a number of models could meet the criteria.

Subsequently, on recommendation of the committee, NCSS endorsed three alternative models (National Council, 1990). In doing so, it left open the possibility that many other models might exist or could be created that met the 24 criteria cited earlier. Like earlier NCSS initiatives, however, the three alternative scope and sequence models identified generated considerable debate, but reflecting the divisions within the field, have failed to attract a consensus.

Apart from meeting the criteria established by the ad hoc committee, the three models are quite different in their designs, emphases, and complexity. Each of them is summarized here.

**The Task Force Model.** One of the three alternatives selected was the model recommended by the earlier 1984 Task Force on Scope and Sequence (1984, 1989): The NCSS Task Force Model. This model conforms closely to the scope and sequence pattern that is currently dominant (discussed earlier) across the United States. Its recommendations are as shown in Figure 3.7.

**The Themes and Questions Model.** The second model that emerged from the NCSS initiative was developed by Hartoonian and Laughlin (1989). They laid out an alternative that is based on the assumption that specific

**Figure 3.7**
**NCSS Task Force Scope and Sequence Model, Grades 6–12**

*Grade 6 — People and Cultures: Representative World Regions*
*Grade 7 — A Changing World of Many Nations: A Global View*
*Grade 8 — Building a Strong and Free Nation: The United States*
*Grade 9 — Systems That Make a Democratic Society Work: Law, Justice, and Economics*
*Grade 10— Origins of Major Cultures: A World History*
*Grade 11— The Maturing of America: United States History*
*Grade 12— One-year course or courses to be required; selection(s) to be made from the following:*
*Issues and Problems of Modern Society . . .*
*Introduction to the Social Sciences . . .*
*The Arts in Human Societies . . .*
*International Area Studies . . .*
*Social Science Elective Courses . . .*
*Supervised Experience in Community Affairs*

*Note.* From "In search of a scope and sequence for social studies" by Task Force on Scope and Sequence, 1989, *Social Education, 53,* pp. 380–382.

scope and sequence decisions should be made by local curriculum committees and teachers. Although the authors did not label their approach, we will characterize it as the *themes and questions model,* since it spells out themes and questions that local decision makers should consider in developing the curriculum. The themes for grades K through 12 are presented in Figure 3.8. The questions that are to be used to shape the 7 through 12 curriculum are presented in Figure 3.9.

**The Global Education Model.** The third model, developed by Kniep (1989), also is untitled. We will refer to it as the *global education model,* since it emphasizes global approaches to all social studies topics. Like the *themes and questions model,* it encourages local decision making with respect to the actual shape of the curriculum. Kniep proposed that the scope of the curriculum be framed around the study of four areas:

1. Human values,
2. Global systems,
3. Global issues and problems, and
4. Global history.

His complex model employs incorporates *conceptual themes, phenomenological themes,* and *persistent problem themes.* He advocates that teachers consider these themes for curriculum organization across the grades. Kniep's conceptual themes are shown in Figure 3.10. Phenomenological themes, which are more complex, include "actors and components playing major roles in the world's systems" (Kniep, 1989, p. 401) and major historical and contemporary events. The persistent problem themes, according to Kniep, address both local and global problems shown in Figure 3.11. He proposes a complex weaving of the three types of themes throughout each grade level from K through 12.

**Figure 3.8**
**Themes and Questions Curriculum Model: Themes for Grades K–12**
*Note.* From "Designing a Social Studies Scope and Sequence for the 21st Century" by H. M. Hartoonian and M. A. Laughlin, 1989, *Social Education, 53,* p. 389. National Council for the Social Studies. Used with permission.

| Grade Levels K 1 2 3 4 5 6 7 8 9 10 11 12 |
| --- |
| ← Cultural heritage → |
| ← Global perspective → |
| ← Political/economic → |
| ← Tradition and change → |
| ← Social history → |
| ← Spatial relationships → |
| ← Social contracts → |
| ← Technology → |
| ← Peace/interdependence → |
| ← Citizenship → |

**Figure 3.9**
**Questions That Shape the Themes and Questions Scope and Sequence Model**

**Middle School Students (Grades 6–8)**
*Viewing the World From Different Perspectives*

How can content from the social studies provide different perspectives when we study events, institutions, and people around the world?

Where can I find and how can I use numeric information about political, social, and economic institutions?

How can we use numeric data to make decisions in our personal lives?

What is culture? How are cultural regions similar and how are they different? What are some issues, crises, and opportunities facing each culture region at present? How might they be resolved?

What is the social nature of human beings? How do leaders exercise power and authority? How have leaders shaped the course of history? How have common people contributed to our well-being? What roles have women played in the creation and development of culture?

What values are important to our culture? How are these values used in personal and national policy-making?

How does the perception we have of ourselves as individuals and as a nation influence the way we behave toward one another?

What is the nature of the earth and its environment today? How will we "protect" space?

How have world regions become increasingly specialized in the production of certain goods, thereby forming systems of economic networks?

What is the nature of our democratic government at the local, state, and national levels? What are some key features of our government?

What roles have people of color played in the development of the United States?

What efforts are made to recognize and appreciate cultural diversity in our country?

What legal rights and responsibilities do individuals and groups have in our country and in other countries?

How has the United States responded to the many challenges facing our country throughout its history?

What challenges does our nation face in the coming years? How might the nation respond?

What relationships exist between the United States and other areas of the globe? How have these relationships changed over the years?

What common challenges are faced by people around the world? How are they likely to respond to ensure our survival on earth?

How has technology influenced our lifestyles, values, and expectations? How might technology shape our lives in the 21st century? How have technological developments changed the lives of people around the world? How has technology changed the ways persons and nations view the world and respond to events?

How might peace be achieved within and among the cultures of the world?

*Note.* From "Designing a Social Studies Scope and Sequence for the 21st Century" by H. M. Hartoonian and M. A. Laughlin, 1989, *Social Education, 53,* pp. 395–397. National Council for the Social Studies. Used with permission.

**Figure 3.9 continued**

**High School Students (Grades 9–12)**

*Assuming Full Citizenship in a Changing World*

How has geography influenced the development of human societies?

How do the histories and cultures of various Western and non-Western societies contribute to our understanding of the world today?

What are the major philosophical, religious, economic, and political ideas of our society? How do they help to explain a world view?

What are some important values that people in various nations and cultures throughout the world hold?

How have the forces of nationalism, industrialism, imperialism, militarism, revolution, technology, and others brought about changes in the attitudes, values, and actions for people in both the Western and non-Western world?

What has democracy contributed to the world? What are some major characteristics of our government and economic system and those of other nations?

How can the histories of the United States and Western civilization be understood as interrelated?

How do people participate actively in political and economic processes and decision making to ensure political, social, and economic justice?

How do the media, government, and private industry use statistical data to inform the public? How can these data be misleading?

What happens when different groups of people come in contact with one another? How have cultural differences led to conflict? How has cultural diffusion benefited humankind?

What major social, political, economic, cultural, scientific, and technological changes have occurred in the United States and elsewhere in the world since World War II? What effects have these changes had on us as individuals, as a nation, and as members of the global community of humankind?

How might these changes influence our values, expectations, and life-styles?

What will our planet Earth be like in the coming years and decades?

How might civil wars and international conflicts be eliminated? How might world peace be achieved?

How can we achieve peace within ourselves? How can we help others achieve peace?

What moral, ethical, and legal obligations do we have toward other human beings and our environment?

What economic, political, humanitarian, and moral roles do international organi-zations play?

How have civil liberties been gained and how are they protected?

Why has there been tension and conflict between and among various minority groups in the United States and elsewhere around the world? How have rising expectations of minority groups brought about change? What challenges remain to be resolved?

How have changes in societies' expectations, values, and life-styles influenced the role of women and the opportunities available to women at present and in coming years?

How can citizens serve their schools and the larger community? What is the good citizen? What is the good person? What is the good society?

**Figure 3.10**
**The Global Education Curriculum Model: Conceptual Themes for Grades K–12**

1. **Interdependence**

   We live in a world of systems in which the actors and components interact to make up a unified, functioning whole.

   *Related concepts:* causation, community, government, groups, interaction systems.

2. **Change**

   The process of movement from one state of being to another is a universal aspect of the planet and is an inevitable part of life and living.

   *Related concepts:* adaption, cause and effect, development, evolution, growth, revolution, time.

3. **Culture**

   People create social environments and systems comprised of unique beliefs, values, traditions, language customs, technology, and institutions as a way of meeting basic human needs; shaped by their own physical environments and contact with other cultures.

   *Related concepts:* adaption, aesthetics, diversity, languages, norms, roles, values. space-time.

4. **Scarcity**

   An imbalance exists between relatively unlimited wants and limited available resources necessitating the creation of systems for deciding how resources are to be distributed.

   *Related concepts:* conflict, exploration, migration, opportunity, cost, policy, resources, specialization.

5. **Conflict**

   People and nations often have differing values and opposing goals resulting in disagreement, tensions, and sometimes violence, necessitating skill in coexistence, negotiation, living with ambiguity and conflict resolution.

   *Related concepts:* authority, collaboration, competition, interests/positions, justice, power, rights.

*Note.* From "Social Studies with a Global Education" by W. M. Kniep, 1989, *Social Education, 53,* p. 401. Used with permission.

## Selecting a Scope and Sequence Pattern

For better or worse, no singular alternative scope and sequence model looms on the horizon to seriously challenge the dominant national curricular pattern outlined earlier—the one on which existing basal texts are based. Similarly no consensus has emerged on the issue of whether it would even be desirable to have a common pattern across all school districts, with all their diversity and disproportionate needs.

**Figure 3.11**
**The Global Education Curriculum Model: Persistent Problem Themes, Grades K–12**
*Note.* From "Social Studies with a Global Education" by W. M. Kniep, 1989, *Social Education, 53,* p. 401. Used with permission.

**Peace and Security**
the arms race
East-West relations
terrorism
colonialism
democracy vs. tyranny

**National/International Development**
hunger and poverty
overpopulation
North-South relations
appropriate technology
international debt crisis

**Environmental Problems**
acid rain
pollution of streams
depletion of rain forests
nuclear-waste disposal
maintenance of fisheries

**Human Rights**
apartheid
indigenous homelands
political imprisonment
religious persecution
refugees

The several alternative models presented, as well as others proposed (see Downey, 1986; Engle & Ochoa, 1986; Stanley & Nelson, 1986), along with the related criteria for selecting a scope and sequence, however, should provide teachers and schools with some basic frameworks for decision making. Ultimately, the development of effective young citizens depends less on the scope and sequence decisions that are made for the nation, states, and local school districts, than on the curriculum that teachers and students construct in individual classrooms.

## GROUP ACTIVITIES

1. Analyze the alternative scope and sequence models discussed in this chapter. Then select one that you find to be most appealing. Discuss what you consider to be its strengths and limitations.
2. Identify two American history textbooks for the same middle-school grade (either 5th or 8th grade) and two for the secondary grades (typically grade 11). Focus on titles of unit topics and compare them for each level. To what extent are the texts similar and how are they different?

3. Discuss the relative advantages and disadvantages of using a basal text in social studies instruction for the middle grades. Then discuss them for the secondary grades.
4. Argue for or against the proposition: State social studies textbook adoptions are preferable to local adoptions.

## INDIVIDUAL ACTIVITIES

1. Determine the specific policies and procedures for adopting social studies texts in either a local school district or at the state level (if applicable). Itemize what you regard as the strengths and weaknesses of the adoption policy.
2. Select a local school district and determine what the scope and sequence pattern is for social studies in grades K through 12. To what degree is it similar or different to the dominant national pattern described in this chapter?

## REFERENCES

Bradley Commission on History in Schools (1988). *Building a history curriculum: Guidelines for teaching history in schools.* Washington, DC: Educational Excellence Network.

Bragaw, D. (1986). Scope and sequence alternatives for the future. *Social Education, 50,* 484–485.

Brophy, J. (1991). *Distinctive curriculum materials in K–6 social studies* (Elementary Subjects Center Series No. 35). East Lansing, MI: Michigan State University, Institute for Research on Teaching, Center for the Learning and Teaching of Elementary Subjects.

Downey, M. T. (1986). Time, space, and culture. *Social Education, 50,* 490–501.

Engle, S. H., & Ochoa, A. (1986). A curriculum for democratic citizenship. *Social Education, 50,* 514–525.

Hanna, P. R. (1963). Revising the social studies: What is needed? *Social Education, 27,* 190–196.

Hartoonian, H. M., & Laughlin, M. A. (1989). Designing a social studies scope and sequence for the 21st century. *Social Education, 53,* 388–398.

*History-social science framework for California public schools kindergarten through grade twelve.* (1988). Sacramento, CA: California State Department of Education.

Joint Committee on Geographic Education. (1984). *Guidelines for geographic education.* Washington, DC: Association of American Geographers and National Council for Geographic Education.

Joyce, B. R. (1972). *New strategies for social education.* Chicago: Science Research Associates.

Joyce, W. W., Little, T. H., & Wronski, S. P. (1991). Scope and sequence, goals, and objectives: Effects on social studies. In J. P. Shaver (Ed.), *Handbook of social studies teaching and learning.* New York: Macmillan.

Keith, S. (1981). *Politics of textbook adoption.* Project Report No. 81-A7. Palo Alto, CA: Stanford University's Institute for Research on Educational Finance and Government.

Kniep, W. M. (1989). Social studies within a global education. *Social Education, 53,* 399–403.

Mehlinger, H. D. (1992). The National Commission on Social Studies in the Schools: An example of the politics of curriculum reform in the United States. *Social Education, 56,* 149–153.

National Commission on Social Studies in the Schools. (1989). *Charting a course: Social studies for the 21st century.* Washington, DC: Author.

National Council for the Social Studies. (1990). *Social studies curriculum planning resources.* Washington, DC: Author.

Needham, N. R. (1989, March). Is there a decent textbook in your future? *NEA Today, 7,* 4–5.

Nelson, M. R. (1992). *Children's social studies* (2nd ed.). New York Harcourt Brace Jovanovich.

Parker, W. C. (1991). *Renewing the social studies curriculum.* Alexandria, VA: Association for Supervision and Curriculum Development.

People for the American Way. (1986). *Looking at history: A major review of U.S. history textbooks.* Washington, DC: People for the American Way.

People for the American Way. (1987). *We the people: A review of U.S. government and civics textbooks.* Washington, DC: People for the American Way.

Peterson, J. F., Natoli, S. J., & Boehm, R. G. (1994). The guidelines for geographic education: A ten-year retrospective. *Social Education, 58,* 192.

Powers, J. B. (1986). Paul R. Hanna's scope and sequence. *Social Education, 50,* 502–512.

Ravitch, D., & Finn, C. (1987). *What do our 17-year-olds know?* New York: Harper & Row.

Sewall, G. T. (1987) *American history textbooks: An assessment of quality.* Washington DC: Educational Excellence Network.

Shaver, J. P., Davis, Jr., O. L., & Hepburn, S. W. (1979). The status of social studies education: Impressions from three NSF studies. *Social Education, 39,* 150–153.

Stanley, W. B., & Nelson, J. L. (1986). Social education for social transformation. *Social Education, 50,* 528–534.

Superka, D. P., Hawke, S., & Morrissett, I. (1980). The current and future status of the social studies. *Social Education, 40,* 362–369.

Task Force on Scope and Sequence. (1984). In search of a scope and sequence for social studies. *Social Education, 48,* 249–262.

Task Force on Scope and Sequence. (1989). In search of a scope and sequence for social studies. *Social Education, 53,* 376–387.

Textbooks today: How sensitive? How accurate? (1992, Spring). *Social Studies Review,* 1–2.

Tyson-Bernstein, H. (1988). *A conspiracy of good intentions: America's textbook fiasco.* Washington, DC: Council for Basic Education.

Viadero, D. (1992, August 5). Texas assesses $860,000 in new fines for textbook errors. *Education Week,* 22.

Welton, D. A., & Mallan, J. T. (1992). *Children and their world: Strategies for teaching social studies* (4th ed.). Boston: Houghton Mifflin.

PART II

# Developing Reflective, Competent, and Concerned Citizens

CHAPTER 4

# Organizing and Planning for Teaching Social Studies

**Basic Issues in Planning Social Studies Instruction**

Identifying a Purpose for Citizenship Education

**Social Studies Goals for Instruction**

Identifying and Stating Goals

**Social Studies Objectives for Instruction**

Identifying and Stating Objectives
Objectives and Student Learning Outcomes
Objectives in the Cognitive and Affective Domains

**Organizing Subject Matter into Units**

Planning and Creating Units
Sources of Units
Resource Units and Teaching Units
Building Units Around Key Social Problems, Questions, and Themes
Incorporating Multiple Perspectives into Units
Using Concept Maps to Plan Units
Planning Units Using Interdisciplinary Teams
Formats for Unit Planning

**Organizing Subject Matter into Lessons**

Lesson Plans
Formats and Procedures for Lesson Planning
The Fundamental Elements of Lesson Planning

**Classrooms as Environments for Learning**

The Uses of Space in Planning Social Studies Instruction
Allocation of Time in Lesson Plans

**Creating and Managing the Classroom Environment**

Student Behavior in the Classroom
Teacher Expectations Concerning Student Behavior
Characteristics of Well-Managed Classrooms

**Balancing Goals and Objectives in the Curriculum: Linking the Head, the Hand, and the Heart**

**Guidelines for Social Studies Program Development**

**Variety in Instructional Planning**

*Consider a teacher, Mr. Olerud, who has traveled throughout Russia over the summer. He wishes to share his experiences and insights with his seventh-grade classes. Further, he hopes to provide them with a per-*

*spective and level of in-depth current information that their social studies text cannot.*

*The idea for a unit on "Russia in the Aftermath of the Breakup of the Soviet Union" begins to take shape. At the outset, the teacher mulls over some basic questions:*

- *How would this unit fit in with my overall purpose in teaching social studies?*
- *Why should my students be asked to learn about this topic?*

*From these initial questions, a basic goal emerges that offers an important rationale for the unit, other than that of merely sharing the teacher's interesting experiences:*

- *What specifically should my class of culturally diverse students gain from the study of the unit?*

*Mr. Olerud ponders the key questions he hopes the unit will answer. He brainstorms and lists his ideas on the chalkboard. Later, after he has given the unit more thought, he will review and revise the set of questions.*

- *Which instructional techniques would be the most effective with the students?*

*Mr. Olerud has a few ideas but later he will more fully flesh out the answers to this question. This will occur as he gets to know his students better and to ascertain their interests, needs, learning styles, and capabilities.*

- *What resources already exist to help create the unit?*

*Some background reading and perusal of the school's and local library's holdings indicates a wealth of recent information and resources. It also reveals some dated political maps that nevertheless will be useful for comparisons.*

*Several telephone calls establish that various community agencies can help provide guest experts. Additionally, a search of the Educational Resources Information Center (ERIC) Clearinghouse for Social Studies/Social Science Education reference materials (discussed later in this chapter) turns up some resource units dealing with the former Soviet Union. Much of this information will be relevant to the study of Russia.*

- *What are the most appropriate ways to determine the quality and quantity of what my students learn from the unit?*

*Mr. Olerud browses through his professional library to gather some initial ideas. Since the school district is sponsoring an in-depth workshop on authentic assessment techniques during the preschool period, he also will have some concrete models available to guide him.*

- *How much time can be spared for such a unit?*

*The answer to this question helps to constrain the scope of the unit. Time is always a limited resource in the curriculum. Further, the amount of time required for a unit often is difficult to estimate accurately, especially for beginning teachers.*

*From the teacher's informed questions, reflections, and initial investigations flow a rationale, specific objectives, related teaching strategies, and authentic assessment procedures. The planning process also identifies student activities, resource materials and speakers, and a schedule that are appropriate for the unit. A new social studies unit is born!*

## BASIC ISSUES IN PLANNING SOCIAL STUDIES INSTRUCTION

One of the major challenges that new social studies teachers face is instructional planning. Carefully prepared, well-designed plans are a key ingredient in all successful teaching.

Experienced teachers often make effective teaching look effortless or spontaneous to an untrained observer. Such teachers even may profess to have done no immediate or sustained planning for their lessons. In reality, through trial and error over the years, seasoned social studies teachers gradually build on their series of successful planning experiences.

Planning involves having a clear rationale for how we intend to proceed and an idea of what we specifically hope to accomplish if our instruction is successful. Planning also requires attention to the prudent use of the limited instructional time available to us during the school day (Borich, 1996).

Planning for social studies instruction may occur at the classroom, departmental, local, or state levels for a day, extended period, or school year. It involves thoughtful consideration of both the nature of what students are to learn and why they are to learn it.

### Identifying a Purpose for Citizenship Education

All social studies planning begins with some *explicit* (conscious or stated) or *implicit* (unconscious or unstated) notion of the purpose of the social studies. In Chapter 1, we examined six alternative perspectives concerning the major purpose of citizenship education; namely, that the emphasis in citizenship education most appropriately might be placed on:

- Transmission of the cultural heritage,
- Social science,
- Reflective inquiry,
- Informed social criticism,
- Personal development, and
- Development of reflection, competence, and concern.

The process of planning social studies instruction should begin with the teacher's adoption of one of these six perspectives or a new one. The statement of purpose then becomes a rudder that guides the remainder of the planning decisions. There should be a clear connection between the teacher's statement of purpose and the individual lessons, activities, and total curriculum that are developed for students.

## SOCIAL STUDIES GOALS FOR INSTRUCTION

The *general* expectations for what educators plan to accomplish in the social studies curriculum over the course of the year or a shorter unit of time constitute curricular **goals.** Establishing goals is an important step toward creating a basic framework for a course of study and for leading the way to more specific curriculum expectations. Brophy and Alleman (1993) have suggested that all aspects of the curriculum should be driven by goals, including questions, subject matter, and evaluation items.

Although, as we have noted, there should be a singular statement of purpose to guide the year's program, there typically will be several goals that it is designed to achieve. Goal statements may be different for each level of the social studies curriculum or they may remain the same across the grades.

### Identifying and Stating Goals

Goal statements are distinguished by their *level of generality*. For example, consider the following goals. The course of study for the year will help students:

1. Prepare for the society of the twenty-first century.
2. Acquire the necessary skills for effective interpersonal relationships.
3. Understand the dominant mainstream culture and the major ethnic subcultures in the United States.
4. Develop an understanding of and tolerance for different values and lifestyles.
5. Exercise their rights and responsibilities as citizens of a democracy.

The preceding goals are important statements of broad concerns that teachers may wish to address in the social studies curriculum, but they require further elaboration and specificity if they are to offer guidance for crafting individual lessons. For example, the first goal statement does not spell out what aspects of our future society will be considered. Nor does the second goal statement indicate the specific skills that will be addressed.

Goals may be related to a particular discipline, such as history. For example, teachers may wish to have their students develop an appreciation of the roles political dissenters and minorities have played over time in changing the laws and policies of our nation. Whether they are related to one discipline or are multidisciplinary in their scope, goal statements are distinguished by their level of generality.

## SOCIAL STUDIES OBJECTIVES FOR INSTRUCTION

Related to goals are the more specific **objectives** that the curriculum is designed to achieve over a school year, single period, or some other unit of time. Whereas goals communicate what the broad general framework for the curriculum will be, objectives translate them into *specific* statements of what students are expected to learn as the outcome of some measure of instruction. Objectives may be stated for individual lessons, for a unit of study, or for the entire year's course of study. The same objective also may be included in more than one lesson.

### Identifying and Stating Objectives

Consider the following sample objectives. Then contrast them with the five goal statements listed earlier. As a result of the lesson (activity), the student will be able to:

- Identify correctly at least five of the countries of Africa by writing in their names on an outline map.
- Create a hypothetical solution to one of the community problems from the list provided that meets 75% of the criteria required.
- Present in writing three causes of World War II, specifying in the answer key actors, roles, places, or events.
- State orally the meaning of the terms *natural resources*, *ozone layer*, *China syndrome*, *radon*, and *smog*.
- Identify examples of the concept "refugee" from an unlabeled set of examples and nonexamples provided.
- Place on a time line a set of 10 events and their corresponding dates with 80% accuracy.

- Construct at least three hypotheses to explain why the American revolution occurred when it did.
- Identify two groups of American citizens who originally were not protected by the Constitution.
- Compare and contrast the positions of the major candidates for president on five major issues by constructing a chart summarizing the data.

## Objectives and Student Learning Outcomes

All of the sample objectives provided indicate some clear and specific student learning outcomes, but some are more precise than others. The first one, for example, is an illustration of a highly specific objective. It states exclusive *criteria* or standards, such as the number of items expected. It also specifies the *conditions* for demonstrating achievement of the objective, such as through writing.

Objectives that provide this degree of specificity and describe clearly the expected behavior of the student are characterized as **behavioral,** or **performance objectives.** All objectives that are stated clearly and specifically can be used effectively in the social studies to plan instruction and to communicate what the expected outcomes of student learning are to be. Some topics lend themselves more to the use of behavioral or performance objectives than others, such as identifying the location of states and listing their corresponding capitals.

**Writing Statements of Objectives.** Sources such as curriculum guides and basal texts often contain examples of the types of social studies goals and objectives for various grade levels and subjects. Typically, statements of objectives begin with the headings similar to the following: The pupil will be able to . . . In other cases, the introductory phrase is assumed, and the objective is stated in a briefer form similar to the following: To (write) (draw) (point to). . . .

Many lists of verbs have been identified to aid teachers in writing objectives. A sample list is provided here to suggest the range of possibilities that can be considered. As a result of the lesson (activity), the student will be able to:

| | | |
|---|---|---|
| rank | identify | defend |
| estimate | assemble | sort |
| predict | match | summarize |
| rate | point to | explain |
| select | organize | demonstrate |
| role-play | classify | locate |
| construct | define | draw |
| write | diagram | modify |

| | | |
|---|---|---|
| state | create | criticize |
| justify | judge | support |
| listen | share | hypothesize |
| debate | convince | map |
| formulate | theorize | internalize |
| conduct | use | argue |
| display | resolve | exhibit |

### Objectives in the Cognitive and Affective Domains

Social studies curriculum planners often classify goals and objectives as being within the cognitive or affective domains. The **cognitive domain** emphasizes thinking processes, and the **affective domain** feelings and emotions. Systems for creating and classifying goals and objectives within these domains were developed by Bloom and his associates four decades ago (Bloom, 1956; Krathwohl, Bloom, & Masia, 1969).

Some goals and objectives indicate directly which of the domains they highlight. The first objective in the set of illustrations in the preceding section, for instance, can be characterized as emphasizing the cognitive domain. Many goals and objectives, however, are not so easily classified and require reference to the context in which they arise.

## ORGANIZING SUBJECT MATTER INTO UNITS

Teachers are typically assigned only the general framework for the subject matter of a course, for example, "world history." In other situations, the complete course of study for the entire year may be laid out, such as when a district, school, or department has adopted a scope and sequence pattern.

In most cases, however, it is possible to augment the existing course outline with supplementary lessons on timely topics, such as local elections or current events. Further, individual teachers have the opportunity to infuse existing curriculum outlines and guidelines with their own sense of purpose, goals, and objectives. In planning, they also will need to consider the background, interests, capabilities, and learning styles of their students (see Chapter 12).

One systematic and direct way to ascertain student interests and concerns as a basis for a unit is to use a structured anonymous survey or questionnaire. An example of how this might be done is given in Figure 4.1.

### Planning and Creating Units

It is possible to organize the subject matter of a course into **units** of study. The essence of a unit is a series of sequenced and related learning activities organized around some theme, issue, or problem, along with goals, objec-

**Figure 4.1**
**Assessing Students' Special Needs**

YOUR ROLE: Teacher ____________ Student ____________ Parent ____________

We are interested in getting your opinion about what special topics might be added to the school's curriculum. We want to be sure that the curriculum includes topics that are important to our students. Listed below are some topics that have been suggested. Consider each one. Then tell us your opinion about whether these topics should be added to the curriculum. Circle one of these answers:

*Definitely:* This topic should *definitely* be added to the curriculum.
*Maybe:* This topic *maybe* should be added, if there is time.
*Not:* This topic should *not* be added to the curriculum.

At the bottom of the page you may list any other topics that you think should definitely be added.

As you answer, keep in mind that if topics are added, then some present topics will have to be dropped or given less time.

The results of the survey will be used by the faculty in determining which changes, if any, should be proposed to the superintendent and the school board.

| **Topic** | **Your Opinion** | | |
|---|---|---|---|
| 1. Avoiding alcohol and drug abuse. | Definitely | Maybe | Not |
| 2. Learning how to be a good citizen. | Definitely | Maybe | Not |
| 3. Making good moral choices. | Definitely | Maybe | Not |
| 4. Learning about careers. | Definitely | Maybe | Not |
| 5. Understanding how families are changing. | Definitely | Maybe | Not |
| 6. Making wise decisions about sex. | Definitely | Maybe | Not |
| 7. Learning how to be a smart consumer. | Definitely | Maybe | Not |
| 8. Knowing how to prevent suicide. | Definitely | Maybe | Not |
| 9. Protecting the environment. | Definitely | Maybe | Not |
| 10. Preparing for college entrance tests. | Definitely | Maybe | Not |
| 11. Improving our community. | Definitely | Maybe | Not |
| 12. Making good use of leisure time. | Definitely | Maybe | Not |
| 13. Understanding the future. | Definitely | Maybe | Not |
| 14. Living in a nuclear age. | Definitely | Maybe | Not |
| 15. Understanding the world's religions. | Definitely | Maybe | Not |
| 16. Learning about world population control. | Definitely | Maybe | Not |
| 17. Valuing our own and others' ethnic heritage. | Definitely | Maybe | Not |
| 18. Reducing conflict between groups. | Definitely | Maybe | Not |
| 19. Selecting and getting into the right college. | Definitely | Maybe | Not |
| 20. Living in peace with other countries. | Definitely | Maybe | Not |

If there are any other topics not listed above that you think should definitely be added, list them here:

21. ______________________________

22. ______________________________

23. ______________________________

*Note.* From *Curriculum renewal* (p. 60) by A. A. Glatthorn, 1987. Reprinted with permission of the Association for Supervision and Curriculum Development and the author. 

**Units should include a mix of activities that involve the head, the hand, and the heart.**

organized around some theme, issue, or problem, along with goals, objectives, resources for learning, and procedures for evaluation.

Resources identified within units frequently include primary source materials, computer software, textbooks, artifacts, maps, periodicals, microfilm, microfiche, and readings. They also may include posters, work sheets, simulation games, transparencies, and drawings. Further, resources may encompass guest speakers, field trips, films, videotapes, videodiscs, audiotape recordings, and assorted other media.

Units may be designed for any length of time. Typically, however, they require from two to six weeks to complete.

**Sample Unit Topics.** Some illustrations of unit titles are:

- "The Two Chinas Problem"
- "The Environmental Crisis in the World"
- "The Causes of the American Revolution"
- "The Role of Women in Developing Nations"
- "International Terrorism"
- "The Homeless in America"
- "The Origins and Aftermath of the Great Depression"

## Sources of Units

Units are available through the national educational clearinghouse, the ERIC Clearinghouse for Social Studies/Social Science Education, Indiana University, 2805 East 10 Street, Bloomington, IN 47408. Additionally, school supply houses that specialize in distributing social studies materials produced by commercial publishers are excellent sources. An example is the Social Studies School Service, 10200 Jefferson Boulevard, PO Box 802, Culver City, CA 90232-0802.

Professional organizations and local school districts also have developed collections of units for different grade levels on a variety of topics. These units typically are located in teacher resource centers and other professional libraries.

"Slavery in the Nineteenth Century" is an example of a unit designed for grades 5 through 8 that is available from a professional organization, the National Center for History in the Schools. The basic goal of the unit is to "make slavery comprehensible to students, showing its oppressiveness and yet explaining how white Southern culture rationalized and sustained it" (Pearson & Robertson, 1991, p. 9). The unit consists of six lessons of varying length with corresponding objectives as follows:

***Lesson 1 Objectives:***

1. To list at least three justifications of slavery used by whites.
2. To speculate on the validity of the justifications of slavery.
3. To explain ways in which white Southerners were legally required to support slavery. (Pearson & Robertson, 1991, p. 15)

***Lesson 2 Objectives:***

1. To study part of a slave inventory.
2. To see how slaves were treated as both people and property.
3. To understand that slaves had various occupations requiring various skills.
4. To compare various forms of slave labor. (Pearson & Robertson, 1991, p. 27)

***Lesson 3 Objectives:***

1. To appreciate African American culture as reflected in stories and crafts.
2. To demonstrate in discussion an understanding of the ways in which African American culture helped give slaves the skills and strength to endure slavery.
3. To identify some aspects of American culture that have African American origins. (Pearson & Robertson, 1991, p. 39)

***Lesson 4 Objectives:***

1. To understand why open rebellion was rarely undertaken.
2. To list different ways slaves resisted their condition.
3. To enact through the *READERS' THEATRE* an example of the minor resistance which pervaded slaves interactions with masters. (Pearson & Robertson, 1991, p. 51)

***Lesson 5 Objectives:***

1. To understand that not everyone accepted slavery.
2. To learn the names and accomplishments of three abolitionists.
3. To explore the diverse arguments for abolition.
4. To appreciate the moral and physical courage of the abolitionists. (Pearson & Robertson, 1991, p. 61)

***Lesson 6 Objectives:***

1. To understand that black and white women were prominent in the struggle for abolition.
2. To express the connection between abolition and the women's rights movement.
3. To list some of the prominent women involved with both abolition and women's rights. (Pearson & Robertson, 1991, p. 75)

A portion of the text of Lesson 4 from the unit is shown in Figure 4.2.

Teachers, themselves, are one of the major developers of individual units. Many of these are shared within a school or district and often are published in curriculum guides and professional texts and journals. An illustration is the set of teacher-generated global studies units detailed in the text, *Teaching about International Conflict and Peace* (Shapiro & Merryfield, 1995).

In developing units, teachers build on their special interests, expertise, or experiences, such as travels. Teacher-created units often begin with a general set of ideas or questions centered around topics that teachers regard as important and that fit within the general framework of their courses. From this base of ideas the other specific details are fleshed out to give the unit shape and focus.

Student textbooks are organized into units that are frequently arranged in chronological order. An illustration taken from the textbook *The American Nation* (Prentice-Hall, 1986) is provided in Figure 4.3. The text is divided into 10 units that normally would be spread over the 36 weeks of the school year. The subject matter of each unit is organized into three to four subtopics or chapters. Each chapter, in turn, is organized into two or more related lessons. Resource materials, follow-up activities, and evaluation measures are provided in each unit.

## Resource Units and Teaching Units

Units are sometimes classified as **resource units** and **teaching units.** Although the two types share many of the same elements, resource units generally are more extensive and detailed than teaching units. Also, they often are designed as multipurpose collections of material to be used by many different teachers for a variety of students. A resource unit typically would list more subtopics, objectives, teaching strategies and activities, resources, and evaluation procedures than an individual teacher needs to use for a topic. Drawing on a resource unit, a teacher can create a teaching

**Figure 4.2**
**Portion of an Instructional Unit on the Resistance of Slaves**

**Slave Resistance**

**A. Objectives**

1. To understand why open rebellion was rarely undertaken.
2. To list different ways slaves resisted their condition.
3. To enact through the Readers' Theatre an example of the minor resistance which pervaded slaves' interactions with masters.

**B. Lesson Background Materials**

Slave resistance ranged from adopting a mask of humility, which gave an illusion of utter dependence, to open revolt, which culminated in the massacre of whites. Students tend to be interested in the sensational forms of resistance. While revolts did occur, they should not be overemphasized. There were hundreds of conspiracies to revolt, but only a few ever actually took place. Nat Turner's Rebellion in Virginia in 1831 is the most famous. Turner's revolt resulted in the murder of 55 white men, women, and children and the deaths of as many blacks in the aftermath. To white Southerners, almost more chilling than the number of deaths was Turner's intelligence and status as the trusted slave of a relatively kind master. If Turner could rebel, then any slave might rise up against any master.

Violent and open rebellions were much more common in Latin America than in North America. This difference was due to weaker military control, easier access to unsettled areas, a greater imbalance of blacks to whites and a greater imbalance of males to females. The existence of families among slaves in the United States was crucial in restraining violent revolts.

Slaves committed countless acts of individual rebellion in day to day living. They often worked slowly or pretended to be stupid when asked to learn a skill. They were careless about property—losing farm tools, damaging equipment and abusing farm animals. Arson was a particularly effective means of revenge; it required little effort and was difficult to detect. Feigning illness was commonplace, especially during harvest or other periods of heavy work. The most pervasive form of resistance was simply masking one's true nature by adopting a role. The role might be a child-like dependence on the master, a stubborn stupidity, or a mask of apathy. Frederick Douglass wrote that he had never heard a slave, while still a slave, say that he or she had a bad master. Masters took comfort in the outward subservience of slaves, but it was a very uneasy comfort bolstered by patrols and the lash.

Running away was another option. Typically, runaways were young males who ran off alone and hid in neighboring woods or swamps. Usually they would be caught or would return on their own after a few days alone without food. But some

*Source:* Reprinted from *Slavery in the Nineteenth Century,* by Jim Pearson and John Robertson, by permission of the National Center for History in the Schools, University of California, Los Angeles, 1991, pp. 51–58.

**Figure 4.2 continued**

slaves managed to escape. There were colonies of runaway slaves in the isolated swamps or mountains of the South, especially in Florida, where they became allied with Seminoles and other tribes of Indians. Another means of permanent escape was the underground railroad, a series of safe houses and stations organized by abolitionists, where slaves could hide on their journey north to freedom. The most famous "conductor," Harriet Tubman, led 300 slaves out of the South on nineteen separate trips.

**C. Lesson Activities**

1. In an exploratory discussion consider why slaves, with a few notable exceptions, did not openly revolt against their condition.
   a. Remind students of the laws reviewed in DOCUMENT B, "The Alabama Slave Code of 1852," which made rebellion difficult.
   b. Explain that masters were brutal to slaves who were even suspected of plotting to rebel and that slaves wanted to protect their families and friends from reprisals. Because most slaves did not openly rebel does not mean they quietly accepted slavery; they resisted in many ways. These acts of resistance were often disguised and typically difficult to prove.
2. Have students read DOCUMENT E, which includes "James Henry Hammond's Slave Rules" and additional excerpts from the "Alabama Slave Code of 1852" (these readings are sufficiently clear that a simplified version is thought unnecessary). These rules and laws suggest ways slaves resisted their masters.
   a. Discuss with students what they would do as slaves to resist their condition. Some students may say they would kill their masters or run away. Slaves did those things, but not as frequently as one might suppose. Explain that slaves disguised their feelings from masters. In the presence of whites, slaves were always playing roles, acting in the ways they believed to be in their best interest. This gave them more private space for living, lulled masters, and gave slaves a measure of control over owners.
   b. Remind students of the patrols and the rules against slaves having weapons or gathering in groups. Also remind students of Bruce's slave inventory, which showed that many women and children were slaves. For the most part, slaves were too tightly controlled and too concerned with the relative well-being of their loved ones to risk open rebellion.
3. Shift the discussion to ways slaves could resist slavery without getting caught. Remind students of the "Tar Baby" story. See if students understand that stories, songs, and other forms of cultural expression were all ways to resist slavery. Often masters were oblivious to resistance of this sort.

**Figure 4.2**
**continued**

Through careful questioning, students should come to recognize some of the more common forms of slave resistance. Questions might include:

a. Why would a master care if a slave or a slave's house was unclean?
b. What does neglect of tools mean?
c. Since all tools eventually wear out or break, could masters or overseers know if a tool was broken on purpose?
d. What difference does it make to the master if slaves drank alcohol?
e. Why was setting a fire punishable by death?
f. Why was breaking into a white person's house at night punishable by death?

Explain that slaves disguised their feelings from masters. In the presence of whites, slaves were always playing roles, acting in the ways they believed to be in their best interest. This gave them more private space for living, lulled masters, and gave slaves a measure of control over owners. Have students list forms of rebellion. These might include:

a. Breaking tools
b. Losing tools
c. Working slowly
d. Running away
e. Feigning illness
f. Pretending stupidity
g. Lying
h. Stealing
i. Arson

4. Pass out DOCUMENT F, "Slavery and the Domestic Slave Trade in the United States." Explain that it is part of a letter written by Ethan Allen Andrews in 1835 and published in 1836 as part of a book about American slavery. The conversation is a distillation of many similar ones Andrews had heard throughout the South.
   a. Divide the class into groups of three. Have students read the document silently.
   b. Have volunteers choose parts for a performance for the class.
5. As a concluding activity, students might write a brief paragraph on slave resistance from a slave's point of view.

**D. Evaluating the Lesson**

Have students imagine they are former slaves explaining to their grandchildren, long after the abolition of slavery, about the ways they resisted slavery. They should write a short paragraph about the way they behaved and why.

**Figure 4.2 continued**

### STUDENT RESOURCE: DOCUMENT E

**James Henry Hammond's Instructions to His Overseer***

(Primary Source)

*The following is the order in which offences must be estimated and punished:*

*1st Running away*
*2nd Getting drunk or having spirits*
*3rd Stealing hogs*
*4th Stealing*
*5th Leaving plantation without permission*
*6th Absence from house after horn blow at night*
*7th Unclean house or person*
*8th Neglect of tools*
*9th Neglect of work*

*The highest punishment must not exceed one hundred lashes in one day and to that extent only in extreme cases. The whip lash must be one inch in width or a strap of one thickness of leather 1½ inches in width, and never severely administered. In general fifteen to twenty lashes will be sufficient flogging.*

*Manual of Rules, [c. 1840–1850] James Henry Hammond Papers, Library of Congress

**Alabama Slave Code of 1852**

(Primary Source)

Additional excerpts:*

1. *Every slave who breaks into and enters a dwelling house in the night time, with the intention to steal or commit a felony, must, on conviction, suffer death.*
2. *Any slave who breaks into and enters a dwelling house in the day time, or any other building in the day or night time, must, on conviction, be punished by stripes, not exceeding one hundred, and by branding in the hand, one or both.*
3. *Every slave who robs, or commits an assault and battery with intent to rob any white person, or willfully maims… any white person, or attempts to poison, or to deprive any white person of life, by any means… must, on conviction, suffer death.*
4. *Every slave who willfully and maliciously sets fire to or burns any dwelling house, or out house appurtenant thereto, store house, banking house, ware house, or other edifice, public or private, corn crib, gin house, cotton house, stable, barn, cotton in the heap to the value of one hundred dollars, or in bale to any value, or any ship or steam boat, must, on conviction, suffer death.*

* From *The Code of Alabama,* prepared by John J. Ormand, Arthur P. Bagby, and George Goldthwaite. Montgomery: Brittain and DeWolf, 1852. (pp. 234–245, 390–393, 589–597)

**Figure 4.3**
**Example of a Course of Study Organized Around Units**

**Unit 1**
**The World of the Americas**
**Chapter 1** The American Land (Prehistory–Present)
**Chapter 2** The First Americans (Prehistory–1600)
**Chapter 3** Europeans Explore America (1000–1650)

**Unit 2**
**Settling the New World**
**Chapter 4** Planting Colonies (1530–1690)
**Chapter 5** English Colonies Take Root (1630–1750)
**Chapter 6** Life in the Colonies (1630–1775)

**Unit 3**
**The Struggle for Independence**
**Chapter 7** Crisis in the Colonies (1757–1775)
**Chapter 8** The American Revolution (1775–1783)
**Chapter 9** Creating a Government (1776–1791)

**Unit 4**
**Strengthening the Nation**
**Chapter 10** The First Presidents (1789–1800)
**Chapter 11** Age of Jefferson (1801–1816)
**Chapter 12** The Nation Prospers (1790–1825)

**Unit 5**
**A Growing Nation**
**Chapter 13** Age of Jackson (1824–1840)
**Chapter 14** Westward Ho! (1820–1860)
**Chapter 15** Two Ways of Life (1820–1860)
**Chapter 16** The Reforming Spirit (1820–1860)

**Unit 6**
**A Nation Divided**
**Chapter 17** The Coming of the War (1820–1860)
**Chapter 18** The Civil War (1860–1865)
**Chapter 19** The Road to Reunion (1864–1877)

**Unit 7**
**America in a Changing Time**
**Chapter 20** Settling the West (1865–1914)
**Chapter 21** Industry Changes America (1865–1914)
**Chapter 22** One Land, Many Peoples (1865–1914)

**Unit 8**
**Becoming a World Power**
**Chapter 23** Calls for Reform (1876–1914)
**Chapter 24** America Looks Overseas (1865–1916)
**Chapter 25** World War I (1914–1919)

**Unit 9**
**A Troubled Time**
**Chapter 26** The Roaring Twenties (1919–1929)
**Chapter 27** The Great Depression (1929–1941)
**Chapter 28** World War II (1935–1945)

**Unit 10**
**Our Nation Today**
**Chapter 29** America in the Fifties (1945–1960)
**Chapter 30** Years of Protest and Change (1960–Present)
**Chapter 31** Challenges to Peace (1960–Present)
**Chapter 32** Pioneers of Today and Tomorrow (1960–Present)

*Note.* From *The American Nation,* 1986, Englewood Cliffs, NJ: Prentice Hall. Copyright 1986 by Prentice Hall. Reprinted by permission.

unit that is tailored for a specific population of students and for a given length of time.

## Building Units Around Key Social Problems, Questions, and Themes

Along with using students' and teachers' immediate interests as the basis for creating units, key social problems, questions, and themes may serve as the foundation for a unit. Using the Revolutionary War period in an American history class as an example, Engle and Ochoa (1988) have provided illustrative questions that teachers might raise to shape the design of a unit (1988; see also Onosko, 1992; Shapiro & Merryfield, 1995).

> Under what conditions is a revolution justified? Did conditions in America in the late eighteenth century fulfill those conditions? Are there better ways than revolution for bringing about social change in society? Under what conditions, if any, should people disobey the law? Is it equally right or wrong for governments to break the law than for individuals to break the law? (p. 156)

As noted in Chapter 1, Hunt and Metcalf (1968) argued that students should be asked to examine reflectively those areas in our culture that traditionally have been closed to scrutiny (see also Chapters 6 and 8). They called these the **closed areas of society.** Closed areas, they maintained, dealt with sex, religion, race and ethnicity, economics, and politics. They encouraged teachers to build lessons and units around issues involving the closed areas.

Similarly, Oliver and Shaver (1966) and Newmann with Oliver (1970) advocated building units around enduring value issues that recur throughout history. For example, a unit might be shaped around the value issue: "When, if ever, should the value of the public's health override personal freedom?" (Oliver, Newmann, & Singelton, 1992, p. 101). This question surfaces in general issues such as whether smoking should be prohibited in public places. How their approach to social issues, sometimes called the **jurisprudential approach,** can be implemented in developing units is considered in more detail in Chapter 8.

## Incorporating Multiple Perspectives into Units

Units also may be constructed around multiple perspectives, that is, different views or interpretations of the same set of events. Noddings (1991), for example, urged that feminist perspectives be included throughout the curriculum to provide a contextually richer analysis. Similarly, Banks (1993) also suggested the study of topics might be advanced and enriched by including the following five perspectives: personal/cultural (students' personal and cultural experiences), popular (mass media, pop culture, and films), mainstream academic (research from mainstream scholars), transformative academic (research that challenges mainstream findings or methodologies), and school (information in school texts and related media).

He illustrated how these five perspectives might be integrated in a unit on the Westward Movement:

> When beginning the unit, teachers can draw upon the students' personal and cultural knowledge about the Westward Movement. They can ask the students to make a list of ideas that come to mind when they think of "The West." To enable the students to determine how the popular culture depicts the West, teachers can ask the students to view and analyze . . . *How the West Was Won*. They can also ask them to view videos of more recently made films about the West and to make a list of its major themes and images. Teachers can summarize Turner's frontier theory to give students an idea of how an influential mainstream historian described and interpreted the West in the late 19th century and how this theory influenced generations of historians.
>
> Teachers can present a transformative perspective on the West by showing the students the film, *How the West Was Won and Honor Lost*. . . . Teachers may also ask the students to view segments of the popular film *Dances with Wolves* and to discuss how the depiction of Indians in the film reflects both mainstream and transformative perspectives on Indians in U.S. history and culture. Teachers can present the textbook account of the Westward Movement in the final part of the unit. (Banks, 1993, pp. 11–12)

Apart from providing an in-depth examination of a topic and promoting multicultural education, this approach introduces students to different types of knowledge. It allows them to use the "perspective glasses" discussed in Chapter 3 as a way to better understand the complexity of determining what occurred during an event.

## Using Concept Maps to Plan Units

One way for the teacher to sketch out the general structure of a unit is through the use of a concept map (Novak & Gowin, 1984). A **concept map** is a listing and an ordering of all of the major concepts to be discussed within a unit. Related concepts are joined in the map, along with a brief statement that explains how they are linked. As I discuss further in Chapters 6 and 9, concept maps have a number of applications in teaching. Our focus in this section is on their application to *unit planning*.

Concept maps offer teachers a planning tool for thinking about all of the important topics they wish to include and connections they wish to make among them in a unit. They provide a comprehensive graphic representation of the unit. Novak and Gowin (1984) have suggested that, in creating a map, teachers should focus on four to seven concepts that are central to the unit. A sample map that represents one instructor's plan for a unit of study on Roman history is shown in Figure 4.4.

To show the evolution of a concept map, a partially completed one depicting initial ideas for a unit on terrorist organizations has been adapted

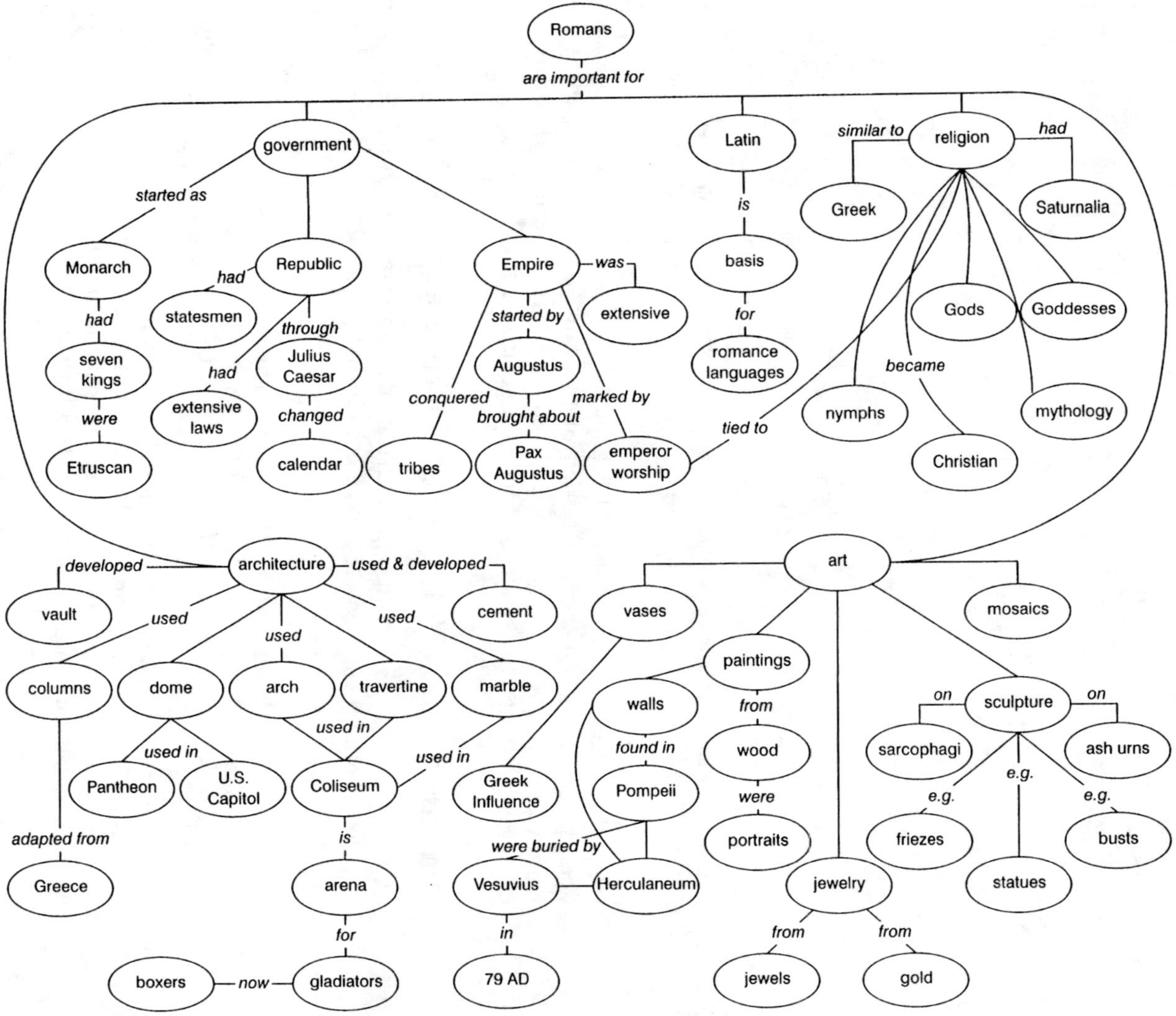


**Figure 4.4**
**Concept Map for Planning a Course of Study**
*Note.* From *Learning How to Learn* (pp. 84–85) by Joseph D. Novak and D. Bob Gowin, 1984. Copyright © 1984. Reprinted by permission of Cambridge University Press.

**Figure 4.5**
**Instructor's Concept Map for a Unit on Terrorism**

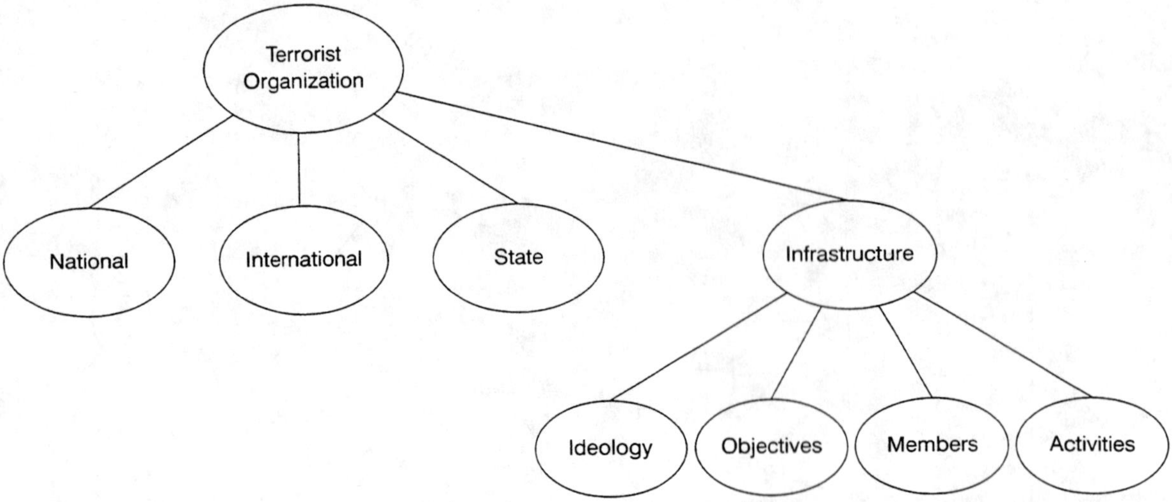


*Note.* From "Teaching About Terrorism: A Conceptual Approach" by M. Kleg, 1986, *Social Science Record, 24,* pp. 36–37. Reprinted by permission.

from Kleg (1986). It is shown in Figure 4.5. As the unit evolves, a teacher would need to fill in the key nodes of the map. For example, the teacher would list the groups to be used as case studies, along with the specific objectives and activities of each terrorist group.

## Planning Units Using Interdisciplinary Teams

"A problem inherent in the structure of the American high school," Merryfield and Remy (1995, p. 48) have concluded, "is fragmentation of the curriculum." They explain:

> For example, students rarely have the opportunity to connect their study of Thoreau's Civil Disobedience in English class in November with their study of the passive resistance tactics of the civil rights movement in U.S. history in March. In most American high schools students are not taught to appreciate important relationships across different academic disciplines or to examine issues holistically. Through the development of interdisciplinary teams such relationships and connections become part of course planning, unit construction, and student thinking. (Merryfield & Remy, 1995, pp. 48–49)

Interdisciplinary teaming also encourages teacher collaboration and sharing and provides greater opportunities for experimentation. In addition, teaming also permits more efficient use of instructional time, since redundancy in topics can be avoided.

**Figure 4.6**
**Sample Format for Unit Planning**

**Unit Plan Format**

I. Descriptive Characteristics
Title:
Student Target Population/Grade Level:
Estimated Time Required:
Rationale and Overview:

II. Goals and Objectives *(Number each for easy referral in constructing lesson plans.)*

Goals:

Specific Objectives:

III. Teaching Strategies and Activities *(Briefly describe the list of possibilities and number them for later reference.)*

IV. List of Resources *(List each item and subdivide by type— e.g., textbooks, speakers, field trips, reference works, various media. Number each for easy reference.)*

V. Evaluation Procedures *(Relate each item to the goals and objectives stated earlier.)*

## Formats for Unit Planning

There are a variety of different unit **formats,** or ways of organizing and presenting the information in a unit. A sample format for developing a unit plan is given in Figure 4.6. The choice of a format to use in unit planning, however, is largely a matter of personal preference. The most practical course of action for teachers is to identify a format in an existing unit that they find easy to follow, and to adopt it.

In summary, the general process of creating a unit can be outlined as follows:

1. Develop an idea for a special topic of study and translate it into a brief, clear statement of your theme or problem focus. (Unit Title)
2. Break the big idea or theme for the unit into a set of more specific ideas and smaller subtopics. (List of Topics)

3. Indicate for which group of students or grade levels the unit is intended and include them in the planning if possible. (Target Student Population)
4. Determine approximately how much time can be spent on the unit. (Time Required)
5. Construct a brief overview of what the unit is to be about and why it is important and useful for the intended class to learn it. (Rationale)
6. Identify a goal or set of basic goals that the unit will be designed to accomplish. (Goals)
7. Outline the specific objectives to be accomplished with the unit and arrange them in sequential order. (Objectives)
8. Identify and develop related significant teaching strategies and activities. (Teaching Strategies and Activities)
9. Identify, locate, and organize all the individuals and the instructional resources that are available and will be needed. (Resources)
10. Develop a plan to evaluate the effectiveness of the unit. (Evaluation Procedures)

## ORGANIZING SUBJECT MATTER INTO LESSONS

As we have seen, one important element of teaching units is the provision for **lessons.** Apart from units, teachers also fashion lessons to achieve discrete objectives that can be achieved over a short period of time. A lesson may last for a single class period or extend over several days.

### Lesson Plans

Lesson planning includes taking into account what has come *before* the lesson and what is to *follow* it, as well as what happens *during* it. Lesson planning requires careful attention to the conditions under which learning is to occur. This includes an awareness of the prior knowledge and special needs of individual students within a class.

Developing effective lessons also requires teachers to give careful thought to the specific details of what is to be achieved. Additionally, it involves consideration of how instructional activities can accomplish objectives in an interesting and meaningful way for a particular group of students.

Above all, in planning lessons, the teacher should have an informed grasp of the subject matter under investigation. In Dewey's (1961) words:

> When engaged in the direct act of teaching, the instructor needs to have subject matter at his fingers' ends; his attention should be upon the attitude and response of the pupil. . . . the teacher should be occupied not with the subject matter itself but in its interaction with the pupils' present needs and capacities." (p. 183)

## Formats and Procedures for Lesson Planning

A quick review of lesson plans found in curricular guides, teacher's manuals for basal texts, and teachers' publications and periodicals will reveal a great deal of variety in forms. As with units, there exist many different notions concerning what written lesson plans should include and which format should be used to construct them. Examples vary in structure, terminology, degree of detail, and in the number of elements they include. The two different types of lesson plans presented in Figures 4.7 and 4.8 illustrate this point.

Similar to the process of adopting a format for unit planning, selecting a format and procedures for lesson planning is largely a matter of a teacher's professional judgment or school requirements. Some schools, for example, request that teachers employ a format and set of procedures that have been standardized in the school or district.

An example of a standardized approach to lesson planning that was adopted by a number of schools across the United States in the 1980s is a seven-step plan developed by and popularized by Hunter (1984). Hunter's lesson plan design, sometimes called the **Theory and Practice (TAP) Model,** provides for the following elements:

1. Establish anticipatory set. (Get students' attention.)
2. Explain the objective of the lesson.
3. Provide instructional input.
4. Model the desired student behavior.
5. Check for understanding. (Get feedback.)
6. Provide for guided practice.
7. Provide for independent practice.

Hunter's model is similar to the seven-step instructional model developed earlier by Gagné and Briggs (1979):

1. Gain attention.
2. Inform the learner of the objective.
3. Stimulate recall of prerequisite learning.
4. Present the stimulus material.
5. Elicit desired behavior.
6. Provide feedback.
7. Assess behavior.

(The sample lesson plan illustrated in Figure 4.8 follows the Gagné and Briggs seven-step format.)

The issue of mandated lesson plan formats and procedures has become controversial among teachers and professional groups. Some of the

**Figure 4.7**
**Sample Lesson Plan Format**

**Patterns of Prosperity**

Creating and using thematic maps require students to gather information, to identify factors for analysis, and to form hypotheses about the geographic theme "regions"—areas defined by certain shared characteristics. This lesson shows students how to create one kind of thematic map and to compare the relative wealth of the various countries in South America. The activity was developed for use with middle-school students.

**Objectives**

- To understand the meaning of the geographic theme *regions* and the term *per capita income.*
- To research data from maps, almanacs, and other sources.
- To map numerical data for geographic regions.
- To analyze and compare patterns of data on quartile maps.

**Background discussion**

Ask students to define the term *region* and to give examples of regions (polar region, the Middle East, Chinatown, an economic region). Encourage students to give some local examples. Tell students they will be comparing per capita income data of the countries of South America and studying regions that share common economic characteristics.

**Materials**

A wall map of South America or an atlas; a current almanac; an outline map of South America; *The Development Data Book,* World Bank Publications, Washington, D.C., 1984. (This book contains social and economic statistics for 125 countries.)

**Schedule of Activities**

*Day 1*

- Have students look at maps of South America and speculate about which might be the wealthiest and the poorest countries. They should write down their predictions, giving reasons for their choices.
- Discuss the term *per capita income,* making sure that students understand how the figures are determined.
- Assign students to look up the per capita income for each country in South America in an atlas or an almanac.
- Have students compare this data with their speculations to see how correct they were.

*Day 2*

- Explain how quartile mapping is done:
  — Rank the per capita income data of each country from highest to lowest.

*Note.* From *Teaching Geography: A Model for Action* (pp. 53–55), 1988, Washington, DC: National Geographic Society. Reprinted courtesy of the National Geographic Society. 

**Figure 4.7 continued**

- Divide the ranked data into four equal parts (as nearly as possible). Each of these parts is called a quartile.
- Define the range (highest to lowest figures) of each quartile.
- Assign a color to each quartile—the darkest colors for the highest figures and lightest colors for the lowest figures.
- Create a key that shows the per capita income range that each color represents.

- Have students fill in the outline map using the four colors from the key.
- Analyze the data on the map.
  - Did the map turn out as predicted? If not, why not?
  - Discuss the factors students think could be related to the per capita income of a country. List these on the board. (Possible answers might include population, resources, value of exports, arable land, labor, literacy, industries, GNP, political or governmental influences. This information is available in an atlas or an almanac.) Keep this list for the next day.

*Day 3*

- Divide the class into small teams. Tell each team that it will be making a second quartile map.
- Review the factors listed on the board on Day 2. Discuss which factors could be represented by numerical data.
- Ask each team to select one factor—literacy, for example—for which numerical data can be found in an atlas or an almanac. Have teams collect data on that factor for each country.
- Have students speculate on which factors they think would be related most closely to per capita income. Discuss why they think so. Have each group map its set of data, using quartiles.
- Have the teams compare their new quartile maps with the per capita income quartile map. How closely do they match? Which data matches most closely? What are some possible reasons for differences?
- Summarize the lesson with the following questions:
  - What is per capita income and what does it tell us about a country or region?
  - Why does per capita income vary in different countries or regions?

**Related Activities**

Have students collect data for other regions of the world or for regions within the United States and follow this same activity.

**Figure 4.8**
**Sample Lesson Plan Format**

**Unit Title:** United States History (Early Beginning through Reconstruction)
**Lesson Title:** Causes of the Civil War Lesson 2.3

**1. Gaining Attention**

Show the following list of wars on a transparency:

French and Indian War 1754–1769
Revolutionary War 1775–1781
Civil War 1861–1865
World War I 1914–1918
World War II 1941–1945
Korean War 1950–1953
Vietnam War 1965–1975

**2. Informing the Learner of the Objective**

Learners will be expected to know the causes of the Civil War and to show that those causes also can apply to at least one of the wars listed on the transparency.

**3. Stimulating Recall of Prerequisite Learning**

Briefly review the causes of both the French and Indian War and the Revolutionary War as covered in Lessons 2.1 and 2.2

**4. Presenting the Stimulus Material**

(a) Summarize major events leading to the Civil War:
- — rise of sectionalism,
- — labor-intensive economy,
- — lack of diversification.

(b) Identify significant individuals during the Civil War and their roles:
- — Lincoln,
- — Lee,
- — Davis,
- — Grant.

(c) Describe four general causes of war and explain which are most relevant to the Civil War:
- — economic (to profit),
- — political (to control),
- — social (to influence),
- — military (to protect).

**5. Eliciting the Desired Behavior**

Ask the class to identify which of the four causes is most relevant to the major events leading up to the Civil War.

**6. Providing Feedback**

Ask for student answers and indicate plausibility of the volunteered responses.

**7. Assessing the Behavior**

Assign as homework a one-page essay assessing the relative importance of the four causes for one of the wars listed on the transparency.

*Note.* Reprinted with the permission of Simon & Schuster, Inc., from the Merrill/Prentice Hall text *Effective Teaching Methods* (3rd ed., pp. 227–228) by Gary Borich. Copyright © 1996 by Prentice Hall, Inc.

reasons schools have given for instituting such policies were to establish minimal teaching standards and to expedite communication among teachers, supervisors, and administrators. For some teachers, however, such a requirement presents a serious constraint. They regard such formats as overly restrictive and inflexible, inappropriate for many types of significant learning activities, and in general an infringement on their professional prerogatives.

## The Fundamental Elements of Lesson Planning

Some fundamental elements to consider in developing a lesson plan structure and format include the following items:

- Lesson title,
- Goals and objectives,
- Initiatory activity,
- Teaching strategies,
- Resources, and
- Transition\Assessment.

To help illustrate the lesson-planning process, for each item, we have included an example taken from the elements of a lesson plan developed by the National Geographic Society (1988, pp. 14–15).

1. *Title.* Giving each lesson a title communicates its focus. Example: "The Geography of Petroleum."
2. *Goals and Objectives.* The lesson should be linked to the larger instructional goals that the teacher has established earlier. The objectives that the lesson is designed to achieve should be stated clearly and as specifically as possible. Although the lesson itself may not explicitly identify for students the goals and objectives it is to achieve, it should be clearly related to them in the prior planning of the lesson. Example: "To use maps and graphs to identify the major areas of world petroleum production and consumption."
3. *Initiatory Activity.* A lesson plan should begin with some brief **initiatory activity** that arouses curiosity, puzzles the students, or somehow focuses attention on what is to be learned. (Onosko, 1992, called this a "grabber".) Example: "Ask students to imagine an end to all international sales of petroleum tomorrow. What would be the impact on the United States? How would students' lives change? What would happen to countries that consume major amounts of petroleum but produce little or none? Use Japan as an example."
4. *Teaching Strategies.* Teaching strategies and activities refer generally to the set of procedures that teachers employ to achieve their instructional

objectives. Different types of strategies exist for different objectives. Strategies incorporate questions, statements, directions, actions, and the sequence in which they are to occur. Strategies also deal with how the teacher plans to structure and present new subject matter and relate it to students' prior knowledge. They also indicate teacher and student roles in the lesson. Example: "Direct students to examine maps in an atlas to identify major petroleum-producing countries. (See *Goode's World Atlas*, page 48.) List their findings on the chalkboard. Have students shade and label these countries on their world outline maps."

5. *Resources.* Somewhere within the lesson for easy reference should be a list of the various resources that will be used during the lesson. The order in which the materials are to be used also should be clearly indicated.
6. *Transition\Assessment.* Each lesson should include some transition to the next one. This may consist merely of a summary of the day's activities, with some indication of what is to follow and how the two lessons are related. It also might consist of some assessment of a phase of learning that has just been completed (see Chapter 13). Additionally, it might provide opportunities for students to apply, extend, or experiment with what they have learned. Example: "Have students research the environmental implications of the widespread use of petroleum as an energy source. (Examples would include air pollution, global warming, oil spills.)"

## CLASSROOMS AS ENVIRONMENTS FOR LEARNING

Although teachers often have limited control over many of the physical features of a classroom, they generally have some freedom, even in the case of shared classrooms, to transform it in ways that facilitate the achievement of their objectives.

### The Uses of Space in Planning Social Studies Instruction

Space in a classroom is an instructional resource to be used prudently like any other. By attending carefully to how space is organized within an area, we can learn much about the kinds of activities that are likely to be encouraged and discouraged within it.

The ways in which teachers and students organize and use their classroom space will either facilitate or impede their mutual objectives. How individuals are located within the space may determine whether productive collaboration, misbehavior, and learning generally are more likely to occur than not. For example, the dynamics of a class likely will be different if a room is filled with tables and chairs rather than desks.

## Allocation of Time in Lesson Plans

In recent years, increasing attention has been paid to how instructional time in classrooms is used by teachers and students. Time, like texts and other instructional materials, represents an important resource for social studies teachers to accomplish their objectives. In planning and executing lessons, teachers need to attend carefully to how time is distributed across various activities. A major issue is the extent to which significant goals and priorities receive the lion's share of attention in the curriculum.

Time is an instructional issue for teachers both on a daily and a long-term basis. Teachers should oversee whether time is portioned out appropriately within individual units and across various topics, as well as throughout the school day and year. They also need to decide whether they will use their annual ration of time to engage students in in-depth examination of a limited number of topics or try to "cover ground."

The sample teacher schedules in Chapter 1 illustrate a conventional approach to organizing class periods. Such traditional school schedules require that a teacher typically monitor how approximately 45 to 50 minutes of total class contact time are used. For example, in the lesson shown in Figure 4.8 designed for a 50-minute period, Borich (1996) recommended that the following distribution of time be used for each of the seven steps in the lesson:

- Step 1. Gaining attention: 1 to 5 minutes
- Step 2. Stating objective: 1 to 3 minutes
- Step 3. Stimulating recall: 5 to 10 minutes
- Step 4. Presenting stimulus material: 10 to 20 minutes
- Step 5. Eliciting desired behavior: 10 to 20 minutes
- Step 6. Providing feedback: 5 to 10 minutes
- Step 7. Assessing behavior: Zero to 10 minutes

**Scheduling Alternatives.** As a way to provide more flexibility in planning social studies instruction, a number of alternatives to the 45- to 50-minute class have been advanced in recent years (Canady & Rettig, 1993). One approach, "the 75-75-30 plan," was initiated as a way to ease the transition from middle to high school. As shown in the example in Figure 4.9, the school year is organized into two 75-day terms and one 30-day session.

Note that social studies classes are offered in a "block" consisting of two periods daily, each 112 minutes in duration for a single 75-day term. "Each block class taught during the 75-day term," Canady and Rettig (1993) have noted, "provides 8,400 minutes of instruction; 112 minutes per day

**Figure 4.9**
**75-75-30 Plan**

| | **Fall Term 75 Days** | **Winter Term 75 Days** | **Spring Term 30 Days** |
|---|---|---|---|
| Block I (periods 1 & 2, 112 minutes) | English | Elective(s) | Elective or Community Service |
| Block II (periods 3 & 4, 112 minutes) | Physical Education | Science | |
| Period 5/L 48 minutes + 24 for lunch) | Band & Lunch | Band & Lunch | Band & Lunch |
| Block III (periods 6 & 7, 112 minutes) | Math | Social Science | Elective & Study |

From "Unlocking the Lockstep High School Schedule," by R. L. Canaday and M. D. Rettig, 1993, *Phi Delta Kappan, 75,* p. 311. Reprinted by permission.

for 75 days is approximately 180 traditional 47-minute class periods" (p. 311).

Such scheduling options afford teachers, students, and administrators opportunities to experiment with different instructional models and to integrate curriculum such as English and social studies. They also permit activities that are not easily compressed into a traditional class period, such as simulations and debates, to be initiated and completed without interruption.

Whatever scheduling options are available to teachers, as they become more skilled in organizing resources and in planning lessons and units, there will be increased opportunities to focus on the needs, interests, and progress of individual students.

## CREATING AND MANAGING THE CLASSROOM ENVIRONMENT

Apart from the issue of how time should be allocated, perhaps one of the most common concerns of beginning teachers is that they will be unable to manage their classes effectively. They often are frightened that their classes will "get out of control." A component of the fear may be the anticipation of possible physical or verbal abuse from students. Beginning teachers may wonder how they would cope in the classroom with extreme behavior such as overt profanity, displays of drugs and drug abuse, assaults, carrying of weapons, and general outbreaks of violence.

An individual or group of students bent on antisocial, violent, or destructive behavior can be frightening for the teacher who is responsible for redirecting the individual or group into constructive learning activities. When a teacher is unsuccessful in doing this, the feeling may be one of complete powerlessness and incompetence.

No effective instruction can occur in the midst of a maelstrom. Communication in a classroom out of control is garbled and coated with tension. Students and teacher lack the sense of security and stability that is necessary for effective teaching and learning to transpire.

A number of comprehensive texts address fears and real problems such as these, as well as the general mechanics of classroom management (e.g., Glasser, 1992; Good & Brophy, 1991; Gordon, 1974; Weber, 1994). A full and adequate discussion of the issues they cover is beyond the scope of this text. Because a successfully managed classroom environment is central to all effective social studies instruction, however, the subject merits at least brief attention in our discussion.

## Student Behavior in the Classroom

Gottfredson, Gottfredson, and Hybl (1993) noted:

> Disruptive behavior in school harms both the misbehaving individual and the school community. Students who misbehave also drop out of school, use drugs and alcohol, and engage in delinquent behavior at higher rates than do their more conforming peers. Later, they tend to make poorer occupational and marital adjustments. . . . (p. 180)

Often beginning teachers receive a countless number of well-intentioned suggestions from their more experienced colleagues on how to be successful in managing a classroom. Those range from maxims such as "Don't smile before Christmas" to lists of specific teacher behaviors to be modeled.

The difficulty for the neophyte in trying to implement such suggestions usually is the lack of an underlying framework or set of principles that can provide a rationale for the teacher's behavior. The absence of such a framework ultimately creates problems when a specific behavior that normally is effective proves to be ineffective. At that point, a teacher is at a loss as to what went wrong and which adjustments should be made.

One central element of a classroom-management framework is awareness of the teacher's expectations concerning what is appropriate student behavior in a classroom. A second basic element is knowledge of well-grounded theory and research concerning characteristics of well-managed classrooms. We will briefly consider each of these points.

## Teacher Expectations Concerning Student Behavior

Good and Brophy (1987) have noted:

> To manage classrooms effectively, teachers need both clear expectations about how students should spend their time and knowledge about what to do when their expectations are not being met. Expectations define classroom management goals and guide decisions about creating, maintaining, and restoring desirable student behavior. (p. 216)

Each teacher has some expectations regarding how his or her students are to behave in the classroom. Some teachers, for example, will accept a high level of noise and a great deal of student movement within the classroom. Others require students to request permission to speak or move about. Students in the middle and secondary grades often have to make quick adjustments from period to period, from one teacher's set of expectations to another.

At best, these adjustments are often just another challenge that students associate with schooling. At worst, they represent for some students a continuing source of confusion and eventual conflict.

Students, themselves, also have their own sets of expectations about appropriate teacher behavior. Those expectations typically include how they expect the teacher to treat them. They also involve what students expect the teacher to do with respect to managing the general classroom environment, including establishing and maintaining rules and policies and handling behavioral problems.

Because teachers' expectations of student behavior may vary within a given school, it often is helpful to make explicit at the beginning of the year the rules, policies, and procedures students are to follow within a given class. These may cover many different areas as the list in Figure 4.10 illustrates.

The process of underscoring expectations can be accomplished simply through the prominent display of a chart, brief statements on assignment sheets, or verbal reminders. In all cases, the teacher should ensure that all students, even chronic absentees, have been briefed.

## Characteristics of Well-Managed Classrooms

What do teachers who have well-managed classrooms do to achieve their results? The answers can be complex and varied, depending on the criteria used for successful management, the subject area, and the ages and personalities of the students. Consequently, answers often appear more in the form of hypotheses that have been partially tested, rather than as definitive prescriptions. Much of the evidence, however, suggests that managerial success involves preventing behavioral problems *before* they occur through specific teacher behaviors (Good & Brophy, 1991).

**Figure 4.10**
**Classroom Rules Related to Conduct and Work**

| | Rules related to classroom conduct | Rules related to academic work |
|---|---|---|
| Rules that need to be communicated first day | 1. where to sit<br>2. how seats are assigned<br>3. what to do before the bell rings<br>4. responding, speaking out<br>5. leaving at the bell<br>6. drinks, food, and gum<br>7. washroom and drinking privileges | 8. materials required for class<br>9. homework completion<br>10. make-up work<br>11. incomplete work<br>12. missed quizzes and examinations<br>13. determining grades<br>14. violation of rules |
| Rules that can be communicated later | 15. tardiness/absences<br>16. coming up to desk<br>17. when a visitor comes to the door<br>18. leaving the classroom<br>19. consequences of rule violation | 20. notebook completion<br>21. obtaining help<br>22. notetaking<br>23. sharing work with others<br>24. use of learning center and/or reference works<br>25. communication during group work<br>26. neatness<br>27. lab safety |

*Note.* Reprinted with the permission of Simon & Schuster, Inc., from the Merrill/Prentice Hall text *Effective Teaching Methods* (3rd ed., p. 478) by Gary Borich. Copyright © 1996 by Prentice Hall, Inc.

Kounin's work (1970) remains one of the most systematic sets of information available on the subject of classroom management, even though his research was limited to elementary classrooms. He found that it was possible to isolate specific teacher behaviors that appeared to be related to managerial success in the classroom. "These techniques of classroom management," he wrote, "apply to the group and not merely to individual students. They are techniques of creating an effective classroom ecology and learning milieu. One might note that none of them necessitates punitiveness or restrictiveness" (Kounin, 1970, p. 143–144).

His findings were that teachers who had a *high* degree of work involvement and a *low* degree of misbehavior in their classrooms demonstrated consistently certain behaviors. Some of those were the following:

1. *Withitness.* Communicating that one knows what is going on in the classroom at all times.
2. *Overlapping.* Being able to attend to two issues simultaneously.

3. *Smoothness.* Managing physical movement from one activity to another without jerkiness, distractions, or halts.
4. *Momentum.* Keeping physical activities moving at an appropriate pace.
5. *Group Alerting.* Attempting to involve nonparticipating students in discussions.
6. *Accountability.* Holding students responsible for their tasks.
7. *Valence.* Pointing out that an activity has something special about it.
8. *Challenge.* Providing intellectual challenges in work.
9. *Seatwork Variety.* Planning varied activities.

## BALANCING GOALS AND OBJECTIVES IN THE CURRICULUM: LINKING THE HEAD, THE HAND, AND THE HEART

In earlier chapters, it was suggested that the purpose of citizenship education was the development of the reflective, competent, and concerned citizen. Further, it was stated that the social studies curriculum should incorporate at each grade level some balance among lessons that seek to develop reflection, competence, and concern. Although individual lessons may not include objectives that address all three dimensions, each unit should include some balance that the teacher considers appropriate. Additionally, it was proposed that the year's program should contain a mix of objectives that reflects the curricular priorities the teacher has established.

The *reflective* citizen was characterized as having knowledge of a body of concepts, facts, and generalizations concerning the organization, understanding, and development of individuals, groups, and societies. Also, the reflective citizen was viewed as being knowledgeable of the processes of hypothesis formation and testing, problem solving, and decision making.

The *competent* citizen was seen as having a repertoire of social, research and analysis, chronology, and spatial skills. The *concerned* citizen was characterized as one who has an awareness of his or her rights and responsibilities, a sense of social consciousness, and a well-grounded framework for deciding what is right and wrong. In addition, the concerned citizen was seen as having learned how to identify and analyze issues and to suspend judgment concerning alternate beliefs, attitudes, values, customs, and cultures.

To illustrate, if a teacher decides that it is most important to emphasize the dimension of competence and is less important to emphasize the dimension of concern during the school year, her distribution of objectives should reflect this fact. That is, *over* one third of them should deal with competence, and the smallest percentage with concern.

Both units and the total curriculum can be analyzed for balance. Figure 4.11 shows a sample of objectives that might be used to frame a 10th-grade unit related to the lesson developed by the National Geographic Society that we considered earlier in this chapter. The theme for the unit would be "The Power of Oil."

In Figure 4.11, note that although all three dimensions are included in the example, one receives greater emphasis (i.e., the reflective dimension).

**Figure 4.11**
**Tenth-Grade Unit: The Power of Oil**

**Sample Unit Objectives that Emphasize the Reflective Citizen Dimension**
Students should be able to:

1. Identify the top 10 nations with respect to concentrations of oil.
2. Rank the top 10 oil-consuming countries.
3. Identify the major uses of oil in the United States.
4. State two ways in which countries that contain large concentrations of oil have exercised power over those who need oil.
5. Predict what would happen if other nations cut off the supply of oil to the United States.

**Sample Unit Objectives that Emphasize the Competent Citizen Dimension**

1. Conduct a cooperative learning activity (see Chapter 5) that reveals the social and economic consequences of discoveries of large oil reserves.
2. Locate on a map the top 10 oil-producing and consuming nations.
3. Construct a chart that shows the average cost of gasoline, excluding state and federal taxes, in the United States over the past 20 years.
4. Identify and use appropriate reference sources, such as *Goode's World Atlas.*

**Sample Unit Objectives that Emphasize the Concerned Citizen Dimension**

1. Take a position on a moral dilemma involving an issue of whether one nation is justified in violating the sovereignty of another to obtain a vital natural resource.
2. Argue either pro or con that the wealthier nations have a moral obligation to help those that are developing nations.
3. Formulate a position on the question: Assuming the United States should continue to give foreign aid, to which nations should it be directed?
4. Judge whether U.S. conservation policies should be directed primarily toward conserving natural resources or making agreements with other nations to secure the resources that we will need in the future.

## GUIDELINES FOR SOCIAL STUDIES PROGRAM DEVELOPMENT

Apart from guides for units and lessons, a number of guidelines for developing complete social studies *programs* at the state and local levels have been developed (e.g., Glatthorn, 1987; Parker, 1991). You should consult the guidelines your state has established regarding the social studies requirements and recommendations for each grade level.

Organizations such as the NCSS periodically issue general guidelines for curriculum planning that cover a range of issues and provide checklists of practical considerations and suggestions. One illustration is the *Revision of the NCSS Social Studies Curriculum Guidelines* (NCSS, 1979). It provides nine basic guidelines for developing a social studies program. Each of the nine guidelines in turn has a related set of more specific subguidelines.

1. The social studies program should be directly related to the age, maturity, and concerns of students.
2. The social studies program should deal with the real social world.
3. The social studies program should draw from currently valid knowledge representative of human experience, culture, and beliefs.
4. Objectives should be thoughtfully selected and clearly stated in such a form as to provide direction to the program.
5. Learning activities should engage the student directly and actively in the learning process.
6. Strategies of instruction and learning activities should rely on a broad range of learning resources.
7. The social studies program must facilitate the organization of experience.
8. Evaluation should be useful, systematic, comprehensive, and valid for the objectives of the program.
9. Social studies education should receive vigorous support as a vital and responsible part of the school program.

A similar set of seven guidelines for program development were created by Engle and Ochoa (1988).

1. The curriculum should have a relatively small number of topics.
2. The topics selected should be those with the greatest potential for stimulating thought or controversy.
3. Students should continually be asked to make value judgments about factual claims and to generate hypotheses.

4. The social science disciplines should be treated as sources of information that can help answer questions rather than truth to be learned.
5. Information from areas other than the social sciences, such as from the humanities, should be used.
6. The curriculum should use varied sources to study in depth a relatively small number of topics.
7. The curriculum should draw on students' experiences to help answer questions.

## VARIETY IN INSTRUCTIONAL PLANNING

Subsequent chapters will offer a variety of different instructional strategies, activities, and materials to engage students and foster exemplary social studies teaching. Chapter 5 examines how the group activities and types of questions we employ affect the quality of our instruction. It also demonstrates how simulations and role-playing techniques can be used effectively to achieve certain objectives. Chapters 6, 7, and 8 detail teaching strategies related to the three dimensions of reflection, competence, and concern.

In applying these strategies in their planning, teachers need to guard against overreliance on any one approach, however successful it may be. They need to ensure that their lesson and unit plans incorporate variety, as well as qualitatively significant activities.

Chapters 9 through 13 will suggest other criteria to consider for monitoring in planning social studies instruction. These include cultural and gender sensitivity, attention to special needs, degree of student engagement in the learning process, authentic assessments, and the inclusion of socially significant subject matter.

## GROUP ACTIVITIES

1. After consulting several sources, identify a format for a lesson plan that you prefer. Discuss the features of the format that you consider to be desirable and explain why.
2. For each of the middle grades and secondary levels, locate either a social studies resource unit or a teaching unit on any topic. Discuss what you consider to be the strengths and weaknesses of the units. Which things would you add?
3. Consult Figure 4.11 and develop two additional objectives relating to the unit theme for each of the three dimensions.
4. Examine the objectives for the six lessons in the unit, "Slavery in the Nineteenth Century," presented in the chapter. Which ones do you con-

sider to be specific and which ones general? How could the general ones be made more specific?

5. React to the quotation from Merryfield and Remy on page 110. Do you agree or disagree? Why?

## INDIVIDUAL ACTIVITIES

1. Select a topic, a grade level, an objective, and a lesson plan format (either those within the chapter or another). Then, develop a sample social studies lesson for either the middle or the secondary grades.
2. Using the format included in the chapter, create your own unit. Identify any grade (from grades 5 through 12) and any topic.
3. Consult the example of a partially completed concept map used for planning a teaching unit that appears in the chapter. Identify a grade level and a topic for a unit. Then create a concept map that incorporates all the subjects you would include in the unit.

## REFERENCES


Banks, J. (1993). The canon debate, knowledge construction, and multicultural education. *Educational Researcher, 22.*

Bloom, B. S. (Ed.) (1956). *Taxonomy of educational objectives, the classification of educational goals. Handbook I: The cognitive domain.* New York: David McKay.

Borich, G. D. (1996). *Effective teaching methods* (3rd ed.). Englewood Cliffs, NJ: Merrill/Prentice Hall.

Brophy, J. E., & Alleman, J. (1993). Elementary social studies should be driven by major social education goals. *Social Education, 57,* 27–32.

Canady, R. L., & Rettig, M. D. (1993). Unlocking the lockstep high school schedule. *Phi Delta Kappan, 75,* 310–314.

Dewey, J. (1961). *Democracy and education.* New York: Macmillan.

Engle, S., & Ochoa, A. (1988). *Education for democratic citizenship: Decision making in the social studies.* New York: Teachers College Press.

Gagné, R. M., & Briggs, L. (1979). *Principles of instructional design.* New York: Holt, Rinehart, & Winston.

Glasser, W. (1992). *The quality school: Managing students without coercion* (2nd ed.). New York: HarperPerennial.

Glatthorn, A. A. (1987). *Curriculum renewal.* Alexandria, VA: Association for Supervision and Curriculum Development.

Good, T. L., & Brophy, J. E. (1987). *Looking in classrooms* (4th ed.). New York: Harper & Row.

Good, T. L., & Brophy, J. E. (1991). *Looking in classrooms* (5th ed.). New York: Harper & Row.

Gordon, T. (1974). *T. E. T. Teacher effectiveness training.* New York: McKay.

Gottfredson, D. C., Gottfredson, G. D., & Hybl, L. G. (1993). Managing adolescent behavior: A multiyear, multischool study. *American Educational Research Journal, 30,* 179–216.

Hunt, M. P., & Metcalf, L. E. (1968). *Teaching high school social studies: Problems in reflective thinking and social understanding.* New York: Harper & Row.

Hunter, M. (1984). Knowing, teaching, and supervising. In P. Hosford (Ed.). *Using what we know about teaching.* Alexandria, VA: Association for Supervision and Curriculum Development.

Kleg, M. (1986). Teaching about terrorism: A conceptual approach. *Social Science Record, 24,* 31–39.

Kounin, J. S. (1970). *Discipline and group management in classrooms.* New York: Holt, Rinehart, & Winston.

Krathwohl, D., Bloom, B. S., & Masia, B. B. (1969). *Taxonomy of educational objectives, the classification of educational goals. Handbook II: The affective domain.* New York: David McKay.

National Council for the Social Studies. (1979). *Revision of NCSS social studies curriculum guidelines.* Washington, DC: National Council for the Social Studies.

National Geographic Society. (1988). *Teaching geography: A model for action.* Washington, DC: National Geographic Society.

Newmann, F. M. with Oliver, D. W. (1970). *Clarifying public controversy: An approach to teaching social studies.* Boston: Little, Brown.

Noddings, N. (1991). The gender issue. *Educational Leadership, 49,* 65–70.

Novak, J. D., & Gowin, D. B. (1984). *Learning how to learn.* Cambridge, England: Cambridge University Press.

Oliver, D. W., Newmann, F. M., & Singleton, L. R. (1992). Teaching public issues in the secondary school classroom. *The Social Studies,* 100–103.

Oliver, D. W., & Shaver, J. P. (1966). *Teaching public issues in the high school.* Boston: Houghton Mifflin.

Onosko, J. J. (1992). An approach to designing thoughtful units. *The Social Studies,* 193–196.

Parker, W. (1991). *Renewing the social studies curriculum.* Alexandria, VA: Association for Supervision and Curriculum Development.

Pearson, J., & Robertson, J. (1991). *Slavery in the 19th century.* Los Angeles, CA: National Center for History in the Schools, University of California at Los Angeles.

Prentice-Hall. (1986). *American Nation.* Englewood Cliffs, NJ: Author.

Shapiro, S., & Merryfield, M. M. (1995). A case study of unit planning in the context of school reform. In M. M. Merryfield & R. C. Remy (Eds.), *Teaching about international conflict and peace* (pp. 41–124). Albany, NY: SUNY Press.

Weber, W. A. (1994). Classroom management. In J. M. Cooper et al. *Classroom teaching skills* (5th ed). Lexington, MA: D. C. Heath.

CHAPTER 5

# Engaging Students in Learning through Small Groups, Questions, Role Playing, and Simulations

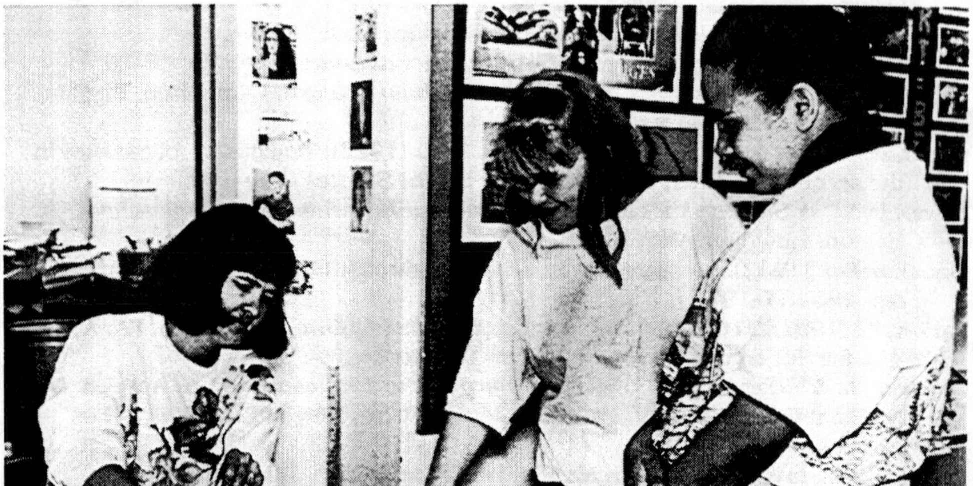

**Grouping Students for Learning**
Planning for Small-Group Work
Small-Group Techniques
Cooperative Learning Group Techniques
The Jigsaw Technique
The Group Investigation Technique

**Using Structured Questions to Aid Learning**
Patterns of Effective Questioning
Effective Use of Time
Effective Selection and Sequencing of Questions
The Taba Questioning Strategies

**Engaging Students in Role Playing and Simulations**
Managing Role-Playing Enactments
Managing Simulations
Sources of Simulations

*Tyrell, Larry, Janice, and Shantel are clustered around a small table. They comprise a group known as the "The Mellow Ones." Each of them is an "expert" on some aspect of the New Deal. The rest of their classmates are similarly organized into groups at other locations in their eighth-grade class.*

*Their teacher, Mr. Karger, has spent the last 10 minutes outlining and evaluating some of the key New Deal programs advanced by President Franklin Roosevelt. For the next phase of the lesson, he asks the experts to leave their groups and meet with other similar experts at designated locations. Each set of experts will be comparing answers to questions about different aspects of the New Deal.*

*A cooperative learning activity is in progress.*

As the previous chapter revealed, in planning exciting and challenging social studies lessons and units, teachers have an assortment of effective tools at their disposal. In this chapter, we consider three sets of instructional strategies that may be used to enrich social studies lessons and activities: the use of *small structured groups, structured questions,* and *role-playing enactments and simulations.*

Each of the three chapters that follow, in turn, identify other specific instructional strategies that focus on developing objectives related to social studies as a matter of "the head, the hand, and the heart." These comprise the three dimensions of the effective citizen that were outlined in earlier chapters: reflection, competence, and concern.

## GROUPING STUDENTS FOR LEARNING

Groups, such as committees, teams, and social organizations, play a major role in our society. In schools, placing students into groups for instructional purposes has a long history (Schmuck & Schmuck, 1983). Traditionally, teachers and administrators have assigned students of all ages to groups to achieve a variety of cognitive and affective objectives. These include completing tasks efficiently, encouraging tolerance of diversity, and providing greater opportunities for in-depth discussions.

Structured group settings that include diversity also afford students an opportunity for social dialogues that can stimulate cognitive growth. They offer the promise of environments where youngsters can explore alternative perspectives, develop new insights, and modify prior knowledge. As Newman, Griffin, and Cole (1989) noted: "When people with different goals, roles, and resources interact, the differences in interpretation provide occasions for the construction of new knowledge" (p. 2).

### Planning for Small-Group Work

Before organizing students into small groups, teachers should consider a number of basic issues. These include making provisions for adequate space and sound control and for avoiding potential distractions. Teachers also should vary grouping techniques to prevent boredom. As a further critical consideration, they need to determine the optimal size of a group in relation to the objective of an activity.

Groups may be as small as two members or as large as the whole class. There is no magic number in determining the optimal size of a "small" group. Five to seven students is a good general rule of thumb for many social studies activities. As we shall see, certain group techniques specify the number of students required and the procedures they must follow.

Members of a group also must be capable of assuming or experimenting with the *roles* they are to play within the group if the group is to function effectively. A simple example is the role of *recorder* in a group, which requires some basic writing, organizing, and reading skills. Students need to practice and experiment with different types of groups and alternate roles within them.

Effective group activities also require as a prerequisite that students possess a number of basic social skills (see Chapter 7). These include:

- Listening,
- Taking turns,
- Working quietly,
- Sharing ideas,

- Asking for information and explanations,
- Accepting others' ideas, and
- Sharing roles and responsibilities.

**Identifying Group Members.** Among the many possible ways of identifying the members for a group are:

- Student self-selection,
- Random assignment,
- Assignment by backgrounds,
- Assignment by special abilities or skills, and
- Assignment by behavioral characteristics.

Aside from student self-selection, the remaining procedures involve some teacher decisions. The alternative procedures require the teacher to assess how certain student characteristics are related to the task and effective operation of the group. Although there is no one best way to identify group members, there are better ways for different objectives.

For instance, consider an activity in which one of the objectives is to improve the level of multicultural understanding within a classroom. Assignment by general background to include a mix of racial or ethnic representatives within each group is likely to be a better choice than student self-selection of groups. Similarly, consider a class where a number of behavioral problems exist at the beginning of a school year. An important grouping consideration for some tasks may be to ensure that potentially disruptive students are not grouped together.

## Small-Group Techniques

Aside from size and composition of the membership, there are other considerations in using small groups for social studies instruction. Certain group techniques have multipurpose applications in the sense that they have relatively flexible designs and are not tied to any particular set of objectives or type of subject matter. Others, such as cooperative learning techniques, are designed to promote specific instructional objectives, such as raising achievement scores or improving interpersonal relationships.

We first consider three multipurpose techniques that frequently are used to facilitate decision making: brainstorming, consensus decision making, and decision making by ratings. Then we examine two cooperative learning techniques that have been designed to promote both cooperative behavior and achievement: Jigsaw II and Group Investigation.

**Brainstorming.** Brainstorming is an effective technique when the objective of a group is to generate as many different solutions to a problem as possible for consideration (Osborn, 1963). The main ingredient for a brainstorming session is a potentially solvable problem, such as How can we get rid of the national debt?

A brainstorming session requires a leader to guide the discussion. A recorder also is needed to list on a large sheet of paper or chalkboard the possible solutions that the group members generate. The ground rules are that all ideas must be accepted and recorded *without* evaluation. Once all ideas have been recorded quickly without comment, they can be discussed. As a final step, the group members can try to agree which are the most useful solutions.

**Consensus Decision Making.** Consensus decision making requires *all* members of a group to agree to support the final solution. The group technique of majority rule with which students are more familiar encourages coalition building and produces temporary subgroups of "winners" and "losers." In contrast, consensus decision making, such as in jury decisions, is a useful technique for ensuring that *all* members' views are considered, since all must agree on the final results.

**Decision Making by Ratings.** The technique of decision making by ratings requires that various choices of individuals within a group be weighted and averaged through ratings. The approach commits a group to accept the decision that receives the best average rating from all members. It is an especially appropriate technique for resolving issues where several attractive alternatives exist, none of which has attracted support of a majority.

Consider the situation in which a group of seven students in a twelfth-grade class are trying to decide which actions the federal government should take to reduce the national debt. Through research, the students have identified and listed five major types of possible actions the government may take. Then they individually rate each of the five actions in order of their first through fifth choices (see Figure 5.1).

Each student's first choice is given a 1, the second a 2, and so on, to their last choice. The individual ratings then are totaled; the action with the *lowest* total score becomes the group's choice. An optional final step in the rating technique is to permit the members to discuss their ratings further and then to conduct a second round of ratings to arrive at the final decision.

The illustration also indicates how the rating technique can produce a *group* position that represents some compromise for everyone. In Figure 5.1, the group's selection through rating (i.e., Freeze All Domestic Spending), was *not* the first choice of any single member. Further, it was only the third choice of a majority of the members.

## Cooperative Learning Group Techniques

A special class of small-group techniques that have been designed to achieve both cognitive and affective objectives under certain conditions is

**Figure 5.1**
**Example of Decision Making by Ratings**

**Issue: How the Federal Government Can Help Reduce National Debt**

| Possible Actions Identified from Research | Individual Ratings of Group Members | | | | | | | |
|---|---|---|---|---|---|---|---|---|
| | Tad | Terry | Ali | Rex | Cy | Peg | Kea | Totals |
| Cut foreign aid | 4 | 1 | 2 | 5 | 1 | 5 | 2 | 20 |
| Increase taxes on poor and middle class | 1 | 5 | 1 | 4 | 3 | 2 | 5 | 21 |
| Cut defense spending | 2 | 4 | 4 | 3 | 5 | 3 | 1 | 22 |
| Freeze all domestic spending | 3 | 3 | 3 | 2 | 2 | 2 | 3 | 18 |
| Reduce all entitlements | 5 | 2 | 5 | 1 | 4 | 4 | 4 | 25 |

called **cooperative (or collaborative) learning.** The term refers generally to grouping techniques in which students work toward some common learning goal in small heterogeneous groups of usually four or five students. Heterogeneity typically includes characteristics such as gender, race, ethnicity, and ability. To be effective, cooperative learning requires that students have been trained for cooperation (Cohen, 1990).

Slavin (1990) has identified seven types of cooperative learning techniques. Some have specific, structured procedures such as those developed at Johns Hopkins by Slavin and his associates: Student Teams Achievement Divisions (STAD), Teams-Games-Tournaments (TGT), and Jigsaw II. Others, such as those developed by Johnson and Johnson (1984) have more flexible structures.

Advocates of cooperative learning techniques assert that they motivate students to do their best, help one another, and organize their thinking through dialogue and elaboration (Newmann & Thompson, 1987; Slavin, 1990; Van Sickle, 1992). Johnson and Johnson (1986) have summarized what they perceive to be the major differences between traditional and cooperative learning grouping techniques. They note that cooperative groups foster interdependence, individual accountability, and group processing of information, whereas traditional types do not.

**Cooperative Learning and Student Achievement.** With regard to the relationship of cooperative learning to academic achievement, Slavin (1990) has concluded, "There is wide agreement among reviewers of the cooperative learning literature that cooperative methods can and usually do have a positive effect on student achievement" (p. 6). It is important to note, how-

**Cooperative learning activities stimulate both cognitive and affective growth.**

ever, that Slavin's analyses of the existing research have revealed there are two essential conditions for cooperative learning techniques to be effective: (a) there must be a group goal that can result in some form of recognition (e.g., class newspaper, certificate, bulletin board, grades, rewards) and (b) success must depend on individual accountability (e.g., individual quiz scores are summed to produce a group score).

**Cooperative Learning and Affective Outcomes.** In addition to achievement outcomes, researchers have discovered that cooperative learning techniques can promote positive intergroup relations and self-esteem. They also can improve attendance and promote positive attitudes toward school and the subjects being studied (Slavin, 1990, 1991). For example, "When students of different racial or ethnic backgrounds work together toward a common goal, they gain in liking and respect for one another. Cooperative learning also improves the social acceptance of mainstreamed academically handicapped students by their classmates . . . " (Slavin, 1990, p. 54). In sum, it appears that cooperative learning techniques that meet the criteria outlined by Slavin can produce both positive cognitive and affective outcomes.

Let us now examine in some detail one specific approach that has wide applicability to all types of social studies subject matter. This cooperative learning strategy, the **Jigsaw technique,** is especially effective with subject matter that has a high degree of factual detail.

## The Jigsaw Technique

Educators and psychologists working in the Austin, Texas, schools in the 1970s to improve relationships among Anglo, Hispanic, and black students devised a cooperative learning technique to reduce racial tensions (Aronson, Blaney, Stephan, Sikes, & Snapp, 1978). The objective of the technique was to encourage children to cooperate, share, and work together effectively, and, in the process, begin to break down interpersonal barriers. It was called *Jigsaw* because it resembled the structure of a jigsaw puzzle.

Jigsaw required students to work in small interracial groups and share parts of a solution to a common challenge. The challenge generally was successful performance on a quiz or assignment given by the teacher. Each member of the group was given only some of the "pieces of a puzzle" (i.e., part of the social studies information that the quiz would address). No single member of the group was supplied with enough information to solve the problem alone. Only through sharing and relying on all the others in the group could each member succeed. At the conclusion of the exercise, all the group members took *individual* tests covering *all* of the collective subject matter that had been shared.

Aronson and his associates (1978) offered a brief example of how they developed their technique:

> For example, in the first classroom we studied, the next lesson happened to be on Joseph Pulitzer. We wrote a six-paragraph biography of the man, such that each paragraph contained a major aspect of Pulitzer's life. . . . Next we cut up the biography into sections and gave each child in the learning group one paragraph. Thus every learning group had within it the entire life story of Joseph Pulitzer, but each child had no more than one sixth of the story and was dependent on all the others to complete the big picture. (p. 47)

After the completion of the experimental program that used Jigsaw, the investigators reported that, in integrated schools, Anglos learned equally well in both Jigsaw and competitive classes. However, blacks and Hispanics performed *better* in Jigsaw classes than in non-Jigsaw ones. Further, it was found that at the conclusion of the study, students liked both groupmates and others in their class better than when the study began. In sum, Jigsaw produced both positive achievement and attitudinal outcomes (Aronson et al., 1978).

**Variations of the Jigsaw Technique.** The original Jigsaw technique can be used for any social studies activity where a body of subject matter can be divided easily into four or five pieces for individuals (see Stahl, 1994). For example, in studying about the Great Depression in the United States, information might be organized into the following categories: causes, solutions, political effects, economic impact, and social consequences, and each student might be given the information for one category.

Often, however, this technique requires extra effort on the part of the teacher to reorganize or rewrite material. Some subject matter also cannot be organized to stand alone without reference to other sections. Additionally, the original Jigsaw was found by researchers to be not as effective as some alternative cooperative learning techniques (Newman & Thompson, 1987).

One variation on the original Jigsaw that often is easier to implement in social studies instruction was developed at Johns Hopkins (Slavin, 1986). Called the **Jigsaw II technique,** it also can be used with any subject matter, including conventional textbook passages, with little or no modifications. Further, it provides more structured group roles and places more emphasis on the achievement of group goals than the original Jigsaw. Other variations exist as well (see Mattingly & VanSickle, 1991).

Jigsaw II requires a group of four or five students selected in the following fashion: one high-ability student, one low-ability student, and two or three average ability students. Further, to the extent possible, Jigsaw II requires that the makeup of the group reflect the ethnic and gender composition of the class as a whole.

Individual accountability in the Jigsaw techniques often is maintained by having each student take a quiz over all the subject matter studied by the group. Procedures in Jigsaw II developed for calculating team scores from students' individual quiz scores require some analysis. Three key concepts are *base score, quiz score,* and *improvement points.*

A base score is one the teacher assigns at the beginning of a Jigsaw II activity, based on the student's social studies grade or some standardized test score. Once a group has finished its Jigsaw II task, individuals typically take a quiz over the subject matter studied and receive a personal quiz score. Each student's new quiz score then is compared to his or her previous or base score. If merited, individuals earn "improvement points" for their group by comparing their quiz scores to their base scores and using the formula shown in Figure 5.2.

For example, consider a group of four students. Suppose Billy's base score was 70, and he receives a 65 on a quiz. Following the scoring procedures described in Figure 5.2, he would be awarded 10 "improvement points."

Tamara had a base score of 100, and her quiz score was the same. She would receive 30 "improvement points." Sarah's base score was 85 and the quiz was 89; she earned 20 improvement points. Steve had a quiz score of 89, compared to a base score of 100; he received 0 "improvement points."

**Figure 5.2**
**Scoring Procedures for Jigsaw II**

| Quiz Score | Improvement Points |
|---|---|
| More than 10 points below base score | 0 |
| 10 points below to 1 point below base score | 10 |
| Base score to 10 points above base score | 20 |
| More than 10 points above base score | 30 |
| Perfect score (regardless of base score) | 30 |

*Note.* Compiled from *Using Student Team Learning* (3rd ed.), by R. E. Slavin, 1986, Baltimore: Johns Hopkins University, Center for Social Organization of Schools.

The group's score consists of the *total of the improvement points of all members of the team*, not their combined raw scores. In this case, the group score was 60 (10 + 30 + 20 + 0). In each new round of Jigsaw II, the prior quiz score becomes a new base score. For example, in the prior illustration, Sarah's new base score for the second round would be 89. If some teams have four members and others have five, the score of the group with five is four fifths of the total.

**An Example of Jigsaw II Procedures.** Let us illustrate an application for Jigsaw II. Our example involves a quiz and a basal text chapter that deals with the development of the New England colonies.

1. Select a chapter within the text and identify four basic topics, themes, or issues that the chapter encompasses.
2. Organize four- or five-member teams according to the group selection criteria given earlier (i.e., ability, ethnicity, gender). Then, allow them to establish their identity and name (e.g., "The Dudes," "Cool Lightning").
3. Distribute to each team a copy of an Expert Sheet that contains a list of the four topics, themes, or issues that have been identified as focusing on some important aspect of the chapter material. (See the example in Figure 5.3.) Each topic should be presented in the form of a question.
4. Assign a topic on the Expert Sheet to each member of each team. Designate these individuals as "experts" on their topics. Where there are five team members, assign one of the topics to two members.
5. Have all students read the chapter selected in class or for homework, focusing on his or her topic on the expert sheet.

**Figure 5.3**
**Sample Expert Sheet for a Jigsaw II Activity on a Chapter Dealing with the New England Colonies**

**Expert Sheet**
**The Development of the New England Colonies**

*Topics:*

I. Who were the pilgrims?
II. How did the Indians and the colonists get along with each other?
III. How did the colonists get along with one another?
IV. How did the Massachusetts Bay Colony develop?

6. Once students have read the chapter, allow experts from different teams who have the same topic to meet and discuss their topic. It may be helpful to provide a discussion sheet similar to the one shown in Figure 5.4 for each expert group.
7. Once the expert group discussions are concluded, have the experts return to their teams. They should take turns teaching the information related to their topics to the other members.
8. When the teaching has concluded, have each student take an individual quiz covering all the topics. All students are to answer all questions.
9. Calculate individual improvement points and report results as team scores (individual scores may be kept for grading purposes). Recognize publicly through such forms as announcements, bulletin board listing, or a newsletter the progress of the teams. Periodically remind students that team scores are based on improvement points.
10. Repeat the preceding steps for subsequent chapters within a unit or until a cluster of chapters has been studied. After each round of

**Figure 5.4**
**Sample Discussion Sheet for Jigsaw II Expert Groups**

**Discussion Group for Expert Group I**

*Topic:* Who were the Pilgrims?

*Points to consider in your discussion:*

1. What is a pilgrim?
2. Why did the pilgrims come to America?
3. When did they leave England for America?
4. Where did they settle in America?
5. Why did they settle at the places they did?
6. What was the Mayflower Compact?
7. What was the significance of the Mayflower Compact?

quizzes, recalculate the team scores based on individual improvement points and publicize the new team standings. At the conclusion, publicly recognize in some fashion the team with the highest score.

Jigsaw and Jigsaw II techniques are versatile. They lend themselves to a number of adaptations in social studies instruction. Slavin (1986) suggested, for example, that teachers might have students do research on topics rather than reference basal texts. Also, instead of using quizzes to ensure student accountability, teachers may assess through such forms as group essays, dioramas, skits, computer databases, or oral reports.

## The Group Investigation Technique

Another cooperative learning strategy that has wide applicability in social studies instruction is the **Group Investigation Technique** (Sharan & Sharan, 1994). In comparison to Jigsaw techniques, the Group Investigation strategy is more open-ended and permits in-depth study of complex problems and issues. It affords groups considerable latitude in how they define and study a topic and report their findings. To achieve its ends, it requires students who already have learned to work effectively in groups.

Leighton (1990) has outlined six steps that Group Investigation involves:

1. Identification of topics and choices by teacher and students,
2. Formation of learning teams based on interests,
3. Investigation of topics selected with teacher assistance,
4. Preparation of presentations for class with teacher assistance,
5. Presentations to whole class, and
6. Evaluation of the work based on predetermined criteria.

An example of how the strategy might be implemented in a social studies class inquiring into the causes of the American Revolution has been provided by Leighton (1990):

> First, students would be divided into temporary brainstorming groups of three or four, each charged with generating a list of questions one might ask in relation to study of the Revolution. The whole class would compile a composite list of questions, which would be sorted into categories. Learning teams would include those who are particularly interested in investigating each category of questions. The teacher's role is to guide the formation of teams so that, to the extent possible, each team includes a fair sampling of students.
>
> The learning teams review the questions in their category and pull together those questions most amenable to the investigation. They set the

> goals for the work and divide the tasks among themselves. Then they begin to study the topic they have chosen. When their studies are complete, they present their findings to the class. A representative from each learning team is delegated to a central coordinating committee to ensure that team reports are presented in orderly fashion and work is equitably distributed within each team.
>
> Evaluation may be designed by the teacher alone or in collaboration with a representative student group. The content on which students are evaluated must reflect the priorities established by the original choice of inquiry topics and by the presentations themselves. Students may be assessed individually on the basis of either the sum of the whole class presentations or the particular material developed within each group. (p. 326)

Sharan and Sharan (1990) offered an illustration of how a research project might proceed using the group investigation technique with a group of five and the topic: How did the different Indian tribes adapt their dwellings to their environment? Each student in the group assumes one of the following roles: coordinator, resource persons (two), steering committee person, and recorder.

The specific questions to be answered are as follows:

- How did the nomadic Apaches design their shelters?
- In what way did hogans suit the Navajo way of life?
- What kind of dwelling did the ancient Indians design?

Resources for the group included a collection of books and reference materials, a set of people to be interviewed, and a list of sites to be visited (see also Sharan & Sharan, 1994).

## USING STRUCTURED QUESTIONS TO AID LEARNING

As we noted at the outset of the chapter, in addition to the decisions associated with the use of grouping techniques to achieve instructional ends, teachers have a number of choices with respect to how they use questions to stimulate learning. Questions are the triggers of reflection. The *type*, *duration*, and the *sequencing* of questions can significantly affect the level of interaction and learning that results from instruction.

Evidence suggests that a great number of the communications between teacher and students consist of questions and answers. More often than not, teachers initiate the questions, read them from texts, or assign them in writing to students (Wilen & White, 1991). Questions are used extensively both in large- and small-group instruction, as well as with individual students.

Effective questions can focus attention on the important objectives of a lesson or activity. They also can encourage students to participate in discussions, move thinking along in a systematic fashion. Questions also can open new avenues of exploration for teacher and students alike.

Questions that originate from students during instruction would appear to be especially helpful for identifying areas that are unclear, need amplification, or were neglected in the teacher's planning. Their spontaneous occurrence in middle and secondary classrooms, however, appears to be rare.

For example, Dillon (1988) reported visiting 27 classrooms containing 721 students in six secondary schools. In these contexts, there were discussions of the seemingly provocative topics of marriage, abortion, smoking, a racist trial, the American Revolution, and environmental pollution. From each classroom, Dillon selected a 10-minute period of dialogue for analysis. Among all the interactions in the classrooms, he found students asked a total of only 11 questions.

## Patterns of Effective Questioning

What types of questions do teachers typically ask or assign to students? Borich (1996, p. 344) has suggested the questions can be organized into seven general categories, those that:

1. Provoke interest or gain attention,
2. Assess state of students' knowledge,
3. Trigger recall of subject matter,
4. Manage instruction,
5. Encourage more advanced levels of thinking,
6. Redirect attention, and
7. Elicit feelings.

Just as with the use of grouping techniques, teachers have a number of decisions to make regarding the use of questions in instruction. The *type, duration,* and the *sequencing* of questions can significantly affect the level of interaction, thinking, and learning that results from instruction. Effective questioning techniques can focus attention on the important objectives of a lesson or activity. They also can encourage students to participate in discussions and move thinking along in a systematic fashion. Teachers can draw on a store of tested principles and strategies in these areas (e.g., Wilen & White, 1991) for sharpening the questioning skills they use in social studies instruction.

Some techniques associated with effective questioning apply to all questions, such as the efficient *use of time* and the appropriate *selection* and *sequencing* of questions. Teachers can draw on a store of tested principles and strategies in these areas for sharpening the questioning skills they use in social studies instruction.

## Effective Use of Time

Ask a friend a question and time how long you have to wait before he or she begins to answer you. A critical element of effective questioning is known as **wait time.** Wait time is the length of time between the teacher's asking of a question and the point at which an answer is expected.

When wait time is short, teachers ask a question and expect an answer immediately. If one is not forthcoming, teachers tend to restate the question, rephrase it, ask a new one, or provide the answers themselves. When wait time is long, teachers ask the question and wait three seconds or longer for an answer. In Tobin's studies (1987), most teachers maintained an average wait time between 0.2 and 0.9 seconds.

Consider the following vignette from a social studies class studying the American Revolution that is taken from a text on questioning by Dillon (1988).

*Teacher:* OK, so we've kind of covered leadership and some of the things that Washington brought with it. Why else did they win? Leadership is important, that's one.
*Student:* France gave 'em help.
*T:* OK, so France giving aid is an example of what? France is an example of it, obviously.
*S:* Aid from allies.
*T:* Aid from allies, very good. Were there any other allies who gave aid to us?
*S:* Spain.
*T:* Spain. Now, when you say aid, can you define that?
*S:* Help.
*T:* Define 'help'. Spell it out for me.
*S:* Assistance.
*T:* Spell it out for me.
*S:* They taught the men how to fight the right way.
*T:* Who taught?
*S:* The allies.
*T:* Where? When?
*S:* In the battlefield.
*T:* In the battlefield? (Dillon, 1988, pp. 87–88)

Dillon (1988) noted that the discussion in the transcript lasted approximately 30 seconds. The teacher asks a total of nine questions, and the student responses last about one second. Given the time required for the teacher to state the question and the students to formulate their responses, we can infer that the wait time in the episode given is quite short.

**The Effects of Increasing Wait Time.** The pioneering research of Rowe (1969) demonstrated the powerful effects of extending wait time. She found that, if a teacher prolonged the average time waited after a question was asked to five seconds or longer, the length of students' responses increased. Conversely, she found that short wait time produced short answers. A review of subsequent studies suggests that at least three seconds is an average threshold of wait time for teachers to attempt to establish (Tobin, 1987).

Rowe also discovered that teachers who learned to use silence found that children who ordinarily said little began to start talking and to offer new ideas. Teachers, themselves, as they extended their waiting time, also began to include more variety in their questions.

Further studies by others have shown that, depending on the type of questions used, extended wait time is associated with longer student responses (e.g., Honea, 1982; Swift & Gooding, 1983; Tobin, 1986) and increased student-to-student interaction. Extended wait time also was found to be associated with greater achievement (e.g., Riley, 1986; Tobin, 1986). Tobin's (1987) analysis of the related research has suggested that teachers can learn to increase their wait time through feedback and analysis of their questioning patterns.

## Effective Selection and Sequencing of Questions

Another important consideration in effective questioning is selecting questions that are *clear, specific,* and *focused.* These types of questions expedite communication, probe for details, keep a discussion on target, and foster sustained critical thinking. They also encourage students to make comparisons, identify causal relationships, see linkages to their own lives, and establish factual claims.

Questions that are improperly worded are a major source of problems both for teachers and students. They frustrate teachers from accomplishing their objectives and are a source of confusion for students. Types of questions that teachers should avoid include those that are: ambiguous, call for a yes or no answer, are slanted, or require students to try to guess what the teacher wants for an answer. Some examples of appropriate and inappropriate ways to phrase questions are illustrated in Figures 5.5 and 5.6.

Another useful questioning technique is learning to order questions in a sequence that stimulates the development of students' thinking. A logical sequence ensures that there is a rationale for the order in which the questions are asked. Brown and Edmondson (1984) have identified a number of questioning sequences that teachers may employ in instruction.

Sequencing is part of the process of developing a set or *script* of questions in advance of teaching a lesson. A **question script** is a basic set of questions that have been constructed, rehearsed, and logically sequenced

**Figure 5.5**
**Desirable Types of Questions**

These are examples of desirable types of questions:

- Why do you agree with the candidate's position?
- What would happen if the world's supplies of oil and natural gas were used up?
- What were some major causes of the Civil War?
- What are some ways neighborhoods change over time?
- What are some ways cities, suburbs, and rural areas are alike and different?
- Suppose you were in Rosa Parks's place. What would you have done?
- What evidence do you have that auto emissions are bad for the environment?

**Figure 5.6**
**Type of Questions to Avoid**

Teachers should be sensitive to the types of questions that generally are *ineffective* in social studies instruction. These types of questions include those that are *ambiguous, require only a yes or no answer,* or are *slanted.* Such questions limit or stifle thinking and often are a source of frustration and confusion for students. The following are examples of the types of questions to avoid:

- What happened in the American Revolution?
- Was George Washington our first President?
- What makes our community the best in the state?
- Where do families live?
- How did Sojourner Truth live her life?
- What does our flag mean?
- What was the first Thanksgiving about?

prior to their use in a lesson or activity. *Rehearsal* refers to the process whereby a teacher reflects on exactly how the questions will be phrased and where in the lesson or activity they are to occur. The function of a script in instruction is to move students from more concrete to more abstract, lower to higher, levels of thinking.

The presence of a questioning script ensures that several well thought out and carefully phrased questions will be used to guide students' thinking, as well as the development of a lesson or activity. Unlike spontaneous questions, which teachers develop as instruction unfolds, a script encompasses a small number of questions, usually three to five, that relate to the subject matter under investigation and that shape the lesson. Scripts, however, may be supplemented by other questions that are needed during a lesson, such as clarification or summarization questions (e.g., What do you mean by "the lunatic fringe"? or Could you sum up your point of view in a single sentence?).

**The Taxonomy of Educational Objectives.** An example of sequencing questions according to the levels of thinking they require is found in the **taxonomies of objectives** developed by Bloom and his associates. The most widely used taxonomy as a guide for framing questions is the one for the cognitive domain (Bloom, 1956). It identifies six levels of thinking, simple (knowledge) to complex (evaluation). The levels, along with an example of a question dealing with the American flag that is matched with them, follows.

| Level of Thinking | Sample Question |
|---|---|
| Knowledge | How many stars does our flag have? |
| Comprehension | Can you explain why our flag has 50 stars? |
| Application | To what extent does the First Amendment apply to those who burn the American flag? |
| Analysis | In what ways are the arguments of those who burn the flag different from those who support it? |
| Synthesis | Under what conditions, if any, would you support an individual's right to burn the flag and why? |
| Evaluation | Assessing the Supreme Court arguments and rulings in flag burning cases, to what extent are they consistent with or opposed to your position on the issue? |

Although it is desirable to have all students ultimately thinking at the highest level possible, most individuals need to move gradually from a lower to a higher level. Getting students to reach a higher level of thinking becomes a matter of asking questions that call for progressively more complex cognitive tasks and allowing sufficient time for reflection.

For example, suppose you and I have just viewed the film *War and Peace* together. As we leave the theater, we begin to discuss the film. My initial question is "Do you remember the names of all the major characters?"

From that conversational opener, we progress to "Which parts did you enjoy the most? Why?" Toward the middle of the discussion, I inquire, "Did this film remind you of any others you have ever seen? In which ways?" We conclude our discussion, by entertaining the final question, "What was the meaning of that film?"

Compare that sequence of questions with a second discussion. In this scenario, as you and I emerge from the film, I inquire concerning this stirring three-hour epic "How would you sum up the meaning of the film in a sentence?"

In the first case, the sequence of questions has helped me organize my thoughts in a way that prepares me for the final complex question. The very same type of question that occurs at the *beginning* of the second discussion, however, is likely to be difficult to tackle at first. Furthermore, even if I could respond to it at the outset, my answer is likely to be less thoughtful and complete than if I had the opportunity to order and build my thinking on a foundation of more concrete and specific details.

Similarly, in unstructured classroom questioning, it is important to engage students in discussions at the appropriate level of questioning. This sometimes requires trial and error, where a teacher discovers that he or she needs to lower the level of questions after drawing a blank from students. Consider the following exchange in which the teacher, Ms. Carpenter, drops back to a lower level after her students fail to respond to the initial question. Later, she begins to work her way back to the original question.

*Ms. Peterson:* What was the significance of the New Deal?
*Class:* (Silence)
*Ms. Peterson:* What were some of the federal programs that were created during the period of the New Deal?
*Roger:* The WPA was started to put people to work on public jobs.
*Julia:* The banks were reformed. I can't remember the name of the program.
*Laronda:* Farmers got loans at low interest.
*Merv:* So did individuals for homes.
*Ms. Peterson:* (After 15 minutes of discussion about the nature and impact of the various New Deal programs) How might our lives be different if the New Deal had never happened?

## The Taba Questioning Strategies

Some educators have developed questioning scripts that are useful for achieving specific instructional objectives. Taba (1969) and her associates developed a series of scripts that are applicable to all topics within the social studies curriculum. Two of the strategies are considered here.

Each includes a set of core questions to be asked in exactly the sequence indicated. Each strategy also is constructed to achieve a specific set of instructional objectives. The first is designed (a) to diagnose what students know and do not know about a topic prior to studying it; (b) to determine what they have learned as a result of studying a topic or experiencing an event; or (c) to encourage all students in the class to participate in a discussion of a topic.

The first strategy uses a simple script consisting of an *opening* question, a *grouping* question, and a *labeling* question as follows.

| Examples | Function of Question |
|---|---|
| ***Opening Question*** | |
| What comes to mind when you hear the word apartheid? | Calls for recollection of information. Allows all students to participate in the discussion on an equal footing. |
| What did you see in the film? | |
| What do you think of when Adolph Hitler is mentioned? | |
| ***Grouping Question*** | |
| Look over our list of items. Are there any that could be grouped together? Why did you group them in that way? | Requires students to organize information on the basis of similarities and differences that they perceive and to provide a rationale for their classification. |
| Are there any things on the board that could be grouped together? Why did you put those items together? | |
| ***Labeling Question*** | |
| Let's look at group A. Can you think of a one- or two-word label or name for it? | Requires students to summarize and further refine thinking. |

Throughout the discussion, questions and statements such as the following types would be used as needed:

**Clarifying Question.** Examples: What sort of strange clothing? Can you give an example of what you mean by liberal?

**Refocusing Statement/Question.** Examples: Let me repeat the original question. Remember what I asked?

**Summarizing Question.** Examples: How could we put that in this space on the board? Could you put that in a single sentence?

In implementing the Taba strategy, the teacher records all students responses on the board or a chart *without* evaluation. Similarly, class members are not permitted to challenge other students' responses. Students' comments are listed verbatim or with minor modifications. When comments are lengthy, students are asked to summarize them. The teacher should accept any rationale that a student provides for grouping items together.

Consider an illustration of how a discussion using this technique might unfold in a secondary class. At the appropriate times in the discussion, as outlined earlier, the teacher asks the following *listing*, *grouping*, and *labeling* questions:

**Listing Question.** Example: What comes to mind when they hear the word *abortion?*

**Grouping Question.** Examples: Are there any things on the board that could be grouped together? (After the student suggests a grouping, ask the question that calls for a rationale.) Why did you put those items together?

**Labeling Question.** Example: Could you suggest a one- or two-word label for each of the groupings?

The students' responses to each question are shown in Figure 5.7.

The second Taba strategy has as its objective that students will be able to summarize data and draw conclusions and generalizations from subject matter examined or from experiences (Taba, 1969). This strategy, like the first, also employs a simple script of three questions: an *opening* question, an *interpretive* question, and a *capstone* question as follows:

| **Examples** | **Function of Question** |
|---|---|
| ***Opening Question*** | |
| What did you see on the trip?<br><br>What did we learn about the Soviets? | Calls for recollections of information. Allows all students to participate in the discussion on an equal footing. |
| ***Interpretive Question*** | |
| What differences did you notice between the two countries?<br><br>How were Roosevelt's feelings about the issue different from Hoover's feelings? | Get students to draw relationships between data being considered and to compare and contrast information. |
| ***Capstone Question*** | |
| What conclusion could we draw from our investigation?<br><br>From our study, what generalizations can you make about institutions? | Asks student to form a conclusion, summary, or a generalization. |

Throughout the discussion, the second Taba strategy uses questions and statements similar to the following as needed:

**Mapping-the-Field Question.** Examples: Have we left out anything? Are there any points that we missed?

**Focusing Question.** Examples: What types of clothing did they wear? How many people actually were affected?

**Substantiating Question.** Examples: What did you see in the film that leads you to believe that? Why do you say that?

**Figure 5.7**
**Illustration of a Classroom Discussion Using the Taba Strategy**

**Listing Question:** What comes to mind when you hear the word *abortion*?

*Student Responses Are Listed on Chalkboard as Follows:*

1. Destroying human life
2. Unwanted pregnancy
3. Committing a sin
4. Population control
5. Rape
6. Abortion referral service
7. Future health and happiness of *all* concerned (mother and child)
8. Mental anguish
9. Father's rights
10. Complications
11. Quacks
12. Costs
13. Self-abortion
14. German measles
15. Why?
16. Why not?
17. Responsibility
18. Misery and depression
19. Women's rights
20. Morning-after pill
21. Contraception
22. Ignorance (not being careful)
23. Sex
24. Methods (vacuum, etc.)
25. The doctor
26. Sterilization

**Grouping Question:** Are there any things on the board that could be grouped together? (After the student suggests a grouping, the teacher asks the next question, which calls for a rationale.) Why did you put those items together? (All rationale are accepted, and are *not* recorded.)

*Student Responses Are Listed on Chalkboard as Follows:*

| | | | |
|---|---|---|---|
| E | 1. Destroying human life | E | 3. Committing a sin |
| DH | 2. Unwanted pregnancy | E | 4. Population control |

**Figure 5.7**
**continued**

| | | | |
|---|---|---|---|
| D | 5. Rape | E | 17. Responsibility |
| H | 6. Abortion referral service | CD | 18. Misery and depression |
| D | 7. Future health and happiness of *all* concerned (mother and child) | A | 19. Women's rights |
| | | AFH | 20. Morning-after pill |
| C | 8. Mental anguish | F | 21. Contraception |
| A | 9. Father's rights | I | 22. Ignorance (not being careful) |
| CDG | 10. Complications | | |
| B | 11. Quacks | I | 23. Sex |
| J | 12. Costs | BF | 24. Methods (vacuum, etc.) |
| F | 13. Self-abortion | | |
| DG | 14. German measles | B | 25. The doctor |
| E | 15. Why? | AEF | 26. Sterilization |
| E | 16. Why not? | | |

**Labeling Question:** Could you suggest a one- or two-word label for each of the groupings?

*Student Responses Are Listed on Chalkboard as Follows:*

A = Women's rights
B = Medical
C = Effects on mother
D = Possible reasons for
E = Personal responsibility
F = Methods of prevention
G = Harm to fetus
H = Where to go
I = Ignorance
J = Money

## ENGAGING STUDENTS IN ROLE PLAYING AND SIMULATIONS

We turn now to the final class of complementary instructional techniques that can be applied across social studies topics: **role playing** and **simulations.** Although they can be used for many types of objectives, role-playing and simulation techniques are especially useful tools for examining issues that are abstract. They also facilitate consideration of affective matters that entail beliefs, attitudes, values, and moral choices. They do this by allowing students to "take on a role," step outside of their usual perspective on issues, and explore alternatives.

Often in social studies classes, we find it necessary to engage students in subject matter that is potentially complex or emotion laden. For example, we may wish to have students understand how supply and demand affect the market price of goods in a capitalist economy. Or we might need to have our students develop more sensitivity to cultural diversity.

## Managing Role-Playing Enactments

Successful role-playing activities require planning and careful attention to the details of how the steps are to unfold. Teachers need to be prepared for the honest emotions that may emerge when students become immersed in a role. Beyond the dramatic enactment of the role playing itself also lie the important stages of setting up, discussing, and internalizing the insights gained during the enactments (Shaftel & Shaftel, 1982).

Introducing role playing in a nonthreatening way is critical to its success as a technique. One approach that Merryfield and Remy (1995) suggest is to:

> seize an opportunity when there is heated discussion over a topic that involves several points of view. Ask Joe, who is strenuously arguing that the U.S. should have bombed the U.S.S.R. during the Cuban Missile Crisis, to take on the role of a Russian missile technician in Cuba. Then call for volunteers who will take roles of other people he might encounter such as a Cuban nurse or a Russian soldier. What would they think about the situation? What would they want to say to the Americans or the Soviet leaders? (p. 25)

Role-playing activities can be broken into five stages:

1. Initiation and direction,
2. Describing the scenario,
3. Assigning roles,
4. Enactment, and
5. Debriefing.

**Initiation and Direction.** Every role-play activity begins with some problem that the class or teacher has identified. Teachers should choose topics of a less controversial or sensitive nature until students become accustomed to the procedures. As students become experienced and comfortable with the technique, they can move on to more urgent concerns.

**Describing the Scenario.** The problem to be discussed should have some clear relevance to a social issue. The actual problem episode that is to trigger the role playing may be presented orally, pictorially, or in writing. A simple story problem may be some reenactment of a historical event, such as Truman's decision to drop the atomic bomb on Japan. It also may center on a contemporary issue, such as a young unwed couple telling one set of parents they are pregnant.

**Assigning Roles.** Role assignment needs to be approached cautiously—to avoid both the appearance of any possible typecasting and the inclusion of any reluctant actors. Using volunteers or drawing by lots eliminates the suggestion of typecasting. At the same time, it has the disadvantage of possibly involving students who cannot function effectively in the roles to be assigned. Often it may be desirable to select certain students who are most likely to give the greatest validity to the roles identified and hence present the problem-solution alternatives most effectively. In any case, assignment requires sensitivity and some experimentation to ensure a productive enactment.

Once assigned, all participants, as well as the rest of the class members (the audience), should briefed on each of the roles. In most cases, this can be an oral briefing. In others, it is important to keep individual roles hidden. Role-profile cards, such as the one shown here, may be supplied and referred to during the role play if necessary.

> **Rochelle:** You are a homeowner who has very unpleasant next-door neighbors. They play their stereo and television late at night, keep old cars parked in their driveway, and seldom cut their lawn. They also are always trying to borrow tools and other things. The prospects are not good that they will soon move. You are unhappy and have decided that something has to be done about the situation.

The students in the audience have roles also, albeit temporarily passive ones. At the conclusion of the enactment, they can be asked to assess whether the roles assigned appeared to be enacted genuinely and suggest alternative ways of playing the roles. They also may be asked to focus on a specific actor and identify vicariously with him or her.

Before moving on to the enactment, the class should be "warmed up" for dramatic activity. Simple pantomime scenes or one-sentence scenarios (e.g., you have just dropped your notebook in a puddle of water) for the students to act out can serve this purpose. Once the class is psychologically prepared, the role play itself can actually be enacted.

**Enactment.** A briefing with the characters individually before the role-play event begins can establish how they plan to enact their roles. Although enactments may be modified during the actual event, rehearsal helps students clarify their roles.

It is important to remind students that during the enactment they should use the names of the characters. This procedure reinforces the fact that individual class members themselves are not the objects of analysis. Similarly, it often is necessary to remind players to *stay in role*—that is, deal with events as their characters actually might. In humorous or anxietyproducing situations, some individuals tend to stop the role-play enactment and respond as an observer.

**Debriefing.** The debriefing phase is a crucial and integral part of role playing. It requires the greatest attention and guidance on the teacher's part to ensure productive and meaningful results. The debriefing period should immediately follow the enactment. The characters should be allowed to share any feelings they had while they were playing their roles and possibly to entertain questions from the audience. At some point, an exploration of alternative ways of handling the characters' roles should occur. If participants are willing, they can be asked to reenact the event in different ways, possibly switching roles.

The debriefing session may take many forms depending on the issue, the maturity of the group, and its experience with role playing. At some point, the issue embedded in the role-play event should be abstracted and clearly addressed so that attention shifts to real experiences, individuals, and places. The teacher then can help students draw parallels between the role-play enactment and real events.

## Managing Simulations

Closely related to role playing is simulation. Often called simulation games, **instructional simulations** are any activity designed to provide lifelike problem-solving experiences in the form of a "game." They provide a representation of some phenomenon, event, or issue that actually exists or existed in the real world. These characteristics distinguish a simulation from a simple game such as Bingo or baseball in which there are rules and some goal, but no representation of real social events. Simulations appear in many forms, including board games and computer software.

A major asset of simulations is that they enable many students to relate easily to and become highly interested in a problem that they might not otherwise take very seriously. Furthermore, they allow students to assume some control over their own learning and to be less dependent on the teacher.

Both a strength and a limitation of simulations is that they permit study of a *simplified* representation of some reality. All simulations limit the number of variables they present to players; otherwise they would be too complicated.

In a simulation of Congress, for example, not all of the actual considerations that weigh on lawmakers in their deliberations could be included and weighed. Similarly, the activity shown in Figure 5.8 deals only with a small number of issues related to the complex world refugee crisis. This basic board-game simulation makes students aware of some of the many difficulties that refugees encounter as they seek asylum in a new nation.

**Figure 5.8**
**Sample Simulation Activity**

**Take Refuge!**

**Materials:** A die
Gameboard
Rules of the game
2 to 4 players

Cut out the playing pieces along the dotted lines. Fold each along the solid line; glue the bottom to a square of lightweight cardboard to form a stand.
To make the gameboard and parts more durable, mount them with rubber cement on cardboard, then cover each with clear plastic adhesive paper. Before you cover them, add color with felt tip markers.

After you play the game, answer these questions:

1) How many good things happened to you as you played this game?
2) Did you find this game frustrating? Why or why not?
3) How would you feel if the things that happened in this game happened to you in real life?

**Rules of the Game**

Each player chooses a token and throws the die. The highest number starts by putting his or her token on square 1. Other players follow accordingly. Whenever a player lands on a shaded square, he or she must follow the instructions for that square.
The first player to reach square 58 is the winner. But to reach that square, you must throw the exact number needed to land on 58. If you throw a number higher than what you need, move to 58 and continue the count by moving backwards. When you reach 58, you have become accepted as a refugee.

3. You forgot your passport! Return to 1.
6. Miss a turn while you look for food.
9. You sprain your ankle on a rugged path. Wait here until all the others have passed you.
11. A fallen tree blocks your path. Miss a turn while you go around it.
14. A wild animal chases you back to 12.
16. You discover a shortcut. Go to 20.
19. You're lost. Return to 17.
22. A scary noise awakens you. Run to safety at 21.
26. Your brother has fallen behind. Find him at 23.
28. A border patrol is looking for you. Hide in 27.
32. You're stuck in a barbed wire fence. Miss one turn.
34. The police arrest you and send you back to your country. Return to 1.
38. You are placed in a transit camp. Miss 2 turns.
40. You are so hungry, you take corn from a field. The farmer chases you back to 39.
44. A heavy storm comes. Take shelter in 42.
48. Miss a turn waiting for a boat to take you across the river.
51. Bad winds slow you down. On your next turn, move forward only 1 space.
53. You left your passport on the other side of the river. Go back to 50.
57. You get a fever. Miss 2 turns.

*Note.* From *Take Refuge!* by Holy Childhood Association, (no date), Washington, DC: Author. Copyright by Holy Childhood Association. Reprinted by permission.

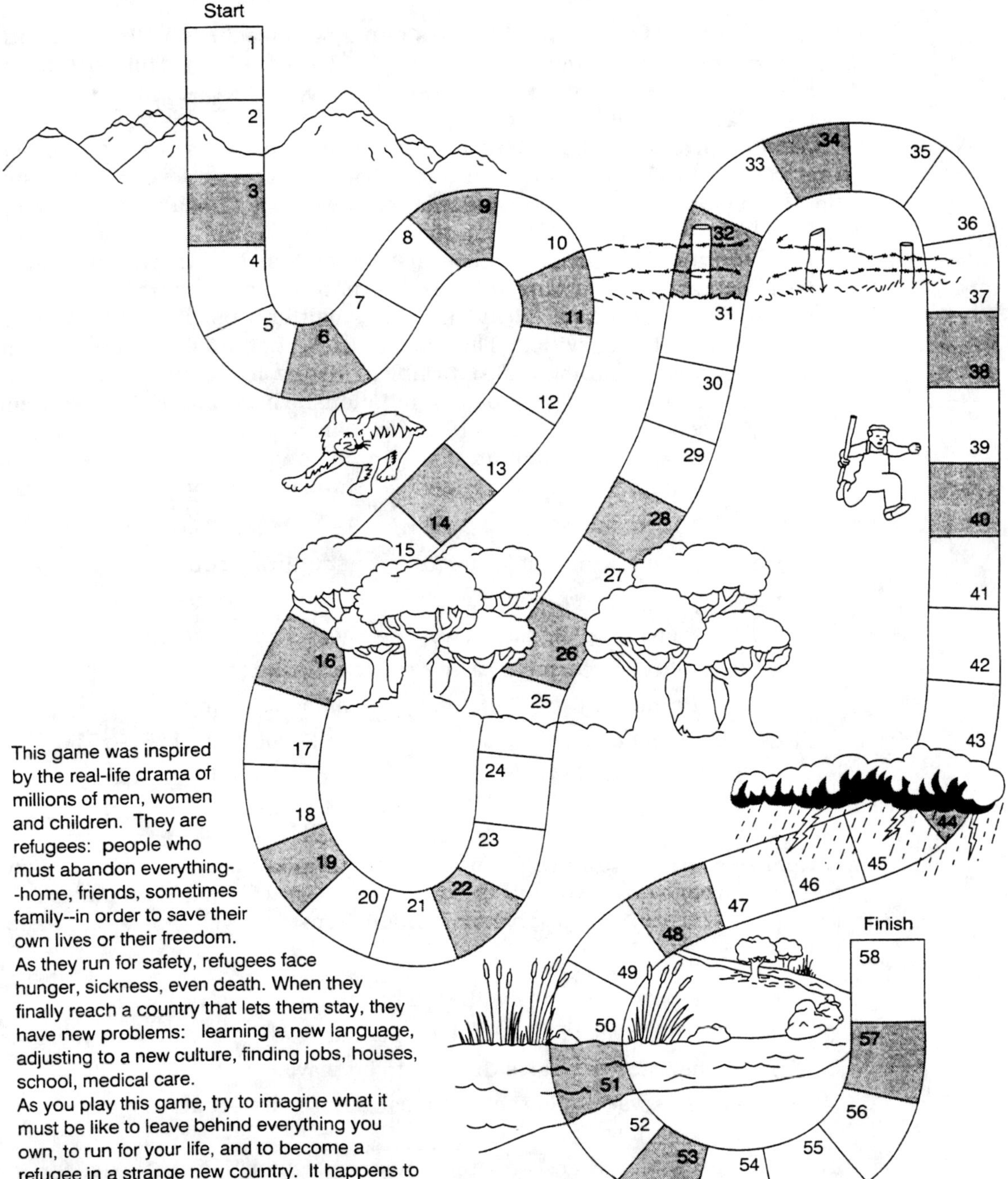


This game was inspired by the real-life drama of millions of men, women and children. They are refugees: people who must abandon everything--home, friends, sometimes family--in order to save their own lives or their freedom.

As they run for safety, refugees face hunger, sickness, even death. When they finally reach a country that lets them stay, they have new problems: learning a new language, adjusting to a new culture, finding jobs, houses, school, medical care.

As you play this game, try to imagine what it must be like to leave behind everything you own, to run for your life, and to become a refugee in a strange new country. It happens to millions of people every year--and for them, it isn't a game.

## Sources of Simulations

In addition to developing their own simulations, teachers have access to a variety of commercial simulations (Horn & Cleaves, 1980). Muir (1980) and Schug and Kepner (1984) have produced a brief selective list and description of a large number of simulations.

Often professional journals also publish simulations that can be used in a variety of different courses and for a variety of grade levels. An illustration is the money and banking simulation developed by Caldwell and Highsmith (1994) for use in a U.S. history course.

Simulations for social studies instruction can be lumped into one of two broad categories: *computerized* formats for one person or a small group and *noncomputerized* formats for small groups that employ board games or role-play activities. The emergence of personal computers, with their capacity for handling many variables quickly, has provided opportunities for an assortment of complex simulations. These often allow students to more closely approximate real events than noncomputerized media. In Chapter 11, we consider computerized simulations.

Some examples of *noncomputerized* simulations, with a brief explanation of each, are:

- *Bafa', Bafa'.* Understanding different cultural groups.
- *Balance of Power.* Four imaginary nations try to keep peace.
- *Dig.* Archaeological dig identifying a former civilization.
- *Discovery 3.* Recreates early American colonization.
- *Equality.* Ethnic group activity in an imaginary city.
- *Independence.* Reenacts the American Revolution, 1763–1776.
- *Starpower.* Analyzes how power is manipulated by groups.
- *Survival and Dominance.* Analyzes international diplomacy.

**Guidelines for Conducting Simulations.** A number of comprehensive texts are available to explain how to construct an effective simulation (e.g., Greenblat, 1987). A summary of the main steps in developing a simulation follows.

1. Define the problem or issue that the simulation is to represent.
2. State the objectives of the simulation as narrowly and clearly as possible.
3. Specify the actors or parts that are to be played.
4. Spell out in some detail the roles that the players are to assume or what they are to achieve.
5. Indicate the resources and the constraints or rules that exist for the players.
6. Specify clearly the decision-making mechanisms or how the simulation is to operate.

7. Develop a trial version of the simulation and field test it.
8. On the basis of the field test, modify the simulation and retest it until all "bugs" have been eliminated.

To employ simulations effectively in instruction, one can follow the same set of guidelines suggested earlier for role playing. Again, the *debriefing* period is a critical and integral phase of a simulation activity. In establishing a time frame for the use of simulations, a teacher must set aside a sufficient block of time to discuss students' insights and reactions. It is also important in this discussion period to relate the simulated events to ones within students' experiences.

## GROUP ACTIVITIES

1. Work in triads and follow the procedures for developing the Jigsaw II activity that are outlined in the chapter. Select a class and a chapter from the class's basal social studies text. Then design a cooperative learning activity. When the activity is completed, list some of the important issues that surfaced. Note what you would do differently.
2. Work in a group of four or five students and select a film that is appropriate for use in a middle-grades social studies class. View it and *individually* develop a brief questioning script consisting of four or five questions. Sequence the questions from simple to complex ones. In your group, compare the different scripts and the rationale for them. Repeat the process with a film for a secondary grade class.
3. Arrange to observe a teacher in a middle-grades or a secondary school during a social studies lesson. In one column on a sheet of paper, list verbatim all the questions that the teacher asks during the class. Also, note the teacher's *wait time* after each question. In an adjacent column, note how the students responded. When you leave the school, analyze your data in relation to the discussion of questioning in the chapter.
4. Arrange with a local teacher to work with a class (grades 5 through 12). Work in dyads and field-test the refugee simulation game in the chapter. Follow the procedures outlined in the chapter. You will need to organize the class into groups and make multiple copies. After you have finished debriefing the class about the game, discuss your experiences and results.

## INDIVIDUAL ACTIVITIES

1. Identify a class of students (grades 5 through 8) and a topic for a social studies lesson. Develop a set of key questions for the lesson, applying the Taba strategy that employs an opening-grouping-labeling question sequence. Also, develop a small set of supplemental questions (e.g., a

clarification question) that you anticipate will be needed during the discussion. Lead a discussion using the script. If possible, record the session on audiotape or videotape and then analyze the outcome.

2. Repeat activity 4 with the following changes: identify a class from grades 9 through 12 and develop a set of questions applying the second Taba strategy.
3. Using any issue or topic, create a role-playing activity for a middle-grades class.
4. Using any issue or topic, create a role-playing activity for a secondary grades class.

## REFERENCES

Aronson, E., Blaney, N., Stephan, C., Sikes, J., & Snapp, M. (1978). *The jigsaw classroom.* Beverly Hills, CA: Sage.

Bloom, B. S. (Ed.) (1956).*Taxonomy of educational objectives, the classification of educational goals. Handbook I: The cognitive domain.* New York: David McKay.

Borich, G. D. (1996). *Effective teaching methods* (3rd ed.). Englewood Cliffs, NJ: Merrill/Prentice Hall.

Brown, G., & Edmondson, R. (1984). Asking questions. In E. Wragg (Ed.), *Classroom teaching skills.* New York: Nichols.

Caldwell, J., & Highsmith, R. L. (1994). Banks and money in U.S. history. *Social Education, 58,* 27–28.

Cohen, G. (1990). Continuing to cooperate: Prerequisites for persistence. *Phi Delta Kappan, 72,* 134–136, 138.

Dillon, J. T. (1988). *Questioning and teaching: A manual of practice.* New York: Teachers College Press.

Greenblat, C. S. (1987). *Designing games and simulations.* Beverly Hills, CA: Sage.

The Holy Childhood Association. (no date). *Take refuge!* Washington, DC: Author.

Honea, M. J. (1982). Wait time as an instructional variable: An influence on teacher and student. *Clearinghouse, 56,* 167–170.

Horn, R. E., & Cleaves, A. (Eds.). (1980). *The guide to simulations games for education and training* (4th ed.). Beverly Hills, CA: Sage.

Johnson, D. W., & Johnson, R. T. (1986). Computer-assisted cooperative learning. *Educational Technology,* 12–18.

Johnson, R. T., & Johnson, D. W. (Eds.). (1984). *Structuring cooperative learning: Lesson plans for teachers.* New Brighton, MN: Interaction Book.

Leighton, M. S. (1990). Cooperative learning. In J. M. Cooper et al., *Classroom teaching skills* (4th ed). Lexington, MA: D. C. Heath.

Mattingly, R. M., & VanSickle, R. L. (1991). Cooperative learning and achievement in social studies. *Social Education, 55,* 392–395.

Merryfield, M. M., & Remy, R. C. (1995). Choosing content and methods for teaching about international conflict and peace. In M. M. Merryfield & R. C. Remy (Eds.), *Teaching about international conflict and peace* (pp. 3–40). Albany, NY: SUNY Press.

Muir, S. P. (1980). Simulation games for elementary social studies. *Social Education, 44,* 35–39.

Newman, D., Griffin, P., & Cole, M. (1989). *The construction zone: Working for cognitive change in school.* New York: Cambridge University Press.

Newmann, F., & Thompson, J. (1987). *Effects of cooperative learning on achievement in secondary schools: A summary of research.* Madison, WI: National Center on Effective Secondary Schools.

Osborn, A. (1963). *Applied imagination* (3rd ed.). New York: Charles Scribner.

Riley, J. P., II. (1986). The effects of teachers' wait-time and knowledge comprehension questioning on pupil science achievement. *Journal of Research in Science Teaching, 23,* 335–342.

Rowe, M. B. (1969). Science, soul and sanctions. *Science and Children, 6,* 11–13.

Schmuck, R. A., & Schmuck, P. (1983). *Group processes in the classroom* (4th ed.). Dubuque, IA: W. C. Brown.

Schug, M. C., & Kepner, Jr., H. S. (1984). Computer simulations in the social studies. *Social Education, 75,* 211–215.

Shaftel, F. R., & Shaftel, G. (1982). *Role playing for social values.* Englewood Cliffs, NJ: Prentice Hall.

Sharan, Y., & Sharan, S. (1990). Group investigation expands cooperative learning. *Educational Leadership,* 17–21.

Sharan, Y., & Sharan, S. (1994). What do we want to study? How should we go about it? Group investigation in the cooperative social studies classroom. In R. J. Stahl (Ed.), *Cooperative learning in social studies: A handbook for teachers.* Menlo Park, CA: Addison-Wesley.

Slavin, R. E. (1986). *Using student team learning* (3rd ed.). Baltimore, MD: Center for Social Organization of Schools, Johns Hopkins University.

Slavin, R. E. (1990). *Cooperative learning: Theory, research, and practice.* Englewood Cliffs, NJ: Prentice Hall.

Slavin, R. E. (1991). Synthesis of research on cooperative learning. *Educational Leadership, 48,* 71–82.

Stahl, R. J. (Ed.). (1994). *Cooperative learning in social studies: A handbook for teachers.* Menlo Park, CA: Addison-Wesley.

Swift, J. N., & Gooding, C. T. (1983). Interaction of wait time feedback and questioning instruction on middle school science teaching. *Journal of Research in Science Teaching, 20,* 721–730.

Taba, H. (1969). *Teaching strategies and cognitive functioning in elementary school children.* Cooperative research project 2404. Washington, DC: U.S. Office of Education.

Tobin, K. (1987). The role of wait time in higher cognitive level learning. *Review of Educational Research, 57,* 69–95.

Tobin, K. G. (1986). Effects of teacher wait time on discourse characteristics in mathematics and language arts classes. *American Educational Research Journal, 23,* 191–200.

VanSickle, R. L. (1992). Cooperative learning, properly implemented works: Evidence from research in classrooms. In R. J. Stahl & R. L. VanSickle (Eds.), *Cooperative learning in the social studies classroom: An invitation to social study.* Washington, DC: National Council for the Social Studies.

Wilen, W. W., & White, J. J. (1991). Interaction and discourse in social studies classrooms. In J. P. Shaver (Ed.), *Handbook of research on social studies teaching and learning.* New York: Macmillan.

CHAPTER 6

# Promoting Reflective Inquiry: Developing and Applying Concepts, Generalizations, and Hypotheses

**Learning and Teaching Concepts**
The Nature of Concepts
Misconceptions and Stereotypes
Concepts in Social Studies Programs
The Process of Learning a Concept
Concept Analyses
Assessing Concept Learning
Instructional Strategies That Promote Concept Learning
Concept Hierarchies

**Learning and Teaching Facts and Generalizations**
The Nature of Facts
The Nature of Generalizations
The Value of Generalizations
Generalizations, Facts, and Hypotheses
Instructional Strategies that Promote the Learning of Generalizations
Using Data Retrieval Charts in Developing Generalizations

**The Reflective Citizen and Problem Solving**
Uses of the Term *Problem* in Instruction
Instructional Strategies for Problem Solving

*Social studies teaching and learning are powerful when they are:*

- *Meaningful,*
- *Integrative,*
- *Value-based,*
- *Challenging, and*
- *Active.*

*As envisioned by the National Council for the Social Studies (1993), "powerful social studies teaching and learning" are essential for the development of reflective, competent, and concerned citizens.*

*To function effectively and advance, a democratic society requires reflective citizens who have a well-grounded body of concepts, facts, and generalizations concerning human behavior, their nation, and the world. In applying such knowledge to civic affairs, citizens must be able to develop and test hypotheses and engage in problem solving using factual data and well-formed concepts. These reflective abilities are acquired cumulatively; they begin early in the home, become more formalized with the onset of kindergarten and schooling, and may develop throughout life.*

*In an earlier chapter, we noted that individuals organized knowledge into structures known as* ***schemata.*** *The elements of these schemata include a complex, interrelated web or network of concepts, facts, generalizations, and hypotheses. We now will consider teaching strategies and learning environments that provide students with subject matter and experiences that stimulate the development of such knowledge structures.*

## LEARNING AND TEACHING CONCEPTS

All learning, thinking, and action involve concepts. They broaden and enrich our lives and make it possible for us to communicate easily with others. Because individuals share many similar concepts, they can exchange information rapidly and efficiently without any need for explaining in detail each item discussed. Similarly, when a communication breakdown occurs, it often is because one of the parties lacks the necessary concepts embedded in the conversation. Not infrequently this happens in social studies textbooks when the author assumes certain knowledge that the student does not actually have.

Concepts are hooks on which we can hang new information. When we encounter new subject matter that does not appear to fit on any existing conceptual hook, we may broaden our idea of what some existing hook can hold or create a new one. These conceptual hangers allow us to tidy up our knowledge structure. They also make it easier to learn and to remember information.

### The Nature of Concepts

In their simplest form, **concepts** may be regarded as categories into which we group phenomena within our experience. Concepts make it easier to sort out large numbers of living beings, objects, and events into a smaller number of usable categories of experience, such as cars, plants, nations, and heroes. As phenomena are sorted into concept categories, we discern their basic or distinguishing characteristics. We may check these characteristics against our memories of past examples or *prototypes* that represent our notion of a typical case of the concept.

Concepts, however, are more than just categories. They have personal as well as public dimensions. The **personal dimensions** consist of the unique individual associations we have accumulated in relation to the concept. Peoples' concepts of money, as an illustration, are attached to their economic goals, perceptions of financial issues, and many other personal associations with money that make their concepts unique.

Considerable evidence demonstrates that culture generally places a large role in shaping this pattern of personal associations (Cole & Scribner, 1974; Hunt & Banaji, 1988; Whorf, 1956). Some investigators also have argued that language specifically is an important influence.

In contrast to the set of unique personal associations that each of our concepts incorporates, some defining properties are shared in common: the **public dimensions** of the concept. The public characteristics distinguish one concept from another and permit easy exchanges of information and experiences. This means that although a professional banker and I, for example, have had different levels of experiences with *money*, we can easily communicate with one another concerning checks, bank drafts, currency, traveler's checks, and credit cards.

## Misconceptions and Stereotypes

Much of the formal learning of concepts in schools often consists of correcting **misconceptions,** that is, incorrect or incomplete concepts, as well as forming new ones. When students focus on the *non*critical properties of concepts and begin to treat them as defining ones, they often develop **stereotypes.** As an illustration, on the basis of a limited range of experiences with Americans classified as *Japanese*, a youngster may have developed the stereotype that Japanese are "people who are shy, hard-working, wear glasses, and are smart." From these limited and isolated experiences, the individual has overgeneralized to *all* Japanese Americans.

## Concepts in Social Studies Programs

By the time they finish high school, students will have encountered thousands of terms in their social studies classes and textbooks. A list of some of the concepts that are commonly encountered in middle and secondary social studies programs, materials, and texts are shown here. Only a fraction of items such as these actually will be learned as concepts and become more than a familiar word (Martorella, 1971).

| | | |
|---|---|---|
| custom | culture | family |
| revolution | earth | assembly line |
| allies | peace | refugee |
| discrimination | justice | country |
| causality | desert | law |
| atlas | tariffs | balance of trade |
| poverty | productivity | artifacts |
| roles | progress | population density |
| conflict | society | social class |
| self | stimuli | attitude |

## The Process of Learning a Concept

It would be difficult for you to recall vividly the experiences that were involved in learning many of the concepts you already possess. To recapture this sensation, I will ask you to learn some new concepts. In doing so, you will be putting yourself in the shoes of a student who is confronted with the same type of task in social studies classes. As you engage in the learning process, reflect on your strategies, your successes and mistakes, and your feelings about the process.

Consider the two concept instruction frames in Figures 6.1 and 6.2 and then answer the questions. When you feel you have learned the concept, compare your responses with the Answer Key at the end of this chapter.

The experiences associated with attempting to learn these new concepts should have sensitized you to some of the problems that students experience. Difficulties often begin with trying to remember (and spell correctly) what appear as strange names. Your experience also may suggest how students sometimes have thoughtful reasons for wrong answers. Most importantly, the exercise should have revealed how *learner problems are often due to the nature of the instruction provided, rather than to student inadequacies.*

**Sources of Difficulty in Concept Learning.** The exercise also should have confirmed that there are different levels of difficulty associated with demonstrating learning of a concept. You will recall I asked you to *state* the

**Figure 6.1**
**Examples and Nonexamples of Slineps**

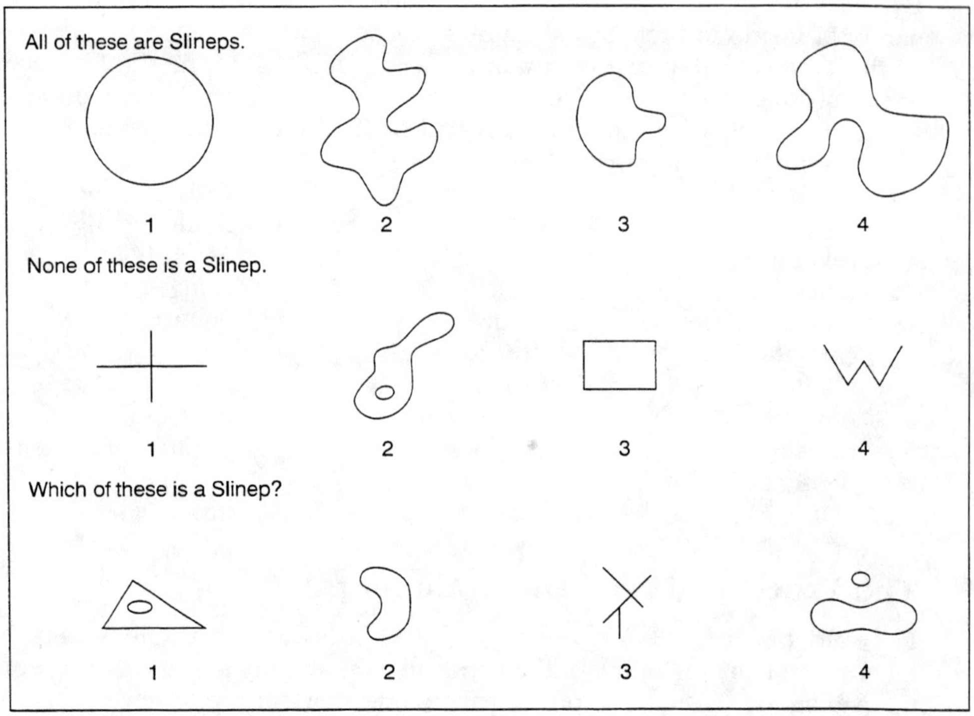

concept rule of each of the two concepts, as well as *identify* examples. Stating the concept rule in your own words or even selecting a correct definition among incorrect ones is a different and more difficult task than identifying examples from nonexamples.

The two examples in the exercise also represented different types of problems associated with concept learning. Two types of concepts were included: *disjunctive* and *conjunctive* (Bruner, Goodnow, & Austin, 1962). Rygs represented disjunctive concepts and Slineps conjunctive concepts.

**Conjunctive, Disjunctive, and Relational Concepts.** Conjunctive concepts, such as Slineps, are the *least* complex type to learn. **Conjunctive concepts** have a single fixed set of characteristics that define the concept, such as those given for Slineps. All the many different examples of Slineps share the same essential set of characteristics. Examples of conjunctive social studies concepts are *ocean, capitalism, century, monarchy,* and *norm.*

**Disjunctive concepts,** such as Rygs, have *two or more* sets of alternative characteristics that define them, rather than a single one. In social

**Figure 6.2**
**Examples and Nonexamples of Rygs**

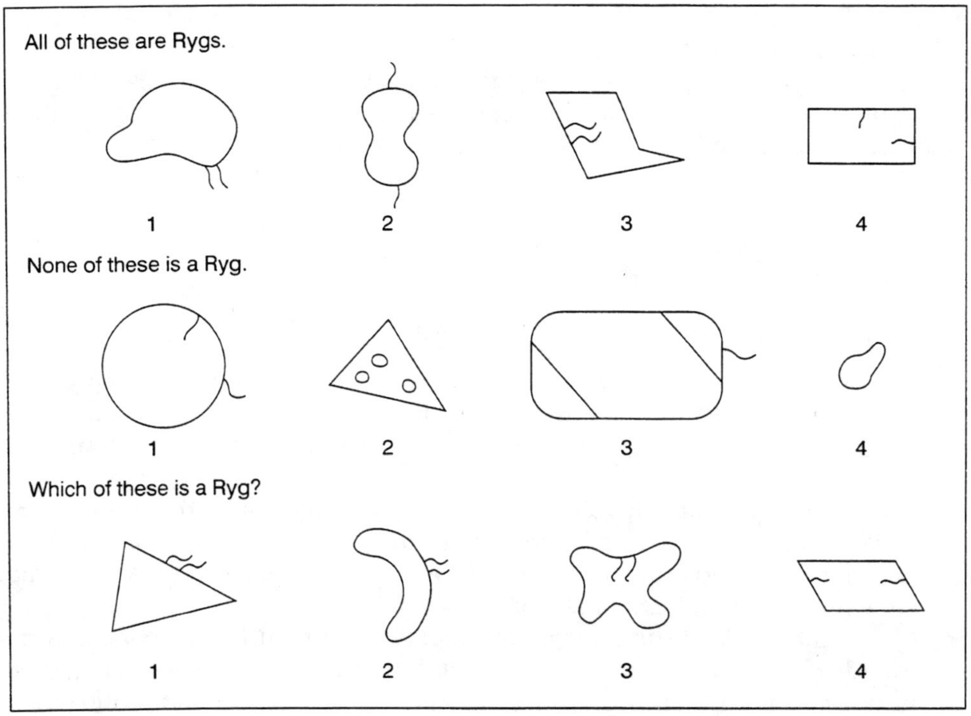

studies, *citizen* is such a concept. Citizens of the United States are those who *either* are born in the country *or* fulfill some test of citizenship *or* are born in another country of parents who are citizens of the United States.

You were not asked to learn the *most* complex type, a **relational concept.** Unlike other types, relational concepts have *no* single fixed set of characteristics. Rather, they can be defined only by comparison to or in relationship to other objects or events. *Justice, far, prosperous, greed, fair,* and *near* are examples of relational concepts in social studies. One cannot tell, for instance, whether a person, place, or thing is "near," only whether it is near to something else, and then only by using some criterion to make a judgment of nearness. Philadelphia may or may not be considered to be near Baltimore. It depends on whether the context of analysis deals with city blocks or planets. In summary, learning a relational concept involves more than identifying a single, simple set of criterial attributes.

**Concrete and Abstract Concepts.** A further source of difficulty associated with learning concepts is their degree of *concreteness* or *abstractness.* **Concreteness** refers to what we can perceive directly through one of our five senses: smell, taste, seeing, feeling, or hearing. **Abstractness** refers to what we cannot directly perceive through our senses.

In practice, the line between what is concrete and what is abstract seldom is so clearly drawn. Consider the list of social studies concepts presented earlier. Some clearly cannot be directly perceived, such as *progress,* and are regarded as abstract; others clearly can be experienced through the senses, such as *atlas,* and are considered to be concrete.

Many concepts, *allies* and *family,* for example, lie however somewhere in between being concrete or being abstract. Aspects of allies and family are visible, such as people, but other important characteristics, the relationships of individuals to one another, are abstract.

## Concept Analyses

A **concept analysis** involves identifying the **name** most commonly associated with the concept; a simplified **rule** or definition that specifies clearly what the concept is; the **criterial attributes** that make up the defining characteristics of the concept; and some **noncriterial attributes** that are characteristics often associated with the concept but nevertheless are nonessential.

An analysis also involves selecting or creating some different **examples** of the concept, including a **best example** or clearest case of the concept, and some related **nonexamples** of the concept. These provide contrast by showing what the concept is not.

Statements of the criterial attributes and definitions of concepts can be found in general dictionaries, specialized dictionaries, such as the *Dictionary of Political Science,* and textbooks. Identifying the noncriterial attributes of concepts requires some reflection, since they take many different forms. As we noted in the illustration relating to Japanese Americans, noncriterial attributes appear in examples of virtually any concept. As a result, their presence often misleads students into believing they are essential features of the concept.

Given the diversity of concepts, there is no specific number of examples that are required to teach a concept. The set of examples provided, however, should adequately represent the range of cases that appear in common usage. For instance, in teaching the concept of *protective tariffs*, the set of examples should include different nations, commodities, and levels.

Nonexamples are most helpful to a learner if they are closely related to the concept being learned in one or more respects. For example, in teaching the concept of *oceans*, it is helpful to use nonexamples such as lakes and rivers and then to point out how they differ from oceans.

Let us consider how a typical concept analysis might proceed using a concept central to discussions of a number of international issues, the concept of *refugee* (Martorella, 1989). Having a firm grasp of the concept of *refugee* opens the door to understanding much of the turmoil, misery, tension, frustration, and complexity that weaves throughout Middle Eastern history. To comprehend why refugee issues of such magnitude persist over decades, both in the Middle East and throughout the world, students require a well-grounded concept on which to build a network of related knowledge.

Refugee problems, of course, are not unique to the Middle East. Estimates of the number of refugees throughout the world exceed 17 million (U.S. Committee for Refugees, 1995). The Middle East, however, is one of the largest centers of refugee populations in the world.

An initial examination of the concept *refugee* will reveal that a clear, legally derived definition of the concept exists. The 1951 United Nations Convention Relating to the Status of Refugees and its 1967 Protocol defined a refugee as:

> any person who, owing to a well-founded fear of being persecuted for reasons of race, religion, nationality, membership of a particular social group or political opinion, is outside the country of his nationality and is unable or, owing to such fear, is unwilling to avail himself of the protection of that country, or who, not having a nationality and being outside the country of his former habitual residence, is unable, or, owing to such fear, is unwilling to return to it. (Ferris, 1985, pp. 2–3)

Although this definition has been adopted by many countries, as Ferris (1985) suggested, it has many limitations. It omits, for example, individuals who have been forced to flee their countries because of violence but who were not individually targeted for oppression. It also excludes those who may flee their homes because of persecution but yet still remain within their own country. Further, it leaves out those whom Stein (1981) regarded as "anticipatory refugees," those who anticipate persecution and leave their country before they are harmed.

Ferris (1985) noted that governments that adhere to the UN definition of refugees use political persecution as the primary basis for granting refugee status. Contending that most definitions are political, Ferris (1985) offered the following example: "In the United States, refugees from communist nations are seen as political refugees, and given refuge while arrivals from El Salvador are treated as economic migrants and usually deported" (p. 9).

Because of the complexity and limitations of the UN definition, it is not potentially useful for initial teaching of the concept of *refugee*. Instead, we will consider a simplified definition that covers most cases and offers a basic foundation for later concept elaboration. In sum, the completed concept analysis appears as in Figure 6.3.

## Assessing Concept Learning

Concept learning can be assessed at several different levels. The most basic level requires students to select an example of the concept from a set of cases that includes nonexamples. For example, a teacher asks a student to identify an example of a *relief map* from a collection of different types of maps. Further levels of testing include:

1. Identifying the criterial attributes of the concept (Illustration: from a list of characteristics, select water, land, and surrounding as those criterial for island);
2. Identifying the noncriterial attributes of the island (Illustration: from a list of characteristics, select climate, size, and vegetation as those noncriterial for island);
3. Identifying the concept rule. (Illustration: from a list of choices, select the correct definition of island);
4. Stating the concept rule. (Illustration: correctly answer the question, What is an island?);
5. Relating the concepts to other concepts. (Illustration: correctly answer the question, How are islands and peninsulas similar and different?); and
6. Locating or creating new examples of the concept. (Illustration: using an atlas, locate five new instances of islands).

The discussion in Chapter 13 will include a complete example of an assessment item for concept learning.

**Figure 6.3**
**A Teacher's Analysis of the Concept of *Refugee***

**Concept Name:** Refugee

**Concept Definition:** A refugee is a victim of persecution who seeks refuge outside his or her country.

**Criterial Attributes:** Victim, persecution, seeking refuge, outside country

**Sample Noncriterial Attributes:** Country of origin, age, gender, educational level, socioeconomic status

**Best Example:** In 1972, 10,000 Jehovah's Witnesses fled Malawi and encamped in eastern Zambia when they were attacked by the Young Pioneers, members of the Malawi Congress Party. This occurred after Hastings Banda, President of the country and leader of the party, denounced the Jehovah's Witnesses.

**Other Concept Examples:** (a) During Israel's war for independence, 1948–1949, more than one-half million Palestinian Arabs fled their homes and were never re-admitted; the contested war-torn areas became the nation of Israel.
(b) Approximately 100,000 to 200,000 Guatemalans fleeing political oppression in their country have taken refuge in southern Mexico. The Mexican government has accepted the refugees, but has not treated them well. (c) As the war in Vietnam ended in 1975, thousands (estimates were in excess of 70,000) of South Vietnamese who feared for their safety when the North Vietnamese gained control were given refuge in several countries. (d) In the course of the Sudanese Civil War, which ended in 1972, over 200,000 citizens sought refuge in nearby countries. The largest percentage settled in Uganda and Zaire. (e) In 1978, approximately 70,000 Muslim Burmese fled from Burma to Bangladesh, contending they had been driven out by Burmese forces at gunpoint and that they had been subjected to rape, torture, and murder. Subsequently, the number of refugees swelled to almost 200,000. (f) The Arab-Israeli War of 1967 lasted six days and resulted in Jordan's loss of control of the West Bank to Israel. As a result of the war, estimates were that over 300,000 people fleeing from the West Bank became refugees. Perhaps as many as half of these had also been refugees from the earlier Israeli war of independence. (g) In the three decades following Israel's war for independence in 1948–1949, more than 800,000 Jews who were citizens of Arab countries sought refuge in Israel. They were fleeing their native countries as a result of conditions such as harassment, persecution, imprisonment, and expulsion.

**Concept Nonexamples:** Nonexamples could include real or contrived cases of citizens of a country who feel policies of their government are repressive but stay in the country; those who feel they are discriminated against in one part of the country and move to another to escape persecution; those who give up their citizenship in one country and become citizens of another; criminals who escape their punishment by fleeing to another country; individuals who are unhappy with their government and who travel abroad; participants in a civil war who are on the losing side.

## Instructional Strategies That Promote Concept Learning

In considering how to teach social studies concepts, Stanley and Mathews (1985) have pointed out that the defining features for most concepts are complex. Further, they observed that category boundaries often are not clear-cut (e.g., Was United States involvement in Korea a *war* or a police *action?*). They also noted that individuals tend to create concept categories based on "best examples," or "prototypes," especially where the concepts have fuzzy boundaries. Concept learning from this perspective is a search for central tendencies of patterns rather than just isolating specific exclusive properties of a concept (Medin & Smith, 1984; Smith & Medin, 1981).

Overall, research concerning how individuals learn concepts has provided a sophisticated empirically based set of instructional guidelines for aiding students in learning concepts (Howard, 1987; Martorella, 1991; Medin & Smith, 1984; Tennyson & Cocchiarella, 1986). From the extensive body of research on concept learning, we can abstract a basic instructional model that consists of the following eight steps:

1. Identify the set of examples and nonexamples you plan to use and place them in some logical order for presentation. Include at least one example that best or most clearly illustrates an ideal type of the concept.
2. Include in the materials or oral instructions several cues, directions, questions, and student activities that draw students' attention to the critical attributes and to the similarities and differences in the examples and nonexamples used.
3. Direct students to compare all illustrations with the best example and provide feedback on the adequacy of their comparisons.
4. If critical attributes cannot be clearly identified or are ambiguous, focus attention on the salient features of the best example.
5. Where a clear definition of a concept exists, elicit or state it at some point in the instruction in terms that are meaningful to the students.
6. Through discussion, place the concept in context with other related concepts that are part of the students' prior knowledge.
7. Assess concept mastery at a minimal level, namely, whether students can correctly discriminate between new examples and nonexamples.
8. Assess concept mastery at a more advanced level; for example, ask students to generate new exemplars or apply the concept to new situations.

**Discovery and Expository Approaches in Teaching Concepts.** **Discovery approaches** encourage students to determine patterns on their own. These approaches consider the act of student discovery to be central to the learning process. In learning concepts, students engaging in discovery approaches determine which attributes are unique to the concept and infer its rule.

By contrast, **expository approaches** make explicit the defining elements of the concept. The teacher, as the major source of information concerning the concept, provides data to students in the most direct way possible (Borich, 1996).

In implementing the eight-step instructional model by using a discovery approach, teachers assume the role of resource persons and guides. Students engaging in learning concepts through discovery approaches try to determine which attributes are critical to the concept and to infer its rule. An alternative is to use an expository approach, wherein teachers assume a more directive role. They make explicit the defining elements of the concept, including the critical attributes and the concept rule. With expository approaches, teachers provide relevant data to students in the most direct way possible (Borich, 1996).

Effective discovery and expository teaching strategies both try to stimulate student curiosity and involvement. They both also use thought-provoking questions and are sensitive to the individual differences among students.

Let us consider how a teacher, Mr. Huber, might teach the concept of *refugee* to a high school class, illustrating first the discovery and then the expository approach. In both cases, he initially completes an analysis of the concept just as shown in Figure 6.3 earlier. Then he consults and applies the eight-step instructional model.

Mr. Huber's discovery lesson might unfold as follows. As a way to *focus attention on the best example,* he asks a series of questions:

- Who can locate Malawi and Zambia on the wall map?
- What caused the Jehovah's Witnesses to leave their native country of Malawi?
- What apparent motives did their attackers have?

Mr. Huber then writes on the board in columns the following headings: the victim, country of origin, cause of flight, location of new settlement. Under each heading, he fills in the relevant information from the concept examples as the lesson progresses.

To *identify the concept name,* Mr. Huber asks, "What do we call persons like the Jehovah's Witnesses who are forced to flee their country because of persecution?" If no one has a correct name, he states, "These types of people are called refugees."

As a way to *identify the concept's criterial attributes and relate it to students' prior knowledge,* Mr. Huber asks, "How is the condition of the Malawi similar to the situation of the Jews during the Third Reich?" Mr. Huber proceeds to introduce a new example of refugees and ask the students to determine how it is similar to and different from the other two cases.

As he introduces each new case, Mr. Huber guides the students to *identify noncriterial attributes that appear in concept examples:* "Notice the things that are different in all of the examples (pointing out such features as the different geographical areas from which refugees come and their ages). These are not important differences. Refugees come from all over the world and are forced to flee their homes for many reasons: their race, ethnicity, religion, political views, or organizational memberships."

Following this step, the teacher *presents additional examples and nonexamples.* He introduces the sets that are found in the concept analysis earlier in the chapter. He also engages the students in a discussion related to the criterial and noncriterial attributes of refugees. In each case, students are asked questions such as these:

- How is this (example) similar to the first one (best example)?
- How is this (nonexample) different from the first one?
- Why is this (new example) also a refugee?
- Why is this (new nonexample) not a refugee?

To get the students to *verbalize the concept definition,* Mr. Huber follows these procedures: "Let's try to list on the chalkboard all the things we can say about all the refugee cases we have considered. Who can complete the sentence I have just written on the board, 'Refugees are ________.'?"

If students do not verbalize the concept rule, the teacher states and writes on the chalkboard a simplified definition: "Refugees are those who seek refuge outside their country because of some form of persecution." This definition might be modified in the future as students encounter new information or issues that suggest that either a broader or more qualified statement is appropriate.

As a way to *assess learning at minimal level,* Mr. Huber instructs the students to identify new examples of refugees as an assignment. He directs students' attention to relevant reference works available in the classroom and the school library. To *assess learning at a more advanced level,* the teacher gives the following directions: "I would like each of you to consult your social studies text. Turn to Chapter 15 and read the discussion concerning immigrants and aliens. From your reading, determine how a refugee is different from an immigrant and an alien."

Had Mr. Huber used an expository approach, he would have included the same elements as a discovery approach. However, he would have attempted to achieve his objectives more directly and explicitly. Wherever possible, he would have called the students' attention to information he regarded as important, rather than expecting them to detect patterns on their own.

For example, he would have pointed out the criterial features of the best example, perhaps by writing them on the chalkboard and referring to them as he introduced each new example. At some point early in the lesson, Mr. Huber also would have written the concept rule on the chalkboard or directed students to a functional definition in the text or reference materials.

Further, as the lesson developed, he would have directed attention to the absence of one or more of the criterial attributes in the nonexamples. Through feedback and practice opportunities, Mr. Huber would have ensured that all students demonstrated an understanding of the criterial attributes and rule of the concept. Assessment of concept learning would proceed in the same fashion as with a discovery approach.

With either a discovery or an expository approach, the eight-step instructional model is applicable to a wide range of social studies concepts. Some concepts, however, are too complex to teach using the model. This is because they are difficult to analyze and define in a clear and unambiguous way that covers all examples of the concept. As an illustration, the attributes of concepts such as *ethnic group, community, Third-World nation,* and *revolution* are not easily identified. The reason is that in each case, although examples of the concepts *resemble* each other, they do not possess the same characteristics in common (Wittgenstein, 1953).

For such concepts, teachers need to be flexible in implementing steps 2, 4, and 5 of the instructional model. They especially need to engage students more in the exploration of the range of variations within examples than in seeking out common attributes. A teacher's ultimate goal should be to assist students in constructing their own schema of the concept.

## Concept Hierarchies

Often it is helpful for both the teaching and learning of concepts to order a series of concepts into a hierarchy. Even when concepts are not learned in a hierarchical fashion, ordering them in this way at some point often makes remembering them and their relationship to one another much easier.

Novak and Gowin's (1984) work with what they identify as **concept mapping** illustrates the application of hierarchies. Developing hierarchies of concepts initially involves placing them in context in an organized way through identifying the most all-encompassing of the concepts in a set. Then the concepts are related to one another in a logical sequence or diagram, along with brief phrases that link them.

Consider the following set of concepts: *sea level, rivers, transportation, mountains, oceans, islands, lakes, earth, land areas, continents,* and *water bodies.* The example in Figure 6.4 depicts a concept map that organizes these concepts in a logical sequence according to their relationship to one another. Kleg's (1986) instructional materials for teaching the concept of *terrorism* (see Chapter 4) also offer a clear example of how concept mapping can be applied to social studies instruction.

**Figure 6.4**
**Concept Map**

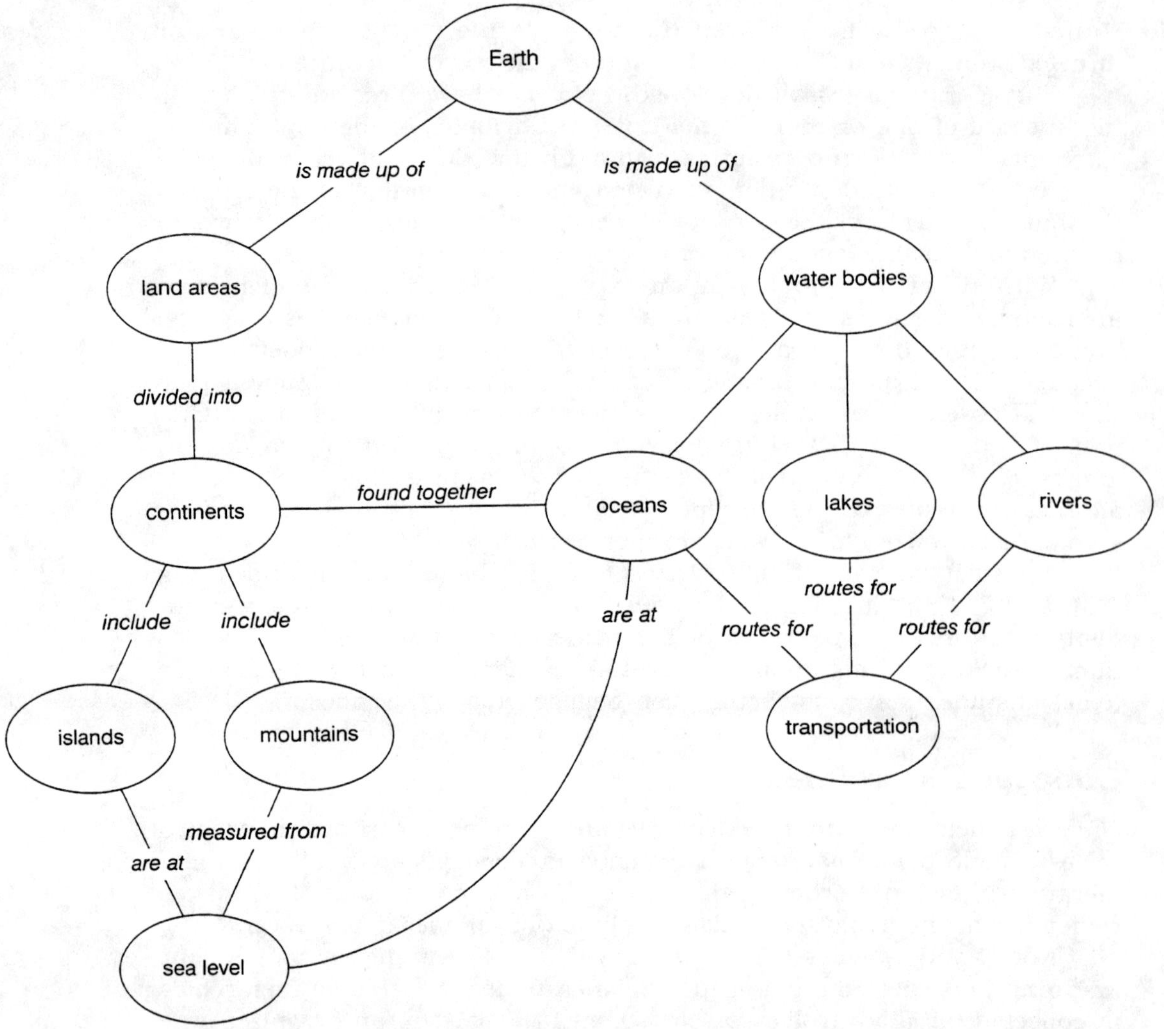


*Note.* From "Teaching Concepts" (p. 179) by P. H. Martorella, 1994, in James M. Cooper (Ed.), *Classroom Teaching Skills* (5th ed.), Lexington, MA: D. C. Heath.

## LEARNING AND TEACHING FACTS AND GENERALIZATIONS

In what ways are facts and generalizations distinguished from concepts? As we have seen, concepts are the building blocks of knowledge. They are part of every fact and generalization that we know. If our concepts are ill formed or incomplete, so will the ideas we build from them be improperly shaped.

When we think, make a decision, or act, we draw on a network of schemata that includes concepts, facts, and generalizations, the major elements of reflection.

## The Nature of Facts

Citizens are bombarded daily with facts and assertions that appear to be *facts*. In our society, facts are valued. Individuals often go to great lengths, spending much time and even money, to get them. People who have knowledge of facts or have access to such knowledge often have considerable power and status; witness heads of countries, inventors, and columnists.

A **fact** is a statement about concepts that is true or verified for a particular case on the basis of the best evidence available. To illustrate, consider a concept cluster that includes *law, court trial,* and *drunken driving.* An example of a fact statement that relates these concepts would be that: In 1988, the North Carolina state courts conducted 132 trials involving drunken driving charges.

Other examples of facts are:

- The Pittsburgh Pirates are a professional baseball team.
- President John F. Kennedy served less than one term.
- The largest state in the United States is Alaska.
- The Supreme Court interprets our Constitution.
- Slavery once was legal in the United States.

Assertions of fact often are accepted on the basis of the best evidence available at one point, only to be proven false later. The notion that atoms were the smallest particles in existence, for example, was long held in the field of science until later discoveries proved it false. Often an assertion will be accepted as a fact by an individual, even though it may not be supported by evidence or may be considered by most people to be false.

**Learning Facts in Meaningful Contexts.** All students need to have experiences in locating identifying, organizing, and verifying significant facts. The facts they are asked to remember also should have practical meaning. A student can learn two lists of 50 pairs of names—one with capitals and states and the other with nonsense words—in the same way. Neither list has any real immediate functional value beyond gaining recognition or success, unless some meaningful context is provided.

Facts learned outside of some meaningful context are often quickly forgotten long before they can be put to any functional use. More importantly, they are not integrated into students' schemata of previously acquired knowledge. This last point is illustrated by the student who had memorized all of the names of American presidents in the correct order, but who could not give the names of any three presidents who had served during the last half of the twentieth century.

Teaching students techniques for more efficiently retrieving meaningful facts from memory is a worthy instructional objective. Citizens frequently need to remember a great number of names, places, events, dates, and general descriptive information to clarify and link new knowledge in functionally meaningful ways. In Chapter 10, we consider some of the general techniques that are useful for helping students to comprehend, communicate, remember, and access factual data acquired in social studies instruction.

## The Nature of Generalizations

From an instructional perspective, a **generalization** is a statement about concepts that is true or verified for all cases on the basis of the best evidence available. Generalizations are similar to facts in that they also are true statements about relationships between or among concepts. However, generalizations summarize and organize a great deal of information obtained from analyses of many sets of facts. The summary results in a single broad, wide-reaching assertion that applies to the past, present, and even future. In contrast, facts assert claims about specific instances.

Consider the assertion of fact from a text:

- Franklin Roosevelt, who in 1932 campaigned for a balanced budget, as President initiated deficit spending to combat the economic crises facing the nation.

Compare it with this generalization:

- Economic well-being is a goal of all nations.

Further, consider each of the generalizations stated in Figure 6.5 with the corresponding factual statement that is related to the generalization.

## The Value of Generalizations

Unlike facts, generalizations have the capacity to *predict* when they appear in the form of "If . . . then" statements. For example: "*If* there is a national election, *then* the turnout of white collar, professional, and business people likely will be greater than that of semiskilled and unskilled workers." The statement predicts that "If certain conditions are present (national elections), a second set of consequences will follow (a pattern of voter turnout)."

As students examine and analyze data for patterns and then summarize their conclusions, they are progressing toward deriving significant generalizations. From the learner's perspective, the understanding that results from the analysis and that is represented by the statement of a generalization is significant.

The synthesis represented by a generalization provides the student with a broad, wide-reaching statement that applies to the past and the present and to all cases everywhere, such as: "Families vary in size and structure." A generalization also may apply to some more limited context, such as: "The nature of democracy in the United States continually evolves as the society grows and changes."

## Generalizations, Facts, and Hypotheses

Unlike facts and generalizations, which are verified assertions, **hypotheses** are untested ideas or guesses. They are potential facts or generalizations, subject to verification. Hypotheses arise when we confront something we wish to explain. They are our attempts to provide plausible explanations for questions such as: What are the causes of poverty? Why does the govern-

**Figure 6.5**
**Sample Social Studies Generalizations and Related Facts**

| Generalization | Example of a Related Fact |
|---|---|
| People in communities are interdependent. | In North Carolina, many small communities must buy water and sewage-processing services from the nearby cities. |
| The climate, topography, and natural resources of a community affect the lifestyle of its people and may determine the types of goods and services the community produces. | Palm Springs in Southern California has been a major recreation center for tourists for years. |
| Geographic factors determine the types of plants and animals that live in a region and influence population distribution. | The Amazon basin possesses many plants and animals that exist nowhere else in the world. |
| Every nation has a unique history that exerts an influence on the events of the present. | The creation of the Constitution and the Bill of Rights gave America a unique form of government and way of life. |
| Throughout history, cultures have borrowed from each other. | In Tokyo, you can find many examples of Americana, ranging from McDonald's to Disneyworld. |
| Technology has exerted a profound influence on all of the cultures in the world. | The invention of air conditioning transformed the population and commerce of states like Florida. |
| Landforms, climate, and the availability of natural resources exert a powerful influence on individual lifestyles and on societies. | Southern Californians are known for their "laid back" lifestyle, created in part by the climate and natural recreational resources. |

*Note.* Generalizations are from *Holt Social Studies* (1986, pp. 8–10).

ment subsidize the tobacco industry at the same time that it requires health warnings on cigarette packs? Why do some people get more upset at burnings of the flag than instances of social injustice?

The process of forming a hypothesis begins when we try to resolve or answer such questions. The hypotheses we propose may be sophisticated and based on a great deal of experience and background or they may be naive and poorly grounded. In either case, hypotheses formed are then *tested* through the gathering and comparing of evidence that supports or refutes them. Not infrequently in the social sciences, as a result of future tests in the context of new evidence, an original hypothesis may be revised or even discarded since some types of evidence are often conflicting and inconclusive. They also may be based on certain unproven assumptions, and as a result, never develop further. The hypotheses to explain why and by whom President Kennedy was assassinated are examples.

Other hypotheses can be verified if one is able or willing to do all that a conclusive test requires to establish cause-effect relationships. Society or researchers, however, may decide the costs of the tests in terms of human resources are greater than the benefits to be derived, or that important ethical principles would be violated by experimentation. To prove the hypothesis that certain environmental factors *cause* individuals to become criminals, rather than to suggest only that a significant *relationship* between them exists, for example, would require humans to be randomly assigned to socially undesirable conditions, whether they wished to assume the risk or not.

Still other hypotheses can never be verified or refuted, since all of the necessary evidence is impossible to obtain. Speculations about "what might have happened" had certain events in history been altered fall into this category. An example would be the hypotheses that "The United States would be far different today had Jefferson not approved the Louisiana Purchase."

Many hypotheses, however, can be tested in social studies classes by gathering and comparing data. When a hypothesis appears to "hold up" or seems to be true in the light of evidence gathered, it tentatively can be regarded as either a fact or a generalization. Which status it achieves depends on whether it applies to a particular case or to all cases within some universe (e.g., the United States).

Students engaged in developing and testing hypotheses need practice and assistance at each grade level. This includes help with generating plausible hypotheses to explain and answer simple but interesting problems and questions. It also implies assistance with gathering and comparing data to test them.

As they progress in developing and testing hypotheses, students can be introduced to the concept of **multiple causality,** which is crucial to the analysis of many issues in the social studies. Understanding multiple causality requires that students recognize and accept that more than one hypothesis may be correct—often several causes explain or account for an event. This relates to events rooted in history (e.g., What caused the American Revolution?), as well as everyday social phenomena (e.g., What causes gang violence?).

Figure 6.6 summarizes the differences among concepts, facts, generalizations, and hypotheses.

## Instructional Strategies that Promote the Learning of Generalizations

As in teaching concepts, strategies that help students develop and test generalizations may employ either *discovery* or *expository* approaches. We have seen the two approaches differ chiefly in the degree to which they place the responsibility on students to identify relationships among cases and to derive the actual generalization. Both approaches involve students in thinking, doing, and learning. Each also guides students in understanding the necessary relationships among items. To provide variety, instruction should include some mix of both discovery and expository approaches.

**Discovery Approaches.** When a discovery approach is used, the teacher withholds the generalization from students. Instructional materials and procedures are structured in such a way that students will infer or discover a generalization from their investigations.

There are no specific steps that a discovery approach follows to teach a generalization. Through whatever means possible, teachers engage and help students in the process of examining sets of data and materials. Additionally, through questioning and explaining, teachers aid students in identifying similarities and differences, patterns, and trends in the data analyzed. Also, teachers assist students in summarizing their conclusions and in discovering or inferring the unstated generalization.

Borich (1996, pp. 297–302) offered a detailed example from a secondary class of a teacher using a discovery approach to aid students in developing a generalization. The teacher begins by asking students whether

**Figure 6.6**
**The Nature of Concepts, Facts, Generalizations, and Hypotheses**

| | |
|---|---|
| Concepts | Categories into which we group people, objects, and events |
| Facts | Statements about concepts that are true or verified for a particular case on the basis of the best evidence available |
| Generalizations | Statements about concepts that are true or verified for all cases on the basis of the best evidence available |
| Hypotheses | Untested ideas or guesses that seek to explain some phenomena |

anyone knows the origins of the phrase, "government of the people, by the people, for the people."

The transcripted portion of the lesson related in Figure 6.7 picks up at this point and reveals the evolution of a lesson on comparative economic systems. Note that in a summary of the lesson at the end of the class, the teacher finally verbalizes the generalization that students have been working toward: "What can distinguish economic systems . . . is the *degree* to which goods and services that affect large numbers of individuals are owned by the government. The most is owned by the government under communism, and the least is owned by the government under capitalism" (Borich, 1996, p. 301).

**Expository Approaches.** Expository approaches may take many different forms. These include calling attention to generalizations in texts and then helping students find evidence to support them. They also encompass having students themselves advance generalizations, which they then test. The basic steps in an expository approach might be summarized as follows:

1. State, write, or call attention to the generalization that is a learning objective for the lesson.
2. Review major concepts that are part of the generalization.
3. Provide instructions, questions, cases, relevant materials, and assistance to illustrate and verify the generalization.
4. Have students identify, find, or create new cases of the generalization.

In contrast to a discovery approach, a teacher using an expository approach might begin a lesson such as the one in Figure 6.7 by first stating the generalization that the students were to learn as a *hypothesis to be tested.* The general approach would be to assist students in locating and examining relevant evidence that supports or refutes the generalization.

## Using Data Retrieval Charts in Developing Generalizations

In using either discovery or expository strategies to teach generalizations, **data retrieval charts** (Taba, 1969) are useful media (see also Chapter 10). Such charts consist of rows and columns of categories and cells of related data. For example, along the left side (rows) of a chart could be listed the names of cities: Pittsburgh, San Francisco, Vancouver, Paris, and Tokyo. Across the top (columns) of the chart could be listed selected characteristics of the cities, such as size, climate, cost-of-living, and major ethnic groups. In the related cells would be the corresponding data for each city.

To provide the structure for the data retrieval chart, the categories of items that will be used for the rows and columns, a teacher first needs to identify the generalization to be taught. As an example of how a generalization can be used to shape the structure of the chart, let us use, "Families around the world differ in their lifestyles" (See "Two Ways," 1988).

To construct the shell of the chart, we need to identify what the two sets of categories, our row and column indicators, will be. In examining the generalization, we can see that we will require data on some *representative families* and some *indicators of lifestyles.* Let us say that we assign the data on families to columns, and that we pick five diverse families from different countries: China, United States, Argentina, Algeria, and Poland.

To the rows we assign four indicators of lifestyle: life expectancy, number of children, per capita income, and number of rooms per dwelling. Our chart shell, with cells to be filled in with data, is shown in Figure 6.8.

The cells of information can be filled in by either the teacher or students or both. The teacher, for example, could begin by partially completing a chart to model for students how data is to be recorded in the cells. Data retrieval charts are particularly appropriate group projects, since tasks can be easily divided, with each member taking responsibility for either a row or a column of data.

When the cells have been filled with information, some further structure is required to analyze, compare, and summarize the material. One procedure for systematically processing the data obtained for each family is to begin by comparing the information by rows (e.g., What is the average number of children in each family), focusing on extremes (e.g., Which family has the largest (smallest) number?).

Once all the rows have been compared, the data sets in columns can be compared, picking each of the families and then comparing it to all of the rest (e.g., How does the United States family compare with the one in China (Argentina), (Algeria), (Poland)?).

If a discovery approach is used, the teacher would have students complete the chart and process the questions. Then, students would be asked to summarize all of the data in the chart in a single sentence or to infer a generalization that the chart data support.

A teacher using an expository approach, in contrast, would share the generalization before the cells in the chart were filled. Once the data were processed, students' attention would be directed to how the information obtained and analyzed supported the generalization.

## THE REFLECTIVE CITIZEN AND PROBLEM SOLVING

The terms *inquiry, critical thinking, the scientific method, reflective thinking,* and *problem solving* all have been used at one time or another to refer to the *process* by which individuals find solutions to problems through reflection. In the process of problem solving, students activate prior schema that include related facts, concepts, and generalizations, and they integrate new subject matter into meaningful knowledge structures.

**Figure 6.7**
**Transcript of a Lesson Using a Discovery Approach to Develop a Generalization**

**Teacher:** Marty.

**Marty:** From Lincoln's Gettysburg Address… I think near the end.

**Teacher:** That's right. Most nations have similar statements that express the basic principles on which their laws, customs, and economics are based. Today we will study three systems by which individual nations can guide, control, and operate their economies. The three terms describing the systems are *capitalism, socialism,* and *communism,* terms which are often confused with the political systems that tend to be associated with them. A political system not only influences the economic system of a country but also guides the behavior of individuals in many other areas, such as what is taught in schools, what the relationship between church and state is, how people get chosen for or elected to political office, what jobs people can have, what newspapers can print, and so on. For example, in the United States we have an economic system that is based on the principles of capitalism—or private ownership of capital—but a political system that is based on the principle of democracy—or rule by the people. These two sets of principles are not the same, and in the next few days you will see how they sometimes work in harmony and sometimes create contradictions. Today we will cover only systems dealing with the ownership of goods and services in different countries—that is, only the economic systems. Later you will be asked to distinguish these from political systems.

Who would like to start by telling us what the word *capitalism* means?

**Robert:** It means making money.

**Teacher:** What else, Robert?

**Robert:** Owning land… I think.

**Teacher:** Not only land, but…

**Robert:** Owning anything.

**Teacher:** The word *capital* means tangible goods or possessions. Is a house tangible?

**Betty:** Yes.

**Teacher:** Is a friendship tangible?

**Betty:** Yes.

**Teacher:** What about that, Mark?

**Mark:** I don't think so.

**Teacher:** Why?

**Mark:** You can't touch it.

**Teacher:** Right. You can touch a person who is a friend but not the friendship. Besides, you can't own or possess a person… So, what would be a good definition of *tangible goods*?

**Betty:** Something you own and can touch or see.

**Teacher:** Not bad. Let me list some things on the board and you tell me whether they could be called capital.
(Teacher writes the following:)

car

stocks and bonds

religion

information

clothes

vacation

OK. Who would like to say which of these are *capital*? (Ricky raises his hand.)

**Ricky:** Car and clothes are the only two I see.

**Barbara:** I'd add stocks and bonds. They say you own a piece of something, although maybe not the whole thing.

**Teacher:** Could you see or touch it?

**Barbara:** Yes, if you went to see the place or thing you owned a part of.

**Figure 6.7**
**continued**

**Teacher:** Good. What about a vacation? Did that give anyone trouble?

**Micky:** Well, you can own it... I mean you pay for it, and you can see yourself having a good time. (The class laughs.)

**Teacher:** That may be true, so let's add one last condition to our definition of capital. You must be able to own it, see or touch it, and it must be durable—or last for a reasonable period of time. So now how would you define *capitalism*?

**Sue:** An economic system that allowed you to have capital—or to own tangible goods that last for a reasonable period of time. And, I suppose, sell the goods, if you wanted.

**Teacher:** Very good. Many different countries across the world have this form of economic system. Just to see if you've got the idea, who can name three countries, besides our own, that allow the ownership of tangible goods?

**Joe:** Japan, West Germany, and Canada.

**Teacher:** Good. In all these countries capital, in the form of tangible goods, can be owned by individuals. Now that we know a little about capitalism, let's look at another system by which a nation can manage its economy. Ralph, what does the word *socialism* mean to you?

**Ralph:** Well, it probably comes from the word *social.*

**Teacher:** And what does the word *social* mean?

**Ralph:** People coming together, like at a party—or maybe a meeting.

**Teacher:** And why do people usually come together at a party or a meeting?

**Ralph:** To have fun. (laughter)

**Teacher:** And what about at a meeting?

**Ralph:** To conduct some business or make some decisions, maybe.

**Teacher:** Yes, they come together for some common purpose and benefits; for example, they make decisions about the things they need to live and prosper. Does that sound like a basis for a kind of economic system? (No response from class) Suppose that a large number of individuals come together to decide on what they needed to live and prosper? What types of things do you think they would consider?

**Billy:** You mean like a car or a home of your own?

**Teacher:** Yes, but let's say that the need for a car or a home of your own among individuals of the group is so very different that this group could never agree on the importance of these for everyone. What types of things could a group of people, perhaps the size of a nation, agree on that would be absolutely essential for everyone's existence?

**Ronnie:** Food.

**Teacher:** Good. What else?

**Billy:** A hospital.

**Teacher:** Very good.

**Sue:** Highways.

**Teacher:** OK. Any others?

**Ricky:** If they couldn't agree on the importance of cars for everyone, then they would have to agree on some other form of transportation, like buses, trains, or planes.

**Teacher:** Yes, they would, wouldn't they? These examples show one of the purposes of a socialist economic system—that is, to control and make available to everyone as many things as possible that (a) everyone values equally and (b) everyone needs for everyday existence.

**Sue:** You mean free, without paying?

**Figure 6.7 continued**

**Teacher:** Yes, or paying very little. In that way both rich and poor can use these services about equally.

**Sue:** But who pays?

**Teacher:** Good question. Who pays for the services provided under a socialist system?

**Mark:** The government.

**Teacher:** And who is the government?

**Mark:** Oh, I get it. The people pay taxes, just like us, and the government uses the taxes to provide the essential services.

**Sue:** So, how is that different from America?

**Teacher:** Good question. Who can answer that one?

**Robert:** It's the same.

**Mark:** No, it's not. Our government doesn't own hospitals, farms, trains, and that kind of stuff.

**Teacher:** Who owns Amtrak?

**Robert:** I think our government does.

**Teacher:** It also, believe it or not, owns some hospitals; and at least some local governments, like ours, own their own bus lines. (The class looks bewildered.) So, if you looked at our country's economic system and compared it to that of a socialist country, you might not see such a big difference. But there is a big difference. What might that difference be? Ralph, you began this discussion.

**Ralph:** I think it's a matter of degree. Almost all of the major things like hospitals and transportation systems that everyone needs are owned and run by the government under a socialist system, but only a few of these things are owned by the government in a capitalist system. On the other hand, there are things like highways, rivers, forests, and so on that are owned by the government under both systems.

**Teacher:** And how would the amount of taxes you pay differ in these two systems?

**Ralph:** You'd pay more taxes under a socialist economy than under a capitalist economy, but some services would be free—or almost—in a socialist system. We'd pay more for these services but we'd also have more money to spend for them after taxes.

**Teacher:** That was a nice way of putting it. Now, what about our third economic system? What's a word similar to communism?

**Billy:** Oh, (hesitating) *community*?

**Teacher:** Yes. And who has ownership under *communism*?

**Robert:** The community.

**Teacher:** ...which is represented by?

**Robert:** The government.

**Teacher:** Yes. Just a moment ago we discovered that much of the difference between capitalism and socialism, as economic systems, was a matter of degree. If this

Problem solving thus is both a way to better organize and interrelate existing knowledge, as well as acquire new information. The elements of reflection are not learned as isolated bits of information, but as part of a pattern of psychologically meaningful knowledge. Students do not first learn facts, for example, *then* engage in problem solving. They use knowledge already acquired and add new elements, such as facts, concepts, and generalizations, *as* they engage in problem solving.

**Figure 6.7 continued**

were also true of the difference between socialism and communism, how might you describe ownership under the communist economic system?

**Sue:** More is owned by the community—I mean by the government.

**Teacher:** Ronnie, you mentioned food before. Do you think food—or the farms on which the food is grown—is owned by the government under communism?

**Ronnie:** I guess so.

**Teacher:** Billy, you mentioned hospitals; Sue, you mentioned highways; and Ricky, you mentioned planes. Who owns these in a communist economic system?

**Class:** The government.

**Teacher:** OK. Now let's create a chart that shows some examples of things likely to be owned by the governments under all three of our economic systems, so that we can see them side by side and compare them.

(Teacher writes the following on board.)

| *Capitalism* | *Socialism* | *Communism* |
|---|---|---|
| highways | highways | highways |
| rivers | rivers | rivers |
| forests | forests | forests |
| | hospitals | hospitals |
| | planes | planes |
| | buses | buses |
| | trains | trains |
| | | food supply |
| | | housing |
| | | industries |

Now, what kinds of things *don't* we find up here?

**Richard:** Personal things, like clothes, watches, and television sets.

**Teacher:** Good. Ownership of these items can never be used to distinguish economic systems. What can distinguish economic systems, however, is the degree to which the goods and services that affect large numbers of individuals are owned by the government: The most is owned by the government under communism, and the least is owned by the government under capitalism. Now, how do you think the amount of taxes paid by individuals living under these three systems would differ?

**Class:** Communism would have the highest, then socialism, then capitalism.

**Teacher:** Good. Tomorrow we will follow this point up and then compare each of these three economic systems with the political systems that represent them. For tomorrow, look up in the encyclopedia the words *democracy* and *totalitarianism* and bring with you a one-page description of the major differences between these two political systems. Be prepared to know the differences between economic and political systems. Then, choose two countries that you think represent these different political systems, and we will discuss and study them further.

Most discussions of reflective thinking or problem solving derive from the work and writings of the American philosopher and educator John Dewey. His ideas on reflective thinking are laid out in detail in two books, *How We Think* (Dewey, 1933) and *Democracy and Education* (Dewey, 1916). In these works, especially the first, Dewey develops clearly the nature of a problem and its relationship to reflective thinking. His ideas have been applied to the teaching of social studies by a number of promi-

**Figure 6.8**
**Sample Shell of a Data Retrieval Chart**

| **Families Around the World** | | | | | |
|---|---|---|---|---|---|
| Indicators of Lifestyles | China | United States | Argentina | Algeria | Poland |
| Life Expectancy | | | | | |
| Number of Children | | | | | |
| Per Capita Income | | | | | |
| Number of Rooms per Dwelling | | | | | |

Adapted from "Two Ways" (1988, pp. 942–943).

nent social studies educators, including Griffin (1992), Engle (1976), and Hunt and Metcalf (1968).

## Uses of the Term *Problem* in Instruction

The term **problem** as it occurs in discussions of problem solving, generally is used in three different ways. It refers to *personal* problems that individuals experience, such as how to become more popular, get along with others, or cope when you lose your job.

The term also is used to refer to significant *social* problems faced by our society or the world. These might be issues such as poverty, inequality of opportunity, crime, or unemployment.

A third usage relates to conditions in which individuals experience a *psychological* state of doubt. The classic example of this usage was provided by Dewey, who cited the case of an individual who comes to a fork in a road and has no sign to guide his direction.

## Instructional Strategies for Problem Solving

Problem-solving instructional approaches may be based on one or more meanings of the term *problem*. One application is to focus on topics that intersect with personal and social problems, such as abortion rights or how wealth should be distributed in a society. This approach, relating to issues dealing with areas such as sex, religion, and economics, that are normally closed to discussion in the classroom, was advocated by Hunt and Metcalf (1968) (see also discussions in Chapters 2, 4, and 8).

The broadest application of problem solving, however, involves the third meaning of problem, creating a state of psychological doubt. It allows the teacher to use *any* subject matter in a problem-solving approach. The teacher's role is to create, in Griffin's (1992) words, "a problematic atmosphere—a set of conditions likely to render the beliefs of students in some degree doubtful" (p. 56).

A psychological problem is created when the teacher succeeds in structuring, displaying, and sequencing subject matter in a special way that casts doubt on students' convictions or conventional wisdom. It is not the subject matter itself, but the way in which it is presented that makes it psychologically problematical. The power of the approach derives from the natural tendency of individuals to want to relieve the psychological disequilibrium they experience by solving the problem or finding explanations to account for it.

Any subject matter can be used for problem solving in this sense if a teacher is able to pose the problem and then help resolve an interesting and intriguing question. Not every lesson or topic, however, lends itself easily to developing problem-solving strategies, since it is often difficult to create a sharp, relevant problem focus for students.

Problem-solving strategies require that teachers create a psychological state of **disequilibrium** in students. A state of disequilibrium is one in which a student perceives that something is peculiar, frustrating, irritating,

**Well-designed computer software can engage students in problem solving.**

puzzling, disturbing, contrary to what is expected, or incongruous. Disequilibrium is induced to cause them to attend to the subject matter being taught, regardless of its topical content or their relative degree of interest in it. Students are asked to resolve the basic issue that puzzles them: Why is this so? or How can this be? or What is the cause of this?

One of the teacher's major roles in creating problem-solving activities is to ascertain what is likely to appear problematical to students in the context of the subject matter to be studied. Unless a teacher has organized material in a way that arouses students' initial curiosity concerning the problem, they are not likely to attend to the problem. If students do not perceive that there is any psychological problem that requires a solution, no real problem solving will occur.

A basic five-step model for problem solving, adapted from Dewey (1933), is presented in Figure 6.9. It outlines the basic sequence of activities that a teacher should follow in engaging students in problem solving.

The general problem-solving instructional model outlined in Figure 6.9 provides only a basic road map. Dewey, himself, suggested that problem solving as it occurs in natural settings does not always follow through steps in a set order. In solving problems, individuals often "jump ahead," temporarily skipping steps, and at other times, may return to a step already passed. He cautioned:

> The five phases . . . of thought that we have noted do not follow one another in a set order. On the contrary, each step in genuine thinking does something to perfect the formation of a suggestion and promote its change into a leading idea or directive hypothesis. It does something to promote the location and definition of the problem. Each improvement in the idea leads to new observations that yield facts or data and help the mind judge more accurately the relevancy of facts already at hand. The elaboration of the hypothesis does not wait until the problem has been defined and an adequate hypothesis has been arrived at; it may come at any intermediate time. (Dewey, 1933, p. 115)

**Creating Problem Scenarios.** Let us consider an example of how the problem-solving model can be applied to the study of international issues in a secondary class. Initially, the Problem Scenario Cards in Figure 6.10 would be shared in some fashion with each student, and a discussion of the related questions within the card would follow.

In both problem scenarios, leaders of a country appear to be interfering in the internal affairs of sovereign nations whose policies they do not like. They also seem to be directly urging, through moral and political suasion, nationals of another country to commit murder.

Another example of a problem-solving approach uses several brief episodes of data and strategic questioning. A class is first presented with the following text excerpt, which is said to represent national sentiment in the early twentieth century:

**Figure 6.9**
**General Problem-Solving Instructional Model**

1. Structure some aspect of the subject matter students are to learn to create a puzzle, dilemma, discrepancy, or doubt.
2. Have the students internalize the problem by asking them to verbalize it. Clarify the problem if necessary.
3. Solicit some hypotheses from the students that might explain or account for the problem. Clarify terminology where necessary, and allow sufficient time for student reflection.
4. Assist students in testing the validity of the hypotheses generated and in examining the implications of the results. Where necessary, assist in providing reference materials, background information relevant to the subject matter, and keeping students on the topic.
5. Aid students in deciding on a tentative conclusion that seems to be the most plausible explanation for the problem, based on the best evidence available at the time. Stress the tentative nature of the conclusion, because future studies and further evidence may lead to a different conclusion.

Adapted from *How We Think* by J. Dewey, 1933, Boston: D. C. Heath.

> The yeoman who owned a small farm and worked it with the aid of his family was the incarnation of the simple, honest independent, healthy, happy human being. Because he lived in close communion with nature, his life was believed to have a wholesomeness and integrity impossible for the depraved population of cities.

In contrast to the quotation, the data in Figure 6.11 are presented to the class as a transparency or a chalkboard entry. With these two sets of data in place, the students can be asked first to identify the nature of the problem (i.e., the discrepancy between the prevalent sentiment about the nature of small farms and the phenomenon of the mass migration to the cities). As a second step, they would be asked to try to hypothesize why the discrepancy existed. Hypotheses that might emerge include the following:

1. When actually given a choice, people choose the glamour of the big city over the monotony and hard work of the country.
2. Immigrants who arrived in great numbers at the turn of the century preferred the country, but had to settle for the cities where the jobs were.
3. People make occupational decisions primarily on the basis of money rather than lifestyle choices.
4. When farmers no longer can make a decent living on the farm, no matter how much they like their lifestyle, they will move to the city.

**Figure 6.10**
**Sample Problem Scenarios**

**Problem Scenario Card A**

Within the space of less than 60 days, two unrelated events occurred in 1989 that shared a similar theme. In the first case, the Ayatollah Khomeini, the functional head of Iran, was reported as being outraged at the publication of a fictional work, *Satanic Verses*, written by Salman Rushdie, a British citizen. Some of the aspects of the fictional work that allegedly outraged Khomeini were its perceived irreverent treatment of the prophet Mohammed and the religion of Islam.

Among the actions Khomeini urged were for Muslims throughout the world to rise up, destroy the book, and kill the author, Rushdie. Muslims around the world responded by burning Rushdie's book, pressuring publishers to discontinue selling it, and threatening to kill Rushdie, who had gone into hiding.

**Questions:**

1. What is your reaction to this event?
2. Whatever you may think of his religious beliefs, do you believe that Khomeini, a reputedly devout Muslim and the acknowledged religious leader of his nation, was being true to his convictions?
3. Given his frame of reference, do you think Khomeini was right or wrong? Why?

**Problem Scenario Card B**

Shortly after the Rushdie affair, national elections occurred in Panama. There were numerous international reports of widespread voting irregularities that favored the existing ruler, General Manuel Noriega. Candidates in opposition to General Noriega had been physically attacked in public in the aftermath of the election. Unconfirmed reports indicate that the CIA spent millions of dollars in the election on behalf of the candidates opposed to Noriega.

President George Bush appeared on American television several days after the election. His perception was that Noriega was attempting to "steal" the election through fraud and bullying. President Bush in his address explicitly called on Panamanians in opposition to General Noriega to do "whatever it takes to get him out of there right now." The President also directly courted the military officials in Panama by promising quick recognition of a new government, if Noriega were removed.

**Questions:**

1. What is your reaction to this event?
2. Whatever you may think of his political beliefs, do you believe Bush, a reputedly devout believer in democracy and the head of his nation, was being true to his convictions?
3. Given his frame of reference, do you think Bush was right or wrong? Why?
4. Many Americans who were outraged at Khomeini and condemned his behavior supported enthusiastically President Bush's statement. What hypotheses can you offer to account for this phenomenon?

**Figure 6.11**
**Ratio of Urban Population to Total Population (Urban = incorporated areas with 2,500 or more people.)**

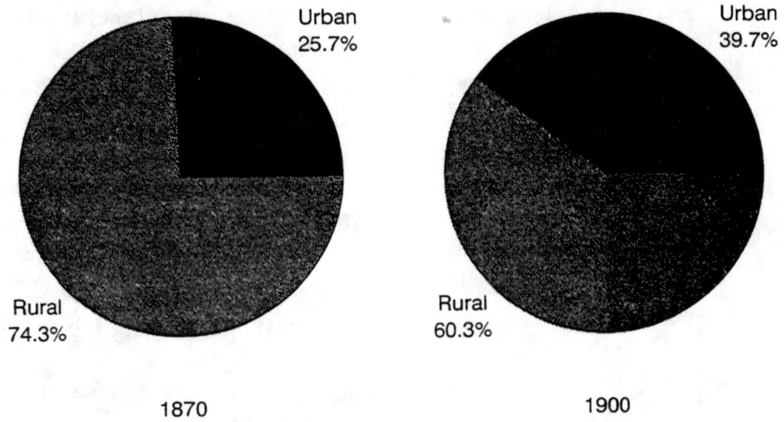


Once the list of hypotheses has been exhausted, students can proceed to test each of them under the direction of the teacher. As with all hypothesis testing in problem solving, students need to be sensitized to the fact that more than one hypothesis may constitute a solution (multiple causation). Similarly, none of the hypotheses volunteered may be a satisfactory explanation. And in any event, all hypotheses are *tentative*, pending receipt of further information.

**Using Case-Study Approaches.** Often effective teaching involves creating totally new instructional materials rather than modifying or restructuring existing texts. This creative process includes adapting relevant materials, such as advertisements or articles, and creating new instructional materials that incorporate media and primary source data. One such type of instructional material is case studies.

**Case studies** are brief sets of data that present a single idea, issue, event, document, or problem in some detail. They attempt to present in-depth coverage of a narrow topic. Further, through concrete examples, they seek to make vivid some general or abstract issue. For example, a case study might include an article examining how an individual was stalked and attacked as a way to begin examining the problem of violent crime in the United States. Or it might incorporate a video episode of a news program that recounts how an innocent victim was able to obtain release from prison to dramatize one dimension of injustices in our criminal justice system.

**Types of Case Studies.** Case studies may be presented through many different media: transparencies, teacher-made sheets, records, video and audio cassettes, films, and various print materials. Four basic types of case studies are (Newmann with Oliver, 1970):

1. *Stories and Vignettes.* These are dramatized accounts of either authentic or fictitious events.
2. *Journalistic Historical Events.* These include original newspaper accounts, recordings, or video records of historical events, eyewitness accounts, and the like.
3. *Research Reports.* These include materials such as the results of studies, statistical tables, and census reports that have been organized and summarized.
4. *Documents.* This category includes a range of different items such as speeches, diaries, laws, and records.

An illustration of a simple case study is presented in Figure 6.12. It uses excerpts from various texts to examine an issue that has intrigued historians for over two centuries: Who actually fired the first shot in what became the American Revolution?

The confrontation between the militiamen and the British at Lexington Green on the morning of 1775 is generally credited as the first battle of the war. What is unclear is which side was responsible for first engaging the battle.

## ANSWER KEY

In Figure 6.1, only number 2 is a *Slinep.* Slineps are single, curved, closed figures.

In Figure 6.2 numbers 2 and 4 are *Rygs.* Rygs are single closed figures with 2 tails and can be formed of either curved or straight lines. A curved-line Ryg always has tails extending *outside* the figure, but a straight line Ryg always has tails extending *inside* the figure.

## GROUP ACTIVITIES

1. Select a basal social studies textbook for any grade, 5 through 12. Identify the text title, the grade level, the author and publisher, and the copyright date. List all of the concepts that are included in 10 pages of the text, beginning with the first page of the chapter. For this exercise include only those concepts that are nouns or adjectives. When you have collected the data, discuss these questions: Which concepts appear most frequently? Which do you consider to be the most difficult? The least difficult?
2. Identify two generalizations from each of the social sciences, other than those found in this textbook. As references you may wish to consult introductory textbooks and specialized reference works. Select only those generalizations that would be suitable for developing social stud-

**Figure 6.12**
**Data Sheet for Case Study**

**Issue:** Who fired the first shot in the Revolutionary War?

Questions to answer in examining different accounts:

1. How many militiamen were involved in the battle?
2. What role did Captain Parker pay in the battle?
3. How many militiamen were killed?
4. Who fired the first shot?
5. What was the significance of claiming who fired the first shot?

**Account 1**

About 70 minutemen were ready to dispute the passage of the British soldiers. They did not withdraw until they were fired upon and 8 of their number killed. Thus began the War of American independence.

**Account 2**

At daybreak of April 19 the British reached Lexington, where they were confronted by about 60 minutemen. Their commander, Captain Parker, told his men: "Don't fire unless you are fired upon; but if they want a war, let it begin here." A shot was fired, but from which side is not certain; then came a volley from the British soldiers which killed 8 men and wounded many others. Unable to oppose a force that outnumbered them ten to one, the minutemen fell back in confusion.

**Account 3**

Pitcairn reached Lexington at sunrise and found himself confronted by some 40 minutemen under Captain John Parker. With an oath he called on them to disperse, but they stood as motionless as a wall, and he ordered his men to fire. (Note: there are different statements as to the opening shots.) The volley laid 7 of the patriots dead and 10 wounded on the village green. Parker was greatly outnumbered, and, after making a feeble resistance, ordered his men to retire.

**Account 4**

At Lexington, 6 miles below Concord, a company of militia, of about 100 men, mustered near the Meeting-House; the Troops came in sight of them just before sunrise; and running within a few rods of them, the Commanding Officer accosted the Militia in words to this effect: "Disperse, you rebels—throw down your arms and disperse"; upon which the Troops huzzaed, and immediately one or two officers discharged their pistols, which were instantaneously followed by the firing of 4 or 5 of the soldiers, and then there seemed to be a general discharge from the whole body; 8 of our men were killed and 9 wounded....

**Account 5**

I, John Parker, of lawful age, and commander of the Militia in Lexington, do testify and declare, that on the 19th [of April], being informed... that a number of regular troops were on their march from Boston... ordered our Militia to meet on the Common in said Lexington, to consult what to do, and concluded not to... meddle or make with the said regular troops [if they should approach] unless they should insult us; and upon their sudden approach, I immediately ordered our Militia to disperse and not to fire. Immediately said troops made their appearance, and rushed furiously, fired upon and killed 8 of our party, without receiving any provocation therefore from us.

**Account 6**

Captain Parker's Company being drawn upon the green before sunrise, and I being in the front rank, there suddenly appeared a number of the King's Troops, about a thousand, as I thought, at the distance of about 60 or 70 yards from us, huzzaing and on a quick pace toward us....

*Note.* Adapted from McMurry (1937, pp. 134–146), as quoted in Gardner, W. E., Beery, R. W., & Olson, J. R. (1969). *Selected case studies in American history* (pp. 60–62, 66–67). Boston: Allyn & Bacon.

ies lessons. Compare your lists and discuss any problems you had in identifying appropriate generalizations.

3. Select one of the four types of case studies described in the text. Identify a class or group in grades 5 through 12 with whom you would use the material and develop a case study on any subject appropriate for that audience. Discuss specifically how you would use the case as a springboard to a problem-solving activity.
4. The full text of the National Council for the Social Studies policy statement concerning powerful social studies, which is referenced at the beginning of this chapter, can be found in the September, 1993, issue of *Social Education*, pp. 213–223. Read the document and discuss your reactions.

## INDIVIDUAL ACTIVITIES

1. Develop a strategy to teach a social studies concept to a seventh-grade student. Use the eight-step instructional model and the concept analysis form provided in the chapter. You may use either a discovery or an expository approach.
2. Repeat the procedures from the previous activity, except substitute an 11th-grade student.
3. Select one of the generalizations identified in group activity 2 and a grade level 5 through 12. Develop a lesson plan to teach one of the generalizations using either a basic expository or a discovery strategy.
4. Consult the example of the problem scenario cards in Figure 6.10 in this chapter and select a grade level 5 through 12. Create a set of problem scenarios using any social studies subject matter that you wish.

## REFERENCES

Borich, G. (1996). *Effective teaching methods* (3rd ed). Englewood Cliffs, NJ: Merrill/Prentice Hall.

Bruner, J. S., Goodnow, J., & Austin, G. A. (1962). *A study of thinking*. New York: Science Editions.

Cole, M., & Scribner, S. (1974). *Culture and thought*. New York: Wiley.

Dewey, J. (1916). *Democracy and education*. New York: Macmillan.

Dewey, J. (1933). *How we think*. Boston: D. C. Heath.

Engle, S. H. (1976). Exploring the meaning of the social studies. In P. H. Martorella (Ed.), *Social studies strategies: Theory into practice* (pp. 232–245). New York: Harper & Row.

Ferris, E. G. (1985). Overview: Refugees and world politics. In E. G. Ferris (Ed.), *Refugees and world politics*. New York: Praeger.

Gardner, W. E., Beery, R. W., & Olson, J. R. (1969). *Selected case studies in American history.* Boston: Allyn & Bacon.

Griffin, A. F. (1992). *A philosophical approach to the subject matter preparation of teachers of history.* Washington, DC: National Council for the Social Studies—Kendall Hunt.

*Holt Social Studies.* (1986). New York: Holt.

Howard, R. W. (1987). *Concepts and schemata: An introduction.* Philadelphia: Cassell.

Hunt, E. B., & Banaji, M. R. (1988). The Whorfian hypothesis revisited: A cognitive science view of linguistic and cultural effects on thought. In J. W. Berry, S. H. Irvine, & E. B. Hunt (Eds.), *Indigenous cognition: Functioning in context.* Boston: Martinus Nijhoff.

Hunt, E. B., & Metcalf, L. E. (1968). *Teaching high school social studies: Problems in reflective thinking and social understanding* (2nd ed.). New York: Harper & Row.

Kleg, M. (1986). Teaching about terrorism: A conceptual approach. *Social Science Record, 24,* 31–39.

Martorella, P. H. (1994). *Concept learning and higher-level thinking.* In J. M. Cooper (Ed.), *Classroom teaching skills* (5th ed.). Lexington, MA: D. C. Heath.

Martorella, P. H. (1971). *Concept learning in the social studies: Models for structuring curriculum.* Scranton, PA: INTEXT.

Martorella, P. H. (1989). Teaching concepts related to the Middle East: Research, theories, and applications. *Social Science Record, 27,* 37–40.

Martorella, P. H. (1991). Knowledge and concept development in social studies. In J. B. Shaver (Ed.), *Handbook of research on social studies teaching and learning.* New York: Macmillan.

McMurry, D. L. (1937). *The evaluation of propaganda by the historical method.* In E. Ellis (Ed.). *Education against propaganda.* Seventh Yearbook of the National Council for the Social Studies. Washington, DC: National Council for the Social Studies, pp. 134–146.

Medin, D. L., & Smith, E. E. (1984). Concepts and concept formation. *Annual Review of Psychology, 35,* 113–138.

National Council for the Social Studies. (1993). *A vision of powerful teaching and learning in the social studies: Building social understanding and civic efficiency.* Washington, DC: Author.

Newmann, F. M., with Oliver D. W. (1970). *Clarifying public controversy: An approach to teaching social studies.* Boston: Little, Brown.

Novak, J., & Gowin, D. B. (1984). *Learning how to learn.* Cambridge, MA: 1984.

Smith, E. E., & Medin, D. L. (1981). *Categories and concepts.* Cambridge, MA: Harvard University Press.

Stanley, W. B., & Mathews, R. C. (1985). Recent research on concept learning: Implications for social education. *Theory and Research in Social Education, 12,* 57–74.

Stein, B. N. (1981). The refugee experience: Defining the parameters of a field of study. *International Migration Review, 15,* 320–330.

Taba, H. (1969). *Teaching strategies and cognitive functioning in elementary school children.* Cooperative research project 2404. Washington, DC: U.S. Office of Education.

Tennyson, R. D., & Cocchiarella, M. J. (1986). An empirically based instructional design theory for teaching concepts. *Review of Educational Research, 56,* 40–71.

Two ways to cope. (December 1988). *National Geographic, 174,* 942–943.

U.S. Committee for Refugees. (1995). *World refugee survey.* Washington, DC: Author.

Whorf, B. (1956). *Language, thought and reality.* Cambridge, MA: Cambridge University Press.

Wittgenstein, L. (1953). *Philosophical investigations.* New York: Macmillan.

CHAPTER 7

# Fostering Citizenship Competency: Developing and Applying Social, Research and Analysis, Chronology, and Spatial Skills

**The Nature of Citizenship Skills**
Lists of Skills for the Social Studies Curriculum, K–12

**Social Skills**
Conflict Resolution Skills

**Research and Analysis Skills**
Interpreting and Comparing Data
Analyzing Arguments
Processing Information from Pictures

**Chronology Skills**
Comparative Conceptions of Time
Recording Events on Time Lines

**Spatial Skills**
The Impact of Spatial Perspectives
Using and Creating Maps in Instruction
Integrating Maps and Globes into All Social Studies Instruction

**Identifying and Using Reference Sources in Developing Skills**
Sample Reference Works for Social Studies
Encyclopedic References

**Activities for Introducing Reference Materials**

*In Ms. Colazzo's seventh-grade world cultures class, students are working in small groups. They are using sets of colored pens and a desk outline map showing nations of the world. Periodically, members of the group consult the sources on the reference table and the large World Hunger Map provided in the Newsweek Education Program.*

*In the context of a unit on world hunger and poverty, the students' objective is to determine which 15 countries in the world had the (1) highest infant mortality rate, (2) the highest population growth rates, (3) the lowest per capita GNP, and (4) the lowest life expectancy. Further, the students are to test the hypothesis that a relationship among these four categories exists (i.e., the same countries appear on each list).*

*Once each group has shaded in the data for each category on four different outline maps using different colors for each, students will analyze the relationships and determine whether the hypothesis is supported. The recorder in each group then will summarize the conclusions. When all of the groups are finished, the entire class will discuss the results.*

*To determine whether there has been a pattern over time, Ms. Colazzo will instruct the groups to identify which 15 countries made the four lists a decade ago. Eventually, individual members of the groups will examine in more depth and report on the countries identified.*

Just as Ms. Colazzo's students, citizens acquire and use skills most effectively in the context of solving meaningful problems and performing tasks that they regard as interesting, functional, or important. Skills facilitate knowledge construction by enabling us to locate, analyze, validate, and apply information efficiently. Effective social studies instruction encourages students to both develop and apply skills. It also provides guidelines for when and why it is appropriate to employ the skills (Brophy, 1992).

## THE NATURE OF CITIZENSHIP SKILLS

Citizens require a repertoire of competencies (skills) to function effectively in our complex society. Over the years, numerous lists of such skills have been advanced for development throughout the social studies curriculum. For example, all basal social studies textbook programs enumerate the various skills that are embedded in the materials. Typically, such lists sequence the skills in the order they are to be taught in kindergarten through grade 12. They also suggest the relative degrees of emphasis that each type of skill should receive (Jarolimek & Parker, 1993).

### Lists of Skills for the Social Studies Curriculum, K–12

One such comprehensive set of skills, shown in Figure 7.1, was produced by the National Council for the Social Studies' Task Force on Scope and Sequence (Task Force on Scope and Sequence, 1989). It provides a detailed inventory of the diverse competencies that students are to develop within their social studies programs.

The list includes three major categories of skills and a number of subcategories. It also suggests the degree of emphasis that each type of skill should receive at different grade levels. This and other similar lists can serve as references for identifying skills to emphasize in planning lessons and units.

The remainder of the chapter will consider ways in which social studies programs across the middle and secondary grades can nurture the development and application of skills in the context of lessons and units. We will focus on a sample of the skills outlined in Figure 7.1 that are organized under four categories of competencies central to effective citizenship: *social skills, research and analysis skills, chronology skills,* and *spatial skills.*

**Figure 7.1**
**Essential Skills for Social Studies**

Suggested strength of instructional effort: Minimum or none · Some · Major · Intense

## I. Skills related to acquiring information

### A. Reading skills

| K–3 | 4–6 | 7–9 | 10–12 | Skill |
|---|---|---|---|---|
| | | | | **1. Comprehension** |
| Major | Intense | Major | Some | Read to get literal meaning |
| Minimum or none | Intense | Major | Some | Use chapter and section headings, topic sentences, and summary sentences to select main ideas |
| Minimum or none | Intense | Intense | Some | Differentiate main and subordinate ideas |
| Minimum or none | Major | Major | Major | Select passages that are pertinent to the topic studied |
| Minimum or none | Some | Major | Intense | Interpret what is read by drawing inferences |
| Minimum or none | Some | Major | Intense | Detect cause and effect relationships |
| Minimum or none | Some | Major | Intense | Distinguish between the fact and opinion; recognize propaganda |
| Minimum or none | Some | Major | Intense | Recognize author bias |
| Major | Major | Major | Some | Use picture clues and picture captions to aid comprehension |
| Minimum or none | Some | Major | Intense | Use literature to enrich meaning |
| Minimum or none | Major | Intense | Intense | Read for a variety of purposes: critically, analytically, to predict outcomes, to answer a question, to form an opinion, to skim for facts |
| Minimum or none | Some | Major | Intense | Read various forms of printed material: books, magazines, newspapers, directories, schedules, journals |
| | | | | **2. Vocabulary** |
| Intense | Intense | Some | Some | Use usual word attack skills: sight recognition, phonetic analysis, structural analysis |
| Minimum or none | Major | Intense | Major | Use context clues to gain meaning |
| Minimum or none | Intense | Major | Major | Use appropriate sources to gain meaning of essential terms and vocabulary: glossary, dictionary, text, word lists |
| Minimum or none | Intense | Intense | Major | Recognize and understand an increasing number of social studies terms |
| | | | | **3. Rate of reading** |
| Minimum or none | Major | Major | Intense | Adjust speed of reading to suit purpose |
| Minimum or none | Major | Major | Major | Adjust rate of reading to difficulty of the material |

### B. Study skills

| K–3 | 4–6 | 7–9 | 10–12 | Skill |
|---|---|---|---|---|
| | | | | **1. Find information** |
| Minimum or none | Intense | Some | Some | Use various parts of a book (index, table of contents, etc.) |
| Minimum or none | Intense | Some | Minimum or none | Use key words, letters on volumes, index, and cross references to find information |
| Minimum or none | Some | Some | Major | Evaluate sources of information—print, visual, electronic |
| Minimum or none | Some | Major | Major | Use appropriate source of information |
| Minimum or none | Some | Major | Major | Use the community as a resource |
| | | | | **2. Arrange information in usable forms** |
| Minimum or none | Some | Major | Major | Make outline of topic |
| Minimum or none | Some | Major | Major | Prepare summaries |
| Minimum or none | Some | Major | Some | Make timelines |
| Minimum or none | Some | Major | Major | Take notes |
| Minimum or none | Some | Major | Major | Keep records |
| Minimum or none | Some | Major | Major | Use italics, marginal notes, and footnotes |
| Intense | Major | Some | Some | Listen for information |
| Intense | Major | Major | Some | Follow directions |
| Minimum or none | Some | Major | Intense | Write reports and research papers |
| Minimum or none | Some | Major | Intense | Prepare a bibliography |

### C. Reference and information-search skills

| K–3 | 4–6 | 7–9 | 10–12 | Skill |
|---|---|---|---|---|
| | | | | **1. The library** |
| Some | Some | Major | Major | Use card catalog to locate books |
| Minimum or none | Some | Major | Major | Use *Reader's Guide to Periodical Literature* and other indexes |
| Minimum or none | Some | Major | Major | Use COMCATS (Computer Catalog Service) |
| Minimum or none | Some | Some | Some | Use public library telephone information service |
| | | | | **2. Special references** |
| Minimum or none | Minimum or none | Some | Major | Almanacs |
| Some | Intense | Some | Minimum or none | Encyclopedias |
| Some | Intense | Some | Minimum or none | Dictionary |
| Minimum or none | Major | Some | Some | Indexes |
| Minimum or none | Minimum or none | Some | Major | Government publications |
| Minimum or none | Minimum or none | Some | Major | Microfiche |
| Minimum or none | Some | Major | Major | Periodicals |

*Note.* From National Council for the Social Studies, 1989. Used with permission.

**Figure 7.1**
**continued**

Suggested strength of instructional effort: —— Minimum or none ▬ Some ■ Major ■ Intense

| K–3 | 4–6 | 7–9 | 10–12 | Skill |
|---|---|---|---|---|
| Some | Some | Some | Major | News sources: newspapers, news magazines, TV, radio, videotapes, artifacts |
| | | | | 3. Maps, globes, graphics |
| | | | | Use map- and globe-reading skills |
| Minimum or none | Intense | Major | Some | Orient a map and note directions |
| Minimum or none | Major | Intense | Some | Locate places on map and globe |
| Minimum or none | Some | Major | Some | Use scale and compute distances |
| Minimum or none | Some | Major | Intense | Interpret map symbols and visualize what they mean |
| Minimum or none | Some | Some | Some | Compare maps and make inferences |
| Minimum or none | Minimum or none | Major | Major | Express relative location |
| Minimum or none | Some | Major | Intense | Interpret graphs |
| Minimum or none | Some | Major | Intense | Detect bias in visual material |
| Minimum or none | Some | Major | Intense | Interpret social and political messages of cartoons |
| Minimum or none | Some | Major | Major | Interpret history through artifacts |
| | | | | 4. Community resources |
| Minimum or none | Some | Major | Major | Use sources of information in the community |
| Minimum or none | Some | Major | Major | Conduct interviews of individuals in the community |
| Minimum or none | Some | Major | Major | Use community newspapers |
| | | | | **D. Technical skills unique to electronic devices** |
| | | | | 1. Computer |
| Minimum or none | Some | Major | Major | Operate a computer using prepared instructional or reference programs |
| Minimum or none | Some | Major | Major | Operate a computer to enter and retrieve information gathered from a variety of sources |
| | | | | 2. Telephone and television information networks |
| Minimum or none | Some | Some | Some | Ability to access information through networks |
| | | | | **II. Skills related to organizing and using information** |
| | | | | **A. Thinking skills** |
| | | | | 1. Classify information |
| Minimum or none | Some | Major | Major | Identify relevant factual material |
| Minimum or none | Some | Major | Major | Sense relationship between items of factual information |
| Some | Some | Major | Major | Group data in categories according to appropriate criteria |
| Some | Some | Major | Major | Place in proper sequence: (1) order of occurrence (2) order of importance |
| Some | Some | Major | Major | Place data in tabular form: charts, graphs, illustrations |
| | | | | 2. Interpret information |
| Minimum or none | Some | Major | Major | State relationships between categories of information |
| Minimum or none | Some | Major | Intense | Note cause and effect relationships |
| Minimum or none | Some | Major | Intense | Draw inferences from factual material |
| Minimum or none | Some | Major | Intense | Predict likely outcomes based on factual information |
| Minimum or none | Some | Major | Intense | Recognize the value dimension of interpreting factual material |
| Minimum or none | Some | Major | Major | Recognize instances in which more than one interpretation of factual material is valid |
| | | | | 3. Analyze information |
| Minimum or none | Major | Major | Major | Form a simple organization of key ideas related to a topic |
| Minimum or none | Some | Major | Major | Separate a topic into major components according to appropriate criteria |
| Minimum or none | Some | Major | Major | Examine critically relationships between and among elements of a topic |
| Minimum or none | Some | Major | Intense | Detect bias in data presented in various forms: graphics, tabular, visual, print |
| Minimum or none | Some | Major | Intense | Compare and contrast credibility of differing accounts of the same event |
| | | | | 4. Summarize information |
| Minimum or none | Some | Major | Major | Extract significant ideas from supporting, illustrative details |
| Minimum or none | Some | Major | Major | Combine critical concepts into a statement of conclusions based on information |
| Minimum or none | Some | Some | Some | Restate major ideas of a complex topic in concise form |

**Figure 7.1**
**continued**

Suggested strength of instructional effort: Minimum or none — Some — Major — Intense

| K–3 | 4–6 | 7–9 | 10–12 | |
|---|---|---|---|---|
| Minimum or none | Some | Major | Intense | Form opinion based on critical examination of relevant information |
| Minimum or none | Some | Major | Intense | State hypotheses for further study |
| | | | | 5. Synthesize information |
| Minimum or none | Some | Major | Major | Propose a new plan of operation, create a new system, or devise a futuristic scheme based on available information |
| Minimum or none | Some | Some | Some | Reinterpret events in terms of what *might* have happened, and show the likely effects on subsequent events |
| Minimum or none | Some | Major | Major | Present visually (chart, graph, diagram, model, etc.) information extracted from print |
| Minimum or none | Minimum or none | Some | Intense | Prepare a research paper that requires a creative solution to a problem |
| Minimum or none | Intense | Intense | Intense | Communicate orally and in writing |
| | | | | 6. Evaluate information |
| Minimum or none | Some | Major | Major | Determine whether or not the information is pertinent to the topic |
| Minimum or none | Minimum or none | Some | Major | Estimate the adequacy of the information |
| Minimum or none | Minimum or none | Some | Intense | Test the validity of the information, using such criteria as source, objectivity, technical correctness, currency |

**B. Decision-making skills**

| K–3 | 4–6 | 7–9 | 10–12 | |
|---|---|---|---|---|
| Minimum or none | Some | Major | Intense | Identify a situation in which a decision is required |
| Minimum or none | Some | Major | Major | Secure needed factual information relevant to making the decision |
| Minimum or none | Some | Major | Intense | Recognize the values implicit in the situation and the issues that flow from them |
| Minimum or none | Some | Major | Major | Identify alternative courses of action and predict likely consequences of each |
| Some | Some | Major | Major | Make decision based on the data obtained |
| Minimum or none | Some | Major | Major | Take action to implement the decison |

**C. Metacognitive skills**

| K–3 | 4–6 | 7–9 | 10–12 | |
|---|---|---|---|---|
| Minimum or none | Some | Major | Intense | Select an appropriate strategy to solve a problem |
| Minimum or none | Some | Major | Intense | Self-monitor one's thinking process |

**III. Skills related to interpersonal relationships and social participation**

**A. Personal skills**

| K–3 | 4–6 | 7–9 | 10–12 | |
|---|---|---|---|---|
| Minimum or none | Some | Major | Intense | Express personal convictions |
| Minimum or none | Some | Major | Major | Communicate own beliefs, feelings, and convictions |
| Minimum or none | Some | Some | Some | Adjust own behavior to fit the dynamics of various groups and situations |
| Major | Major | Major | Major | Recognize the mutual relationship between human beings in satisfying one another's needs |

**B. Group interaction skills**

| K–3 | 4–6 | 7–9 | 10–12 | |
|---|---|---|---|---|
| Minimum or none | Some | Some | Major | Contribute to the development of a supportive climate in groups |
| Major | Major | Major | Major | Participate in making rules and guidelines for group life |
| Major | Major | Major | Major | Serve as a leader or follower |
| Major | Major | Major | Major | Assist in setting goals for the group |
| Minimum or none | Some | Major | Major | Participate in delegating duties, organizing, planning, making decisions, and taking action in a group setting |
| Some | Some | Major | Major | Participate in persuading, compromising, debating, and negotiating in the resolution of conflicts and differences |

**C. Social and political participation skills**

| K–3 | 4–6 | 7–9 | 10–12 | |
|---|---|---|---|---|
| Minimum or none | Some | Major | Intense | Keep informed on issues that affect society |
| Minimum or none | Some | Major | Intense | Identify situations in which social action is required |
| Minimum or none | Some | Major | Intense | Work individually or with others to decide on an appropriate course of action |
| Minimum or none | Some | Major | Intense | Work to influence those in positions of social power to strive for extensions of freedom, social justice, and human rights |
| Minimum or none | Some | Major | Intense | Accept and fulfill social responsibilities associated with citizenship in a free society |

## SOCIAL SKILLS

Whether at home, at school, on the job, or at a party, having good relationships with others or "getting along" requires social skills. They are the glue that binds groups and society as a whole together harmoniously and productively. In whatever we hope to accomplish cooperatively with other individuals, social skills are instrumental in achieving our goals.

If our social environment is rich in positive models and experiences as we mature, we continuously acquire and integrate sets of valuable social skills. Once mastered, such skills are often applied to settings different from the ones in which they were learned. In this fashion, over time, many people manage to assimilate naturally the basic social competencies necessary to navigate successfully through life.

### Conflict Resolution Skills

Arguably, one of the most important skills that socially competent citizens in a democratic society have is the ability to resolve conflicts in a nonviolent and socially acceptable manner. Conflicts surround us. In all regions of our nation, youngsters of every age and from every social strata are exposed to conflict in a variety of forms.

Nightly, on television they can view episodes of conflict between parents and among other adults, between ethnic groups or countries, among politicians, and between neighborhood gangs. The alarming national statistics on child abuse and gang deaths also suggest that many students often experience violent conflict firsthand and are themselves the victims of conflict and misplaced aggression.

Classroom activities that encourage students to experiment with alternative peaceful ways of resolving conflicts can help prepare them to cope with the larger conflicts that reside within our society. These include helping them to understand the sources of disagreements and confrontations and to work out constructive solutions to their own conflicts. It also includes aiding them in developing, applying, and observing rules.

Approaches to teaching conflict resolution skills should communicate to students that the presence of some conflict is a normal everyday occurrence in a complex, interdependent society and world. Conflicts arise when the goals of individuals or groups clash. The resolution of conflict can be destructive (e.g., a fight or battle) or constructive (e.g., a compromise or a treaty).

A number of practical programs, guidelines, and strategies exist to help teachers address conflict resolution. For example, Scherer (1992) has outlined 10 basic negotiating skills that teachers can help students develop. These are shown in Figure 7.2. Another example of an excellent resource is Byrnes' (1987) book, *Teacher, they called me a ________!* It includes activities appropriate for middle grades students that involve conflict themes. Many schools also have instituted peer mediation programs. In these, students are trained to serve as mediators in conflicts.

**Figure 7.2**
**Basic Negotiating Skills**

- Check whether you understand the other person correctly and whether he or she understands you.
- Tell the other person what you think: don't try to read another's mind or tell others what you think they think.
- Talk about needs, feelings, and interests, instead of restating opposing positions.
- Recognize negotiable conflicts and avoid non-negotiable ones.
- Know how you tend to deal with most conflicts and recognize others' styles.
- Put yourself in the other's shoes.
- Understand how anger affects your ability to handle conflict and learn how to avoid violence even when you're angry.
- Reframe the issues; talk about them in other ways to find more common ground between yourself and the other person.
- Criticize what people say, rather than who or what they are.
- Seek win-win solutions, not compromises; find solutions where all parties get what they need, rather than solutions where all get some of what they need.

*Note.* From "Solving Conflicts—Not Just for Children" by M. Scherer, 1992, *Educational Leadership, 50,* p. 17.

## RESEARCH AND ANALYSIS SKILLS

Research and analysis skills are interrelated and often are inseparable in applications. **Research** can be viewed as the process of both locating and finding information in response to some question. It often includes the identification, isolation, and recording of data, consistent with some agreed upon conventions.

**Analysis,** on the other hand, may be regarded as chiefly the process of examining, verifying, and comparing data to arrive at some conclusion. Analysis also includes reaching a conclusion.

The ability to select appropriate information, record it accurately, and organize it in some accessible fashion constitutes one of the social scientist's most important collection of skills. This ability also is a vital competency for effective citizens, since we all occasionally need to have a complete, correct, and easily accessible account of some event.

For these reasons, social scientists and others often develop common systems for categorizing and reporting information. Some of these are quite elaborate and complicated. Still others may seem strange to students initially, such as the procedures for citing footnotes and bibliographic references. Students should have opportunities to experiment with different conventions used by social scientists for categorizing, recording, and sharing data.

Three subcategories of research and analysis skills that we will examine in more detail are *interpreting and comparing data*, *analyzing arguments*, and *processing information from pictures*.

## Interpreting and Comparing Data

A key aspect of research and analysis is interpreting and comparing data accurately and meaningfully. This skill requires paying careful attention to what is heard, seen, felt, and even tasted or smelled. Data are encountered through all of our senses. We may process these data firsthand through personal encounters, such as attending a concert or a meeting, and also indirectly, as when we read a book that describes a person, place, or event.

**Cultural Filters in Interpreting and Comparing Data.** Effective processing and interpreting of data requires a recognition that each of us also filters what we experience through our individual "lenses," which in turn, have been shaped by our experiences and culture, including our gender.

We all are familiar with the phenomenon that different individuals processing the same data often focus on different aspects, and as a result, report different accounts of what was experienced. These lenses or cultural filters are considered in more detail in Chapters 9 and 12, but they merit brief attention here as well.

An activity from a social studies text illustrates how students can be helped to develop this recognition of the biases that observers bring to any event they view. As part of tracing the events leading up to the end of the Revolutionary War, the authors of the text *The American Nation* (Prentice-Hall, 1986, p. E8), for example, ask students to compare the views of Washington and Cornwallis concerning the Battle of Yorktown. Through the activity, the students both acquire a skill and further insights into how the long and debilitating war was viewed by both sides.

Students using the text are provided with the excerpts shown in Figure 7.3. They also are given guidelines for comparing points of view and a set of questions that include these:

- What is Cornwallis' view of the events at Yorktown?
- What reason or reasons does Cornwallis give for surrendering?
- What is Washington's view of the events at Yorktown?
- Why did Cornwallis and Washington have different points of view?

The different accounts of the same event by Cornwallis and Washington may be reasonably accurate reports of what each person actually experienced, but they are clearly different. Students should learn to recognize that any single account is not necessarily more accurate, representative, or factual than another. Taken as a whole, however, collective accounts may present a more complete account than any single report.

**Figure 7.3**
**Comparing Two Points of View**

These two excerpts are from reports on the Battle of Yorktown. Read them carefully. Then, using the guidelines for comparing two points of view in Skill Lesson 8, answer the questions that follow.

**Report of Cornwallis to the commander of British forces in America, October 19, 1781.**

I have the shameful task to inform your Excellency that I have been forced to surrender the troops under my command to the combined forces of America and France.... [Cornwallis then describes how his outnumbered forces were surrounded and attacked by the American and French forces.]

Our numbers had been reduced by the enemy's fire, but particularly by sickness and by the fatigue of constant watching and duty. Under these circumstances, I thought it would have been inhuman to sacrifice the lives of this small body of gallant soldiers by exposing them to an assault [by the enemy] which could not fail to succeed. I therefore proposed to surrender. I enclose the terms of the surrender. I sincerely regret that better could not be obtained, but I have neglected nothing in my power to lessen the misfortune and distress of both officers and soldiers.

**Report of Washington to the President of Congress, October 19, 1781.**

I have the honor to inform Congress that the defeat of the British army under the command of Lord Cornwallis is most happily achieved. The tireless devotion which moved every officer and soldier in the combined army on this occasion has led to this important event sooner than I had hoped....

I should be lacking in gratitude if I did not mention the very able help of his Excellency the Count de Rochambeau [a French commander] and all his officers. I also feel myself indebted to the Count de Grasse [the French admiral] and the officers of the fleet under his command.

*Note.* From *Teacher's Resource Guide* (p. E8), 1986, Englewood Cliffs, NJ: Prentice Hall.

**Interpreting and Comparing Written Materials.** In our roles as citizens, we often must process and interpret information from sources such as texts and books, articles, charts, graphs, tables, and pictures. In the social studies, it is especially important that students early on begin to develop the skills to carefully interpret and compare a variety of written materials reflecting different perspectives. This includes identifying the perspective of the author.

As competent citizens, students need to be able to distinguish fact from opinion, bias from objectivity, reality from fiction, and extraneous from essential information. Students also must be able to differentiate neutral from emotion-laden terms and to consider what is excluded, as well as included, in written material.

Written material especially often presents students with special problems in making interpretations and comparisons. Frequently this is because they have difficulties with reading in general, an issue that is discussed in depth in Chapter 10.

All of the skills considered in the preceding section are called into play when analyzing subject matter such as biographical accounts. Students cannot possibly avoid reading biographies that suffer from flaws, nor should teachers try to prevent them. To attempt to shield students completely from inaccurate or distorted biographical accounts would be both undesirable and unrealistic. Doing so would cut them off from dealing with the same kind of deficiencies that abound in the mass media and everyday experiences that they encounter.

As an alternative, teachers can engage students in exercises that involve comparative analyses of biographical accounts. For example, students can be asked to read several biographical accounts of the same person and compare the discrepancies. This can be followed with discussion of questions such as these:

1. What did each of the books say about __________ with respect to the nature of his or her childhood and teenage years, important people in his or her life, educational background, interests and aspirations, and major accomplishments?
2. What things were similar in the books you read?
3. What things were different in the books you read?
4. How would you sum up what you have learned from reading all of the books about __________'s life?

**Interpreting and Comparing Charts, Graphs, and Tables.** In our society, much of the information we share with one another is communicated through charts, graphs, and tables. Each edition of a local paper will carry numerous examples of each. They abound in newspapers and periodicals such as *The New York Times, USA Today, Time, Newsweek,* and *U.S. News and World Report,* as well as student editions of newspapers. They also appear in televised newscasts.

Citizens, journalists, newscasters, and social scientists alike use charts, graphs, and tables to summarize information or to simplify communication. For example, if economists wish to cut through reams of statistical data and complex discussions to show the relationships between gender and education and earnings, they often use a graph such as the one in Figure 7.4.

However, for students, extracting facts, generalizations, and hypotheses from charts, graphs, and tables frequently is a difficult task. This is particularly the case when the chart, graph, or table contains many details.

In addition to assistance in skillfully interpreting the data of others, students need guidance in representing their own analyses in the form of charts, graphs, and tables. They need first to gain competency in handling

**Figure 7.4**
**Mean Money Earnings, by Educational Attainment and Sex, 1990**

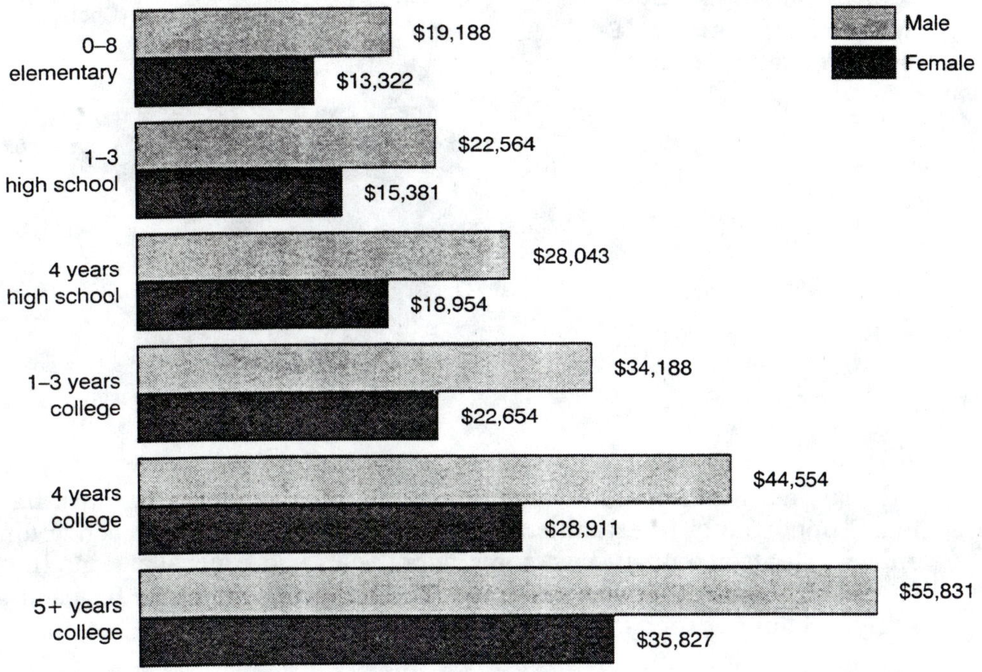


*Note.* From *Statistical Abstract of the United States: 1992,* (112th edition), table 713, by U.S. Bureau of the Census, 1991, Washington, DC: Author.

small, simple sets of data rather than being overwhelmed at the outset. Teachers can help provide natural experiences by incorporating charts, graphs, and tables into all of their lessons and current affairs discussions to help explain a point, answer a question, or frame a problem.

Students also may experiment with computer tools to help them represent data in the form of charts, graphs, and tables. An example is the pie chart in Figure 7.5. It was completed by a sixth-grade student using a basic computer software graphing program called *Data Plot.*

**Using Charts, Tables, and Graphs in Instruction.** Charts, graphs, and tables, when accompanied by probing questions and teacher-guided analysis, can serve as springboards to reflective thinking within lessons and units. For example, consider the table in Figure 7.6. The data are potentially interesting to middle or secondary level students, but they lack a focus.

**Figure 7.5**
**Pie Chart Showing Percentages of Time Spent by a Sixth Grader During a 48-Hour Weekend Period**

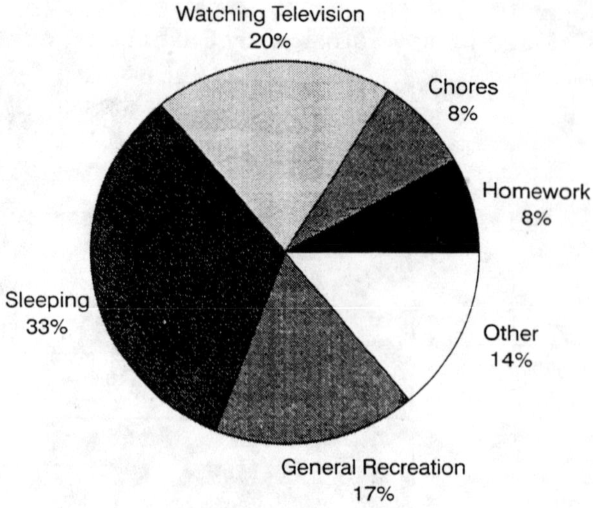


The addition of some focusing questions, after students have had an initial opportunity to examine the data, would provide an objective for the analysis. It also could suggest some hypotheses and generalizations that the students might not otherwise generate. The following might be used as a sample set of questions:

1. In which state is life expectancy longest for males? Females?
2. In which state is life expectancy shortest for males? For females?
3. How does the life expectancy of males and females in our state compare with states having the highest and lowest figures? With the national averages for men and women?
4. How do you account for the differences in life expectancies between males and females?
5. How do you account for the differences in life expectancies between the states that have the highest and the lowest figures?
6. Did you find any surprises? Why were you surprised?
7. Based on the information in the table, what can we conclude about the life expectancy of men and women?

## Analyzing Arguments

Whether presented in written or oral form, arguments often suffer from bias, distortion, and faulty logic. The ability to detect these elements in argumentation is critical to effective citizenship. Developing these skills requires continuous practice and application in the context of the research and analysis of subject matter. It also involves wide exposure to bias and distortion in all its forms, including that in the mass media, arguments of respected figures and demagogues alike, and even textbooks.

**Figure 7.6**
**Table of Data on Life Expectancy, by State**

**Where Life is Longest**

The chart shows life expectancy at birth for each state, based on a study of death rates from 1979–1981. By that method, the national average was 70.1 years for men and 77.6 for women.

| State | Male | Female | State | Male | Female |
|---|---|---|---|---|---|
| Alabama | 68.3 | 76.8 | Montana | 70.5 | 77.7 |
| Alaska | 68.7 | 76.9 | Nebraska | 71.7 | 79.3 |
| Arizona | 70.5 | 78.3 | Nevada | 69.3 | 76.5 |
| Arkansas | 69.7 | 77.8 | New Hampshire | 71.4 | 78.4 |
| California | 71.1 | 78.0 | New Jersey | 70.5 | 77.4 |
| Colorado | 71.8 | 78.8 | New Mexico | 69.9 | 78.3 |
| Connecticut | 71.5 | 78.6 | New York | 70.0 | 77.2 |
| Delaware | 69.6 | 76.8 | North Carolina | 68.6 | 77.4 |
| District of Columbia | 64.6 | 73.7 | North Dakota | 72.1 | 79.7 |
| Florida | 70.1 | 78.0 | Ohio | 69.9 | 77.1 |
| Georgia | 68.0 | 76.4 | Oklahoma | 69.6 | 77.8 |
| Hawaii | 74.1 | 80.3 | Oregon | 71.4 | 78.8 |
| Idaho | 71.5 | 79.2 | Pennsylvania | 69.9 | 77.2 |
| Illinois | 69.6 | 77.1 | Rhode Island | 71.0 | 78.3 |
| Indiana | 70.2 | 77.5 | South Carolina | 67.6 | 76.1 |
| Iowa | 72.0 | 79.6 | South Dakota | 71.0 | 79.2 |
| Kansas | 71.6 | 79.0 | Tennessee | 69.2 | 77.5 |
| Kentucky | 69.1 | 77.1 | Texas | 69.7 | 77.7 |
| Louisiana | 67.6 | 75.9 | Utah | 72.4 | 79.2 |
| Maine | 70.8 | 78.4 | Vermont | 71.1 | 78.5 |
| Maryland | 69.7 | 76.8 | Virginia | 69.6 | 77.3 |
| Massachusetts | 71.3 | 78.5 | Washington | 71.7 | 78.6 |
| Michigan | 70.1 | 77.3 | West Virginia | 68.9 | 76.9 |
| Minnesota | 72.5 | 79.8 | Wisconsin | 71.9 | 78.9 |
| Mississippi | 67.7 | 76.4 | Wyoming | 70.0 | 78.2 |
| Missouri | 69.9 | 77.7 | | | |

*Note.* National Center for Health Statistics.

**Detecting Bias and Distortion.** It is far more effective for students to encounter bias and distortion in their natural constructions, rather than in an abstracted or edited forms that typically appear in student texts. This suggests that a social studies classroom should be a forum for a wide array of materials from a diverse assortment of individuals and groups. Students also should be encouraged to share cases of bias and distortion that they have encountered in materials.

If the assortment of such materials collected is rich in examples, it may evoke controversy and even possible criticism, unless the purpose for its presence is clearly established. The teacher needs to make clear at the outset and reiterate periodically that *in no way does the presence of material imply either endorsement of its content or authors and sponsors.* Similarly, it may be necessary to establish some ground rules, consistent with school policies, concerning the types of materials that must be excluded and under what circumstances (e.g., pornographic material, racial hate literature in an emotionally charged multiracial class).

**Logical Reasoning.** Arguments that are free from bias and distortion, nonetheless may be flawed in their reasoning. Helping students detect errors in reasoning requires some work with logic. This in turn demands translating assertions and arguments into some form where they can be analyzed. One such form is a syllogism. **Syllogisms** are statements arranged in the following order:

> All men and women are mortal.
>
> Catherine is a woman.
>
> Therefore, Catherine is mortal.

**Casting Arguments in the Form of Syllogisms.** Although most assertions and arguments do not appear neatly in a syllogistic form, they often can be recast with minor revisions and reorganization. Consider this hypothetical conversation between Harry and Sarah during the height of the Cold War:

*Harry:* What are those sly Communists up to? They have just advocated more nuclear arms limitations.
*Sarah:* Yeah? So what's the problem with that?
*Harry:* You know the Reds can never be trusted.
*Sarah:* You mean if they are pushing disarmament, there must be something wrong with it?
*Harry:* You got it.
*Sarah:* I see your point.

Organized as a syllogism, the argument mutually advanced by Sarah and Harry appears as follows:

> If Communists support an action, something must be wrong with it.
>
> They support disarmament.
>
> Therefore, something must be wrong with disarmament.

In this case the *major premise,* the first statement in the syllogism, was inferred but never actually stated in the conversation—a frequent occurrence in discussions. When confronted with the inferred premise, Harry and Sarah likely would disavow it, since the Soviets supported many things with which we would find nothing wrong, including breathing, eating, and motherhood.

If one were to accept the unstated major premise of the argument, it *would* logically follow that "There must be something wrong with disarmament." Thus, this example also illustrates how a logically *valid* argument can result from a premise that is *false*.

**Testing the Validity of Syllogisms.** One way that students can be helped to ascertain whether an argument is valid (i.e., the conclusion follows from the major premise) or invalid is through the use of circle diagrams. The one shown in Figure 7.7 diagrams the first syllogism that we presented. It demonstrates that the circle representing "Catherine" *must* be placed within the largest circle representing "mortal people," since she has been placed within the circle, "men and women."

The circle diagram shown in Figure 7.8 similarly illustrates how the circles can be used to uncover *invalid* arguments. Therein, the example diagrammed proceeded in this fashion:

> All mechanical things are made by people and computers.
>
> Airplanes are made by people and computers.
>
> Airplanes, therefore, are mechanical things.

Since "airplanes" may be placed *anywhere* within the circle, "things made by people and computers," it need not follow that they are one of the "mechanical things."

**Figure 7.7**
**Circle Diagram Showing Argument Is Logically Valid**

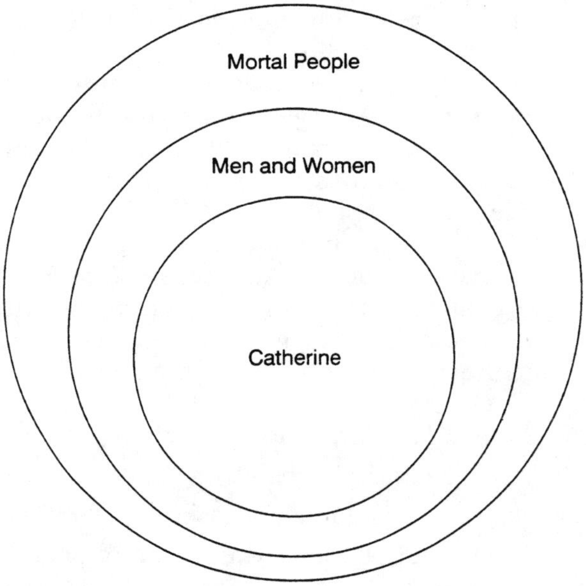

**Figure 7.8**
**Circle Diagram Showing Argument Is Logically Invalid**

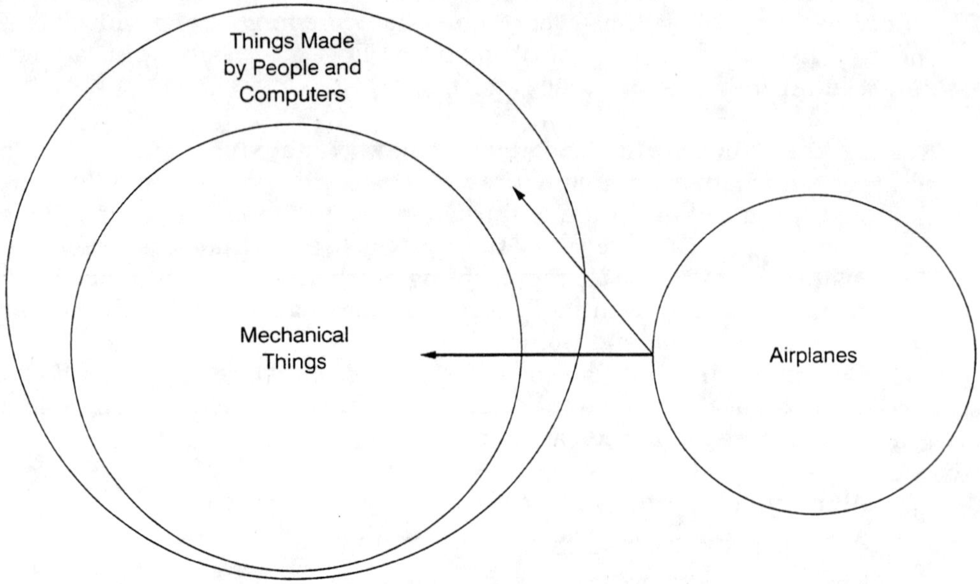


**Programs to Develop Logical Reasoning Skills.** Providing students with appropriate experiences involving logical reasoning extends beyond analyzing deductive arguments. The acquisition of such skills is a complex process that occurs slowly over time. Further, stage theorists argue these skills are related at least in part to the developmental level of the students (Cole & Cole, 1989).

Social studies teachers should become familiar with the range of instructional strategies and activities that are now available within the comprehensive programs that have been developed. Those are available for youngsters across all ages and developmental abilities, and they cover a wide variety of skills.

One such program, *Philosophy for Children*, has been developed by the Institute for the Advancement of Philosophy for Children (*Philosophy for Children*, 1987). The program includes materials for elementary, middle, and secondary grades students. Some of the skills that the program attempts to develop include the following:

- Classifying and categorizing,
- Defining terms,
- Drawing inferences from premises,
- Finding underlying assumptions,
- Formulating causal explanations,

**Debates are a strategy for aiding students in developing and applying reasoning skills.**

- Searching for informal fallacies,
- Predicting consequences,
- Working with contradiction, and
- Identifying and using criteria.

## Processing Information from Pictures

Pictures also represent a form of data that must be processed in order to extract meaning from them. Some of the most interesting teaching materials in the social studies are pictures or pictorial print materials. Visual materials can enrich and enliven instruction. Research data also suggest that imagery facilitates learning (Somer, 1978; Wittrock & Goldberg, 1975).

**Types of Pictures.** Teachers use many different types of pictures in teaching. Five types common to social studies instruction are noted here.

- Informational pictures,
- Tell-a-story pictures,
- Open-ended pictures,
- Expressive pictures, and
- Political cartoons.

Many pictures, such as one showing mountains or the Washington Monument, appear to be self-explanatory and *informational.* Some help students see relationships or *tell a story.* Others are more *open-ended,* permitting different viewers to read many varied interpretations of what is being communicated. These types of pictures can serve as springboards for discussion of issues.

Still other photos are *expressive;* they portray human emotions or arouse them in the viewer. Shots of starving people, war-ravaged areas, and little children are examples of expressive pictures. An additional type of picture, often containing a caption, makes a social or political statement and is typically characterized as a *political cartoon.*

**Using Political Cartoons in Instruction.** **Political cartoons** are a visual form that can be especially effective for dramatizing an issue in social studies instruction. However, they often are difficult for students to process (Steinbrink & Bliss, 1988). This is because they frequently embed complex concepts, require considerable prior knowledge, and employ visual metaphors.

Heitzman (1988) has provided a comprehensive annotated list of sources of political cartoons for use in the classroom. The cartoon by Auth shown in Figure 7.9, for example, encapsulates the rich irony that accompanies the cruel and endless tragedy of religious warfare in Lebanon. The following questions could be used to process this and (with slight revisions) similar political cartoons:

1. What do you see in the picture?
2. What does each of the figures and items in the picture stand for?
3. What is the issue that is represented in the picture?
4. What do you think the cartoonist thought of each of the figures in the picture?
5. What would be an appropriate caption for the cartoon?

## CHRONOLOGY SKILLS

Much of what we typically do both in our daily lives and in social studies classes involves *chronology,* some understanding of how people, places, items, and events are oriented in time. As adults, we are comfortable with related time concepts such as "a long time ago," "recently," "in the past," and "infinity." From a very young child's perspective, a basic concept of time involves understanding which items came first, which came last, and what typically happens as the result of the passage of units we call hours, days, weeks, months, or years.

**Figure 7.9**
**Political Cartoon**

*Note.* From *Behind the Lines* by Tony Auth. Copyright © 1975, 1976, 1977 by Tony Auth. Copyright © 1971, 1972, 1973, 1974, 1975 by the Philadelphia Inquirer. Reprinted by permission of Houghton Mifflin Company.

For middle and secondary school students, chronology competencies evolve to include an understanding of the interrelationship of events and individuals over a temporal period. They also include a sense of what is meant by a unit such as a century. Eventually, it includes an understanding of the abstractness and arbitrariness of all units of time, whether they be measured in nanoseconds (billionths of a second), eons, or some new standard.

## Comparative Conceptions of Time

In each society, the larger culture and various subcultures shape the ways in which individuals both conceive of time and respond to its passage. Thus, a Bostonian may come to characterize the pace of life in rural South Carolina as "slow" and that of Manhattan as "fast." On an international scale, this generalization means that diverse nations often view the past, present, and future in different terms.

On a planetary scale, different views of time also are possible. Hawking (1988), in *A Brief History of Time*, has pointed out that contemporary physicists' perspectives on time in space are quite different from those people on Earth use to guide their daily lives:

> Consider a pair of twins. Suppose that one twin goes to live on the top of a mountain while the other stays at sea level. The first twin would age faster than the second. Thus, if they meet again, one would be older than the other. In this case, the difference in ages would be very small, but it would be much larger if one of the twins went for a long trip in a spaceship at nearly the speed of light. When he returned, he would be much younger than the one who stayed on Earth. This is known as the twins paradox, but it is a paradox only if one has the idea of absolute time at the back of one's mind. In the theory of relativity there is no unique absolute time, but instead each individual has his own personal measure of time that depends on where he is and how he is moving. (p. 33)

## Recording Events on Time Lines

Activities that require students to arrange and view people, places, objects, and events as occurring in sequence—such as time lines—help to establish the perspective of chronology. Time lines provide a simple system for listing, ordering, and comparing events over some period. They function as a summary statement of a series of events. Also, they can represent a schema of how an individual has organized data into a meaningful chronological pattern.

Time lines may be horizontal or vertical. Also, any unit of time may be used, ranging from a day to centuries. Similarly, any context or theme may be the basis for a time line, for instance: "What I did today in the order I did it" or "The chronology of Constitutional amendments."

Time lines function cognitively in several ways. Completed ones provide students with a summary of information concerning a series of occurrences over time. When students themselves construct time lines, they must first compare events and then structure them in a meaningful pattern.

To illustrate the differences in the two applications, consider the simple time line shown in Figure 7.10 that summarizes for a reader some major events over two decades. Processing the figure requires only that the reader *note* the order of events.

Alternately, entertain a task that calls for you to *create* a time line. For example, begin by placing in the correct order of occurrence the following events: President Nixon's visit to China, the end of the Vietnam War, the first flight of the Wright brothers, the beginning of the Civil War, the assassination of President Kennedy, the invention of xerography, and the premiere of *Gone With the Wind*.

Compare your sequence with the following, arranged in ascending chronological order:

- The beginning of the Civil War
- The first flight of the Wright brothers
- The premiere of *Gone With the Wind*
- The invention of xerography
- The assassination of President Kennedy
- President Nixon's visit to China
- The end of the Vietnam War

Often time lines can be used to illustrate *causal relationships*, as well as temporal sequences. Genealogies are examples of such applications.

## SPATIAL SKILLS

In an increasingly interdependent nation and world, citizens have greater need than ever before for skills that can better orient them in space. Competent citizens must be able to locate themselves and others spatially in order to travel, exchange ideas, and access artifacts. Spatial skills most often appear in social studies in the discipline of geography, but they are distributed throughout all areas of the curriculum. Identifying political boundaries, the locations of cities, landmarks, and land masses and determining the relationship of one object in space to another are all part of spatial understanding.

### The Impact of Spatial Perspectives

Citizens also need to become more aware of how our spatial perspectives and vocabularies influence many of our social, political, and economic perspectives. Whether we view something as far away, densely populated, or growing, for example, may affect whether we decide to visit a region, seek a job there, or change our residence. Even the language we use in describing an area can skew our perspective. Collins (n. d.) has noted, for example,

**Figure 7.10**
**Simple Time Line**

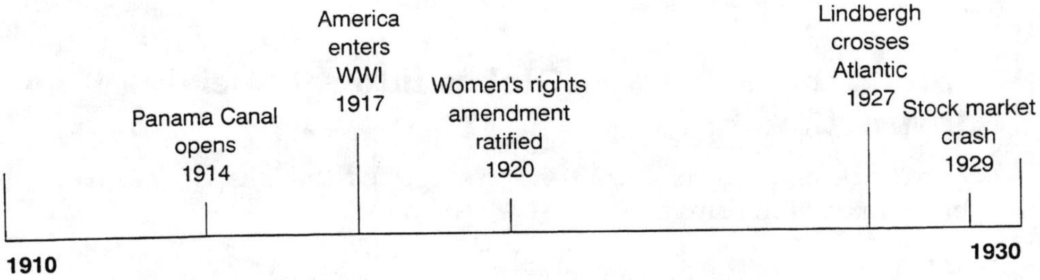

"Terms we select to describe other nations—and the present state of their social, economic, political development—influence student's perception of those nations."

As an illustration, for years Africa was characterized by teachers and texts as "the dark continent," creating a host of negative associations. Further, unlike most other regions of the world, the continent, rather than the nations within it, was studied as a whole, creating the misperception that there was a high degree of uniformity among all Africans.

## Using and Creating Maps in Instruction

The most common ways that individuals use to orient themselves spatially are through the application of existing maps and the creation of new ones. To a lesser extent, individuals reference globes. Maps and globes represent some region on the Earth. They do so, however, with varying degrees of distortion.

**Map and Globe Distortions.** Students should be sensitized to the relevant distortion and measurement issues associated with different projections. In representing regions on the Earth, maps and globes do so with varying degrees of distortion. Since the creation of the first maps, nations often have deliberately distorted the maps they used for political purposes. They have done this, among other ways, by extending or reshaping boundaries and rerouting rivers, as suits their interpretation of historical claims. Apart from those deliberate distortions, all projections of areas on the Earth's surface are functionally distorted in some ways because of the problem of translating a curved surface to a flat one.

The National Geographical Society in 1989 adopted the **Robinson projection** (see Figure 7.11) as one that produced the least distortion for most nonspecialized map applications. It is compared with the traditional **Van der Grinten projection,** shown in Figure 7.12, that the Society had used since 1922 for most of its world maps.

Note the differences in the sizes and shapes of Greenland and the United States shown in each of the projections. Because of its location on the Earth, given seven different projections, the shape and size of Greenland will be different in each of them. Even in the Robinson projection shown in Figure 7.11, Greenland is still 60% larger than it should be. In the Van der Grinten projection, it is 554% larger.

## Integrating Maps and Globes into All Social Studies Instruction

Jarolimek and Parker (1993) have suggested that maps can furnish eight basic types of information:

**Figure 7.11**
**A Robinson Projection**

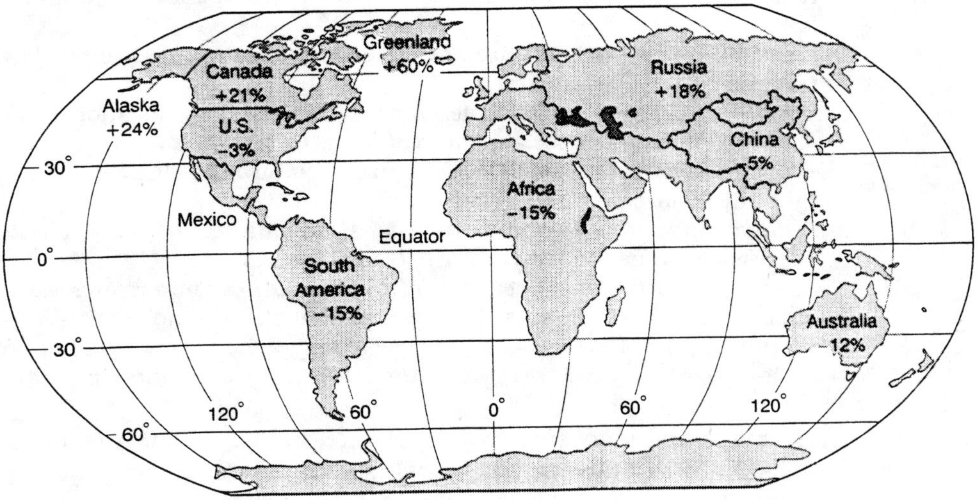


**Figure 7.12**
**A Van der Grinten Projection**

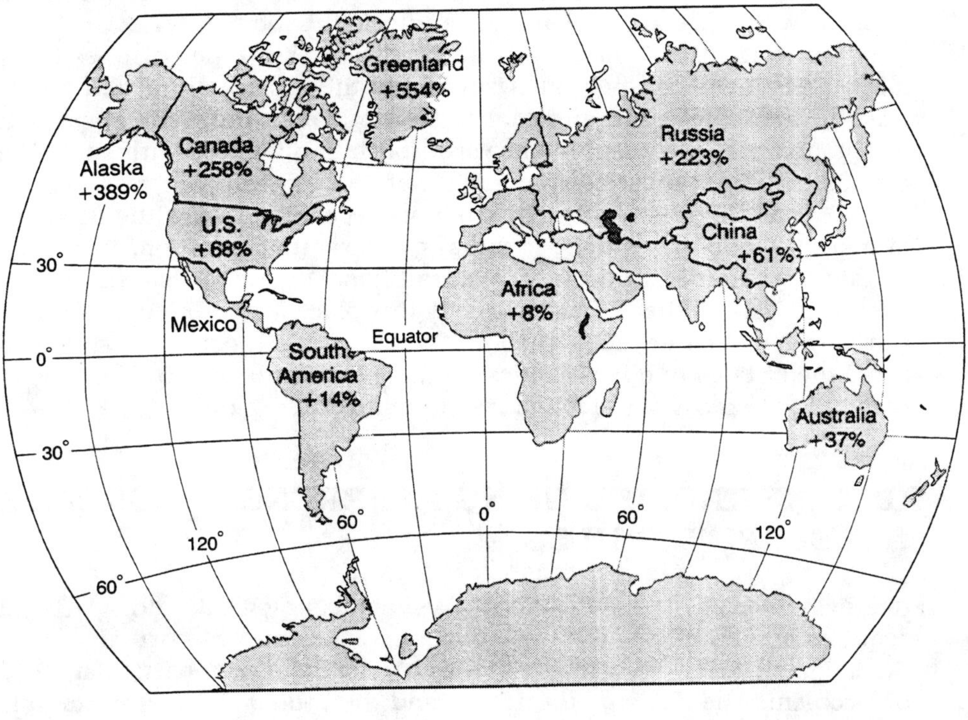

1. *Land and water forms.* Continents, oceans, bays, peninsulas, islands, straits.
2. *Relief features.* Plains, mountains, rivers, deserts, plateaus, swamps, valleys.
3. *Direction and distance.* Cardinal directions, distance in miles or kilometers and relative distance, scale.
4. *Social data.* Population density, size of communities, location of major cities, relationship of social data to other factors.
5. *Economic information.* Industrial and agricultural production, soil fertility, trade factors, location of industries.
6. *Political information.* Political divisions, boundaries, capitals, territorial possessions, types of government, political parties.
7. *Scientific information.* Locations of discoveries, ocean currents, location of mineral and ore deposits, geological formations, air movements.
8. *Human factors.* Cities, canals, railroads, highways, coaxial and fiber-optic cables, telephone lines, bridges, dams, nuclear power plants. (p. 174)

Ideally, maps and globes should be an integral part of all social studies instruction. As they examine issues for which spatial perspectives would be instructive, students should be introduced to the wide range of maps and globes that exist. Teachers also should combine the development of spatial skills with others.

An example of a lesson that integrates spatial, as well as research and analysis, skills is provided in Figure 7.13. The issue that the lesson centers upon is: What special problems do landlocked nations face?

Students also should learn about the diverse types of questions that maps and globes can help answer. One of the most natural and functional ways to integrate maps and globes continuously into daily social studies instruction is to use them to answer important questions with spatial implications that the teacher or students generate while studying a subject.

Teachers also should help students recognize that, although one type of map or globe may suffice to answer a particular question, it may not be suitable for another. Apart from the traditional spatial questions of "How do I get from here to there?" or "Where is this place located?" maps and globes can help answer questions such as "What are the most promising areas in the United States to open businesses that cater to the elderly?" or "Where in the world are most of the followers of the major religions?"

## IDENTIFYING AND USING REFERENCE SOURCES IN DEVELOPING SKILLS

Acquiring social, research and analysis, chronological, and spatial skills requires students to use a variety of reference sources. Virtually anything, including an individual, may serve as a reference for a particular question or problem. The *JCPenney Catalog* and the *Yellow Pages* are examples of reference sources that individuals commonly have around their homes.

**Figure 7.13**
**Lesson That Integrates Spatial Skills Development and Application**

## Understanding the Dilemma of Landlocked Nations

Thirty of the world's independent nations are without access to the sea—they are landlocked. With some exceptions, landlocked nations are generally small, developing countries with numerous social and economic problems. This lesson plan explores the background essential to understanding the problems that landlocked nations face.

### Objectives

- To define the geographic theme "location."
- To define the term "landlocked" and to identify the world's landlocked nations.
- To identify advantages and disadvantages of being landlocked in both a historical and a contemporary context.
- To research social and economic data about landlocked countries and to draw conclusions about the economic development of such countries.
- To identify the origin of problems that landlocked nations face.
- To investigate how certain countries came to be landlocked.
- To speculate on places that could become landlocked in the future.

### For Discussion

- What is a landlocked nation?
- Many goods in international trade are shipped by sea for at least part of their journey. What does this mean to countries without coastlines? (Examples: Dependence on neighboring countries; delays in receiving goods; tariffs; and transportation costs.)
- Identify some countries that lost their coastlines in war.
- Using examples from current events, identify places that could become landlocked in the future.

### Follow-up Activities

- Divide the class into two groups. Assign one group to report on the historical and current advantages of being landlocked. Assign the second group to report on the disadvantages. Discuss the relative merits of each viewpoint.
- Ask the class to do research on landlocked countries, using almanacs, encyclopedias, textbooks, and other resources. Display information about each country on a chart. List generalizations that can be made about landlocked nations. Point out exceptions.
- Have each student select two countries—one that is landlocked and one that is not—and use a data book or an almanac to analyze statistics about them. Suggest that students pay special attention to indicators of social and economic development, such as life expectancy, adult literacy, population growth rate, and GNP per capita. Then have each student write an essay comparing the two countries.
- Have students select and read about a landlocked nation and then prepare an oral report about the country's problems. Have students include the importance of relative location on each country's problems.

*Note.* From *Teaching Geography: A Model for Action* (pp. 36–39), 1988, Washington, DC: National Geographic Society.

Increasingly, electronic references sources, such as electronic card catalogs and databases, also are gaining acceptance in our society schools. Entire encyclopedias and collections of assorted reference works are available on a single CD-ROM, for example *Comptons' Picture Encyclopedia* and *Encarta*, both of which include sound and animation. In Chapter 11, which explores the role that newer technologies can play in the social studies curriculum, we will consider electronic reference sources in more detail.

Because the range of reference materials available in their homes often is limited, students need to be encouraged to go beyond them. This involves learning about the nature and use of specialized reference works typically found in libraries (usually in the "Reference Materials" section). Where computer-based references are used, technology skills also are required.

The notion that many sources can and should be considered as appropriate reference possibilities is an important one for students to learn. Similarly, they should understand that the basic criterion for judging the value of a reference work is "How useful and authoritative is it for solving a problem or answering a question?"

## Sample Reference Works for Social Studies

A sample of the numerous print reference works that both teachers and students have found to be useful in the social studies follows:

- *Album of American History.* This multivolume history of the United States is composed of pictures arranged chronologically.
- *Dictionary of American Biography.* This is a multivolume source of information on nonliving Americans who have made some significant contribution to American life. Included are politicians, artists, musicians, writers, scientists, educators, and many other types.
- *Dictionary of American History.* This multivolume work is arranged alphabetically and includes articles on a variety of historical topics, some famous and some not so well known.
- *Discoverers: An Encyclopedia of Explorers and Explorations.* This single volume includes details on a number of individuals who were pioneers in their time, along with descriptions of their exploits.
- *Goode's World Atlas.* This is an authoritative and comprehensive atlas of the world.
- *The Illustrated History of the World and Its People.* In 30 volumes a wealth of information is presented on the geography, people, history, arts, culture, and literature of individual countries of the world. There is also information on such topics as foods, religions, dress, holidays, festivals, customs, and educational systems of the countries.
- *Statesman's Yearbook.* A succinct thumbnail sketch of each country is provided in one volume.

- *The Story of America: A National Geographic Picture Atlas.* An extensive collection of visual, spatial, and narrative data on each of the states.
- *The Timetables of History.* In a chronologically organized single volume, a wide variety of important dates are included, covering seven major categories of American life.
- *Worldmark Encyclopedia of the Nations.* This multivolume guide to nations is arranged alphabetically by the name of the country and provides basic information on the social, political, historical, economical, and geographical features of a country.

### Encyclopedic References

To promote a well-balanced understanding of individuals or groups, teachers should alert students to the limitations of encyclopedic references. Because of their attempt to be comprehensive yet concise, they are severely constrained in the amount of space they can devote to any single topic. No matter how authoritatively and carefully any topic has been researched and written, an encyclopedia entry must omit a great deal of material. This limitation applies to print encyclopedias and, to a much lesser extent, their electronic counterparts. Increasingly, because of the capabilities of CD-ROMs, electronic reference collections are far less limited in the amount of material they can include on a single CD disk.

Consider, for example, if you were asked to sum up your life in an essay that someone will use to learn about you. The restrictions are that the essay must be no more than 250 words; all of the information must be accurate and objective; the reading level must be no higher than the fourth grade; and you must include everything the readers need to know. They will have no other information about you. If you feel at all uncomfortable about having to record your life's history under these limiting conditions, keep in mind that entire *groups* or *nations* are often described in encyclopedias under the same constraints.

## ACTIVITIES FOR INTRODUCING REFERENCE MATERIALS

One way to introduce reference materials in a meaningful context is to create interesting, puzzling, or intriguing questions for students that require them to use such sources. The difficulty of the questions may be varied for different age and ability groups by providing more of fewer clues. The actual reference resources to be used in answering the questions may be made available within the classroom. As alternatives, students may be given a list of helpful reference materials or be allowed to use the school library to identify resources on their own.

One type of activity that can be used to introduce reference materials in the context of solving interesting problems is a Problem Sheet. Consider the activity in Figure 7.14.

The Problem Sheet could contain some additional information that would make the solution easier. For example, the following additional pieces of data could be inserted into the paragraphs of the original description to give students more clues. These would make it easier to limit the list of countries that could match the description.

1. There are fewer than four people per square mile in the country.
2. One third of the country is a desert, but only a small part of it is sandy. There is sufficient vegetation in the desert to support the feeding of camels and horses.
3. The lack of abundant raw materials and suitable transportation systems restricts industrial growth.
4. The major occupation of the country is herding, though some small-scale industries have been started.

**Figure 7.14**
**Problem Sheet**

**Problem Sheet**

*Directions:* You are to discover the identity of Country X, a real country, described below. Use any reference sources that you wish. The ones that have been identified for you may be especially helpful. After you have discovered which country it is, list all of the references you consulted. Then tell whether each of the references helped you learn the identity of the country and in which way.

*Data on Country X:*

**Country X**

Country X differs from many other nations in several ways. It covers an area of 600,000 square miles with approximately 2,000,000 people. It is one huge plateau with the eastern half consisting mainly of plains with some mountains, while the western half is largely mountainous with some plains. Hundreds of lakes exist throughout the country, especially in the mountains, and in the hilly and mountainous regions, there are forests.

In climate, Country X suffers from cold winds that sweep across the treeless plains and from great temperature extremes. For example, the temperature has risen to 105° (Fahrenheit) in the summer and to –50° in the winter. Though there are many fish, the people have not really cultivated a taste for them, and exist chiefly on their livestock products and game.

*Identity of Country X:*

Reference sources used to determine identity:

Which were useful and in which way:

5. The people of the country are largely nomadic, customarily dress in long flowing robes called *dels*, and live in canvas huts called *yurts*.
6. Infant mortality is relatively high, 66 per thousand births.

The country, by the way, is the Mongolian People's Republic, sometimes called Outer Mongolia.

Any similar set of data that presents a puzzle or problem— whether it deals with a country, a city, an event, or an individual —can satisfy the same objective. The aim is to have students discover the functional value of reference sources through an interesting and challenging activity.

## GROUP ACTIVITIES

1. Locate five political cartoons. In your group, discuss how each might be used as a springboard for discussion in a secondary class.
2. Select a topic and create a Problem Sheet for a seventh-grade class. Use a real country, city, or person as the subject. Also, create a list of clues similar to those in the text that could be used to help students identify the subject. Try out the Problem Sheet with the members of the group and discuss possible modifications.
3. Examine the chart of social studies skills provided in the chapter. Among the list of skills, which do you consider to be the most important to develop? Which skills would you add to the list and why?
4. Locate from newspapers or magazines instances of bias or distortion in reporting an event. Explain how such materials might be analyzed in a middle grades social studies class.

## INDIVIDUAL ACTIVITIES

1. Identify five social studies reference works similar to the ones listed in the chapter that are suitable for students in grades 5 through 8 to use. After each source, write a brief description of the type of material that is referenced and a sample question that the book could answer.
2. Repeat group activity 4, this time targeting grades 9 through 12.
3. Develop a collection of different types of maps (either originals or copies) that could be used with middle grades and secondary students. To locate them, consult newspapers and periodicals, as well as reference works. For each map, list the types of questions that the map answers.
4. Examine a collection of different maps and identify the map symbols they employ. From them, construct a poster appropriate for grades 5

through 8 that includes an assortment of map symbols. Next to each symbol, place the name of the object that the symbol represents.

5. Develop a collection of different types of tables, charts, and graphs that deal with issues suitable for discussion with students in grades 9 through 12. To locate the materials, consult newspapers and periodicals, as well as library reference works. For each table, chart, and graph, list the types of questions that it could answer. Also, indicate how each item might be used as a springboard for discussion with students.
6. Develop an activity for engaging students in grades 5 through 8 in mapping some spatial area such as their neighborhood. Field-test the activity with a group of five students for whom it is appropriate. Indicate the school and grade level of the students; provide copies of their maps; and describe and evaluate the results.
7. Using any source, identify examples of logically invalid arguments. For each argument, use the circle technique illustrated in this chapter to show that the arguments are invalid.

## REFERENCES

Auth, T. (1977). *Behind the lines.* Boston: Houghton Mifflin.

Brophy, J. (1992). Probing the subtleties of subject-matter teaching. *Educational Leadership, 49,* 4–8.

Byrnes, D. (1987). *Teacher, they called me a ________!* New York: The Anti Defamation League of B'nai B'rith.

Cole, M., & Cole, S. R. (1989). *The development of children.* New York: Scientific American.

Collins, H. T. (n. d.). What's in a name? *Resource pack: Project LINKS.* Unpublished manuscript, George Washington University.

"Essential Skills for Social Studies." National Council for the Social Studies.

Hawking, S. W. (1988). *A history of time: From the big bang to the black holes.* New York: Bantam.

Heitzman, W. R. (1988). Sources of political cartoons. *The Social Studies,* 225–227.

*Philosophy for children.* (1987). Upper Montclair, NJ: Institute for the Advancement of Philosophy for Children, Montclair State College.

Prentice-Hall. (1986). *The American nation.* Englewood Cliffs, NJ: Author.

Scherer, M. (1992). Solving conflicts—not just for children. *Educational Leadership, 50,* 14–15; 17–18.

*Simply Japan.* (1989, May). Atlanta, GA: Consulate General of Japan. Somer, R. (1978). *The mind's eye.* New York: Dell.

Steinbrink, J. E., & Bliss, D. (1988). Using political cartoons to teach thinking skills. *The Social Studies, 79,* 217–220.

Task Force on Scope and Sequence. (1989). In search of a scope and sequence for social studies. *Social Education, 53,* 376–387.

*Teacher's resource guide: The American nation.* (1986). Englewood Cliffs, NJ: Prentice-Hall.

*Teaching geography: A model for action.* (1988). Washington, DC: National Geographic Society.

U.S. Bureau of the Census. (1991). *Statistical Abstract of the United States: 1992.* (112th edition). Washington, DC: Author.

Wittrock, M. C., & Goldberg, S. G. (1975). Imagery and meaningfulness in free recall: Word attributes and instructional sets. *Journal of General Psychology, 92,* 137–151.

CHAPTER 8

# Nurturing Social Concern and Ethical Growth: Analyzing, Developing, and Acting on Beliefs, Attitudes, and Values

**Social Concern and Citizenship Education**

The Morally Mature Citizen

**The Dimensions of Concern**

The Nature of Beliefs
The Nature of Attitudes
The Nature of Values
The Nature of Value Judgments

**Instructional Strategies for Examining Beliefs, Attitudes, and Values**

Attitude Inventories
Challenging Beliefs and Attitudes
Value Analysis

**Promoting Ethical Growth**

The Moral Development Theories of Jean Piaget and Lawrence Kohlberg
Alternative Strategies for Moral Education in Public Schools

**Social Issues as a Curricular Focus**

Curricular Framework for Analyzing Social Issues in the Classroom
Freedom of Speech and Social Concern
Social Issues and Controversy
Teacher Positions on Controversial Issues

**Academic Freedom in the Classroom**

Challenges to Academic Freedom
Handling Complaints Concerning Social Studies Materials

*Who, if anyone, should be required to submit to compulsory testing for deadly communicable diseases such as AIDS?*

*How can we prevent nuclear destruction?*

*How can the nations of the world work together to prevent the "greenhouse effect"?*

*What would be required to bring about lasting peace and stability in the Middle East?*

*How can governmental policies more adequately provide equal opportunities for all Americans in such areas as jobs, housing, schooling, and legal justice?*

Citizens who are cognizant of and responsive in an informed manner to issues such as those above may be characterized as *concerned citizens.* Their concern extends beyond local and personal issues to those at the regional, national, and international levels that affect the destinies of all humankind.

Concerned citizens also establish personal priorities and make ethical decisions with respect to issues they care about (see Benninga, 1991). Additionally, they can make and keep commitments. Making a commitment involves choosing from among the various social issues identified, those about which we personally plan to do something. It is a decision to go beyond extending our knowledge of a subject; it involves acting on our conclusions.

When we fulfill a commitment to do something we have decided is important, we become a social *actor.* Action may take many forms, depending on our age, talents, and resources. For example, simply doing what we have concluded is "the right thing" can be a form of action. As we progress from awareness to action, we become increasingly efficacious.

## SOCIAL CONCERN AND CITIZENSHIP EDUCATION

I argued in earlier chapters that the three dimensions of reflection, competence, and concern characterize the effective citizen. Reflection and competence alone, without concern, are incomplete. To many Americans, it is obvious that among our citizens some people are highly reflective and competent—witness embezzlers, slumlords, drug lords, and tax evaders—but who lack a basic grounding in social concern. In carrying out our citizenship roles, the dimension of concern provides a focus for the exercise of reflection and competence.

The dimension of concern also heightens awareness that we are members of a pluralistic democratic society in an increasingly interdependent world where sensitivity for the welfare of others and our planet arguably should become the norm. It further reflects the assumption that, if our nation is to prosper and survive, the knowledge and skills we possess must be guided by our feelings and concern for others and the common social good, as well as our personal needs and aspirations.

### The Morally Mature Citizen

During the past decade, educators, parents, and civic groups have expressed alarm over the lack of social concern evidenced by many youngsters in our society. In addressing this issue, the Association for Supervision and Curriculum Development (ASCD) developed a set of standards for what it labeled the *morally mature person*.

The ASCD standards (1988) summarized in Figure 8.1 can be viewed as a general description of the ideal concerned citizen.

In this chapter, we examine illustrative areas in which teachers may contribute to the development of concerned citizens. Additionally, we consider some of the basic issues that arise from related classroom activities. As we shall see, analysis of matters of social concern may involve one or more of the instructional strategies we examined in earlier chapters.

## THE DIMENSIONS OF CONCERN

In a pluralistic society, citizens should be able to view issues from others' perspectives and to identify and resolve value conflicts. To make and act on social choices and commitments, concerned citizens also need well-grounded systems of beliefs, attitudes, and values. Additionally, since an important aspect of citizenship is deciding what are the right and the wrong things to do in a situation, individuals need to develop a sound ethical framework.

### The Nature of Beliefs

Each of us holds to some set of interrelated beliefs, attitudes, and values. We each have thousands of different beliefs, some important and some trivial, some objectively verifiable, and some not. A **belief** may be defined as any assertion an individual makes that he or she regards as true (Rokeach, 1968). A belief may not actually be true or a fact, but a person must think, feel, or act as if his or her assertions are factually correct for them to be beliefs.

Illustrations of beliefs that some individuals hold include these assertions:

- There is life on Mars.
- The series of events known as the Holocaust never occurred.
- Wagner was the greatest composer who ever lived.
- Democracy is the best political system.
- It is time to trade in my car.

The sum of all those things we believe may be regarded as a **belief system.** Throughout our lives, our belief systems typically undergo many changes as evidence gives us reason to cast aside old ones and acquire new ones. If our belief system is receptive to change, it can be called *open.* Those systems that resist change may be characterized as *closed.*

### The Nature of Attitudes

**Attitudes** are closely related to beliefs. They are clusters of related beliefs that express our likes and dislikes, general feelings, and opinions about some individual, group, object, or event (Rokeach, 1968). We can have attitudes toward all sorts of items—Japanese, Jews, peace, scuba diving, the environment, beers, or even toward nonexistent entities, such as elves and centaurs. Beliefs and attitudes are derived from many sources, including relatives and friends, the mass media, and peers, and different experiences (Triandis, 1971).

**Figure 8.1**
**The Morally Mature Person**

What kind of human being do we want to emerge from our efforts at moral education? What are the characteristics of the morally mature person?

A moment's reflection tells us that moral maturity is more than just knowing what is right. The world is full of people who know what is right but set moral considerations aside when they find it expedient to do so. To be moral means to *value* morality, to take moral obligations seriously. It means to be able to judge what is right but also to care deeply about doing it—and to posses the will, competence, and habits needed to translate moral judgement and feeling into effective moral action.

We submit that the morally mature person has six major characteristics, which are derived from universal moral and democratic principles. These characteristics offer schools and communities a context for discourse about school programs and moral behavior.

The morally mature person habitually:

1. *Respects human dignity,* which includes
   - showing regard for the worth and rights of all persons,
   - avoiding deception and dishonesty,
   - promoting human equality,
   - respecting freedom of conscience,
   - working with people of different views, and
   - refraining from prejudiced actions.
2. *Cares about the welfare of others,* which includes
   - recognizing interdependence among people,
   - caring for one's country,
   - seeking social justice,
   - taking pleasure in helping others, and
   - working to help others reach moral maturity.
3. *Integrates individual interests and social responsibilities,* which includes
   - becoming involved in community life,

*Note.* From "Moral Education in the Life of the School" by ASCD Panel on Moral Education, 1988, *Educational Leadership, 45,* p. 45. Reprinted with permission of the Association for Supervision and Curriculum Development. 

## The Nature of Values

We will consider **values** to be the standards or criteria we use in making judgments about whether something is positive or negative, good or bad, pleasing or displeasing (Shaver & Strong, 1976). The standard we have, for example, for determining whether an individual's conduct is good or bad derives in part from our value of *honesty*.

**Figure 8.1 continued**

- doing a fair share of community work,
- displaying self-regarding and other-regarding moral virtues—self-control, diligence, fairness, kindness, honesty, civility—in everyday life,
- fulfilling commitments, and
- developing self-esteem through relationships with others.

4. *Demonstrates integrity,* which includes
   - practicing diligence,
   - taking stands for moral principles,
   - displaying moral courage,
   - knowing when to compromise and when to confront, and
   - accepting responsibility for one's choices.
5. *Reflects on moral choices,* which includes
   - recognizing the moral issues involved in a situation,
   - applying moral principles (such as the Golden Rule) when making moral judgments,
   - thinking about the consequences of decisions, and
   - seeking to be informed about important moral issues in society and the world.
6. *Seeks peaceful resolution of conflict,* which includes
   - striving for the fair resolution of personal and social conflicts,
   - avoiding physical and verbal aggression,
   - listening carefully to others,
   - encouraging others to communicate, and
   - working for peace.

In general, then, the morally mature person understands moral principles and accepts responsibility for applying them.

Each of us shares a number of basic or core values. According to Rokeach (1968), they include:

| | | |
|---|---|---|
| independence | freedom | wisdom |
| courageousness | salvation | pleasure |
| social recognition | self-respect | honesty |
| cleanliness | happiness | true friendship |

| | | |
|---|---|---|
| helpfulness | equality | broadmindedness |
| cheerfulness | mature love | responsibility |

Teachers should make clear for students the distinction between values and *rules.* Rules, which schools and other institutions routinely establish and enforce, may imply tacit support for certain values such as honesty, punctuality, cleanliness, politeness, and obedience. As individuals, however, we can elect for pragmatic reasons to observe the rules without necessarily internalizing or supporting the values that undergird them.

## The Nature of Value Judgments

In contrast to the values themselves, we also have value judgments—the actual assertions or claims we make based on the values. **Value judgments** are ratings of people, objects, or events that reflect values. Figure 8.2 summarizes the contrasts among beliefs, attitudes, values, and value judgments.

Value judgments may be positive or negative and directed at any object. They apply our value standards to some individual, group, event, or item. Consider the following value judgments:

- Ronald Reagan was a great communicator.
- The United States should not have dropped the atom bomb on Japan.
- Porsche makes the finest car in the world.
- Gilda is a fantastic woman.
- Tom is an honest man.
- *Gone With the Wind* is a superficial account of the South.

**Figure 8.2**
**The Nature of Beliefs, Attitudes, Values, and Value Judgments**

| | |
|---|---|
| Beliefs | Any assertions individuals make that they regard as true |
| Attitudes | Clusters of related beliefs that express our likes, dislikes, general feelings, and opinions about some individual, group, object, or event |
| Values | The standards or criteria we use in making judgments about whether something is positive or negative, good or bad, pleasing or displeasing |
| Value Judgments | Ratings of people, objects, or events that reflect values |

Contrast the foregoing value judgments with statements of fact, such as "Ronald Reagan was elected President for two terms." Distinguishing statements of fact from value judgments is a useful exercise relating to value analysis. Beyond this step, students can begin to analyze and validate their own value judgments and contrast them with those of others.

## INSTRUCTIONAL STRATEGIES FOR EXAMINING BELIEFS, ATTITUDES, AND VALUES

Teaching strategies often combine objectives relating to beliefs, attitudes, values, and ethical issues. Teaching materials and texts similarly often lump them together under headings such as "values education." Since beliefs, attitudes, and values all are interrelated, a teaching strategy that focuses on one invariably has some impact on the others. The practical import of these interrelationships for classroom instruction is that objectives directed toward any one of them automatically involve the others to some extent (Bennett, 1990).

A starting point for instruction in the area of beliefs and attitudes is identifying where individuals stand on issues. Consider the following statements of economic beliefs and identify the ones with which you agree.

- One of the most important motivating forces in human beings is the search for economic self-gain.
- Government should have only minimal control over the economy.
- Whatever benefits business benefits everyone.
- It corrupts people to get something for nothing.
- Because of subsidies, tax breaks, special legislation, and other governmental favors, the rich get richer and the poor get poorer.
- Most people on welfare could be self-supporting if they really wanted to be.

One of the ways in which beliefs and attitudes may be examined, compared, and discussed is through simple surveys or inventories, such as the one you just took. Through the process of examining the positions of others, it often is easier for students to become aware of and clarify their own beliefs and attitudes.

Student debates are another way to help students clarify their positions on complex social issues. Evans (1993) describes in Figure 8.3 how he uses debates with middle-school students dealing with issues such as "John Brown: Criminal or Hero?"

Curriculum materials that present differing perspectives on important contemporary issues, such as the *Opposing Viewpoints* Series (see Figure 8.4), also are effective ways to introduce students to attitudes and values.

**Figure 8.3**
**Classroom Debates as a Strategy to Analyze Complex Social Issues**

**Using Classroom Debates as a Learning Tool**

Student debates are effective ways to foster cooperation, critical thinking, and enthusiasm for learning among middle school students. Teachers can use debates in almost any discipline, include students of all reading levels, and, when properly orchestrated, help students comprehend important and complex issues.

Political debates during election years can help students assess candidates and issues, whether at the presidential, congressional, or local levels. Student debates, however, are equally useful at any time and in any classroom. The curriculum itself should be a good source of topics—competing theories or historical disputes, for example—or current social and political controversies, such as abortion, women's rights, unemployment, foreign affairs, AIDS, education, and taxes.

I usually schedule debates at the end of a unit of study. As students investigate their debate topics and then listen to the debates of others, they add knowledge to the foundation of classroom lessons. Holding debates at the end of a study unit also provides me with an alternative form of evaluation, in lieu of a test, to help assess how well students have learned the material. I choose three interrelated topics relevant to the study unit just completed. For example, following a study of events leading to the Civil War, debate topics might be: "John Brown: Criminal or Hero?" "States Rights: Should States Be Allowed to Secede?" and "The Kansas-Nebraska Bill: Pro or Con?"

To stage a debate, I begin by dividing the class into three groups. I select members of these groups systematically to distribute evenly students of varying abilities. I then divide each group into two teams, one of which will argue for their chosen topic and the other, against it. Each group then randomly selects a debate topic from among the preselected subjects. This random selection enables them to explore perspectives that may differ from their own.

Prior to the debate, students should spend at least one week investigating their particular issue and rehearsing opening statements and presentations. During this preparation phase, I provide research assistance appropriate to the aptitude of each class. For example, in some classes, it is enough to furnish students with magazines, newspapers, and other information. In other classes, I must highlight this material and explain how the students could use it effectively in a debate.

As homework assignments, I ask students to bring in any relevant information they can find about their topics. I also remind them to prepare for the unexpected by learning as much as possible about their opponent's topic.

After students have coordinated and gathered their information, they make posters and signs to illustrate their position and begin rehearsing their presentations. One or two days before the debate, I schedule a short rehearsal.

*Note.* From "Classroom Debates as a Strategy to Analyze Complex Social Issues" by M. D. Evans, 1993, *Social Education, 57*(7), p. 370. 

**Figure 8.4**
**Example of Curriculum Materials That Present Opposing Views on an Issue**
*Note.* From *Opposing Viewpoints* Catalog, Greenhaven Press: San Diego, CA, 1993, p. 21.

**Causes of Crime**

*Distinguishing Between Fact and Opinion*
Four issues are debated:
- Does Poverty Cause Crime?
- Does Genetics Determine Who Causes Crime?
- Does the Use of Illegal Drugs Cause Crime?
- Does Easy Access to Guns Cause Crime?

They are a refreshing alternative to basal texts, which often present only one side of an issue—typically the consensus view. At the same time, teachers should be cautioned that often the original sources are so abridged that students are getting only the "60-second newsclip version" of issues.

## Attitude Inventories

An **attitude inventory** can be a composite of beliefs from many sources organized as an individual position. Additionally, it may include statements quoted from various sources or ones the teacher has created. Students also may be able to organize their own surveys and collect and analyze the results.

The work of Osgood, Suci, and Tannenbaum (1957) has provided teachers with a useful tool for analyzing general attitudes called the **semantic differential.** This technique employs sets of scales or rating sheets through which an individual's attitude concerning any object—people, events, experiences, and the like—can be assessed. The scales are easy to construct, use, and score.

Individual or group scores can be used to compare individual attitudes with those of other groups, such as a class or series of classes in a school, or with the position taken by someone in a text or in the mass media. The semantic differential technique can be used either as a springboard to discussions or as one aspect of evaluation to *measure* the effects of a unit of instruction.

**Constructing Attitude Inventories.** An inventory is constructed by first identifying some attitude object. This may include objects such as persons, groups, places, or things (e.g., Abraham Lincoln; illegal aliens; Washington, DC; abortion clinic protesters). The name of the attitude object also may be replaced with a picture of it. Objects should be chosen after considering the levels of knowledge, maturity, and interests of the students and the nature of the scope and sequence of the curriculum.

Along with the object, pairs of adjectives are selected that express opposites—for example, happy-sad, rich-poor, or good-bad (see Figure 8.5). Any adjectives that make sense in relationship to the attitude object being analyzed may be used.

No particular number of pairs must be used, but no fewer than 5 and no more than 10 is a suggested rule of thumb. At the top of the sheet, the name of the topic is placed, followed by the set of adjective pairs placed at the opposite ends of a continuum that allows seven rating options. Each student then is given a copy of the inventory and completes his or her ratings, as illustrated in Figure 8.5.

**Scoring a Completed Attitude Inventory.** Each point on the continuum in Figure 8.5 is assigned a number from 1 to 7, with the space next to the *positive* adjective (for example, "good") being assigned the number 7. The space next to the opposing *negative* adjective, "bad," is assigned the number 1. The spaces in between are numbered accordingly.

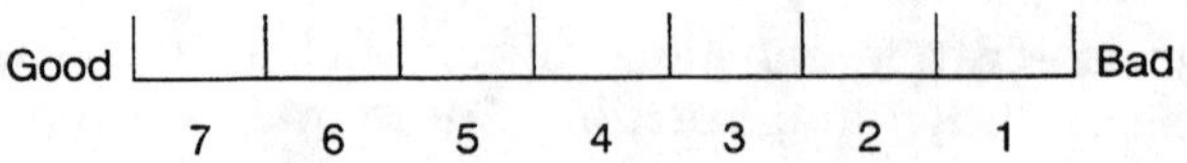


After students have completed the inventory, it is possible to measure whether each individual's attitudes toward the object are generally positive or negative. Since the inventory has 10 pairs, the highest possible score is 70, which would indicate an extremely *positive* attitude toward unwed mothers. The lowest possible score is 10, which would indicate an

**Figure 8.5**
**Attitude Scale**

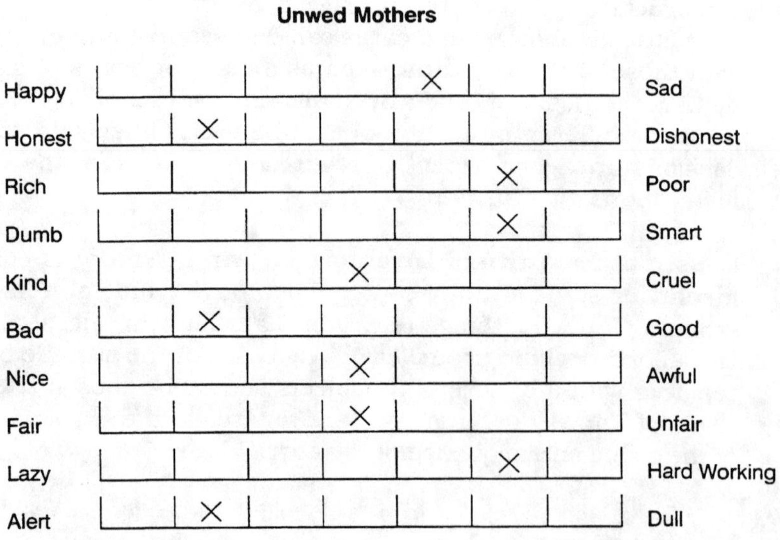

extremely *negative* attitude. A score of 40 would suggest a moderate view. The student who completed the inventory in Figure 8.5 had a score of 43, which indicates a slightly positive attitude toward unwed mothers.

A composite score representing the overall attitude of the class also can be obtained. This is done by summing all of the individual scores and then dividing the total by the number of respondents. Class scores can then be compared with those of other classes within a school.

## Challenging Beliefs and Attitudes

Once beliefs and attitudes have been identified, they can be analyzed. In a classroom guided by the spirit of inquiry, all verifiable beliefs and attitudes are fair game for challenge and investigation. The basic strategy for accomplishing this is to separate beliefs from individuals, raise them to the level of consciousness, and then examine them in the light of evidence that supports or refutes them.

Challenging what often passes for conventional wisdom, not only in a classroom but in the larger community, requires sensitivity and skill on the part of the teacher. Some guidelines for challenging beliefs follow (Martorella, 1977):

1. The beliefs or attitudes must be verifiable through rational means. This excludes assertions such as "God exists" or "There is life after death."
2. Both the teacher and the students must be able to deal with the subject in a rational and nonemotional manner.
3. The beliefs or attitudes should be at least partially inaccurate. Otherwise analysis becomes an exercise in sophistry.
4. The purpose of challenges is to engender examination and modifications in the light of evidence, not to substitute "right" for "wrong" views.
5. Some ways to isolate beliefs or attitudes for investigation are to look to sources such as talk shows on radio, letters to the editor, as well as the mass media in general and students' remarks.

## Value Analysis

Since values are more enduring than beliefs and attitudes, they are highly resistant to change (Rokeach, 1968). In dealing with values, both in the formal and the informal curriculum of the schools, teachers often swing to either of two extremes. They may try to *inculcate* a particular set of values that seem reasonable, inoffensive, or sanctioned by the local community. Alternately, they may encourage the point of view that all values are *relative*, that one set of standards for making judgments about whether something is good or bad is as good as another.

Neither extreme is defensible or functional in a democratic and pluralistic society. As suggested earlier, our pluralistic society supports many competing sets of values as legitimate. Further, as Hunt and Metcalf (1968) have argued, value *conflicts* abound in our society and in our personal lives. Schools must sustain, without supporting, a variety of citizens' value structures that cut across a swath of political, economic, social, and religious lines. At the same time, no responsible individual or institution can be mute in the presence of evil under the principle of supporting all persons' rights to hold whatever values they wish.

We do students a serious disservice if we suggest that learning values either by rote or arbitrarily is an appropriate course of action. The alternative approach is to aid students in a rational analysis of both the values they hold and the bases for them, as well as identifying the values they cherish the most.

This approach includes comparing our existing values and priorities with competing sets and examining how we handle value conflicts, such as when in battle our respect for human life conflicts with obeying orders to kill. It also involves examining the implications of the judgments we make based on our values. Additionally, it encompasses attending to the discrepancies between what we assert as values and the values that are reflected in the decisions we make and the actions we take.

**Identifying and Applying Value Hierarchies.** Which value in life is the most important to you? Which is the least important? Developing value hierarchies, determining what is more important and what is less significant in our system of values, helps make us more aware of our priorities and concerns. When we compare our value preferences with those of others, we also gain a broader perspective concerning how others view the world.

Value hierarchies can be approached by providing students with a list of value terms and asking them to organize an item in some order from most important to least important. Suppose we consider this set of values provided by Rokeach (1968): wisdom, freedom, national security, material comforts, equality, family security, and salvation.

All of these are important values, but which do you regard as the *most* important? Try a simple exercise to determine your value hierarchy. Record your choice at the *left* end of the continuum in Figure 8.6. Arrange the remaining values in the order of your choice. Ask a friend to complete the same sorting process and then compare your choices. Any set and number of values may be used, although the larger the number the more difficult the task.

Beyond offering a general insight into our value structure, value hierarchies can be used prior to the study of social issues to alert students to the frame of reference they are bringing to their analyses. As they define their position on an issue, they can be asked to assess the extent to which their

**Figure 8.6**
**Value Continuum**

| 1 | 2 | 3 | 4 | 5 | 6 | 7 |
|---|---|---|---|---|---|---|
| Most important | | | | | | Least important |

value structure shaped the outcome. Correspondingly, they can compare alternative positions through the lens of other value structures.

**Analyzing Value Conflicts.** We often must choose between virtue and pleasure, honesty and kindness, obedience and wisdom, and to make countless other choices in life where there are two or more cherished but competing values. Such value conflicts often can be resolved only by appeal to one or more other values that occupy a place of greater importance in our value hierarchy. What teachers should help students recognize is that value conflicts, like controversy in general, cannot be avoided and that they seldom occur in the form of stark choices between good and evil, justice and injustice.

Newmann with Oliver (1970) offered an example of how simple exercises can be constructed to provide students with experience in identifying and analyzing value conflicts through the use of analogies. In the first illustration in Figure 8.7, students are asked to construct an analogy that represents a value in conflict with the one presented (Newmann with Oliver, 1970).

In the second exercise shown in Figure 8.8, the teacher presents students with both the values and the analogies and asks to students to match them (Newmann with Oliver, 1970).

**Figure 8.7**
**Analyzing Value Conflict**

For each following claim, think up a situation, a historical event, or a short story that would contradict or pose an exception to the claim.

| **Value Claim** | **Challenging Analogy** |
|---|---|
| *Example:* It is wrong to kill | An innocent man is attacked by a thief with a knife. The man shoots the thief in self-defense. |

1. You should never tell a lie.
2. The majority should rule.
3. Each person is entitled to an equal share of the necessities of life.
4. We all deserve freedom of speech.
5. We should always obey the law.

*Note.* From Newmann with Oliver (1970, p. 276).

**Figure 8.8**
**Identifying and Analyzing Value Conflicts Through the Use of Analogies**

After reading the statements by Boris and Doris, decide for each analogy whether it challenges Boris's position (mark B); challenges Doris's position (mark D); or does not clearly challenge either position (mark N).

**Boris:** Opposing sides of public issues should be given equal time so that citizens can decide their views carefully.

**Doris:** But we should never restrict freedom of the press.

**Analogy 1:** Suppose Grand Trunk, a small town, is served by one newspaper and one television station, owned by the same man. He allows advertisements, news, and speeches favorable only to Republican candidates. He ignores publicity given to Democratic candidates and their views. Shouldn't something be done about that?

**Analogy 2:** All three newspapers in Watertown were accused by the police of publishing information from the secret police files. The police chief filed suit for breach of contract, charging the reporters had broken their promises. Do you think the reporters should be punished?

**Analogy 3:** Representatives from the government of North Vietnam request free time on television and free space to publish editorials in the newspapers to match all the United States opinion against their country. Do you think that should be allowed?

*Note.* From Newmann with Oliver (1970, p. 277).

Instructional strategies for helping students identify and resolve value conflicts are intertwined with issues of right and wrong. Often, discussion in the educational literature use the terms *value conflicts* and *moral dilemmas* interchangeably. In the section that follows, we will consider specifically the ways in which beliefs, attitudes, and values enter into the ethical development of young citizens.

**Analyzing Comparative Value Judgments.** Chadwick and Meux (1971) developed a detailed eight-step model for analyzing value judgments that focuses on a single issue and requires students, individually and then as a class, to list, rank, and discuss positive and negative statements about an issue. Once they have completed these stages, students must formulate final positions and make observations and recommendations, seeking out information in the process.

Let us consider how the Chadwick and Meux procedures might be initiated with a secondary class (Martorella, 1977). Due to the lengthy process involved, we will sketch only the initial stages of the strategy.

The teacher and the students have been discussing a news report that the federal government would begin limiting the use of automobiles in some national wilderness areas in order to help protect the environment. Most students applauded the action as a necessary restriction to reduce the effects of pollution and congestion and to preserve the natural beauty of the recreational areas.

Some students asked why the government was instituting the policy now; others were indifferent. A vocal minority, however, directly challenged the government's plan to limit automobile access to some areas as an infringement on individual rights. They pointed out that national recreational areas were created to serve all of the people and that the only fair policy would be one that a majority of all Americans supported. The minority believed that most people preferred driving in recreational areas to walking; besides, they argued, only a small percentage of the total population would have the physical stamina or training to explore on foot.

From the discussion, it was clear to the teacher that few students had much solid information to support their value judgments and arguments. Only a few students had firsthand experiences with national parks, forests, and wilderness areas, and the others knew little about the nature and operation of such areas. As the class ended, the teacher informed the class that they would resume the discussion as soon as the teacher could assemble some suitable resource materials.

When the discussion resumed, the teacher distributed copies of a map identifying the national wilderness areas across the United States. After a careful analysis of the locations and an extended discussion of the nature of wilderness areas, each student was asked to consult resources identified in the school library and to construct an individual folder containing lists of positive and negative statements about wilderness areas. Further, the students were asked to rank the statements in order of perceived importance.

Tom, a student who supported the government's policy, completed his folder as shown in Figure 8.9. At this stage, his list was vague at points and uneven.

When this stage of the analysis was completed, the teacher compiled a class list summarizing all of the students' ideas. Discussion of the positive and negative statements follows. The students then were asked to formulate individual folders with possible solutions for the *negative* statements that received the highest ratings by the class. Solutions were to be ranked in order of importance, and, as with the first folder, students were to list below the solutions a list of positive and negative statements about each of them.

During the final stage, the students had an opportunity to discuss further their second folders, consult with the teacher and other resources, and arrive at a final position. When their analysis was complete, each student constructed a final folder similar to the one shown in Figure 8.10, reflecting his or her observations and recommendations.

**Figure 8.9**
**Tom's Lists of Statements About the Preservation of Wilderness Areas**

| Positive Statements | Negative Statements |
|---|---|
| 1. Gives those who want to make the effort a real special nature experience | 1. Closes off scenic beauty from a majority of people |
| 2. Guarantees open spaces for future generations | 2. Makes it tough or impossible for disabled people to see the special nature areas |
| 3. Protects and preserves wildlife | 3. Impedes progress (e.g., electricity-producing dams) |
| 4. Preserves purity of water—an important natural resource | 4. Discourages development of natural resources |
| 5. Provides a place for different kinds of outdoor activities | 5. Prevents needed management of environment to counter effects of civilization |
| 6. Keeps areas in an unspoiled natural state | 6. Takes up land that could be used for more important things |
| 7. Helps keep the ecological balance from being upset | 7. Based on unrealistic view of nature—man is an intruder |
| 8. Lets scientists have a kind of laboratory to study nature | 8. Gives in to conservation pressure-group demands |
| 9. Maintains the public trust given to the national park and the national forest service | 9. Reduces number of recreational management jobs |
| 10. Provides a cheap recreation area | 10. Reduces sale of nonwilderness recreational equipment |
| 11. Helps sale of wilderness recreational equipment | |

*Note.* Martorella (1977, p. 151).

## PROMOTING ETHICAL GROWTH

The analyses of our beliefs, attitudes, and values eventually intersect with basic matters of *ethics* or *morals*. Ethical issues require us to make decisions about what should be done, what course of action should be taken when competing choices are available. Determining what is the right course of action, especially in a complex, rapidly changing world, often involves more than looking to tradition or to what immediately benefits us personally, a group, or a nation for decision. **Ethics** includes questions such as: What is proper? What is just? What is the fair thing to do?

Our body of ethical principles guides us in answering basic moral questions such as these as they recur throughout our lives. In turn, the network of beliefs, attitudes, and values that undergird our ethical framework is pressed into action whenever we confront a basic dilemma concerning what is the right and the wrong thing to do.

**Figure 8.10**
**Tom's Observations and Recommendations**

**Observations**

1. It will be difficult to preserve all areas that currently exist in their wilderness state, and still satisfy everyone's recreational needs.
2. Keeping a balance between pro and anti-wilderness demands can't always be settled by dividing a recreational area. Sometimes dividing an area simply destroys its value to both sides.
3. Often decisions about the preservation of the wilderness are made on the basis of political pressures.
4. It is hard to settle wilderness preservation issues in a way that satisfies both the majority's and the minority's rights.

**Recommendations**

1. A national advisory board should be set up to determine what the country's recreation needs are likely to be. The board should make recommendations for needed laws to maintain wilderness areas in a way that will serve all of the people.
2. Until the board makes its recommendations, all lands designated as wilderness should be kept as they are.
3. Environmental education should be included in the curriculum, K–12.

*Note.* Martorella (1977, p. 154).

Initially, many of us derive our moral codes from our parents or our parent surrogates. They point the way to what is right and wrong behavior. In some form, they reward us when we respond correctly and rebuke us when we err. As children, we learn early on a host of moral "dos and don'ts" in this fashion.

If we never progress beyond this stage of imitation and repetition of behavioral patterns as responses to moral issues, our ethical framework does not mature. Morality for such an individual is largely a matter of imitating patterns of responses that were learned long ago and that have been refined and reinforced over the years.

On the other hand, in those cases where individuals develop without clear guidelines, they may face life without an ethical compass to guide their decisions. They are likely to skip from situation to situation doing what seems prudent at the time. What is right becomes a matter of what is expedient. Each moral decision bears little relationship to the last one or to the next one. If nothing happens to change the behavior of such individuals, they remain ethically rootless.

## The Moral Development Theories of Jean Piaget and Lawrence Kohlberg

Kohlberg and his associates developed, refined, and tested a theory of **moral development** that drew from Piaget's earlier work (Kohlberg, 1976). One aspect of Piaget's developmental research dealt with the ways in which individuals reason about matters of right and wrong. As they mature, Piaget argued, children begin to understand that the needs of others must be taken into account in making moral judgments.

He discovered that children over time exhibit qualitatively different types of moral reasoning. For instance, young children are prone to pay attention to what an authority figure, such as a parent, says to determine what is the right or the wrong thing to do in a situation. As they grow older, however, children are more likely to take into account the principles of reciprocity and cooperativeness in making a moral decision (Piaget, 1965).

**Kohlberg's Stages of Moral Development.** In building on Piaget's research, Kohlberg identified six closely related stages of moral development, which are summarized in Figure 8.11.

Kohlberg contended that individuals proceed from stage to stage with each stage building on the preceding one. No stage may be skipped, and

**Figure 8.11**
**Kohlberg's Stages of Moral Development**

| | Stage | What Is Right |
|---|---|---|
| Stage 1 | Heteronomous Morality | To avoid breaking rules; be obedient for its own sake; avoid harm to persons and property |
| Stage 2 | Instrumental Purpose, Exchange | To follow rules when in your interest; do what is fair |
| Stage 3 | Mutual Expectations, Interpersonal Conformity | To measure up to expectations of those you respect; observe the Golden Rule. |
| Stage 4 | Social System, Conscience | To observe the law and rules; contribute to society. |
| Stage 5 | Social Contract | To observe the social contract; evidence respect for core values such as life and liberty. |
| Stage 6 | Universal Ethical Principles | To uphold universal ethical principles: justice, equality of human rights, and respect for individual human dignity. |

*Note.* Adapted from "Cognitive-Developmental Approach to Moral Education" by L. Kohlberg, 1976, in *Social Studies Strategies: Theory Into Practice,* edited by P. Martorella, pp. 127–142. Copyright 1976 by L. Kohlberg.

Kohlberg maintained that progression through the stages is not inevitable. Also, he argued that moral development may be retarded at any stage. Attaining higher levels of moral reasoning, he concluded, requires increasing capability in logical reasoning and perspective taking.

**Onset of Stages of Moral Development.** Kohlberg's theory postulates that, as a rule of thumb, the probabilities are that children in the primary grades would be at stages 1 and 2 and those in the intermediate grades would be at stages 2 and 3. Most middle grades students are likely to be at stage 3, with some at 2 and a few at 4. Most secondary students will be at stages 3 and 4. Kohlberg maintained that the majority of all individuals, youngsters and adults, typically never advance beyond the third or fourth stages of development.

**The Role of Moral Dilemmas in Moral Development.** Moral development, according to Kohlberg's theory, is stimulated through confrontations and dialogue concerning moral dilemmas (Kohlberg, 1976; 1980). The dilemmas consist of brief episodes involving matters of right and wrong in which only two courses of action are available. An individual must take a position on one side of the argument or the other, offer reasons for the choice, and entertain the competing position and alternative rationale.

Kohlberg's sample dilemmas were based on traditional ethical issues drawn from moral philosophy. They centered around such matters as fairness, equity, honesty, obedience, observance of laws, and property rights. Each dilemma briefly and clearly framed a simple issue that called for a direct categorical answer.

Neither of the two possible positions regarding a dilemma is considered to be morally preferable or indicates a more advanced stage of moral reasoning. Rather, it is the *type* or *quality* of reasoning that individuals use to defend their positions that indicates the dominant stage of moral development that has been reached.

For example, consider the situation in which two small children are asked whether it is right to take a dollar from the billfold of a rich man if he is out of the room and cannot see the child taking the money. One child says no, because a promise was made to a parent never to take anything that belonged to someone else. The other child says yes, because the rich man will never know and no punishment will result. *Both* children reflect only stage 1 reasoning, as described in Figure 8.11. Neither child reasons beyond the point of obeying an authority or avoiding punishment.

**Kohlberg's Critics.** Kohlberg's theories have attracted a broad range of criticisms (e.g., Gibbs, 1977; Kurtines & Grief, 1974; Noddings, 1984). Some of the major complaints concern whether his studies truly apply across all cultural groups and both genders. Gilligan (1982), for example, has challenged whether males and females have similar moral perspectives.

Other critics have raised serious questions about whether reasoning relating to dilemmas posed in classroom exercises indicates how individuals would respond to real moral crises (e.g., Colby & Damon, 1992). Still others have challenged the validity of the stages themselves. Cole and Cole (1989) have captured the essence of this vein of criticism:

> Despite its comprehensiveness and its ability to inspire research, Kohlberg's theory of moral development has had a somewhat stormy history. . . . Although several studies have confirmed that children progress through Kohlberg's stages of moral reasoning in the predicted order . . . others have failed to support the idea that Kohlberg's stages follow each other in an invariant sequence from lower to higher. Instead of a steady progression upward, subjects sometimes regress in their development or seem to skip a stage. (p. 578)

## Alternative Strategies for Moral Education in Public Schools

Between two extreme positions—supporting the modeling of authority figures or encouraging rootlessness—lies an alternative role in moral education for public schools in a pluralistic democracy. This approach rejects the

**In our complex, rapidly paced society, students are confronted with a variety of ethical issues.**

notion that students should be indoctrinated to respond to moral questions with prescribed or consensus answers (see Lickona, 1991). It also rejects the position that students should be taught that one moral course of action is as good as another.

An appropriate moral education program for schools is one that is compatible with the goals of a democratic society. Such a program engages students in the consideration of realistic moral issues and then provides them with opportunities for dialogue in groups under the guidance of the teacher. In describing such an approach, Damon (1988) has observed: "In such groups, the teacher poses the problem and guides the discussion, but the children are encouraged by the peer dialogue to express their own views and to listen to each others' feedback" (pp. 150–151).

A number of social studies educators, most notably Oliver and Shaver (1966), Newmann with Oliver (1970), and Lockwood (1985), have advocated that teachers provide ample opportunities for students to discuss and debate moral issues that arise from conflicts within our society. Such strategies require students to consider and take a stand on basic moral issues in which cherished values are in conflict. They then are required to engage in rational dialogue with others to defend their positions.

As one application of this approach, Lockwood and Harris (1985) have developed a series of case studies built around specific historical incidents that involve ethical issues. These are woven into the traditional American history curriculum.

> For example, a story based on the life of Quaker Mary Dyer embodies the theme of religious tension in Puritan New England. In addition, the focus on her decision to face death for her beliefs is an instance of the conflict between the values of authority, life, and liberty. Similarly, a story based on President Eisenhower's decision to permit issuance of a false cover story regarding the U-2 incident reflects themes of the Cold War era and presents conflicts involving the values of truth, life, and authority. (Lockwood, 1985, p. 267)

**Guidelines for Constructing Moral Dilemmas.** Teaching strategies that capitalize on students' natural interest in fundamental issues of right and wrong, like those presented, focus on competing moral choices. Such approaches help students of all ages develop an ethical framework grounded in reason by engaging them in analyzing, discussing, and taking a stand on realistic dilemmas.

Construction of a moral dilemma includes the following considerations:

1. The issue should be appropriate for the students' age and interests and should be related to subjects they are studying (e.g., considering whether it is ever appropriate to break a law in a unit on laws).
2. The issue presented should offer students only two basic choices for a decision: Should A or B be done?

3. Both choices for the dilemma should be likely to attract some support within the class. (If there is no difference of opinion at the outset, it will be difficult to generate discussion.)
4. The dilemma must involve an issue of what is a just or fair course of action. Right or wrong in the case of a dilemma does not mean factually correct or incorrect.
5. All of the material to be used to present the dilemma, whether written, oral, or visual, should be succinct and clear. The focus should be clearly on the dilemma and the decisions that are required.

A specific example of an ethical dilemma, one that dramatizes a choice some parents in the United States currently are facing, is shown in Figure 8.12. It suggests the form that the presentation of any ethical dilemma might take and includes some sample probing questions for students to consider.

**Guidelines for Presenting and Discussing Moral Dilemmas.** For the presentation and discussion of a dilemma, the following procedures are suggested:

1. Present the dilemma to students in the form of a handout statement, an oral reading, a role-play scenario, or other media formats.
2. Organize the students into discussion groups and allow them to take a position with respect to the issue raised in the dilemma. Be sure that in each group both positions on the issue are represented at the outset.
3. Use a series of probing questions to follow up the dilemma. When it appears there is convergence on one point of view, raise questions that force consideration of the other. Act as a "devil's advocate" to argue whatever position is currently not popular.
4. Keep the focus on the dilemma. It is important to keep students' attention on the issue they are trying to decide. If necessary, arbitrarily eliminate options that might draw students off the hard choice to be made.
5. Encourage the students to try to put themselves in the shoes of all the characters in the dilemma.

## SOCIAL ISSUES AS A CURRICULAR FOCUS

The term *social issue* is used loosely in the social studies. Its meaning ranges from any topic that has social implications, to social problems, to any item of controversy (see Olner, 1976). Social issues invariably touch on beliefs, attitudes, values, and ethical dilemmas. Issues may change over time, as old ones no longer affect large numbers of people and as new social phenomena arise.

**Figure 8.12**
**An Ethical Dilemma Involving Alleged Parental Child Abuse**

Today there is an increasing problem of child abuse, which covers a range of maltreatments that include emotional, physical, and sexual abuse. Some of this abuse even occurs at the hands of a child's own parents. Often it is very difficult to convict a parent of child abuse, particularly sexual abuse in the case of a very young child, when there are no overt signs or witnesses. This difficulty is due, among other factors, to the age of the child and the related issues of ignorance, fear of recriminations, or credibility of testimony.

In cases where the parents are divorced and the courts have not been able to establish culpability for abuse, a further problem arises. If the courts do not have sufficient evidence to establish that one parent has abused a child, the offending parent may upon request be granted partial or full custody of the child. The courts then often have acted to enforce these custody rights, and, in some cases, have incarcerated those parents who refuse to recognize them.

This creates a dilemma for the parent who believes the child has been abused and who is caught between observing the law and safeguarding the welfare of the child. Ms. Colbert is a parent caught in this dilemma. She believes there is clear evidence that her former husband, who has been granted shared custody of their son Tom, age 3, has sexually abused the child.

The court has ruled that there is insufficient evidence to support her charge. She has elected to defy the court order and run away with Tom because she believes Mr. Colbert will abuse the boy.

Is Ms. Colbert doing the right or the wrong thing? Why?

**Sample Probing Questions**

1. Does the nature of the alleged abuse make a difference?
2. What evidence of abuse would you accept as reasonable evidence of sexual abuse?
3. Should Tom's age be an issue?
4. Does it matter that the courts do not agree with Ms. Colbert?
5. Is Ms. Colbert's action fair to her husband? To Tom?

From an instructional perspective, we will consider a **social issue** to be any matter in dispute that affects a sizable group of people and is solvable. Once a matter is resolved to the satisfaction of most of those involved, the issue ceases to exist. These are somewhat subjective and general criteria for identifying social issues; they leave teachers with wide latitude to select topics for discussion and analysis. Also, they permit teachers to include topics for investigation that may be largely of local or regional import, such as gang violence.

Social issues are often most clearly expressed in the form of questions. Examples are:

- How can we provide adequate shelter for the homeless?
- How can we make our system of taxation fair for all social classes?

## Curricular Framework for Analyzing Social Issues in the Classroom

As we considered in earlier chapters, several social studies educators have provided distinctive frameworks for identifying and shaping social issues for investigation within the social studies curriculum. We will consider briefly two such approaches. One, by Hunt and Metcalf (1968), focuses on what they called the **closed areas** of our society. The other, advanced by Oliver and Shaver (1966), centers on enduring social issues and is labeled the **jurisprudential approach.**

**Closed-Areas Approach.** Hunt and Metcalf (1968) have argued that in our society certain areas of personal and social conflict are closed to rational examination. Writing over a quarter-century ago, they wrote:

> Certain areas of conflicting belief and behavior are largely closed to thought. In these areas, people usually react to problems blindly and emotionally. Closed areas are saturated with prejudices and taboos. Inconsistency or mutual contradiction in beliefs and values rule behavior in any closed area. There is usually a reluctance to examine certain ideas because it is believed that they are "impractical," "theoretical," or "in violation of common sense." Those areas of belief which are most important to individuals are likely to be those in which rational thought is least valued. In our culture, irrational responses commonly occur in such areas as power and the law; religion and morality; race and minority-group relations; social class; sex; courtship and marriage; nationalism and patriotism; and economics. (Hunt & Metcalf, 1968, pp. 26–27)

Hunt and Metcalf argued that these areas were most likely to intersect with the personally felt problems of students. The authors recommended the **closed-areas approach,** the technique of selecting instructional materials on the basis of their potential for developing and resolving problems for students within the context of the closed areas. Beliefs, attitudes, and values were to be the objects of investigation.

As a starting point, they suggested that teachers probe the *conflicts* in the closed areas. For example, consider the contradiction: "It is believed that the United States is a land of opportunity and that anyone can get ahead if he tries hard enough; but it is also believed that a person cannot move upwards nowadays unless he gets lucky breaks or knows the right people" (Hunt & Metcalf, 1968, p. 376).

**Jurisprudential Approach.** Oliver and Shaver (1966) advocated a **jurisprudential approach** to the social studies curriculum, one that is similar in some respects to that urged by Hunt and Metcalf. Oliver and Shaver suggested that students should be exposed to general areas of conflict or public problems in our society. Further, they stated, "the student should be taught to analyze these public issues within some useful political and social framework. We are suggesting that initially the appropriate framework grows out of a Western constitutional tradition" (1966, p. 13).

Through case studies, Oliver and Shaver employed legal-ethical dilemmas that emphasize the conflicts within our society that persist over time. A sample outline of a curriculum unit presented in Figure 8.13 using 14 cases illustrates their approach. Other units currently available from the Social Science Education Consortium include the following:

- The American Revolution: Crisis of Law and Change
- The Civil War: Slavery and the Crisis of Union
- The Rise of Organized Labor: Workers, Employers, and the Public Interest
- Immigration: Pluralism and National Identity

## Freedom of Speech and Social Concern

For concerned citizens to explore social issues unfettered requires a climate of freedom secured by their government. The First Amendment in the Bill of Rights is a concise and powerful guarantee of some of the most vital aspects of our daily lives, including freedom of speech.

> Congress shall make no law respecting an establishment of religion or prohibiting the free exercise thereof; or abridging the freedom of speech, or of the press; or the right of the people peaceably to assemble, and to petition the government for a redress of grievances.

Freedom of speech is central to all other freedoms to which we are entitled under our Constitution. Historically this right has been interpreted broadly by the courts and extended to a variety of different forms of expression. Exercising the right of freedom of speech traditionally has meant that citizens expect to be able to say without fear of reprisal generally whatever is on their minds—in public and in private, in conversations, and through the media—about whatever and whomever they please. The further expectation is that this right exists no matter what the issue or position or station in life of the person being discussed.

Although most of us cherish the right of freedom of speech, some individuals often have difficulty accepting the *reciprocal responsibility* that accompanies the right. For example, local mores may serve to restrict First Amendment guarantees by permitting free speech only for some, at certain times, and under specified conditions.

In a pluralistic democracy, individuals often may swim against the tide of conformity, both in the content of their views and in the form in which

**Figure 8.13**
**Case Studies for a Unit Using the Jurisprudential Approach**

**Unit Four**
**Application of Analytical and Political Concepts Using Specific Controversial Cases**

| *Document* | *Description of Content* |
|---|---|
| | [Most of these cases are based on Supreme Court decisions] |
| "Lunch Counter" | Fictitious case of a Negro sit-in demonstration |
| "Sidewalk Speech" | Incident involving free speech, based on a constitutional case: *Feiner* v. *New York*, 340 U.S. 315 (1951) |
| "Davis Lumber" | Incident in which a lumber dealer challenges the constitutionality of Fair Labor Standards Act, based on a constitutional case: *United States* v. *Darby*, 312 U.S. 100 (1941) |
| "The House" | Story about housing discrimination against an American citizen of Chinese ancestry |
| "Flag Salute" | Incident in which a Jehovah's Witness refuses to allow his child to salute the flag in public school, based on two constitutional cases: *Minersville School District* v. *Gobitis*, 310 U.S. 586 (1940), and *West Virginia Board of Education* v. *Barnette*, 319 U.S. 624 (1943) |
| "The Job" | Incident in which California prosecutes a man for helping his unemployed brother-in-law enter the state, based on a constitutional case: *Edwards* v. *California*, 314 U.S. 160 (1941) |
| "Radios and Buses" | Incident in which two men contest the right of a bus company to install radios on public buses |
| "Smittites" | Story of a religious sect which obtains special tax privileges because of a broadened definition of "religious property" |
| "Rabin Case" | Incident in which a counterfeiter's desk is searched when he is arrested (Does this constitute unreasonable search and seizure?), based on a constitutional case: *United States* v. *Rabinowitz*, 339 U.S. 56 (1950) |
| "Out of Bounds" | Story about housing discrimination against a Negro doctor. |
| "Ota Case" | Fictional account of a Japanese family relocated from the west coast at the beginning of World War II, based on a constitutional case: *Korematsu* v. *United States*, 323 U.S. 214 (1944) |
| "Loudspeaker and the Union" | Incident in which a city restricts the right of a labor organization to use a loudspeaker to take its case to the public, based on a constitutional case: *Kovaks* v. *Cooper*, 336 U.S. 77 (1949) |
| "Hours" | Incident in which the government restricts a woman's right to work or be hired for as many hours as she wants, based on a constitutional case: *Adkins* v. *Children's Hospital*, 261 U.S. 525 (1923) |
| "The Voyage" | Story of a long-time non-citizen resident of the United States who is refused readmission to the United States after visiting his native country behind the iron curtain, based on a constitutional case: *Shaughnessy* v. *United States*, ex. rel. Mezei, 345 U.S. 206 (1953) |

*Note*. From *Teaching Public Issues in the High School* (pp. 250–251) by D. W. Oliver and J. P. Shaver, 1966, Boston: Houghton Mifflin. Reissued, Utah State University, 1974. Reprinted with permission.

they are expressed. Although their ideas may offend the sensibilities of the majority, that fact does not detract from their right and our responsibility.

Students should recognize that in a democracy there is only one true defense against being influenced or mislead by ideas that are antithetical to the majority or to those in power. That is the cultivation of reason and the protection of the right to offer divergent arguments. When we responsibly support others' freedom of speech, it is *our* common right that we safeguard.

In social studies classes, as students engage in open and candid discussions, teachers periodically will need to stress some key principles concerning the right of freedom of speech:

1. It is a special right that historically has distinguished our nation from many others. Without this right, our life and our society would be much different.
2. It is a right that Americans continually have had to safeguard since the founding of the Republic. Inevitably some individuals and groups in our society have objected to the content of someone's point of view, the way in which it was expressed, or even their nonexpression of a view, when one was expected.
3. The right would be meaningless for most citizens if it did not entail the responsibility to entertain the views of others or to let them exercise the right as well.
4. Part of the vitality of a society in which freedom of speech is championed and protected by law is that diverse opinions freely expressed and widely circulated give rise to innovations and creativity.
5. In exercising our right, we may seriously entertain divergent points of view—even those with which we strongly disagree—without subscribing to, being sympathetic with, or planning to act on the ideas expressed.

The rights and reciprocal responsibilities that flow from our constitutional guarantees of freedom of speech have considerable significance for the social studies curriculum in middle and secondary schools. They provide a framework within which teachers can nurture development of the dimension of concern through an open examination of beliefs, attitudes, values, ethical dilemmas, and social issues.

## Social Issues and Controversy

The analysis of social issues and the exercise of our freedom of speech frequently generate controversy in an open society. Johnson and Johnson (1988) define *controversy* in academic contexts as "conflict that exists when one student's ideas, information, conclusions, theories, and opinions are incompatible with those of another and the two seek to reach an agreement" (p. 59).

Controversy is a normal part of life in a democracy. In our society, the rights and privileges we share as citizens provide us with the tools to peacefully and constructively debate or resolve controversial issues. The opportunities for controversy result naturally through the normal exercise of our rights and responsibilities. We do not have to seek them out. Acts as simple as fertilizing our lawn with chemicals, renting our house to whomever we wish, or even contracting certain diseases can involve us in controversy.

Controversy over matters of concern is one sign that our democratic system is functioning properly. Societies that are closed, that have little tolerance for divergent points of view, or that have rigidly circumscribed rights have little controversy. Such societies punish those who create it and also attempt in other ways to suppress and eradicate it.

Students need to accept controversy as a dimension of democracy, rather than always seeking to avoid it. Young citizens should be exposed to it early in a form that takes into account their level of maturity and experiences. They also should recognize there are likely to be times in every responsible citizen's life, regardless of age, when he or she creates controversy. They also need to be able to deal with controversy in social studies classes.

**Guidelines for Handling Discussions of Controversial Issues.** A number of guidelines and positions exist concerning the treatment of controversial issues in social studies classes (Kelly, 1986; Muessig, 1975). For example, Johnson and Johnson (1988) have developed an elaborate six-step model that involves students working in groups. The NCSS ("Academic freedom," 1967) also has produced a comprehensive position statement and set of guidelines to aid teachers in handling controversy. Among its recommendations are that teachers:

> Protect the right of students to express and defend opinions without penalty.
> Establish with students the ground rules for the study of issues.
> Promote the fair representation of different points of view.
> Insure that activities do not adversely reflect upon any individual or group because of race, creed, sex, or ethnic origin.
> Teach students *how* to think, not *what* to think.
> Adhere to written policy concerning academic freedom established by the Board of Education.
> Give students full and fair consideration when they take issue with teaching strategies, materials, requirements or evaluation practices.
> Exemplify objectivity, demonstrate respect for minority opinion, and recognize the function of dissent. ("Academic freedom," 1967, p. 2)

## Teacher Positions on Controversial Issues

Invariably, at some point in the discussion of controversial issues, students wish to know what the teacher thinks. For a teacher to suggest that he or she had *no* opinion would be silly or dishonest. It also is likely to puzzle students. If it is important for them to form a position on the issue, why hasn't the teacher done so?

Teachers have several options when such a question arises. They may state their positions at that point or suggest that they have a tentative position but would like to hear all of the students' arguments before making a final decision. Alternately, they may indicate that they have a position but would rather not state it until the discussion is finished and students have made their own decisions. When teachers really have no opinion because of the nature of the issue, they should share this fact and the reasons.

It is important for students to understand that in a controversy the positions of those in authority, including that of the teacher, are not necessarily the best or the correct ones. Moreover, in many controversies, authority figures (and often "authorities" on the subject of the controversy) take competing positions. The most prudent course for all citizens is to seek out all points of view, to consider the facts, to come to a tentative conclusion, and to keep an open mind to new arguments.

## ACADEMIC FREEDOM IN THE CLASSROOM

In dealing with social issues that may engender controversy, social studies teachers require a degree of autonomy in the classroom. One of the important freedoms for all social studies teachers to safeguard is **academic freedom.** "A teacher's academic freedom," the NCSS noted, "is his/her right and responsibility to study, investigate, present, interpret, and discuss all the relevant facts and ideas in the field of his/her professional competence" (NCSS, 1967).

### Challenges to Academic Freedom

Challenges to academic freedom occur when individuals seek to constrain the free and open airing of different points of view in the classroom. This happens when either discussions or the use of instructional materials that a teacher considers relevant to the study of an area are curtailed. Some of the basic types of threats to academic freedom in the social studies classroom include:

1. Teacher self-censorship because of fear of criticism or reprisals,
2. Prohibitions against using certain individuals or groups as resource persons in the classroom,
3. Prohibitions against the study of certain topics, areas, or individuals, and
4. Selection, alteration, or exclusion of curricular materials in ways that impede free and open inquiry in the classroom.

## Handling Complaints Concerning Social Studies Materials

Challenges to a teacher's right to use certain materials in social studies classes are particularly common threats to academic freedom. One study estimated that, during the 1992–1993 school year, there were over 300 attempts to restrict or ban the use of teaching materials from school. Approximately 4 out of 10 were successful ("4 of 10," 1993). Objects of censorship were varied and targeted by a range of protest groups, as the case involving a middle-grade class in Figure 8.14 attests.

When criticisms or challenges surface, it is important for teachers to distinguish between those that are based on misinformation and those that are attacks on academic freedom. A school or a district should have in place a policy and procedures for handling complaints that requires individuals to document the specific details of allegations. All social studies teachers should have a copy.

One of the elements of the school's set of procedures should be a form that those airing complaints are asked to complete and file formally. A sample form, shown in Figure 8.15, has been developed by the NCSS ("Academic freedom," 1967).

Filing a formal complaint puts an individual or group on record with respect to the specific nature of the complaint, its perceived degree of seriousness, and the desired action. It also forces the critic to actually examine the alleged offensive material, rather than rely on secondhand accounts.

**Figure 8.14**
**Example of Complaint Concerning Controversial Social Studies Material**

**Witches Want Tale to Vanish from School**

Two self-proclaimed witches have asked the [Mount Diablo, California] schools to ban the story "Hansel and Gretel" because it degrades witches and suggests it's all right to kill them.

"This story teaches that it is all right to burn witches and steal their property," said Karlyn Straganana, high Priestess of the Oak Haven Coven....

The controversy arose after a class of fifth graders staged a mock trial charging Hansel and Gretel with murder in the death of a witch who took them in after they became lost in the forest.

The student jury found the children innocent because they acted in self-defense. ("Witches," 1992, p. 5a)

**Figure 8.15**
**Suggested Model of a Complaint Form**

**Request for Reconsideration of Social Studies Materials**

Type of material (book, film, pamphlet, etc.):

______________________________________________

Title of material: ______________________________

Author (if known): ______________________________

Publisher: ____________________________________

Date of publication: ____________________________

Request initiated by (name, address, phone number):

______________________________________________

______________________________________________

______________________________________________

Do you have a child in the school concerned? ☐ Yes ☐ No

Complainant represents:

______________________________ (self)

______________________________ (organization—name)

______________________________ (other group—identify)

1. To what in the material do you object? (Please be specific. Cite words, pages, and nature of content.)
2. Why do you object to this material?
3. Are you acquainted with the range of materials being used in the school system on this general topic?
4. Do you approve of presenting a diversity of points of view in the classroom?
5. What would you like your school to do about this material?
   (a) Do not expose or assign it to my child.
   (b) Withdraw it from all students as well as my child.
   (c) Send it back to the appropriate school department for reevaluation.

Signature of Complainant ______________________________

Date: ______________________________

*Note.* From *Academic Freedom: A Policy Statement* (p. 1) by National Council for the Social Studies, 1967, Washington, DC: Author. © National Council for the Social Studies. Used with permission.

## GROUP ACTIVITIES

1. Find a case that was decided before the Supreme Court in the past five years that involved First Amendment rights. Discuss the ways in which the case extended or limited personal freedoms.
2. How much freedom do you think a teacher in the middle grades should have regarding social studies lessons and materials? In the secondary grades?
3. In your own community, identify five significant social issues that you believe a concerned citizen should examine or become involved in. Also, develop a rationale for why you think these issues are especially important. Discuss your conclusions.
4. Select some area in which attitudes might be analyzed in a middle or secondary grades class. Use one of the topics listed earlier in the chapter or one of your own choosing.
5. Develop an attitude inventory related to the topic you have selected that is appropriate for children in grades 5 through 12. Then identify a class to field-test the inventory. Discuss the results and any changes you would make based on your experiences.

## INDIVIDUAL ACTIVITIES

1. Using the criteria found in the chapter, construct a moral dilemma suitable for use with middle-grades students. Then develop related discussion questions for each.
2. Repeat the activity in group activity 5, except create a dilemma suitable for students in the secondary grades.
3. Select one of the lists of values identified in the chapter and identify a group of 12th-grade students. Explain each of the values and then ask each of the students to arrange them in order of importance. Ask students to share their lists and their reasons. Record and evaluate your findings.
4. Using the definition within the chapter, identify what you consider to be some of the current "closed areas" in our society. Be as specific as possible.

## REFERENCES

ASCD Panel on Moral Education. (1988). Moral education in the life of the school. *Educational Leadership, 45*(8), 4–8.

Bennett, C. (1990). *Comprehensive multicultural education: Theory and practice* (2nd ed.). Boston: Allyn & Bacon.

Benninga, J. (Ed.). (1991). *Moral character and civic education in the elementary school.* New York: Teachers College Press.

Chadwick, J., & Meux, M. (1971). Procedures for value analysis. In L. E. Metcalf (Ed.). *Values education.* 41st yearbook. Washington, DC: National Council for the Social Studies.

Colby, A., & Damon, W. (1992). *Some do care: Contemporary lives of moral commitment.* New York: Free Press.

Cole, M., & Cole, S. R. (1989). *The development of children.* New York: Scientific American Books.

Damon, W. (1988). *The moral child.* New York: Free Press.

Evans, M. D. (1993). Using classroom debates as a learning tool. *Social Education, 57,* 370.

4 of 10 censorship attempts succeed. (September 2, 1993). Raleigh, NC. *The News & Observer,* p. 9a.

Gibbs, J. (1977). Kohlberg's stages of moral development: A constructive critique. *Harvard Educational Review, 47,* 43–61.

Gilligan, C. (1982). *In a different voice.* Cambridge, MA: Harvard University Press.

Hunt, M. P., & Metcalf, L. E. (1968). *Teaching high school social studies: Problems in reflective thinking and social understanding* (2nd ed.). New York: Harper & Row.

Johnson, D. W., & Johnson, R. T. (1988). Critical thinking through structured controversy. *Educational Leadership, 45*(8), 58–64.

Kelly, T. E. (1986). Discussing controversial issues: Four perspectives on the teacher's role. *Theory and Research in Social Education, 14,* 113–138.

Kohlberg, L. (1976). The cognitive-developmental approach to moral education. In P. H. Martorella (Ed.), *Social studies strategies: Theory into practice.* New York: Harper & Row.

Kohlberg, L. (1980). Educating for a just society: An updated and revised statement. In B. Munsey (Ed.), *Moral development, moral education, and Kohlberg.* Birmingham, AL: Religious Education Press.

Kurtines, W., & Grief, E. B. (1974). The development of moral thought: Review and evaluation of Kohlberg's approach. *Psychological Bulletin, 81,* 453–470.

Lickona, T. (1991). *Education for character.* New York: Bantam.

Lockwood, A. L. (1985). A place for ethical reasoning in the curriculum. *The Social Studies, 76,* 264–268.

Lockwood, A. L., & Harris, D. E. (1985). *Reasoning with democratic values: Ethical problems in United States history.* New York: Teachers College Press.

Martorella, P. H. (1977). Teaching geography through value strategies. In G. A. Manson & M. K. Ridd (Eds.), *New perspectives on geographic education: Putting theory into practice.* Dubuque, IA: Kendall/Hunt.

Muessig, R. H. (Ed.). (1975). *Controversial issues in the social studies.* Washington, DC: National Council for the Social Studies.

National Council for the Social Studies. (1967). *Academic freedom and the social studies teacher.* (1967). Washington, DC: Author.

Newmann, F. M., with Oliver, D. W. (1970). *Clarifying public controversy: An approach to teaching social studies.* Boston: Little, Brown.

Noddings, N. (1984). *Caring: A feminine approach to ethics and moral education.* Berkeley, CA: University of California Press.

Oliver, D. W., & Shaver, J. P. (1966). *Teaching public issues in the high school.* Boston: Houghton Mifflin.

Olner, P. (1976). *Teaching elementary school social studies.* Orlando, FL: Harcourt.

Osgood, C. E., Suci, G. J., & Tannenbaum, P. H. (1957). *The measurement of meaning.* Urbana, IL: University of Illinois Press.

Piaget, J. (1965). *The moral judgment of the child.* M. Gabain (Trans.). New York: Free Press.

Rokeach, M. (1968). *Beliefs, attitudes and values: A theory of organization and change.* San Francisco: Jossey-Bass.

Shaver, J. P., & Strong, W. (1976). *Facing value decisions: Rationale-building for teachers.* Belmont, CA: Wadsworth.

Triandis, H. C. (1971). *Attitude and attitude change.* New York: John Wiley.

Witches want tale to vanish from school. (May 28 1992). Raleigh, NC. *The News & Observer,* p. 5a.

# PART III

# Analyzing and Improving Social Studies Teaching and Learning

CHAPTER 9

# Preparing Students to Live in a Global and Culturally Diverse World

*What role should our nation play in the world?*

*In the twenty-first century, what will be the relationship of the United States to the rest of the world?*

*To what extent is our national identity sacrificed as we become globally interdependent?*

*Will heightened global awareness foster cooperation or breed divisiveness?*

*Will our cultural diversity enrich us or fragment us into competing ethnic enclaves?*

*Reflective, competent, and concerned citizens of the twenty-first century increasingly will be confronted with questions such as these. In answering, they will need to balance immediate national interests with those of the world as a whole. As members of an interconnected world, they also must be sensitive to the cultural differences that exist among nations.*

## BALANCING NATIONAL AND GLOBAL CONCERNS

Appeals to citizens to advance our national interests often invoke themes that emphasize *patriotism* (i.e., support for your country) and *nationalism* (i.e., place interests of your country above others). In contrast, advocates for a global perspective challenge us to consider "the greatest good for the greatest number" or the concerns of *all* nations, including our own.

One of the positive aspects of patriotism and nationalism is the creation of a sense of community, of belonging to a larger enterprise and sharing in a collective tradition. We identify with our nation's victories and defeats, pride and shame in such events as the Olympic games, wars, explorations in space, and concern for the environment.

Patriotism and nationalism also can be cohesive forces that bind citizens together. These forces can encourage people to work cooperatively, contribute to the next generation's welfare, and if necessary, be willing to sacrifice their lives for the common good.

Extreme patriotism and nationalism, however, can lead to the oppression of dissident minorities and hatred and distrust of other nations. These forces can create barriers to greater understanding across cultures and reduce the opportunities for people to work together to achieve common goals. They also can create an exaggerated sense of superiority, as occurred in Nazi Germany. Additionally, in an era where an increasing number of nations possess both nuclear weapons and unstable political leadership, excessive patriotism and nationalism can threaten the very existence of the world.

In addition to constructively channeled patriotism and nationalism, a heightened level of global awareness in an increasingly interdependent and shrinking world also is essential (Anderson, 1991; Tye & Tye, 1992). Potentially, the benefits of increasing and strengthening global linkages are enormous, including vast economic, cultural, and environmental gains. At the same time, global awareness reveals our national stake in finding solutions to problems that require the attention of all nations.

Ramler (1991) has stated:

> Now, at the edge of the 21st century, all the countries of the world are interconnected in virtually every aspect of life. World markets have been developed [that] offer consumer goods, labor, technology, and energy. The global economy irrevocably ties the economic health of the U.S. to events abroad. Thus, the U.S. must continually redefine its position within the context of global development.
>
> Today the flow of ideas, information, and services is linked globally; and these linkages reach each household and every person. The flow includes the arts, the sciences, sports, medicine, tourism, and entertainment, as well as such unfortunate phenomena as drug traffic, disease, and environmental damage. (p. 44)

## Global Education in an Interconnected World

Global concern involves both an understanding of the nature and interdependence of other nations and an interest in their welfare. It also means a willingness to identify and make important decisions that may provide long-term benefits for the lot of the world at the expense of short-term national interests. Global education, in turn, refers to the process of engendering global concern in our citizens.

> Global education refers to efforts to cultivate in young people a perspective of the world which emphasizes the interconnections among cultures, species, and the planet. The purpose of global education is to develop in youth the knowledge, skills, and attitudes needed to live effectively in a world possessing limited natural resources and characterized by ethnic diversity, cultural pluralism, and increasing interdependence. (National Council, 1981, p. 1)

Angell and Avery (1992) have emphasized the importance of tying world issues to events and objects within students' immediate environment in global education (see also Merryfield & Remy, 1995). One of the ways that this can be accomplished is for students to discover social, political, and economic linkages between their community and the rest of the world (Chartock, 1991).

Some social studies educators have urged that the entire social studies curriculum adopt a global focus. For example, Kniep (1989) has proposed such a program developed around the five themes of *interdependence, change, culture, scarcity,* and *conflict* and four categories of persistent problems: *environmental concerns, human rights, peace and security,* and *national/international development.* His ideas are discussed in more detail in Chapter 3.

Several projects have developed special materials for addressing salient global issues. Two examples are the *Choices for the 21st Century Education Project* and the *Refugee Awareness Program* (TRAP). The *Choices Project* at the Watson Institute for International Studies at Brown University (Box 1948, Providence, RI 02912) has produced a series of inexpensive units for secondary students that address America's global policies. Sample units, which are updated periodically, are:

- *U.S. Immigration Policy in an Unsettled World*
- *Global Environmental Problems: Implications for U.S. Policy*
- *U.S. Trade Policy: Competing in a Global Economy*
- *The Role of the United States in a Changing World*

The Center's materials engage students in analyzing alternative future scenarios based on certain assumptions and value choices. For example, in the unit *The Role of the United States in a Changing World*, students explore four alternate paths for U.S. policy over the next decade and assert and defend their choice. A sample segment from one of the activities in the unit is shown in Figure 9.1.

TRAP at North Carolina State University (Department of Curriculum and Instruction, Box 7801, Raleigh, NC 27695-7801) focuses on refugee

**Figure 9.1**
**Sample from "The Role of the United States in a Changing World"**

**The Futures in Perspective—Teacher's Guide**

| | *Future 1* | *Future 2* | *Future 3* | *Future 4* |
|---|---|---|---|---|
| What is the greatest threat facing the United States beyond its borders? | Aggressive dictatorships present the greatest threat to the United States. Ruthless tyrants not only terrorize their own people but strive to expand their power at the expense of their neighbors by building up dangerous military machines. | International instability presents the greatest threat to the United States. In a world on the brink of chaos, sudden changes in the international order may upset the world's economy and plunge still more countries into conflict, even nuclear war. | Global crises, such as environmental problems, refugees, and AIDS, present the greatest threat to the United States. The growing interdependence of the planet means that U.S. problems cannot be separated from the problems affecting the world as a whole. | Overseas entanglements, which divert us from the problems we face at home, present the greatest threat to the United States. We cannot afford to pour money into foreign affairs while our cities decay and our educational system declines. |
| What should we learn from the Cold War? | The Cold War showed that U.S. resolve and commitment are capable of defeating the forces opposed to freedom and democracy. | The Cold War showed that cautious diplomacy, even with our enemies, maintains stability and prevents war between military superpowers. | The Cold War showed that competition for world domination sparks wars and conflict throughout the globe. | The Cold War showed that placing foreign affairs at the top of our priorities allows our so-called allies to take economic advantage of us. |
| What principles should guide our policy on economic aid to developing countries? | We should use aid to encourage governments to adopt democratic principles and respect human rights. | We should give aid to countries that are willing to serve U.S. foreign policy interests. | We should give greater amounts of aid to international organizations to help improve conditions in poor countries and to address environmental problems. | We should end foreign aid, except for humanitarian emergencies, and redirect the money toward solving problems here at home. |
| What should be the U.S. role in the UN? | The United States should steer the UN toward taking a more active stance in promoting the American values of democracy, human rights, and tolerance for diversity throughout the world. | The United States should use the UN as a tool to restrain the ambitions of Russia, China, and other potentially dangerous powers, and to maintain international stability. | The United States should support efforts to strengthen the UN's ability to maintain international peace, address global problems, and improve economic conditions in the developing world. | The United States should withdraw its troops from UN peacekeeping operations and reduce its overall involvement in the UN. |

From *Teacher's Resource Book,* Choices Education Project, p. 14. Center for Foreign Policy Development at Brown University, Box 1948, Providence, RI 02912.

issues and their implications for world peace (Martorella, 1993). Around this theme, TRAP has developed instructional materials for the middle and secondary grades. These consist of cooperative learning materials and interactive video kits that incorporate laserdiscs and HyperCard stacks (see Chapter 11).

In Chapter 11, we also consider some illustrations of how electronic networks that link schools and students around the nation and the world are being used to spur global education. These involve the transmission from computer to computer of information that includes print, video, and audio data. *World Classroom* is an example of a program that attempts to engage students in developing a world community using telecommunications.

## Peace Education

A number of organizations have promoted the theme of world peace as a focus for global education. These include *Peace Links Educators for Social Responsibility, The Center for Teaching Peace, The International Center for Cooperation and Conflict Resolution,* and *The United States Institute for Peace.*

The concerns of these organizations include teaching students about the ways that wars, violent acts, and general conflicts are initiated and how they can be avoided and controlled. These organizations also seek to acquaint students with the threat of potential nuclear destruction and the effects of warfare. They also promote alternative strategies for maintaining peace and stability throughout the world.

Some organizations also produce curriculum materials that promote peace education. Examples of materials and programs that have been developed, along with their sources, are shown in Figure 9.2.

**Figure 9.2**
**Examples of Peace Education Materials**

J. McGinnis and K. McGinnis, *Education for Peace and Justice: A Manual for Teachers*, 4 vols., St. Louis, MO: The Institute for Peace and Justice, 2747 Rutger Street, St. Louis, MO 63104.

G. C. Abrams and F. C. Schmidt, *Peace Is in Our Hands*, Philadelphia: Jane Addams Peace Association, 1213 Race Street, Philadelphia, PA 19107.

Educators for Social Responsibility, *Perspectives: A Teaching Guide to Concepts of Peace*, Cambridge, MA: Educators for Social Responsibility, 23 Garden Street, Cambridge, MA 02138.

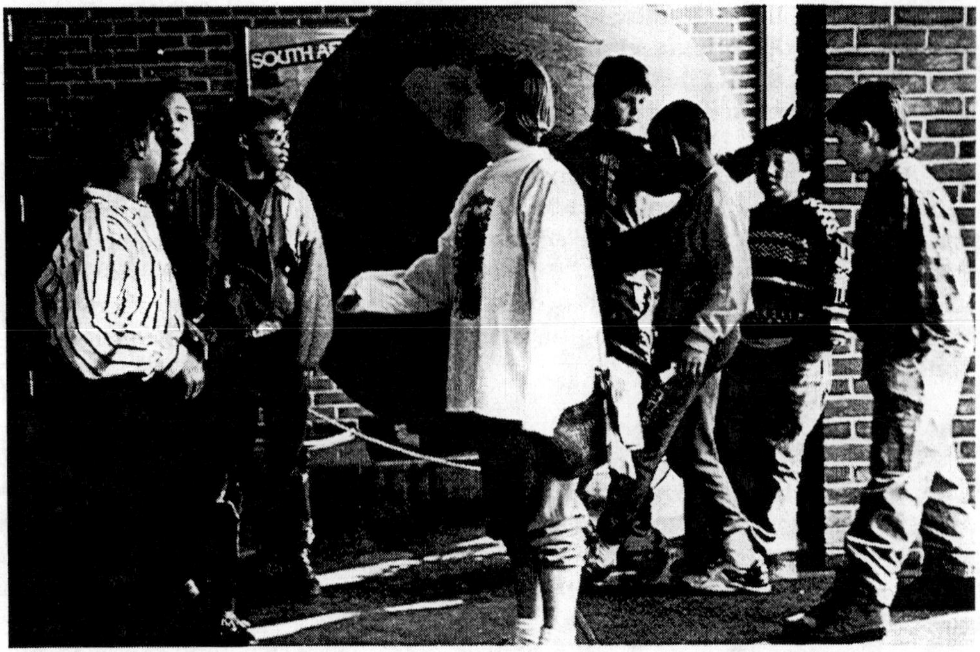


**The challenge of multicultural education is to capitalize on our diversity to enrich social studies instruction.**

## MULTICULTURAL EDUCATION

Each day's wave of current events reinforces our awareness that our globally interdependent world is a melange of people of different colors, religions, languages, and customs. Our own nation is a microcosm of this diversity. Gaining insights into these ongoing events and their social, political, and economic implications is the essence of *multicultural education.*

Multicultural education has special significance for our nation because of its rich mix of racial and ethnic groups. Also, multicultural education intersects with the major themes in our history and our abiding national commitment to equity in the treatment of citizens.

In the past half-century, the move for equity for all racial and ethnic groups in our society received a dramatic impetus from the civil rights struggles of the 1950s and 1960s and the attendant legislation and judicial rulings that they spawned. The wave of moral indignation and political restructuring generated by the succession of historic, often tragic, events that came to be known as "the civil rights movement" forced the nation to attack the roots of racism.

The movement began as a series of concrete, dramatic steps by a few brave individuals on behalf of fundamental justice for African Americans.

By the 1980s, it had blossomed into an international outcry on behalf of people and groups everywhere who suffered oppression or injustice at the hands of those in power. In the United States, this movement included an introspective analysis of the treatment of ethnic groups that had suffered dramatically, consistently, and extensively from racism, such as Native Americans, Hispanic Americans, Latino Americans, and Asian Americans, as well as African Americans.

The outcry also forced an examination of our treatment of ethnic and religious minorities in general. By the close of the decade, American ideals were globalized into a passion for social justice for all human beings and an increasing sensitivity for the rights of minorities across the world. Apartheid in South Africa and the treatment of Palestinians in the Middle East, for example, became hotly debated political issues in our nation. The amorphous mass of displaced Americans, the homeless, and the homeless of the world, upwards of 18 million refugees who have neither home nor country, became part of the American political agenda.

During the 1990s, in the wake of the dissolution of the Soviet Union, the reorganization of Eastern Europe, ethnic violence throughout the world, and the Cold War's demise, there was a renewed pragmatic urgency to our efforts for multicultural understanding. There also are increasing global political and economic reasons for our schools to emphasize multicultural education. As Sobol (1990) underscored: "[W]e live in a small and multicultural world. If we wish to communicate effectively with the majority of the world's people—who are not white and who don't speak English—we must know more about how they see the world, how they make sense of experience, why they behave as they do" (p. 28).

Sensitizing students to the rich American tradition of cultural pluralism and its implications is a fundamental part of the process of multicultural education. As Bennett (1986) observed:

> A basic assumption of multicultural education is that different ethnic groups can retain much of their original culture if they so choose, and can be multicultural at the same time. In other words, it is believed that people can learn about multiple ways of perceiving, behaving, and evaluating so that they can conform to those aspects of the macroculture that are necessary for societal well-being, without eroding acceptance of their original ethnicity. It is assumed that ethnic traditions and beliefs can be preserved under conditions of intercultural contact that will reduce myths and stereotypes associated with previously unknown groups. These are big assumptions. (p. 56)

Banks (1984) has contended that, in its role of supporting cultural pluralism and promoting multicultural education, the school should "help students to break out of their cultural enclaves and to broaden their cultural perspectives. Students need to learn that there are cultural and ethnic alternatives within our society that they can freely embrace" (p. 9). He observed further: "The major goal of multicultural education is to change the total educational environment so that it promotes a respect for the wide range of cultural groups and enables all cultural groups to experience equal educational opportunity" (p. 23).

What multicultural education advocates have proposed requires an ongoing commitment on the part of all teachers and schools, as well as key actors—such as parents—in the social environment beyond the school. Many skills associated with multicultural education are developed slowly over time. Some, such as perspective taking, are acquired only when students reach the appropriate developmental stage. And all are affected by the training individuals receive in the home and the experiences they have outside of the school.

Even preschoolers learn from their home and neighborhood environment to imitate and promote attitudes of tolerance and intolerance, appreciation and rejection of individuals and groups that are culturally different (Byrnes, 1987; King, 1990). Byrnes (1988) has warned that, for example, in some families: "Children may be told that people belonging to certain minority groups will kidnap them or hurt them if they aren't careful. Some children are scolded or even beaten if they play with children of different races, religions, or socio-economic status" (p. 268).

## Emerging Issues in Multicultural Education

Is there such a thing as "an American culture"? To some extent, we all share in an amorphous cultural framework that makes us "American" (Spindler & Spindler, 1990). In addition, we have potential points of cultural reference, should we care to use them, that allow us to distinguish ourselves from the larger cultural American framework. We may choose to identify with one or more subcultures that are distinguished by distinctive ways of acting, thinking, and feeling (Kleg, 1993).

Cultural groups that are identified by ethnicity, **ethnic groups,** for example, view themselves as belonging together and gaining identification by virtue of their ancestry, real or imagined, and common customs, traditions, or experiences, such as language, history, religion, or nationality. Individuals often use the terms *cultural* or *ethnic* interchangeably in referring to themselves and others. Because many of the different groups in our nation prize those distinguishing characteristics that give rise to their individuality, we regard our nation as being *culturally pluralistic* or *multicultural.*

Our distinctive differences often divide us, as well as enrich us. The hatred and violence that spewed forth from Eastern Europe in the aftermath of Yugoslavia's disintegration is a chilling reminder. Racism, prejudice, and hostility still stalk the world, including our own nation: "Today racial and ethnic prejudices, discrimination, scapegoating, and other forms of aggression continue to characterize the human experience" (Kleg, 1993, p. 1).

Kleg has provided an excellent sample list of concepts that are central to students' understanding of issues related to prejudice. These appear in Figure 9.3.

**Figure 9.3**
**Sample of Concepts**

| | | | |
|---|---|---|---|
| 1. affirmative action | 14. discrimination | 25. perception | 36. self-fulfilling prophecy |
| 2. anomie | 15. ethnic group | 26. projection | 37. self-hate |
| 3. anti-locution | 16. ethnicity | 27. predilection | 38. Social Darwinism |
| 4. anti-Semitism | 17. ethnocentrism | 28. prejudice | 39. social distance |
| 5. apartheid | 18. ethnocide | 29. race | 40. stereotype |
| 6. aryan | 19. frustration-aggression hypothesis | 30. racism* | 41. tolerance |
| 7. assimilation | 20. genocide | 31. relative deprivation | 42. vicious circle of discrimination |
| 8. attitude | 21. human rights | 32. scapegoating | 43. xenophobia |
| 9. bifurcation | 22. integration | 33. segregation | |
| 10. bigotry | 23. (social) majority | 34. selective exposure | |
| 11. civil rights | 24. (social) minority | 35. selective perception | |
| 12. cultural relativism | | | |
| 13. desegregation | | | |

* including averse and dominative racism

*Note.* From *Racism and Hate Prejudice* (p. 246) by M. Kleg, 1993, Albany, NY: State University of New York Press.

The key issue in multicultural education for many is: How can we celebrate the richness and uniqueness of our diversity and the multiple perspectives that differing groups offer, while at the same time stress the common bonds that unite and strengthen our nation politically, economically, and socially? The impassioned debate that continues over this issue touches many areas (Banks, 1991; Bullard, 1992; Martel, 1992; Ogbu, 1992; Ravitch, 1992). The fallout has implications for how textbooks, instructional materials, and curriculum in schools will be shaped in the future.

The heated debate includes disagreements over such matters as the language that is used be to label groups, the factual accuracy of the existing alternative historical perspectives (e.g., "Eurocentric vs. Afrocentric"), whose perspectives should be represented, and which perspective should be the dominant or "mainstream" one. The argument also has taken on a note of urgency. As Banks (1992) has noted: "People of color, women, and other marginalized groups are demanding that their voices, visions, and perspectives be included in the curriculum" (p. 33).

Addressing the issue of perspectives is crucial to multicultural understanding and, in fact, an informed analysis of all social data. For example, in his seminal text, *Red, White, and Black: The Peoples of Early America*, Nash (1982) argued that:

> [T]o cure the historical amnesia that has blotted out so much of our past we must reexamine American history as the interactions of many peoples from a wide range of cultural backgrounds over a period of many centuries. . . . Africans were not merely enslaved. Indians were not merely driven from the land. . . .
>
> To break through the notions of Indians and Africans being kneaded like dough according to the whims of invading European societies, we must abandon the notion of "civilized" and "primitive" people. . . .
>
> Africans, Indians, and Europeans all had developed societies that functioned successfully in their respective environments. None thought of themselves as inferior people. (pp. 2–3)

Similar to Nash, Benitez (1994) has advocated that teachers employ an "alternative perspectives approach" in teaching history. "With this approach," she wrote,

> the teacher presents historical events from alternative, i.e., non-male, non-Judaeo-Christian, or non-Northwestern European, perspectives. . . . The following are examples using this approach:
>
> - **Pre-colonial**. Discuss the concept of discovery with the students. Point out that Asians immigrated via Alaska and that more than 500 native cultures thrived before the Europeans landed in North America.
> - **Colonial.** Point out that the Spanish colonized more than one-third of the present United States, including Florida, Louisiana, Texas, New Mexico, Arizona, and California, and that some Spanish settlements preceded British settlements by almost a century. . . .
> - **Seventeenth century through today**. Review the history of European settlements in North America from the perspective of the mainland American Indian. Ask students to write about or discuss how they would feel as an American Indian at several different historical junctures and vis-a-vis different groups of Europeans, taking into account the changing perceptions American Indians had of the white newcomers. Then ask students to write an essay entitled "The Invasion from the East" from the perspective of an American Indian. (p. 143)

Merryfield and Remy (1995) have emphasized the importance of involving students in firsthand experiences with people from different cultures as a way to gain insights into their perspectives. Samples of the strategies the authors advocate are:

> Students practice active listening by interviewing people from another culture.
> *Example:* Students interview a Vietnamese immigrant about his perspectives on refugees and political asylum.
>
> Students work cooperatively with people from another culture toward common goals.
> *Example:* Students work with employees from a local Honda plant to develop a video on "cross cultural understanding and economic cooperation." . . .

Students are immersed in another culture.
*Example:* Students raise money and plan a study tour to visit rain forests in Costa Rica. (Merryfield & Remy, 1995, p. 20)

## Designing Strategies for Multicultural Education

Henderson (1992) offered an apt illustration of how Ms. Smiley, a middle-grade teacher, reflectively brought a multicultural education perspective to both her planning and development of a social studies lesson (see Figure 9.4).

Similarly, Banks (1993) has suggested that in social studies classes multicultural education might be advanced by including five different perspectives that represent different sources of information (see Figure 9.5). Each perspective offers students a different insight from which to construct a more informed grasp of an historical event. Chapter 4 includes an illustration of how these five perspectives could be incorporated into a unit dealing with the Westward Movement.

Apart from including multiple perspectives, some experiences that effective multicultural education programs might offer students include:

1. Learning how and where to obtain objective, accurate information about diverse cultural groups.
2. Identifying and examining positive accounts of diverse cultural groups or individuals.

**Figure 9.4**
**Sample Multicultural Lesson**

As she [Ms. Smiley] plans her unit on Columbus, she looks for materials that help her critically examine the topic. She reads Kirkpatrick Sale's *The Conquest of Paradise: Christopher Columbus and the Columbian Legacy*.... [New York: Knopf, 1990], which questions Columbus' motives and ecological values. Based on this examination, she decides to include activities that will broaden her students' multicultural perspectives. She shows students a segment of an old cowboy movie in which Native Americans are portrayed as savages. Then she asks students to list adjectives that express how they feel about Native Americans. While teaching the unit, Ms. Smiley will present information from the Native American as well as the European point of view. When the students have completed the unit, she will ask them to make another list of adjectives expressing how they feel about Native Americans. She will analyze and discuss any differences between the two lists with her students. (p. 7)

*Note.* From *Reflective Teaching: Becoming an Inquiring Educator* (p. 7) by J. G. Henderson, 1992, Englewood Cliffs, NJ: Merrill/Prentice Hall.

**Figure 9.5**
**A Multiperspective Approach to Multicultural Education**

| *Perspective* | *Source of Information* |
|---|---|
| Personal/Cultural | Students' personal and cultural experiences |
| Popular | Mass media, pop culture, and films |
| Mainstream Academic | Research from mainstream scholars |
| Transformative Academic | Research that challenges mainstream findings or methodologies |
| School | Information in school texts and related media |

*Note.* Adapted from "The Canon Debate, Knowledge Construction, and Multicultural Education" (p. 7) by J. Banks, 1993, *Educational Researcher,* 4–14.

3. Learning tolerance for diversity through experimentation in the school and classroom with alternate customs and practices.
4. Encountering, where possible, firsthand positive experiences with diverse cultural groups.
5. Developing empathic behavior (trying to put yourself in the shoes of a person from a different cultural group) through role playing and simulations.
6. Practicing using "perspective glasses;" that is, looking at an event, historical period, or issue through the perspective of another cultural group or gender.
7. Improving the self-esteem of all students.
8. Identifying and analyzing cultural stereotypes.
9. Identifying concrete cases of discrimination and prejudice, including those taken from students' experiences.

These nine types of experiences all aim to heighten students awareness of the diversity among us while respecting their own cultural anchors.

## Guidelines for Selecting Appropriate Curriculum Materials for Multicultural Education

As they observe and participate in the evolving debates concerning the most appropriate forms of multicultural education, teachers should consider several general propositions. These may prove helpful in identifying and examining subject matter and working with students:

1. All historical accounts are only selective representations of an event, and they reflect the background or perspective of the recorder.

2. Obtaining a variety of different perspectives on an event often extends our understanding of it. Each perspective may provide information the others missed or dismissed as unimportant. Depending on our objective and the issue, one perspective also may be more helpful than another.
3. Often multiple perspectives of an event are directly contradictory. In that event, we must make a judgment as to which is the most informed or reliable.
4. For many issues, we may not have access to all of the different perspectives that exist. For others, the perspectives we would like to have do not exist or have not been discovered.
5. Regardless of which perspectives are obtained and whether they are shared in oral or written form, we should hold them to the standards of the best available scholarship.

To aid in the selection of multicultural curriculum materials, a number of detailed guidelines exist. As an example, Etlin (1988) provided a basic five-point checklist for teachers to consider in assessing the appropriateness of multicultural materials.

> 1. Does the text or other items [instructional material] give proportionate coverage to our country's different ethnic groups?
> 2. Does it present them in the variety of roles and situations that all our country's people deal with, rather than limit them to one or two stereotypical contexts?
> 3. Does it present stories and historical incidents from the point of view of the people concerned, whatever their ethnic group, rather than that of the traditional single-culture U.S. society?
> 4. Does it use language that recognizes the dignity of the groups involved, not using demeaning slang terms? Does it avoid using dialect unless it's presented respectfully and serves a necessary purpose?
> 5. If it's fiction or a reader, does the story line avoid distributing power and competence on the basis of ethnic group stereotypes? (p. 11)

The National Council for the Social Studies (NCSS) also has published a more extensive set of guidelines for multicultural education: *Curriculum Guidelines for Multicultural Education* (National Council, 1992). The document provides 23 categories of guidelines for evaluating a school's program, along with a rating form. The NCSS guidelines also develop a rationale for multicultural education.

## Resources for Multicultural Education

A fine assortment of instructional materials also is available to aid teachers in dealing with multicultural issues. The references at the end of the chapter include a selection of books that have lists of student materials, organizations that provide resources, and reference materials and periodicals for teachers.

Many organizations, including the NCSS, also provide collections of written materials and media that are periodically updated. The NCSS, for example, each year in the April/May issue of *Social Education* publishes a list of notable trade books that includes a selection of works with multicultural themes.

Examples of materials and organizations that provide resources for multicultural education include the following ones.

### *Instructional Materials*

- *Building Ethnic Collections: An Annotated Guide for School Media Centers and Public Libraries,* Libraries Unlimited, PO Box 263, Littleton, CO 80160.
- *Ethnic American Minorities: A Guide to Media and Materials,* R. R. Bowker, PO Box 1807, Ann Arbor, MI 48106.
- *Materials and Resources for Teaching Ethnic Studies: An Annotated Bibliography,* Social Science Education Consortium, 855 Broadway, Boulder, CO 80302.
- *Our Family, Our Friends, Our World: An Annotated Guide to Significant Multicultural Books for Children and Teenagers,* R. R. Bowker, 121 Chanlon Road, New Providence, NJ 07974.
- *Multicultural Perspectives in Music Education,* Music Educators National Conference, 1902 Association Drive, Reston, VA 22091.
- *Multicultural Education,* Caddo Gap Press, 3145 Geary Boulevard, San Francisco, CA 94118.

### *Organizations*

Afro-Am Educational Materials
809 Wabash Avenue
Chicago, IL 60605

The Anti-Defamation League of B'nai B'rith
823 United Nations Plaza
New York, NY 10017.

Asia Society
469 Union Avenue
Westbury, NY 11590.

Asian/Pacific American Heritage Council
Box 11036
Alexandria, VA 22312

Council for Indian Education
517 Rim Rock Road, PO Box 31215
Billings, MT 59107

The Council on Interracial Books for Children
1841 Broadway
New York, NY 10023.

National Council of La Raza
1725 Eye Street, NW
Washington, DC 20006

Stanford Program on International and Cross-Cultural Education
Littlefield Center, Room 14
Stanford University
Stanford, CA 94305-5013

## GENDER ISSUES IN MULTICULTURAL EDUCATION

Multicultural education embraces the analysis of gender issues (King, 1990). As a reflection of the broader social ferment concerning equity for all groups within our society, discrimination on the basis of gender has come under increasing attack. **Sex-role stereotyping** is one aspect of gender issues. It refers to the practice of attributing roles, behaviors, and aspirations to individuals or groups solely on the basis of gender.

Discrimination based on gender may surface in any number of ways in school contexts. It may occur, for example, through teachers' patterns of activity assignments, group placements, the content of compliments and criticisms, and types of behavior tolerated. Examples range from the treatment of females in textbooks and curriculum materials (e.g., women are absent from historical periods or have stereotyped roles); to differential treatment of males and females in the classroom (e.g., girls are asked to bake the cookies for the party and the boys to set up the tables); to erroneous assumptions about attitudes and cognitive abilities (e.g., girls are assumed to be more emotional than boys); to institutional practices that appear to favor one gender over another (e.g., males are favored over females for administrative positions).

Where sex-role stereotyping occurs in instructional materials, textbooks, and the mass media, probably one of the most effective ways for teachers to combat it is to challenge it directly. They can first sensitize students to its presence through a newspaper activity similar to the one in Figure 9.6 and then examine analytically factual data and counterexamples. This approach can have the residual effect of alerting students to stereotypes of all varieties, including those that are racial, ethnic, or political.

Another strategy is to provide students with curriculum materials and trade books that reflect the perspectives, contributions, and achievements of women (Zarnowski, 1988). A case in point is the book *The Gentle Tamers* by Dee Brown (1981), which includes firsthand accounts of women

**Figure 9.6**
**Activity to Sensitize Students to Sex-Role Stereotyping**

**Newspapers Look at Females and Males**

1. In a group, conduct an audit of gender representation in your newspaper. Look at the pictures, read the news stories, and answer the following questions about the way females and males are depicted:

| | Females | Males |
|---|---|---|
| How many individuals are pictured in photos? | ____________ | ____________ |
| What are they doing? | ____________ | ____________ |
| Why are they pictured? | ____________ | ____________ |
| In what section did you find the photos? | ____________ | ____________ |

2. Compile your information and display it in a way that can't be analyzed: a graph, a data retrieval chart, or a Venn diagram like the one on the right.

3. Discuss your findings. How were the two genders represented? How would you explain your findings?

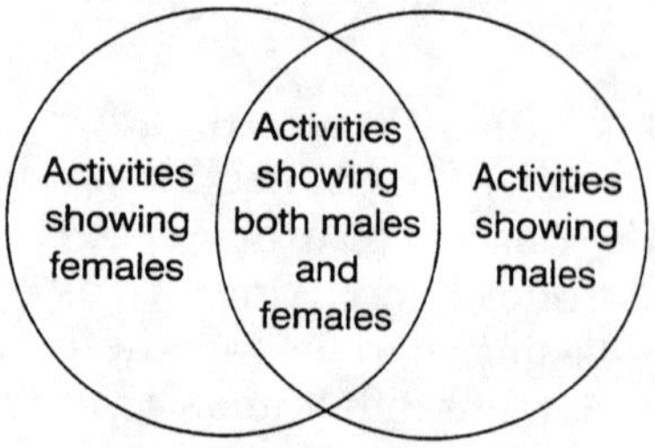


Reprinted with permission from the Newspaper Association of America Foundation.

who helped build the West. Included are stories from the accounts of Elizabeth Custer, Carry Nation, Virginia Reed, and Josephine Meeker.

## Women's Perspectives in History

Gender issues extend beyond identifying stereotypes to include the subject of women's perspectives on events and issues. Noddings (1991/1992) noted: "If women's culture were taken more seriously in educational planning, social studies and history might have a very different emphasis. Instead of moving from war to war, ruler to ruler, one political campaign to the next, we would give far more attention to social issues" (p. 68). She has called for more attention in the social studies curriculum to issues and practices that she considers central to women's experiences (e.g., intergenerational responsibility and nonviolent conflict resolution).

As a special effort to redress the relative absence of women and their contributions and perspectives in written history, the field of women's history has developed. Underscoring the neglect of women in the history of our nation, the Congress, in declaring March *Women's History Month* wrote:

> American women of every race, class, and ethnic background helped found the Nation in countless recorded and unrecorded ways as servants, slaves, nurses, nuns, homemakers, industrial workers, teachers, reformers, soldiers, and

> pioneers; and . . . served as early leaders in the forefront of every major progressive social change movement, not only to secure their own right of suffrage and equal opportunity, but also in the abolitionist movement, the emancipation movement, the industrial labor union movement, and the modern civil rights movement; and . . . despite these contributions, the role of American women in history has been consistently overlooked and undervalued in the body of American history. . . .

The National Women's History Project (PO Box 3716, 77838 Bell Road, Windsor, CA 95492-8515) and the Upper Midwest Women's History Center (6300 Walker Street, St. Louis Park, MN 55416) are examples of attempts to expand the focus of traditional history. These two organizations provide a woman's perspective on historical events as well as information concerning the vital roles that women have played in history. Both projects have produced an array of curriculum materials for K through 12 social studies classes. These include biographies, videos, posters units, photo, and reference books. Materials deal with women in the U.S. and other nations.

*Women in the World Curriculum Resources* (1030 Spruce Street, Berkeley, CA 94707), in contrast, uses dramatized accounts from world history to provide a female voice (see sample activity in Figure 9.7). Using data from different periods in women's history, the project has created a series of teaching units that recount historical events through the eyes of fictitious young women.

One result of students's increased awareness of global and multicultural issues often is a developing sense of **social consciousness.** Social consciousness is an awareness that in society citizens have both a right and a responsibility to identify and redress some social needs, in short, to help build a better world.

Social consciousness may be directed toward situations that can be easily changed and to actions that will have minimal impact on society. It also can be focused on problems that require complex changes and whose alterations will have far-reaching consequences. Ultimately, social consciousness also breeds social responsibility. Citizens of any age exhibit consciousness of social issues when they decide something in their society requires redress.

In a democracy, each citizen is relatively free to identify the social issues he or she wishes to address. In developing concerned citizens, teachers have the responsibility to encourage youngsters to identify areas of social need and the corresponding strategies for change. This requires giving students "the opportunity to contribute to the lives of others and to the improvement of the world around them" (Berman, 1990, p. 78).

The general message that a student should derive from activities that encourage social consciousness is that, for a society to prosper and improve, citizens must in some way give, as well as receive: "Through citizenship, we receive a number of privileges as our birthright. At the same time, we also inherit the reciprocal responsibility to make some continuing contribution to our society."

**Figure 9.7**
**Sample Activity: Including a Female Voice in Studying World History**

**Women's Rights**
**Ancient Egypt and the United States**

I. Read this definition:

*Rights:* A right is a privilege which a person is owed. It is guaranteed by law.

*Examples:* right to vote; right to a free education.

II. Hold a class discussion about the meaning of a *right.* What are some rights we have in the United States? Do students have any rights? Do children have any rights? Can rights be taken away? Do you think rights have to sometimes be fought for? Do the rights people have differ according to the society in which they live? Can you give an example of this?

III. Compared to women in other ancient civilizations, Egyptian women had many rights. The following *Rights of Women in Ancient Egypt and United States* form lists some of the rights women had in ancient Egypt. Use this form to compare their rights to women's rights today by asking the opinion of your mother or of any adult woman. Read her the rights of women in ancient Egypt listed on the form and ask if she also has these rights. Write her answer, "yes," "no," or "don't know" in the space provided.

IV. Then ask her: what other rights do you think women in the United States have? What other rights do you think women would like to have that they do not have now? Which of the rights listed do you think women had in the United States in the nineteenth century?

V. In class, poll the students to discover everyone's answers. Write the results on the chalkboard. *Discuss:* Were women's rights in ancient Egypt similar to those women have today? What additional rights do women have today? What changes have there been in women's rights in the United States since the nineteenth century? How do you think these changes came about?

**More Research:**

1. Using the rights listed on the *Rights of Women in Ancient Egypt and United States* form find out if women in nineteenth century America had these rights. Find out how women achieved the rights they did not have in the past.
2. Find out if women in classical, ancient Greece had the rights listed on the form.
3. Find out the meaning of these terms: *equal rights, civil rights, birthright, human rights, women's rights, copyright.* Have these rights always existed for everyone? Which groups have had to struggle for these rights?

*Note.* From *Spindle stories: Three units on women's world history, book two* (pp. 1–2) by Lyn Reese, 1991, Berkeley, CA: Women in the World Curriculum Resource Project. Reprinted by permission.

**Figure 9.7**
**continued**

| Rights of Ancient Egyptian Women | Rights of Women in the United States: |
|---|---|
| I. *In Egypt women had a right to:* | *Do American women have the same rights?* Answer no, yes or don't know. |
| • keep anything they inherited from their parents when they married. | ________ |
| • share equally with their husband any wealth both partners acquired within their marriage. | ________ |
| • conduct business on their own. | ________ |
| • own and sell property. | ________ |
| • be a witness in a court case. | ________ |
| • represent themselves in court. | ________ |
| • make a will giving their wealth to whomever they wish. | ________ |
| • adopt children. | ________ |
| • go out in public and be in mixed company with men. | ________ |
| • keep their own name after their marriage. | ________ |
| • be supported by their ex-husband after a divorce. | ________ |
| • work at jobs other than being a "house-wife." | ________ |
| • seek any employment they are qualified for. | ________ |

II. What other rights do women in America have? ____________________

____________________

III. What other rights do you think women would like to have but do not now?

____________________

____________________

IV. Which of the rights listed do you think women had in the United States in the nineteenth century? ____________________

____________________

## Social Service Projects

An illustration of what an individual school can do to promote social consciousness and responsibility is a program implemented by the Ravenscroft School in Raleigh, NC. Ravenscroft has made social service part of the required curriculum.

Each month, students in the middle grades engage in **social service projects.** These include activities such as recycling, making sandwiches for a local soup kitchen, visiting the elderly, collecting toys and clothes for the needy, and spending time with disabled students from other schools. Teachers then build on the experiences and reflections of students and encourage them to do follow-up research on subjects such as the causes of poverty.

Other schools and consortia of schools across the United States are engaged in similar curricular efforts to encourage the development of social responsibility (Lewis, 1991). In 1992, Maryland became the first state to mandate community service by all students as part of graduation requirements. The law requires that all students in the middle and secondary school grades perform 75 hours of service in their communities.

# CURRENT AFFAIRS

Engaging students in significant current affairs discussions invariably involves some aspects of global education, multicultural education, or social consciousness. By guiding students through an analysis and interpretation of the "news," as reported by the media, teachers can use current events as vehicles to address significant curricular objectives.

Our students live in a society in which we are inundated with current affairs information through the popular media, especially television. No matter where one lives in the United States or the world, it is possible to access televised news throughout the day by cable, satellite, or antenna reception. The various print media similarly afford us multiple opportunities to learn about current affairs.

## Strategies for Analyzing Current Affairs

It's Friday. Time for current events!

Too often it happens that a certain day—usually the first or last of the week—is set aside in classrooms for "current events." When this practice occurs, students gain the impression that contemporary affairs are not an ongoing, vital part of everyday life.

Contemporary affairs at the local, national, and international levels should be incorporated naturally into the social studies curriculum throughout the year. Teachers should read a local paper regularly to identify significant events and issues. When current affairs have special significance, either for the local community, nation, or world, they also should be allowed to take precedence over the regularly scheduled subject matter.

Incorporating emerging current developments into the existing curriculum can demonstrate the vitality of the social studies and how the past, present, and future are linked. Merryfield and Remy (1995) illustrated how one teacher, Connie White, at Linden McKinley High School in Columbus, Ohio, reflectively and flexibly fused emerging events with the existing curriculum. White was concluding a discussion of the Crusades just as the Gulf War erupted.

> Although she had planned to teach a unit on African civilizations next, she decided to continue with the Arabs and focus on their achievements and their connections to the world today. She began with a discussion in which her students began to make connections with their previous work on Arab civilizations and the current conflict in the Persian Gulf. The students then worked in cooperative groups to develop timelines of historical antecedents and the role of the area in global conflicts. They used their information from the timelines to make transparencies of the changing borders in the Middle East so that as a class they could examine how power had changed hands over hundreds of years and the role of conflict in the region. (pp. 37–38)

To provide different viewpoints and stimulate discussion, Ms. White invited guest speakers. She also had students simulate a peace conference after they determined which countries should be included. Later, as a culminating activity, students shared their views concerning global conflicts with their counterparts in Geneva, Switzerland, using a computer and a modem (discussed later in this chapter and in Chapter 11).

**Bulletin Boards, Activities, and Current Events.** Students, especially in the middle grades, should be encouraged on an ongoing basis to bring to class or place on a special **living bulletin board** (i.e., one that grows as the class feeds it) pictures and articles that represent events that especially interest or puzzle them. Similarly, as each new unit or lesson is introduced, a teacher may encourage the class to identify materials or share information from the news that relates to the subject matter under study.

A teacher periodically also may stimulate an analysis of contemporary affairs by action-oriented activities. An example is a simulated newscast where the class is divided into "news desks." These might be the local, state, national, and international "desks."

Students can be assigned to one of the four desks and asked to prepare the evening's report of events at these levels. After brainstorming what the news is at their desk, each of the groups can select a newscaster to report the news. After the "newscast," the results can be discussed by the whole class for inaccuracies, interrelationships, and omissions—much like they might analyze real newscasts.

## Using Newspapers and Print Materials

Some of the major sources of print materials for learning about contemporary affairs are newspapers and periodicals. Many of the printed materials that are available at the "adult" level actually are written at a very low reading level, and they contain a number of instructive visual and chart materials. However, their intelligent use requires some understanding of how newspapers select, construct, often bias and distort, and feature stories (Kirman, 1992). We will consider these and other issues related to printed materials in more detail in Chapter 10.

Many newspapers and periodicals feature local or "colorful" news at the expense of national and international affairs. Among the major exceptions are *The New York Times* and the *Washington Post*. These are sold throughout the United States in most major metropolitan areas and are excellent sources of information for social studies teachers and secondary students.

**Student Versions of Newspapers and Periodicals.** Some publishers also have produced versions of weekly newspapers and periodicals for students that have an instructor's guide for the teacher. These publications are especially adapted for students in the middle and secondary grades and include materials that attempt to be both objective and interesting. Nonetheless, they have some of the same limitations as other printed materials.

Two examples of student newspapers are *Junior Scholastic* and *World-Wise*. Illustrations of periodicals are *COBBLESTONE* and *CALLIOPE*. These publications include teacher's manuals that suggest activities and discussion topics.

## Using Technology in Teaching About Current Affairs

Computer, video, and related technologies also make it possible for students to enrich current affairs activities by linking resources and individuals across the United States and in other countries over the **Internet** to create an **electronic global classroom** (Kurshan, 1991). A number of companies now provide easy access to the Internet, including world linkages and transmission of text, sound, and even video. Global Learning Corporation, for example, markets a program called WorldClassroom. This combines social studies and science projects that students in different countries share via computers, modems, communications software, and phone lines. AT&T's The Learning Network has a similar structure. In Chapter 11, we consider applications of the Internet and other computer-based technologies to global education in more detail.

Using simpler technologies, some schools have integrated the use of shortwave radios into the social studies curriculum. For example, students in Redford, Michigan, tuned into broadcasts in English from such countries as Australia, the Vatican, England, and Switzerland, and correlated the information they obtained with geographic instruction. Since world band radio reception is better in the evenings, students were permitted to sign out radios for home use.

For those schools that have access to cable television (about 70% of elementary and secondary schools), a wealth of resources exist. C-SPAN, for example, includes programming that covers both national and international issues (see Figure 9.8). Some television networks also have created special news programs for schools that have access to cable television. Turner Broadcasting System, producer of *CNN Newsroom*, The Discovery Channel, producer of *Assignment: Discovery*, and Whittle Communications, producer of *Channel One*, now provide news programs that may be taped free of charge under certain conditions.

For example, *CNN Newsroom* is a 15-minute, commercial-free program available daily over cable at no charge to schools. The program airs each weekday at 3:45 A.M. ET over the CNN cable network. Teachers can record the program on their VCR and use it later that morning or when they choose.

Each edition of the program begins with a news segment that covers the day's top stories. In addition, programs include topical features or "desks" as follows:

*Futures Desk*. A forecast of emerging trends in the world.

*International Desk*. An investigation of international news and events around the world.

*Business Desk*. An explanation of finances, economics, and the world of work.

*Science Desk*. A focus on latest developments in science and technology.

*Editor's Desk*. An in-depth analysis of the week's biggest stories.

## Guidelines for Developing Current Affairs Activities

Following are some general guidelines for developing current affairs activities. They include criteria for designing activities that can make a contribution to young citizens' understanding and use of current affairs information.

Current affairs activities should:

1. Develop a broad framework for viewing and linking contemporary affairs from the local, to the regional, to the state, to the national, to the international level.
2. Demonstrate the links between the events that swirl about us and our lives.
3. Assess the factual dimensions of contemporary affairs from those that are opinions and biases.
4. Identify issues among general accounts of events.
5. Illustrate what is meant by a *point of view* concerning an issue.

**Figure 9.8**
**Short Subject Lesson Plan from C-SPAN**

## The First Amendment

### Introduction

This "Short Subject" pertains specifically to the First Amendment to the Constitution. After viewing the videotape, students should be able to identify the major guarantees of the amendment and the extent and limitations of these guarantees.

As they view the "Short Subject" tape, students will be introduced to events in which examples of First Amendment rights are involved. Commentary is provided by Professor Greg Ivers of The American University.

### Goals

1. To present an overview of the First Amendment, focusing on the four basic freedoms incorporated in the text.
2. To show concrete examples of the issues involved in dealing with the First Amendment.
3. To explain the Supreme Court's relationship to the First Amendment.

### Objectives

At the conclusion of this lesson, students will:

1. be able to identify and explain the four primary rights incorporated in the First Amendment.
2. be able to cite examples of specific issues and cases involving the First Amendment as presented in the "Short Subject" videotape.
3. recognize and be able to explain various technical terms relating to the First Amendment.
4. recognize the limits of the basic freedoms of the First Amendment as imposed by the Supreme Court.

### Materials

1. C-SPAN "Short Subject" videotape: The First Amendment.
2. Students should have a copy of the First Amendment, or the text may be written on the board.

### Lesson

***Background to Lesson***

The issue of a bill of rights was raised in the Constitutional Convention by George Mason of Virginia but opposed by many.

When the original Constitution was sent out for ratification, many states called for a bill of rights.

Sources of the Bill of Rights:

1. State constitutions written from 1776–1787
2. Recommendations that emerged from the state conventions that ratified the Constitution
3. The traditions of English common law

On October 2, 1789, the proposed Bill of Rights was sent to the states for ratification.

James Madison wanted the "rights" interspersed throughout the original document, but Roger Sherman suggested that they be placed separately at the end of the document.

*Source: C-SPAN in the Classroom: Short Subject Lesson Plan,* Vol. III, no. 1. © 1991, C-SPAN.

**Figure 9.8 continued**

### Lesson

1. Write the following words on the board and tell students to listen for them in the "Short Subject" tape:

   *symbolic speech*
   *Pentagon Papers Case*
   *establishment clause*
   *clear and present danger*
   *prior restraint*
   *unpopular speech*
   *government being neutral*

2. Read the text of the First Amendment, with students paying particular attention to the four freedoms.
3. Tell students to note the specific cases cited in the videotape as they relate to each of the major freedoms cited in the First Amendment.
4. Show the "Short Subject" videotape.

### Follow-Up Questions

1. What are the specific freedoms referred to in the First Amendment?
2. Why do you think the founders chose to put these particular guarantees of freedom first in the Bill of Rights?
3. What is the difference between *speech* and *expression?*
4. Why would putting the First Amendment and the rest of the Bill of Rights separately at the end of the original Constitution be significant?
5. The word *construction* as applied to documents is a technical legal term meaning how a document is interpreted. How do you think the following would apply to the First Amendment? *Strict construction? Loose construction?*

### Follow-Up Activities

Have students check their newspapers and television newscasts for issues related to the First Amendment, and bring these to the attention of the class.

As you and your students view C-SPAN programs throughout the school year, look for issues relating to the First Amendment. Discuss these in class.

Identify specific issues in your local community that relate to the First Amendment. Discuss these in class.

In a class discussion, have students explore ways in which they are personally affected by the First Amendment.

Have students tape C-SPAN and other network programs that deal with First Amendment freedoms.

### Additional Follow-Up Questions

1. What do the following terms mean?

   *establishment clause*
   *clear and present danger*
   *symbolic speech*

2. Does freedom of speech allow one to say anything he or she chooses about others?
3. Since the First Amendment guarantees freedom of religion, could a group practice human sacrifice as part of their religion? Could a group use illegal drugs as part of their religion? Why or why not?

6. Encourage students to take positions on issues of concern and identify courses of action they plan to take.
7. Illustrate examples of controversies and constructive ways to resolve them.
8. Distinguish between trivial and significant news.
9. Develop a functional concept of *news*.
10. Identify alternative sources of information for contemporary affairs and some ways to gauge the relative merits of each.
11. Develop the principle that all citizens can and should be participants in events, as well as concerned spectators.
12. Support and demonstrate the general principle that contemporary affairs are an ongoing, vital part of daily life and the social studies curriculum.

## GROUP ACTIVITIES

1. Refer to the discussion of the *CNN Newsroom* in the chapter. Arrange to tape and critique an edition of the special free news program for students. Discuss what you consider to be the strengths and limitations of the newscast.
2. Focusing on the world scene, identify five significant issues that you believe a concerned citizen should examine or become involved in. Also, provide a rationale for why you think these issues are important. Discuss your conclusions.
3. Consider how your own hometown community or some segment of it is linked with other nations. How is it dependent on other countries? How are they dependent on your community? Make a list of all of the goods, services, human exchanges, and the like that come into your community from the rest of the world. Then construct a similar list showing the resources going from the community to the rest of the world. Compare your results.
4. Consult your local reference librarian to obtain the addresses of the publishers of the student newspapers and periodicals listed in the chapter. Write to them and request a sample copy of each. When you receive them, analyze their strengths and weaknesses for use with middle grades and secondary students. Discuss your conclusions.
5. Locate the quotation in the chapter that is taken from Gary Nash's book, *Red, White, and Black.* What are your reactions to his observation?

## INDIVIDUAL ACTIVITIES

1. Consult a reference librarian to obtain the addresses of the various organizations noted in the chapter that distribute teaching materials

relating to global education, peace education, gender issues, and multicultural education. Write them and request a list of their current curriculum materials and books.

2. Create three lists of possible activities similar to those described in the chapter that would encourage social consciousness in students. Develop one list of five or more activities for grades 5 through 8 and another for grades 9 through 12. Give a title to each of the activities and describe specifically how students would undertake it. Also indicate the preparation and follow-up discussions that should accompany each activity.
4. Identify four developing countries and create a research folder for each. Collect and organize pictures, articles, and materials that can be used as background by a teacher or as subject matter by students. For each country, begin your search for material by contacting the appropriate embassy, consulate, or related international agencies.
5. Locate a cartoon, letter to the editor, or article from the local newspaper that you feel reflects racial, ethnic, or gender bias. Identify what you view as the bias and explain why.

## REFERENCES

Anderson, L. (1991). A rationale for global education. In K. Tye (Ed.), *Global education: From thought to action.* Alexandria, VA: Association for Supervision and Curriculum Development.

Angell, A. V., & Avery, P. G. (1992). Examining global issues in the elementary classroom. *The Social Studies, 83,* 113–117.

Banks, J. (1984). *Teaching strategies for ethnic studies* (3rd ed.). Boston: Allyn & Bacon.

Banks, J. (1991). Multicultural literacy and curriculum reform. *Educational Horizons,* 135–140.

Banks, J. (1992). Multicultural education: For freedom's sake. *Educational Leadership, 49,* 32–36.

Banks, J. (1993, June–July). The canon debate, knowledge construction, and multicultural education. *Educational Researcher,* 4–14.

Benitez, H. (1994). Globalization of United States history: Six strategies. *Social Education, 59,* 142–144.

Bennett, C. I. (1986). *Comprehensive multicultural education: Theory and practice.* Boston: Allyn & Bacon.

Berman, S. (1990). Educating for social responsibility. *Educational Leadership, 48,* 75–80.

Brown, D. (1981). *The gentle tamers: Women of the old wild west.* Lincoln, NE: University of Nebraska Press.

Bullard, S. (1992). Sorting through the multicultural rhetoric. *Educational Leadership, 49,* 4–7.

Byrnes, D. A. (1987). *Teacher, they called me a _________?* New York: Anti-Defamation League of B'nai B'rith.

Byrnes, D. A. (1988). Children and prejudice. *Social Education, 52,* 267–271.

Chartock, R. K. (1991). Identifying local links to the world. *Educational Leadership, 49,* 50–52.

Choices for Education Project (1994). *Teacher's Resource Book: The role of the United States in a changing world.* Providence, RI: Author.

Etlin, M. (1988, May–June). To teach them all is to know them all. *NEA Today,* pp. 10–11.

Henderson, J. G. (1992). *Reflective teaching: Becoming an inquiring educator.* Englewood Cliffs, NJ: Merrill/Prentice Hall.

King, E. W. (1990). *Teaching ethnic and gender awareness.* Dubuque, IA: Kendall/Hunt.

Kirman, J. M. (1992). Using newspapers to study media bias. *Social Education, 56,* 47–51.

Kleg, M. (1993). *Racism and hate prejudice.* Albany, NY: State University of New York Press.

Kniep, W. M. (1989). Social studies within a global education. *Social Education, 53,* 399–403.

Kurshan, B. (1991). Creating the global classroom for the 21st century. *Educational Technology,* 47–50.

Lewis, B. (1991). *The kid's guide to social action.* Minneapolis, MN: Free Spirit Publishers.

Martel, E. (1992). How valid are the Portland Baseline Essays? *Educational Leadership, 49,* 20–23.

Martorella, P. H. (1993). Refugee issues in a globally interdependent world. *Educational Horizons.*

Merryfield, M. M., & Remy, R. C. (1995). *Teaching about international conflict and peace.* Albany, NY: State University of New York Press.

Nash, G. (1982). *Red, white, and black: The peoples of early America.* Englewood Cliffs, NJ: Prentice Hall.

National Council for the Social Studies. (1981). *Global education.* Washington, DC: Author.

National Council for the Social Studies. (1992). Curriculum guidelines for multicultural education. *Social Education, 56,* 274–293.

Noddings, N. (1991/1992). The gender issue. *Educational Leadership, 49,* 65–70.

Ogbu, J. U. (1992). Understanding cultural diversity and learning. *Educational Researcher, 21,* 5–14.

Ramler, S. (1991). Global education for the 21st century. *Educational Leadership, 49,* 44–46.

Ravitch, D. (1992). A culture in common. *Educational Leadership, 49,* 8–11.

Sobol, T. (1990). Understanding diversity. *Educational Leadership, 47,* 27–30.

Spindler, G., & Spindler, L. (1990). *The American cultural dialogue and its transmission.* Philadelphia: Falmer Press.

Tye, B. B., & Tye, K. A. (1992). *Global education: A study of school change.* Albany, NY: State University of New York Press.

Zarnowski, M. (1988). Learning about contemporary women: Sharing biographies with children. *The Social Studies, 79,* 61–63.

CHAPTER 10

# Comprehending, Communicating, and Remembering Subject Matter

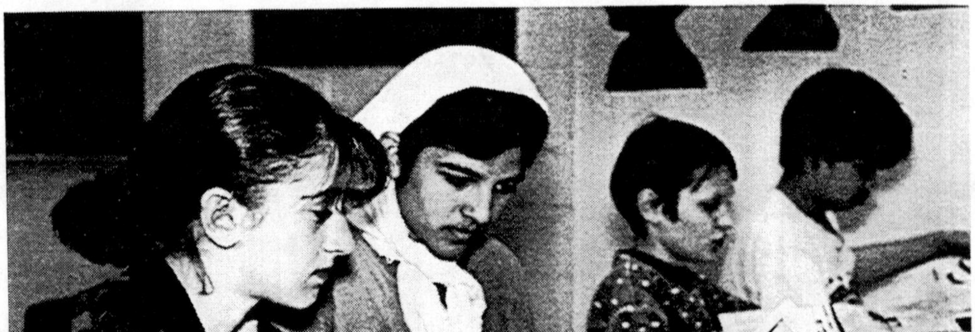

**Comprehending Social Studies Subject Matter**

Building on Existing Knowledge in Reading
Strategies for Improving Reading Comprehension
The Reading-Social Studies Connection

**Reading and Social Studies Text Materials**

Using Adolescent Literature in Social Studies Instruction
Reading Newspapers and Periodicals
Visual Literacy
Metaphors and Other Figures of Speech in Social Studies Instruction
Traditional Measures of Readability

**Communicating Social Studies Subject Matter**

Listening and Speaking
Integrating Writing into the Social Studies Curriculum
Word Processing Tools in Writing

**Remembering Social Studies Subject Matter**

Imagery and Memory
Structured Mnemonic Techniques
Notetaking Techniques

*Testifying before a congressional committee in 1989, Dexter Manly, age 30, broke down in tears. He was embarrassed because he could not read more than a paragraph of the prepared statement before him.*

*What made this case so unusual was that Dexter Manly was a highly successful professional football player. Moreover, he had graduated from high school and spent four years at a major university. As a closet illiterate, he finally had sought professional help three years before his testimony and was diagnosed as reading at the second-grade level.*

*His case helped dramatize the plight of the massive number of illiterates in our nation, estimated at more than 23 million people. Many of these are in our middle and secondary schools, and the number appears to be growing. Such statistics, reflecting our national reading problem, have become the object of serious social controversy in the United States.*

*Student reading problems pose an especially serious obstacle to learning in the area of social studies, since much of the subject matter appears in written form. Further, reliance on nonprint materials, even when they do exist, often limits students' opportunities for reflective analysis and precludes use of primary source data. Reading competencies also are required in everyday citizenship roles, from being an informed consumer to comprehending the ballot in a voting booth.*

*As we have considered in earlier chapters, social studies instruction directed toward developing the reflective, competent, and concerned citi-*

*zen incorporates many elements of planning. It includes strategies for organizing and presenting subject matter in ways that achieve the teacher's goals and objectives. Such instruction also aids students in comprehending, communicating, and remembering the social studies subject matter they encounter.*

## COMPREHENDING SOCIAL STUDIES SUBJECT MATTER

Contemporary perspectives on reading underscore that readers are not passive receivers of information from printed materials. Rather, they interact with text and construct meaning from it. The result may or not be the same meaning that the author intended.

**Comprehension,** as reading educators use the term, is a complex act representing a number of different cognitive processes. These include recognizing words and relating them to previously learned information and making inferences. What readers actually comprehend from a passage of text "depends upon their knowledge, motives, beliefs, and personal experiences" (Camperell & Knight, 1991, p. 569).

It also should be noted that the subject matter of social studies often deals with places and cultural practices that students may never have encountered. Additionally, the field draws heavily on abstract concepts (e.g., democracy, detente, alienation). Social studies also embraces subject matter that includes many specialized concepts and complex visual and tabular data (e.g., filibuster, political cartoons, GNP tables).

### Building on Existing Knowledge in Reading

Regardless of their ages or abilities, students' existing knowledge (i.e., *prior knowledge*) is a critical variable in reading comprehension: "All readers, both novices and experts, use their existing knowledge and a range of cues from the text and the situational context in which the reading occurs to build, or construct, a model of meaning from the text" (Dole, Duffy, Roehler, & Pearson, 1991, p. 241). Often this knowledge base is incomplete or students fail to relate it the information in text. Also, the existing knowledge may be inaccurate or at variance with texts, in which case students are likely to ignore or reject the new information.

### Strategies for Improving Reading Comprehension

Beyond their existing knowledge, students bring to the reading process various strategies that they use with varying degrees of effectiveness to construct meaning from text.

Dole, Duffy, Roehler, and Pearson (1991) have summarized five powerful strategies, supported by cognitively based research, that students can use to improve their comprehension of any texts, including social studies materials:

- Determining importance,
- Summarizing information,
- Drawing inferences,
- Generating questions, and
- Monitoring comprehension.

*Determining importance* involves assessing which items the author considers to be important. This may include understanding how a text is structured, as well as how to look for clues as to what is important.

The strategy of *summarizing information* relates to selecting what is significant, synthesizing data, and then representing passages of text, either orally or in writing.

*Drawing inferences* involves integrating prior knowledge with the information given in text to draw conclusions (e.g., inferring the character is male on reading "the Catholic priest blessed the little girl").

The strategy of *generating questions* in this context refers to students generating their own questions about text.

*Monitoring comprehension* consists of students being aware of how much they understand about text and how to remedy omissions or confusion.

## The Reading-Social Studies Connection

Helping students comprehend social studies subject matter typically involves aiding them in reading textbooks, newspapers, periodicals, reference works, and adolescent literature. Approaches that incorporate well-grounded instructional strategies in reading and social studies can advance teachers' goals for both areas. Five techniques that meet these criteria are the *K-W-L technique*, *discussion webs*, *concept (or semantic) maps*, *graphic organizers*, and *data retrieval charts*.

**The K-W-L Technique.** The **K-W-L technique** (Carr & Ogle, 1987; Ogle, 1986) is a basic way to (1) initiate study of a unit by motivating students and activating their prior knowledge, and (2) assess what they have learned after the unit is concluded.

Consider a unit of study on the Bill of Rights. At the outset of the unit, a sheet similar to the one shown in Figure 10.1 is given to each student or group (see Young & Marek-Schroer, 1992). After brainstorming, a cumulative list of *known* items is compiled. The process then is repeated for the items students *want to know* about the Bill of Rights. At that point, the teacher also may include additional questions that the text analysis will address.

In the following stage, students consult the list of items in the W column. They also confirm or refute the accuracy of the items in the K column. As a final step, the students list in the L column what they have *learned* from their readings. Alternately, the teacher may use some of the different forms of assessment discussed in Chapter 13 to determine what students have learned.

**Discussion Webs.** A **discussion web** (Duthie, 1986) may be used to help students organize arguments or evidence from text. It is suitable for issues or questions that are not resolved or for which there are balanced pro and con arguments.

An example of a web is given in Figure 10.2. As shown, a web begins with a teacher question related to materials that students have read: Should the United States have dropped the atomic bomb on Japan? The format that follows is flexible, but students, individually or in small groups, need to locate information that supports both sets of answers; for example, under the "No" column, a student writes "Thousands of innocent civilians were killed or maimed in some way."

After completing the web, students discuss the findings and then take an individual position on the issue (e.g., "Yes. Without the bomb, it would have taken an invasion of Japan to end the war. This would have caused a lot of casualties on both sides").

**Concept Maps.** **Concept (or semantic) mapping** is a flexible technique that has several different applications in social studies instruction, including aiding students' comprehension (see also Chapters 4 and 6). The tech-

**Figure 10.1**
**Illustration of the K-W-L Technique**

**K-W-L Chart**

Bill of Rights

| K (What we know about the Bill of Rights) | W (What we want to know) | L (What we learned) |
|---|---|---|
| | | |

**Figure 10.2**
**Should the United States Have Dropped the Atomic Bomb on Japan?**

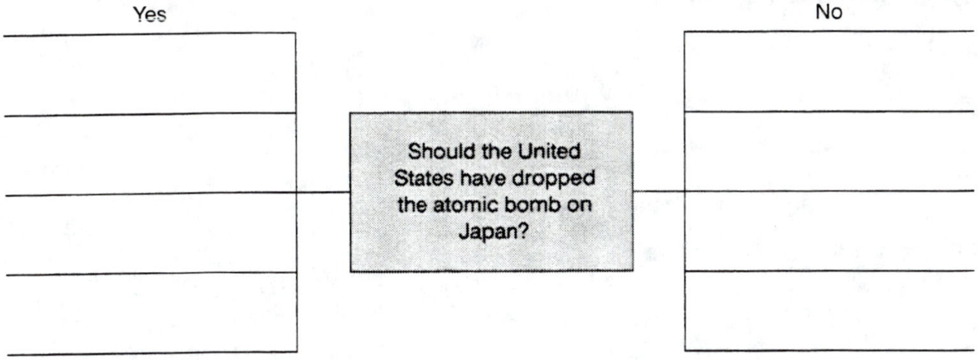


nique encourages students to organize categories of concepts and identify relationships among them.

Many variations of the concept mapping technique exist (e.g., Novak & Gowin, 1984). Basically it begins with the teacher or students identifying a series of major concepts in a narrative (e.g., a chapter), including one that is the central concept. These concepts then are organized and linked through a diagram that illustrates logical connections.

The organization of the concepts typically is hierarchical, but some applications omit this condition. In some way, however, the central or overarching concept should be identified, either by assigning it the largest circle or placing it at the top or the center of the page. In one variation, the teacher creates a partial map. This shows some of the concepts and linkages to demonstrate relationships and model the technique, and then students are asked to complete the map.

Figure 10.3 illustrates the application of this approach with a concept map made by a sixth-grade student characterized as a "low achiever" (Novak & Gowin, 1984, p. 41). The map represents the student's organization of information after reading a textbook chapter. The teacher supplied the concepts of *feudalism, kings, guilds,* and *church* shown in the figure, and the student then completed the map.

In a different type of application, Ms. Devereaux, a ninth-grade teacher, began the study of the federal budget by listing the target term *Federal Budget Expenditures* on the board in the center circle. Then she asked students to brainstorm some of the specific items that are included in the federal budget. Their responses, which include items such as student loans, interest on savings bonds, and social security, were recorded on the board. Ms. Devereaux also added some of her own items to the list. After the brainstorming and listing, she and the class also constructed some simple categories of the federal budget under which their responses were grouped:

**Figure 10.3**
**A Concept Map for History Prepared by a Previously Low-Achieving Student in Sixth Grade**

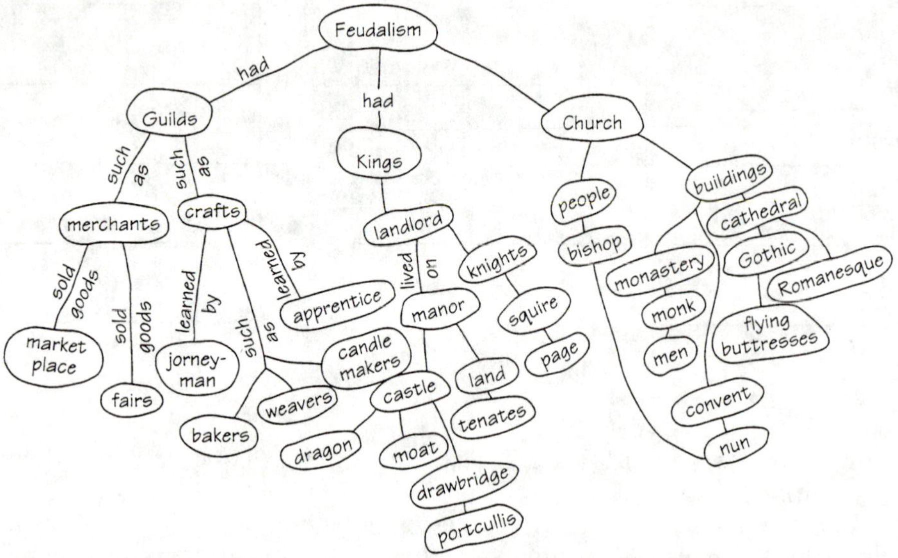


From *Learning How to Learn* (p. 41) by J. D. Novak and D. Bob Gowin, 1984, Cambridge, UK: Cambridge University Press. Reprinted with the permission of Cambridge University Press.

Entitlements,

Defense spending,

Interest on the national debt, and

Other programs.

Then, she asked the class to construct individual maps that later were used to organize the information. One student's partially completed map is shown in Figure 10.4. Students also were instructed to include new items as they are encountered in readings and discussions.

**Graphic Organizers.** **Graphic organizers,** similar to concept maps, are representations of the relationships among major themes in a reading passage. They can be used by students before reading material as a way to discern how the teacher or author has structured information. Alternately, they can be used at the end of a reading session to serve as a summary.

Typically, graphic organizers appear as hierarchical diagrams or verbal overviews that show relationships. For example, in an American history class, a teacher might begin a discussion of the "New Deal" programs by first overviewing the ways in which the actions of the Roosevelt administration constituted a departure from the past administrations. Similarly, an

**Figure 10.4**
**Partially Completed Concept Map**

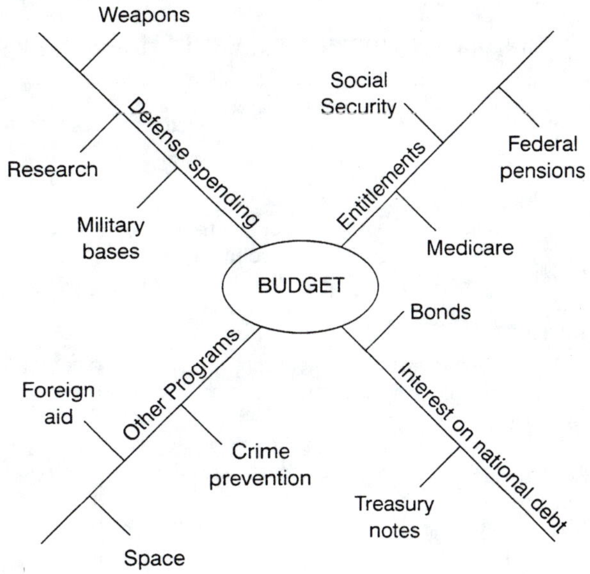


American government class could be given a chart outlining the structure of the executive branch before examining each of the major units.

Bean, Sorter, Singer, and Frazee (1986) provide a clear example of a diagram used in a world history class that serves as an organizer (shown in Figure 10.5). Whereas the text for the class discussed several specific revolutions, such as the French Revolution, the authors used the organizer to show students the general properties of all revolutions.

**Data Retrieval Charts.** **Data retrieval charts,** which we considered earlier in Chapter 6, allow teachers and students to organize data from written text in a way that highlights important relationships. The format they employ offers comparisons and analyses that are not included in typical text discussions. The data retrieval chart, shown in Figure 10.6, illustrates how a teacher can offer students a skeleton that aids them in organizing information in their social studies textbook chapter.

## READING AND SOCIAL STUDIES TEXT MATERIALS

An extensive body of research has documented the limitations of existing social studies text materials from a variety of perspectives (e.g., Armbruster & Gudbrandsen, 1986; Beck & McKeown, 1988, 1991; Garcia, 1993; Siler, 1986–1987). From a cognitive perspective, for example, one major criticism of social studies textbooks—especially history texts—is that they lack depth, compartmentalize information, and fail to aid students in linking passages

**Figure 10.5**
**Graphic Organizer for a World History Class**

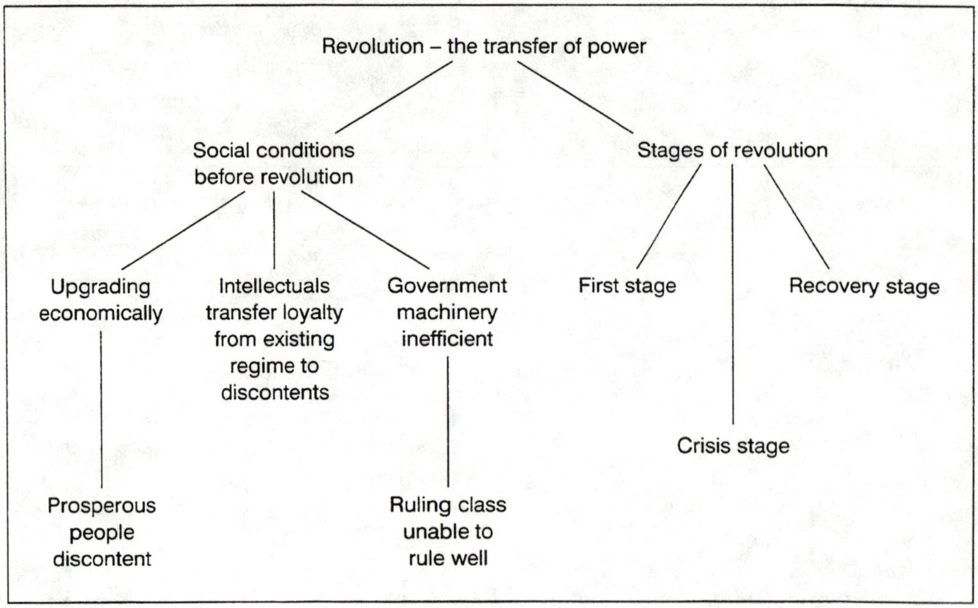


**Figure 10.6**
**Sample Data Retrieval Chart**

| | Natural Resources | Standard of Living | Major Social Problems | Major Exports |
|---|---|---|---|---|
| *Countries* | | | | |
| Costa Rica | | | | |
| Mexico | | | | |
| Argentina | | | | |
| Guatemala | | | | |

and discovering cause-effect relationships. Another charge is that they discourage hypothesis development and problem solving.

What characteristics specifically would make social studies texts seem "**considerate**" or "friendly" to a reader? Singer (1986) summarized the features of such texts in five categories: *text organization*, *explication of ideas*, *conceptual density*, *metadiscourse*, and *instructional devices* (see also Armbruster, 1984; McCabe, 1993).

*Text organization* refers to statements of purpose and rationale, organization of material, suggestions concerning how to learn from the text, and the like, provided for the reader. Included are a uniform writing style throughout the text and consistent use and placement of questions and rhetorical devices. Other such aids would be time lines and cause-effect and comparison charts.

*Explication of ideas* refers to straightforward statements of facts and ideas. Included is the definition of new terms as they are introduced, the provision of necessary background information, and the relating of new knowledge to prior knowledge. Included also is the explication of some organizing point of view or theory for the text, if one exists.

*Conceptual density* refers to the number of new concepts, ideas, and vocabulary items included in the text. The greater the number of these and the fewer the explanations through the introduction of main ideas and examples, the more complex is the learning task for the student.

*Metadiscourse* has been likened to a conversation between the author and the reader about the text. The discussion may cover any topic and typically uses the first person form of narration.

*Instructional devices* refer to text features that help the user better comprehend its meaning. Among these features are tables of contents, headings, cues, annotations in the margins, inserted questions, indices, and the like.

Researchers (Armbruster & Anderson, 1984; Armbruster, Anderson, & Meyer, 1991) have identified strategies for helping students identify and use the organizing structures in their texts. These are known as **frames,** ways of visually conceptualizing significant content of texts.

Frames represent important ideas and relationships in text. They may take many forms: data charts, tables, diagrams, and concept maps. Since authors of texts seldom provide frames, teachers and students have to create them. Once they are constructed, evidence suggests that they facilitate learning from social studies texts (Armbruster, Anderson, & Meyer, 1991), as well as other subjects.

Consider the following application of frames to a social studies text describing the Westward Movement, as shown in Figure 10.7. The teacher has identified for major categories of information that structure the text's narrative concerning the Pioneers and Native Americans: *goals*, *plans*, *actions*, and *outcomes*. four

## Using Adolescent Literature in Social Studies Instruction

Pick up a social studies textbook for any grade and read a sample chapter. Did it hold your interest?

Apart from their structural limitations, which we have already discussed, some of the most biting criticisms of social studies textbooks are

**Figure 10.7**
**Frame for the Westward Movement**

| The Westward Movement | Pioneers | Native Americans |
|---|---|---|
| What were their goals? | | |
| What were their plans? | | |
| What actions did they take? | | |
| What was the outcome of their actions? | | |

that they are dull, lifeless, disjointed, and lack a point of view. They also have been criticized for omitting the pageantry, myths, stories, issues, and anecdotes that are part of the vitality of social studies. Further, their critics charge that they provide only a single, allegedly objective, account of events; they also lack an "acknowledgment that there even exists more than one lens through which to examine social and political events and phenomena" (Beck & McKeown, 1991, p. 488).

*Adolescent literature* is an antidote to some of the major problems that textbooks have. A wealth of books designed for middle and secondary grades youngsters exist. They offer the promise of exciting and colorful in-depth alternative portrayals of issues, ethical dilemmas, social models, events, persons, and places by outstanding authors and illustrators.

**Adolescent literature can enrich and enliven social studies.**

To help middle and secondary grades social studies teachers locate outstanding books, the National Council for the Social Studies (NCSS) has published *An Annotated Bibliography of Historical Fiction for the Social Studies, Grades 5 through 12* (Silverblank, 1992). Also, each year in the April/May of *Social Education*, the NCSS publishes a list of notable trade books in the field of social studies during the past year, some of which are appropriate for the middle grades. The list includes works written for grades K through 8 that emphasize human relations and different cultural groups.

**Biographies.** *Biographies* designed for youngsters are especially useful in social studies. Zarnowski (1990) provided a detailed set of strategies for using biographies in social studies instruction in her book *Learning about Biographies*. One of the techniques she recommended is drawing relationships between the events in the life of the subject and those in history.

Semantic maps, discussed earlier, can be used to structure the analysis of adolescent literature. Norton (1993) provided a detailed illustration of how a middle-grade class used maps in their study of World War II in conjunction with reading Lois Lowry's *Number the Stars*. This is an account set in Denmark of how the Resistance aided Jews. The teacher placed the title of the book in the center of the map, with four spokes extending from it: conflict, themes, setting, and characterization. After students, working in groups, completed the book, they filled in details as shown in Figure 10.8.

## Reading Newspapers and Periodicals

*Newspapers and periodicals* have many of the same problems as textbooks. On the one hand, they offer students a wealth of data on contemporary affairs and help bridge the gap between the real world and that of the school curriculum (see examples in Chapter 9). To properly interpret and process the information these media contain, however, most students—even good readers—need assistance.

Although they share many elements in common with textbooks, newspapers and periodicals present some special reading challenges. Effectively reading newspapers and periodicals includes being able to:

1. *Separate headlines from the substance of an article.* This involves being aware that a headline is often an interpretation of what the article is about made by someone other than the author.
2. *Identify and correctly use common colloquialisms, metaphors, acronyms, and cryptic expressions.* This includes an awareness of how frequently such expressions are used.
3. *Locate new concepts in stories and dismantle sentences packed with difficult concepts.*

**Figure 10.8**
**A Semantic Map Showing Conflict, Themes, Setting, and Characterization**

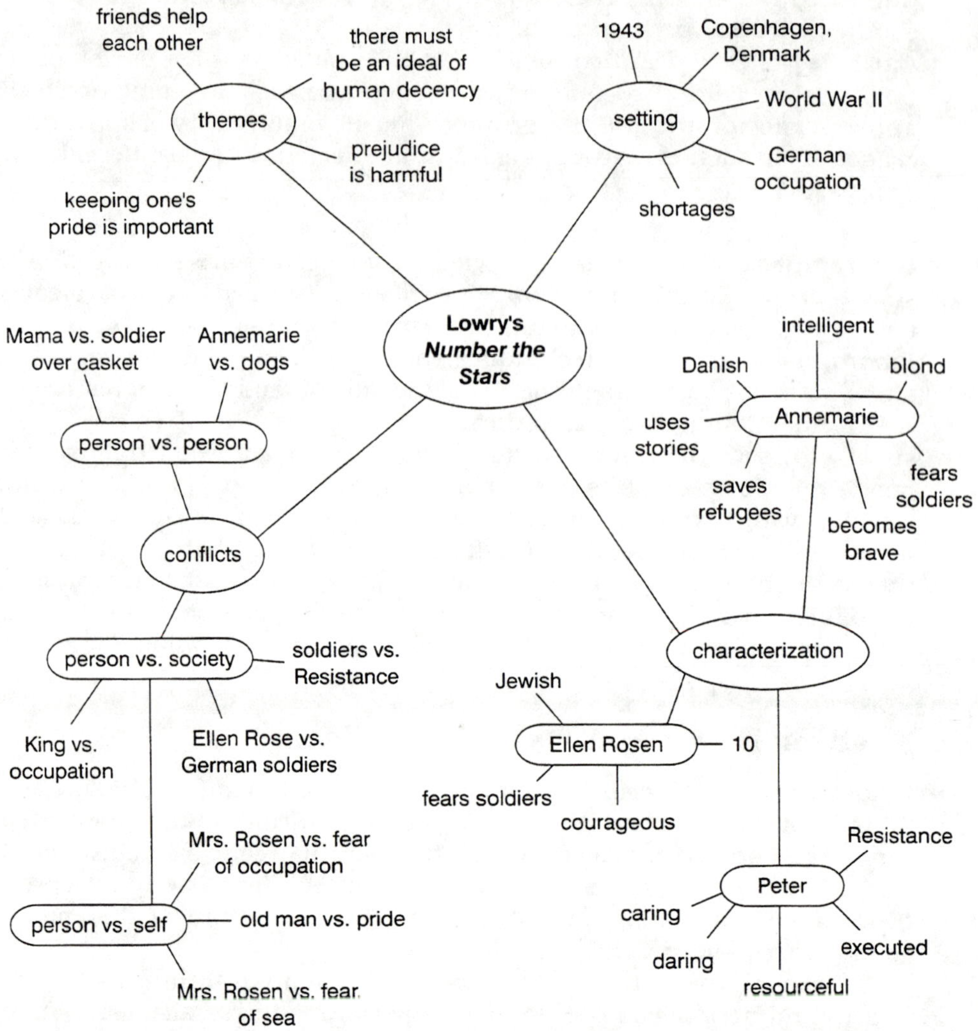


*Note.* From "Webbing and Historical Fiction" by D. Norton, 1993, The Reading Teacher, 46(5), 433. Reprinted by permission.

4. *Compare different accounts of the same event.* This involves searching for cause-effect relationships and separating what appears to be fact from opinion.
5. *Identify the big idea in a story.* This involves separating the important points from the peripheral or colorful but nonessential ones.
6. *Recognize how information is categorized and organized.* This includes identifying the structure of newspapers and periodicals and recognizing the nature of the contents within each section.

## Visual Literacy

Research data suggest that learning through imagery, such as pictures, often is easier than through other forms. Pictorial data enliven lessons and spark interest in social studies activities. There are a variety of still pictures and visual materials available for teaching social studies, including paintings, photos, slides, drawings, dioramas, transparencies. Old magazines and newspapers, as well as commercially prepared materials, are treasure troves of visual materials that can be used as springboards for social studies lessons. For students to comprehend visual data with social data effectively, however, they need to understand how to *read* pictures.

**Techniques for Reading Still Pictures.** Reading visual material effectively requires some of the same techniques that print reading does. It involves more than merely perceiving what is visually present. In reading visual materials, viewers try to answer a series of basic questions. These include points such as:

- Identifying which data the picture presents (What is presented?),
- Distinguishing whether the information represents fact or fiction (Is this an actual or recreated version of reality?),
- Relating the data to other information (What bearing does this have on what is known already?), and
- Summarizing the data (What would be an appropriate title or caption for the item?).

In Chapter 7, other considerations for processing pictures and constructing meaning from them are discussed. These encompass an examination of the varieties of pictures that appear in the social studies, including political cartoons.

## Metaphors and Other Figures of Speech in Social Studies Instruction

"The cold war has ended." "The United States can't be the world's police officer." These statements are two examples of figures of speech frequently used in social studies text materials and classroom discussions. **Figures of speech** are expressions that force students to go beyond the literal meaning of each concept in a statement to fathom the intent of the author.

**The Nature of Metaphors.** Among the most common figures of speech that students encounter in social studies discussions are *metaphors* and *similes* (Mahood, 1987; Martorella, 1988). A **metaphor** is a phrase in which something well known is used to explain or expand the meaning of another item less well known, for example: "Reagan was the Teflon president." The familiar no-stick quality of Teflon illustrates how criticisms of the President did not stick.

Other social studies terms that require metaphorical thinking are these (Pugh, Hicks, Davis, & Venstra, 1992, p. 127):

| | |
|---|---|
| muckrakers | pocket veto |
| spoils system | gag rule |
| bandwagon | Underground Railroad |
| domino theory | checks and balances |

**Similes** are similar to metaphors. They also compare unlike sets of items but use the terms *like* or *as* in the comparisons. For example, "The President is *like* the captain of a ship" is a simile.

**Metaphors in Instruction.** Metaphors are interwoven throughout texts, media reports, and discussions. Howard (1987) observed that metaphors are used to clarify points or define a concept, for example: A revolution is an exploding volcano. Metaphors apparently act as a cognitive puzzle. To solve the puzzle, students need to discover the similarity between two seemingly dissimilar sets of concepts in the metaphor.

Metaphors also stimulate the generation of new knowledge. That is, in confronting a metaphor, an individual is puzzled and reflects on old knowledge to create new; he or she finds ways to tie existing conceptual networks to fresh subject matter. When a metaphor ceases to be novel and passes into common usage, it is *dead* or in effect no longer is a true metaphor except for someone who has never before heard the expression. An example of a dead metaphor might be "The bill was dead on arrival."

Ortony (1975) has noted that metaphors serve us in several ways. One is by transferring elements of experience from well-known to less well-known contexts. Another is by permitting a more memorable learning experience as a result of the imagery involved in metaphors. A third function of metaphors, Ortony argued, is to supply us with meanings that we otherwise typically might not be able to encode in language. Witness the references during the Reagan administration to a "Star Wars" defense policy as metaphorical shorthand for a host of complex ideas.

Drawing on the work of researchers, it is possible to infer a general comprehension strategy that teachers could employ in helping students with metaphors (Martorella & Spires, 1992). It might be hypothesized as follows:

1. Draw students' attention to the nonliteral meaning of the metaphorical statement. (Example: For the statement "A revolution is an exploding volcano," ask if volcanoes actually explode during a revolution).
2. Model your thinking for the students as you note that a nonliteral interpretation has been made intentionally by the author. (Example: Point out that the author described a revolution in an unusual way to draw attention to its unusual qualities.)

3. Help students identify the appropriate matching attribute in the topic and the vehicle. (Example: Let's list on the board some things we think of when we hear the word *volcanoes*. Now, let's list some things we think of when we hear *revolutions*.)
4. Instruct students to disregard matching attributes that are trivial or inappropriate to comprehending the metaphor. (Example: Which items do we have in both lists? Which items do you think are most important?)
5. Provide ongoing feedback as students engage in each phase of the comprehension process.

A sample activity that engages students in examining economic metaphors that are common in social studies instruction is outlined in Figure 10.9.

**Figure 10.9**
**Using Metaphors in the Classroom**

**Activity:**

Discuss the mental pictures evoked by the following economic terms. Look for current terms in business publications to increase this list.

*Stock market crash:* the 1929 "fall" of the Dow-Jones index led to "smashed" hopes, "broken" dreams, "ruined" lives, and the Depression. What about the more recent "crash" of 1987?

*"Prosperity is just around the corner":* President Franklin D. Roosevelt's metaphor for how soon America would return to normalcy was intended to evoke belief in "happy days," an antithesis to the "depression days."

*New Deal:* FDR's metaphor for the programs that he was instituting to improve the economy told people that the game was changing. If they did not like the "cards" they had been dealt, they could have a "new deal."

*Inflation:* In contrast to depression, inflation refers to "ballooning" costs and wages.

To understand the power that these metaphors conveyed when they were first used, students should consult with relatives and neighbors who lived during the thirties and forties.

- Ask your relatives or neighbors about their feelings toward these terms. Invite them to reminisce about those years and about other slogans that they may recall. Ask them about their attitude toward President Roosevelt and his policies and why they think he was reelected three times.
- What power do slogans have over people's emotions and intellects? Prepare a presentation on the power of slogans by using examples from today's newspapers, television programs, and other media.

*Note.* From *Bridging: A teacher's guide to metaphorical thinking* (p. 126) by S. L. Pugh, J. W. Hicks, M. Davis, & T. Venstra, 1992, Urbana, IL: National Council of Teachers of English.

## Traditional Measures of Readability

Text publishers and teachers alike often feel the need to have some mechanical, relatively objective yardstick to gauge the general level of difficulty in reading materials. Numerous measures use mathematical formulas to calculate the approximate reading level of reading materials. Frequently, texts are associated with a particular reading level that has been identified by using one or more of those popular measures.

Reading formulas provide a basic standard to compare different materials, usually based on two aspects of writing style—sentence length and word difficulty. They offer only a *probability estimate* of whether a set of social studies materials is likely to be easy or difficult for a given student to process.

Professionals who deal with severe reading difficulties in students recognize that assessing accurately and comprehensively the dimensions of individuals' actual reading capabilities and limitations is far more complex than assigning scores (Armbruster, 1984; Calfee & Drum, 1986; Meyer, 1984).

# COMMUNICATING SOCIAL STUDIES SUBJECT MATTER

In addition to becoming more effective readers, students need to communicate effectively in their citizenship roles. Communication involves *listening*, *speaking*, and *writing*. In the home, the marketplace, at work or play, in addition to reading, all of us must listen, speak, and write effectively to achieve some of our most fundamental goals and live in harmony with others.

Reading, listening, speaking, and writing are interrelated. "Each informs and supports the other" (Strickland, 1990, p. 20). Instructional approaches that attempt to integrate all these elements into meaningful activities for students are often characterized as **whole-language approaches.** By integrating these four dimensions throughout the social studies curriculum, teachers can better prepare students for their roles as citizens.

## Listening and Speaking

Much of students' cognitive development depends on opportunities to engage in social discourse. This includes interactions within and presentations to groups, where feedback is available. As they engage in dialogue with others, students clarify and advance their own thinking, as well as influence and persuade others. Part of the social studies curriculum should assist students in becoming effective in communicating their ideas through listening and speaking to other individuals and interacting in small and large groups.

Some students, as they enter school, appear to be skillful listeners; they already have learned to wait quietly until another finishes speaking. Becoming a good listener, just as with becoming a good speaker, requires practice. The basic characteristic of good listeners seems to be that they allow senders to complete their messages without interruption and they interpret correctly the senders' main points. Both conditions are necessary for effective listening.

In the classroom, helping students become good listeners includes teaching them to take turns in talking and to wait for acknowledgment before speaking. It also requires that the teacher delay calling on impulsive speakers. Posting a simple set of rules to encourage listening and speaking in structured teacher-led discussions can be a helpful reminder to students.

Some techniques that help foster effective listening and speaking are:

- Requiring that all students periodically to restate or review what another said earlier,
- Providing criteria for self-analysis of speaking abilities,
- Emphasizing frequent oral reports,
- Creating games or role-playing enactments to provide practice in letting everyone speak and listen,
- Asking students periodically to take notes when others give reports or short presentations,
- Having students listen to public speakers or media figures and then quizzing them on what was said, and
- Encouraging students to practice giving their reports at home using a tape recorder.

A self-evaluation form that students may use to monitor their own discussion habits in groups is shown in Figure 10.10.

## Integrating Writing into the Social Studies Curriculum

Like reading, speaking, and listening, writing is an integral part of effective citizenship (Bragaw & Hartoonian, 1988; Civitas, 1991). Stotsky (1990) has written:

> [W]riting has been as much a part of the history of democratic self government as reading, and is essential to public speaking. In the course of American history, as local self government developed, so too did the kind and amount of writing that people needed to do as citizens. . . .
>
> Writing is also a vital support for the most direct way that citizens can express themselves and participate in civic or political life; as public speakers. Finally, writing for academic purposes can stimulate the moral reasoning and the independent reading and thinking that lie at the heart of both academic study and responsible public discourse. (p. 72)

**Figure 10.10**
**Pupil Self-Evaluation Form for Discussions**

**What Do I Do in Discussions?**

| | *Sometimes* | *Always* | *Never* |
|---|---|---|---|
| 1. Do I do most of the talking? | ____ | ____ | ____ |
| 2. Do I usually talk only a little? | ____ | ____ | ____ |
| 3. Can I follow the suggestions of others? | ____ | ____ | ____ |
| 4. Do I get angry when others do not agree with me? | ____ | ____ | ____ |
| 5. Do I interrupt others? | ____ | ____ | ____ |
| 6. Do I take turns talking? | ____ | ____ | ____ |
| 7. Do I stay on the subject? | ____ | ____ | ____ |
| 8. Am I a good listener? | ____ | ____ | ____ |

Stotsky suggested some of the basic ways that students can use writing in their citizenship roles.

- To personalize civic relationships and/or express civic identity (e.g., thank-you letter to a civic official),
- To provide information or services,
- To evaluate public services, and
- To advocate a position on a public issue.

In addition to these types of civic writing, teachers could integrate the following types of writing into social studies activities:

Recording in journals,
Writing poems,
Constructing data retrieval charts,
Preparing information for databases in computer programs,
Creating captions for cartoons,
Notetaking,
Writing book reviews,
Writing reports,
Developing scripts for slide shows,
Constructing advertisements, and
Writing newsletters.

Some roles or audiences that students might assume for their writing activities are outlined in Figure 10.11.

**Figure 10.11**
**Audiences for Social Studies Writing**

| | | |
|---|---|---|
| ad agencies | characters in novels | movie stars |
| administrators | doctors | pen pals |
| artists | historical figures | politicians |
| athletes | hospital patients | salespersons |
| cartoonists | journalists | scientists |
| Chamber of Commerce | lawyers | teachers |
| community figures | older or younger students | television stations |

*Note.* From *Content Reading Including Study Systems: Reading, Writing and Studying Across the Curriculum* (p. 121) by C. M. Santa, L. Havens, M. Nelson, M. Danner, L. Scalf, & J. Scalf, 1988, Dubuque, IA: Kendall/Hunt.

**The RAFT Technique.** An example of a basic technique to make students more effective writers in the context of the social studies curriculum is *RAFT*, developed by Vandervanter (cited in Santa et al., 1988). The technique helps students improve their essays by teaching them to consider four major dimensions in their writing, the:

- *R*ole they are assuming, such as a woman in Colonial times or the inventor of the polio vaccine,
- *A*udience to whom they are writing, such as an employer or a patient,
- *F*ormat for the written communication, such as a diary or an advertisement, and
- *T*opic (plus an action verb), such as urge an industry to stop polluting a stream or clarify a misunderstanding with a friend.

## Word Processing Tools in Writing

Among the tools that teachers can use to assist students in improving their writing are various types of word processing computer programs. These encourage students to experiment with language, sentence and paragraph structure, and the sequencing of ideas and to construct multiple drafts. Such programs also allow students to prepare banners and newsletters.

Some examples of the software programs that are appropriate for students in the middle and secondary grades are *Bank Street Writer, ClarisWorks, Word, MacWrite,* and *Print Shop* (see also Chapter 11).

# REMEMBERING SOCIAL STUDIES SUBJECT MATTER

An adjunct to helping students comprehend subject matter as they read text materials is aiding them in *remembering* such information (Mastropieri &

Scruggs, 1991; Torney-Purta, 1991). To the extent that teachers and text authors systematically organize data for more efficient remembering, they assist students in creating schemata and referencing, activating, and applying prior knowledge.

The subject of memory traditionally has suffered from association with the rote learning of nonfunctional information. In reality, students frequently are required in social studies classes to remember a great number of names, places, events, dates, and general descriptive information to clarify and link new knowledge in meaningful ways. This need includes remembering names, places, events, dates, patterns, and general descriptive information.

## Imagery and Memory

Creating an image related to an element of subject matter often can assist us in remembering of information (Bower, 1972; Richardson, 1980; Wittrock, 1986). In an extensive review of 23 studies, Levie and Lentz (1982) concluded that drawings and pictures have a powerful effect on learning from printed instructional materials. In all but one study, students learned more from materials that included related illustrations or pictures than from materials without illustrations. Research also indicates that spatial information may be learned more effectively from maps than from verbal descriptions.

Wittrock's (1986) model of generative learning predicts that both memory and comprehension are facilitated when students relate new information to be learned to their prior knowledge and generate a representation of the relationship. Students who wished to remember the various battles of the Civil War, for example, might visually imagine Bull Run as a bull, Gettysburg as a Getty gasoline station, and so on.

## Structured Mnemonic Techniques

Several specific memory strategies, or **mnemonic techniques,** exist for social studies applications, some dating back to the early Romans and Greeks (Bellezza, 1981; Wittrock, 1986). Mnemonics involve either imagery or verbal devices or some combination of the two. Two mnemonic strategies that have applications to social studies instruction are the *first-letter technique* and the *keyword technique*.

**First-Letter Technique.** The **first-letter technique** involves taking the first letter of each word to be remembered and composing a word or sentence from the letters. For example, to remember the list of American presidents in correct chronological order, one may remember a rhyme such as, "*W*atch *a* *j*olly *m*an *m*ake . . . " (Washington, Adams, Jefferson, Madison, Monroe).

Another application of the first-letter technique is to create an acronym composed of the first letters of the items you wish to remember. For example, suppose you wish to remember the names of the Great Lakes: Huron, Ontario, Michigan, Erie, and Superior. Remembering the simple acronym *HOMES*, which is composed of the first letters of the names, will help you recall the five lakes.

**The Keyword Technique.** Another mnemonic device, the **keyword technique,** initially was used for learning foreign language vocabulary (Atkinson, 1975). It since has been applied to a variety of types of information, including social studies data, and has several variations (see Mastropieri & Scruggs, 1991). This technique involves first identifying a word to be related to the one to be remembered and then generating an interactive image between the two words (Levin & Pressley, 1985).

Based on their extensive review of the related research, Pressley, Levin, and Delaney (1982) concluded: "The evidence is overwhelming that use of the keyword method, as applied to recall of vocabulary definitions, greatly facilitates performance" (pp. 70–71). Their conclusion was based on the analysis of studies in which both concrete and abstract words were the learning tasks and the subjects were of varying ages.

Mastropieri and Scruggs (1991) suggested that the application of the keyword technique consists of three steps as outlined here:

1. Create a keyword by casting the terms to be learned into a term that sounds similar and which can be represented visually in some concrete way. (Example: Apples to represent Annapolis, the capital of Maryland.)
2. Relate the keyword to the information to be learned in an picture, image, or sentence. (Example: Visualize apples getting married.)
3. Verbally review the relationships by first recalling the keyword, noting the relationship in the visual image, and then stating the correct response. (Example: Recall the word *apples*, note what the apples were doing in the image, and assert that Annapolis is the capital of Maryland.)

## Notetaking Techniques

Effective notetaking techniques also can facilitate both comprehension and remembering of subject matter in social studies texts and lectures (see Slater, Graves, & Piche, 1985). One effective notetaking technique uses a **split-page approach,** as illustrated by Spires and Stone (1989) in Figure 10.12.

Students are directed to divide the page into two columns. The left column, which takes up one third of the page, is for listing key concepts and ideas. The right column is for related supporting information.

**Figure 10.12**
**Split-Page Method of Notetaking**

| Lecture topic: "Social Control" | |
|---|---|
| Definition of social control | Ways of conditioning or limiting actions of individuals to motivate them to conform to social norms. |
| Two types of social control | (1) internalized<br>(2) externalized |
| Internal control | Individuals accept norms of group or society as part of own personality (e.g., refrain from stealing not because afraid of arrest but because believe stealing is wrong). |
| | Most effective means of socially controlling deviant behavior. |
| External control | Set of social sanctions (informal or formal) found in every society. |
| Informal sanctions | Applied through actions of people we associate with every day (i.e., the *primary* group). |
| | May range from gesture of disapproval to rejection by primary group. |
| Formal sanctions | Applied by agents given that function by society (e.g., law enforcement). |

From Spires & Stone (1989).

Spires and Stone (1989) found that the notetaking strategy was particularly effective when students learned to ask themselves the following questions before, during, and after a lecture.

> PLANNING (before taking notes)
> How interested am I in this topic?
> If my interest is low, how do I plan to increase interest?
> Do I feel motivated to pay attention?
> What is my purpose for listening to this lecture?
>
> MONITORING (while taking notes)
> Am I maintaining a satisfactory level of concentration?
> Am I taking advantage of the fact that thought is faster than speech?
> Am I separating main concepts from supporting details?
> What am I doing when comprehension fails?
> What strategies am I using for comprehension failure?
>
> EVALUATING (after taking notes)
> Did I achieve my purpose?
> Was I able to maintain satisfactory levels of concentration and motivation?
> Did I deal with comprehension failures adequately?
> Overall, do I feel that I processed the lecture at a satisfactory level? (p. 37)

## GROUP ACTIVITIES

1. Select a social studies basal text for any grade, 5 through 12. Create (a) a graphic organizer for any chapter within the text; (b) a data retrieval chart for another chapter; and (c) a frame for another chapter. Compare your results.
2. Locate an eighth-grade social studies text and select any chapter within the text. Then, using either the first-letter or keyword techniques, develop a mnemonic device to help remember the names of important individuals, places, and events within the chapter. Compare your results.

## INDIVIDUAL ACTIVITIES

1. Identify five metaphors in newspapers or periodicals. Then explain how you would try to explain them to a middle-school student using the guidelines in the chapter.
2. Identify and read four trade books for students in grades 5 through 8 that address significant social issues. List the author, title, publisher, and copyright date for each, along with a brief summary of the book and the issue it raises. To identify some appropriate works, consult the references in the chapter or the following sources: A. F. Gallagher, "In Search of Justice . . . ," *Social Education*, November/December, 1988, pp. 527–531; R. W. Evans & V. O. Pang, *The Social Studies*, May/June, 1992, pp. 118–119.
3. Work with a student in grades 5 through 12 and help him or her construct a concept map using any concept for the organizing theme.

## REFERENCES

Armbruster, B. B. (1984). The problems of "inconsiderate" text. In G. G. Duffy, L. R. Roehler, & J. Mason (Eds.), *Comprehension instruction: Perspectives and suggestions.* New York: Longman.

Armbruster, B. B., & Anderson, T. (1984). Structures of explanations in history textbooks or so what if Governor Stanford missed the spike and hit the rail? *Journal of Curriculum Studies, 16,* 181–194.

Armbruster, B. B., Anderson, T. H., & Meyer, J. L. (1991). Improving content area reading using instructional graphics. *Reading Research Quarterly, 26,* 393–416.

Armbruster, B. B., & Gudbrandsen, B. (1986). Reading comprehension instruction in social studies programs. *Reading Research Quarterly, 21,* 36–48.

Atkinson, R. C. (1975). Mnemonics in second language learning. *American Psychologist, 30,* 821–828.

Bean, T. W., Sorter, J., Singer, H. G., & Frazee, C. (1986). Teaching students how to make predictions about events in history with a graphic organizer plus options guide. *Journal of Reading, 29,* 739–745.

Beck, I. L., & McKeown, M. G. (1988). Toward meaningful accounts in history texts for young learners. *Educational Researcher, 17,* 31–39.

Beck, I. L., & McKeown, M. G. (1991). Research directions: Social studies texts are hard to understand: Mediating some of the difficulties. *Language Arts, 68,* 482–489.

Bellezza, F. S. (1981). Mnemonic devices: Classification, characteristics, and criteria. *Review of Educational Research, 51,* 247–275.

Bower, G. H. (1972). Mental imagery and associative learning. In L. W. Gregg (Ed.), *Cognition in learning and memory.* New York: Wiley.

Bragaw, D. H., & Hartoonian, H. M. (1988). Social studies: The study of people in society. In R. S. Brandt (Ed.), *Content of the curriculum.* Alexandria, VA: Association for Supervision and Curriculum Development.

Calfee, R., & Drum, P. (1986). Research on teaching reading. In M. C. Wittrock (Ed.), *Handbook of research on teaching* (3rd ed.). Englewood Cliffs, NJ: Merrill/Prentice Hall.

Camperell, K., & Knight, R. S. (1991). Reading research and social studies. In J. P. Shaver (Ed.), *Handbook of research on social studies teaching and learning.* New York: Macmillan.

Carr, E., & Ogle, D. (1987). K-W-L-plus: A strategy for comprehension and summarizing. *Journal of Reading, 30,* 626–631.

*Civitas: A framework for civic education.* (1991). Calabasas, CA: Center for Civic Education.

Dole, J. A., Duffy, G. G., Roehler, L. R., & Pearson, P. D. (1991). Moving from the old to the new: Research on reading comprehension instruction. *Review of Educational Research, 61,* 239–264.

Duthie, J. (1986). The web: A powerful tool for the teaching and evaluation of the expository essay. *History and Social Science Teacher, 21,* 232–236.

Garcia, J. (1993). The changing images of ethnic groups in textbooks. *Phi Delta Kappan, 75,* 29–35.

Howard, R. W. (1987). *Concepts and schemata: An introduction.* Philadelphia: Cassell.

Levie, W. H., & Lentz, R. (1982). Effects of text illustrations: A review of research. *Educational Communication and Technology Journal, 30,* 195–232.

Levin, J., & Pressley, M. (1985). Mnemonic vocabulary instruction: What's fact, what's fiction. In R. Dillon (Ed.), *Individual differences in cognition* (Vol. 2, pp. 145–172). New York: Academic Press.

Mahood, W. (1987). Metaphors in social studies instruction. *Theory and Research in Social Education, 15,* 285–297.

Martorella, P. H. (1988). Students' understanding of metaphorical concepts in international relations. *Social Science Record, 25,* 46–49.

Martorella, P. H., & Spires, H. A. (1992). Minding metaphors: Instructional strategies for production and comprehension. *Teaching Thinking and Problem Solving, 14,* 1, 3–5.

Mastropieri, M. A., & Scruggs, T. E. (1991). *Teaching students ways to remember: Strategies for learning mnemonically.* Cambridge, MA: Brookline Books.

McCabe, P. P. (1993) Considerateness of fifth-grade social studies texts. *Theory and Research in Social Education, 21,* 128–142.

Meyer, B. J. F. (1984). Organizational aspects of text: Effects on reading comprehension and applications for the classroom. In J. Flood (Ed.), *Promoting reading comprehension.* Newark, DE: International Reading Association.

Norton, D. E. (1993). Webbing and historical fiction. *The Reading Teacher, 46,* 432–436.

Novak, J., & Gowin, D. B. (1984). *Learning how to learn.* Cambridge, MA: Cambridge University Press.

Ogle, C. (1986). K-W-L: A teaching model that develops active reading of expository text. *The Reading Teacher, 39,* 564–570.

Ortony, A. (1975). Why metaphors are necessary and not just nice. *Educational Theory, 25,* 45–53.

Pressley, M., Levin, J. R., & Delaney, H. D. (1982). The mnemonic keyword method. *Review of Educational Research, 52,* 61–91.

Pugh, S. L., Hicks, J. W., Davis, M., & Venstra, T. (1992). *Bridging: A teacher's guide to metaphorical thinking.* Urbana, IL: National Council of Teachers of English.

Richardson, J. T. E. (1980). *Mental imagery and human memory.* London: Macmillan.

Santa, C. M., Havens, L., Nelson, M., Danner, M, Scalf, L., & Scalf, J. (1988). *Content reading including study systems: Reading, writing and studying across the curriculum.* Dubuque, IA: Kendall/Hunt.

Siler, C. R. (1986–1987). Content analysis: A process for textbook analysis and evaluation. *International Journal of Social Education, 1,* 78–99.

Silverblank, F. (1992). *An annotated bibliography of historical fiction for the social studies, grades 5 through 12.* Dubuque, IA: Kendall/Hunt.

Singer, H. (1986). Friendly texts: Description and criteria. In E. K. Dishner, T. W. Bean, J. E. Readance, & D. W. Moore (Eds.), *Reading in the content areas: Improving classroom instruction* (2nd ed.). Dubuque, IA: Kendall/Hunt.

Slater, W. H., Graves, M. F., & Piche, G. L. (1985). Effects of structural organizers on ninth grade students' comprehension and recall of four patterns of expository text. *Reading Research Quarterly, 20,* 189–202.

Spires, H. A., & Stone, D. (1989). Directed notetaking activity: A self-questioning approach. *Journal of Reading, 33,* 36–39.

Stotsky, S. (1990). Connecting reading and writing to civic education. *Educational Leadership, 47,* 72–73.

Strickland, D. S. (1990). Emergent literacy: How young children learn to read and write. *Educational Leadership, 47,* 18–23.

Torney-Purta, J. (1991). Schema theory and cognitive psychology: Implications for social studies. *Theory and Research in Social Education, 19,* 189–210.

Wittrock, M. C. (1986). Students' thought processes. In M. C. Wittrock (Ed.), *Handbook of research on teaching* (3rd ed.). New York: Macmillan.

Young, T. A., & Marek-Schroer, M. F. (1992). Writing to learn in social studies. *Social Studies and the Young Learner, 5,* 14–16.

Zarnowski, M. (1990). *Learning about biographies: A reading and writing approach for children.* New York: Teachers College Press.

CHAPTER 11

# Using Technology to Enhance Social Studies Instruction

**Infusing Microcomputer Applications into the Social Studies Curriculum**

**Identifying and Evaluating Appropriate Social Studies Software**

Types of Social Studies Software
Simulation Software
Analyzing Information Using Databases and Spreadsheets
Using Groups with Computer-Based Instruction
Evaluating Social Studies Software

**Telecommunications and Online Information**

The Internet
Electronic Mail (E-Mail)
Two-Way Video Conferencing
Social Studies Resources on the Internet

**Multimedia in the Age of Emerging Computer Technologies**

Interactive Multimedia Systems in Social Studies Instruction
Microcomputers and CD-ROM Technology
Cable Television and Social Studies Instruction
Distance Learning
Teacher- and Student-Made Video Materials

**Using Traditional Media Effectively**

**Emerging Technologies and the Challenge of the Future**

*When juniors at Fullerton [California] Union High School arrived for U.S. history class last September, many found the traditional rows of student desks had given way to individual tables with computers and separate chairs that could be grouped to accommodate varied lessons. Their textbooks had been replaced by primary source documents, supplementary readings, and encyclopedia information provided via computer. (OERI Bulletin, Spring/Summer, 1993, p. 3)*

Among the many challenges that educators face as they approach the twenty-first century is how to effectively and creatively harness modern technology to significant instructional ends. Apart from the social, economic, and even political changes they have spawned, computers and related microprocessor-based technologies have shown the potential to revolutionize learning and assist us in performing an endless variety of complex tasks. Although they have not yet engendered a revolution in our classrooms, microcomputers have demonstrated they can provide forms of instruction and reinforcement beyond the capability of alternative media. They can simulate patience, humor, and excellent memories and can provide personalized assistance and immediate feedback on demand. Computers also have extended our vistas concerning schools: "In the era of electronic learning, school is where the learner is" (Mecklenburger, 1990, p. 107).

## INFUSING MICROCOMPUTER APPLICATIONS INTO THE SOCIAL STUDIES CURRICULUM

In social studies classes, computers also have proven they can help students quickly access in structured ways great amounts of information to aid in hypothesis development and problem solving. They also can simulate important social issues (Budin, Kendall, & Lengel, 1986; Vockell & Brown, 1992). Above all, computers can challenge and excite students.

With some exceptions, however, the full potential impact of computers on the array of required subjects and topics in the curriculum has not been fully realized (Mecklenburger, 1990). Newer computer-related technologies have yet to emerge as significant instruments of curricular change in our classrooms.

Traditional technological tools such as overhead, film, and slide projectors and duplicating and xerography machines continue to dominate as the preferred electronic tools for facilitating social studies instruction. Increasingly, however, they will share a role with the developing computer-based technologies that have touched the lives of every American and forged a communications revolution outside of the classroom (Tyre, 1990).

Microcomputers, along with a variety of peripheral devices, have the potential to become important electronic allies with social studies teachers in their pursuit of instructional objectives. Apart from their utility as instructional tools, microcomputers also represent an important *object* of instruction in the social studies curriculum because of their impact on the world. The political, social, and economic consequences of the micro revolution, as well as its fascinating history and geographical dispersion, constitute an important dimension of contemporary American and world history.

Students should address, for example, the issues created by the rapid growth of data banks and computer networking and the relative ease with which proprietary materials may be copied. Some of the topics students might consider in social studies classes include:

- The economic implications of increased computer usage,
- The fears and anxieties that computers produce in many people,
- The real and imagined potential of computers for dehumanization,
- The uses and misuses of online networks,
- The nature of a computerized society of the future,
- The effects of computers on privacy, and
- Gender and SES inequities in access to computers.

# IDENTIFYING AND EVALUATING APPROPRIATE SOCIAL STUDIES SOFTWARE

An assortment of software programs with individual lessons, exercises, and activities exist for most popular microcomputers. Increasingly, software programs require more memory, storage capability, and peripherals, such as CD-ROM units and video disk units (discussed in later chapters). There are, however, a limited number of software programs available that match well with the entire scope and sequence of a typical K through 12 social studies curriculum (Ehman & Glenn, 1987). This means that teachers must select software carefully, choosing only programs that address important curricular objectives, regardless of their other merits.

## Types of Social Studies Software

Software programs often are categorized according to the instructional technique they employ (e.g., simulations, tutorials, drill-and-practice) or the functions they perform (e.g., word processing, database management, graphing). Listed in Figure 11.1 is a cross section of programs and applications for the middle and secondary grades. These illustrate the variety of objectives that existing software can satisfy. Throughout other chapters, where appropriate, social studies software programs have been identified. However, new software is rapidly being developed and old titles are being retired. For lists of current social studies titles, consult publications such as *Multimedia Source Guide* (1995–96) and *Only the Best: The Annual Guide to Highest-Rated Education Software/Multimedia for Preschool–Grade 12* (Association for Supervision and Curriculum Development, 1995).

The list in Figure 11.1 includes the title, publisher or distributor, and a brief description of each program. More complete descriptions of the programs, as well as many others, along with hardware requirements and the current addresses of the publisher or distributor can be found in the comprehensive reference *TESS: The Educational Software Selector*, published by EPIE Institute, at Teachers College Press, New York, NY 10027. Some individual school districts also have prepared guidelines identifying social studies software that is appropriate for each grade level. An example is the guide prepared by Erickson (no date) for the San Juan (CA) Unified School District: *Macintosh Educational Software Correlation Guide to the History-Social Science Framework for California Public Schools.*

## Simulation Software

In Chapter 5, we considered *non*computerized simulations as an effective way to explore social issues in social studies classes. The increasing capacity of microcomputers to quickly store and manipulate many variables

**Figure 11.1**
**Cross Section of Social Studies Software for Middle and Secondary Grades**

**Middle Grades**

| Title | Publisher | Description |
|---|---|---|
| *One World Countries Database* | Active Learning Systems | Database on countries of the world |
| *The Other Side* | Tom Snyder Productions | Simulation that teaches information concerning global tensions |
| *Hometown: A Local Area Study* | Active Learning Systems | Database shell that enables students to enter and access data on their hometown |
| *Where in the World is Carmen Sandiego?* | Broderbund | Simulation that teaches facts and reference skills related to countries |
| *Oregon Trail* | MECC | Simulation that requires problem solving |
| *Archaeotype* | Dalton School | Simulation of archaeological exploration |
| *Nystrom Desk Atlas* | Nystrom | Major Atlas |

**Secondary Grades**

| Title | Publisher | Description |
|---|---|---|
| *Polls and Politics* | MECC | Analysis of survey data |
| *Election of 1912* | Eastgate Systems | Simulation of an election using HyperCard environment |
| *Presidential Fever* | DATAWIN | Simulation of presidential elections |
| *The U.S. Constitution: Nationalism and Federalism* | Focus Media | Tutorial covering U.S. Constitution |
| *Washington's Decisions* | Educational Activities | Role play decisions relative to Revolutionary War |
| *Ancient Lands* | Microsoft | Database on Rome, Ancient Egypt, and Greece |
| *Encarta* | Microsoft | Encyclopedia with sounds, photos, and animation |

offers opportunities for presenting complex simulations. This gives them a major edge over their board-game counterparts.

Among other features, computer simulations afford students the opportunity to explore roles, positions, and opinions and obtain feedback in privacy. They also can engage students, individually or in groups, in the kind of challenges and opportunities for problem solving and success that the electronic games outside of the classroom present. Computer simulations also have the capacity to stimulate lively discussions, whether used as a individual, small-group, or whole-class activity with a large monitor.

An example of effective simulation software is *Wagon Train 1848*. It engages students in a simulation of a covered wagon journey along the famous Oregon Trail that ran from Independence, Missouri to Oregon City, Oregon, as shown in Figure 11.2. As they venture forth in a caravan of wagon trains, students encounter sickness and disease, water shortages, and assorted calamities. To survive, they must plan and work cooperatively and use the information they are given for problem solving.

Another exceptional software item is *SimCity*, available through Broderbund. It simulates the workings of a major urban area and the decisions policymakers confront.

As with non-computerized simulations, teachers need to structure activities carefully and engage students in reflection and generalization. As a general procedure for effective use of a computer simulation, teachers should follow the five-step guidelines for enactments discussed in detail in Chapter 5:

**Figure 11.2**
**Example of Type of Map Included in the Software Program *Wagon Train 1848***

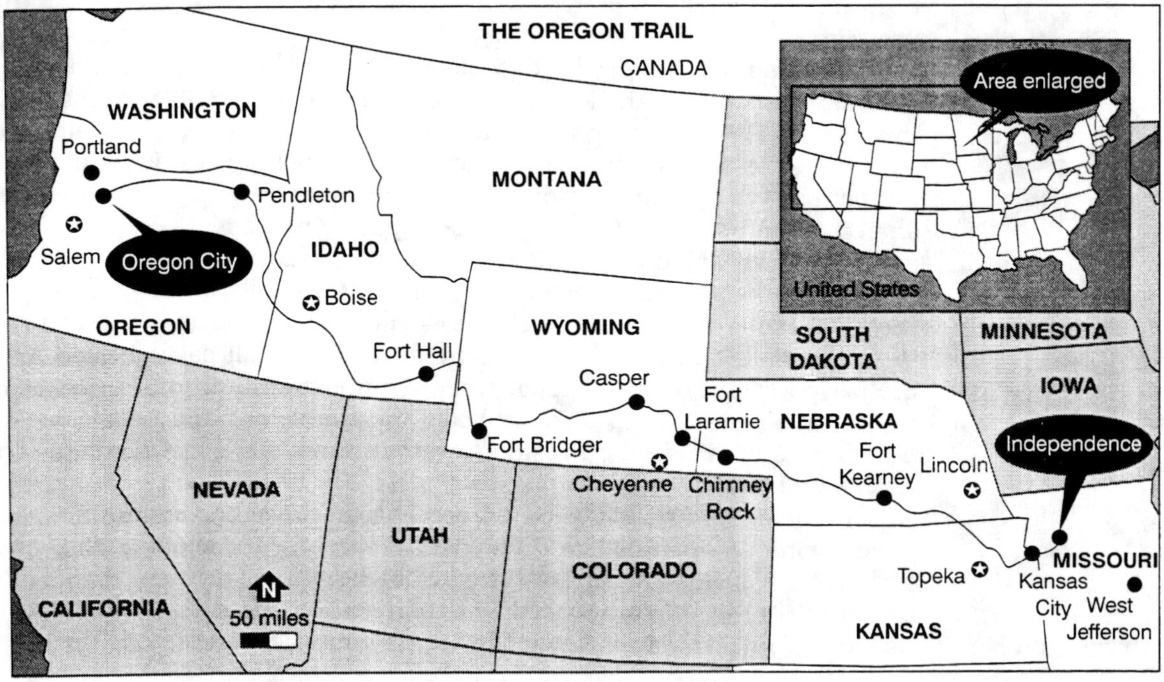

1. Initiation and direction,
2. Describing the scenario,
3. Assigning roles,
4. Enactment, and
5. Debriefing.

## Analyzing Information Using Databases and Spreadsheets

The computer is an ideal tool for those social studies topics that involve information retrieval, analysis, organization, and processing (Bilof, 1987; Hunter, 1985). These processes require accessing, creating, and manipulating **databases.** "A social studies teacher can use a database to find factual information (Who was the oldest delegate at the Constitutional Convention?); to show trends over time (What were the changes in immigration to the United States during the period 1890–1960?); and to seek relationships between variables (Do nations with the high rates of population growth tend to be poor or wealthy?)" (*The Macintosh Advantage*, no date). Ehman and Glenn (1987) have called databases "one of the most powerful computer tools available for social studies instruction" (p. 37).

Informational databases exist in the form of software programs such as several of those shown in Figure 11.1. This type of software provides a small-scale database of information on a selected set of topics. These may be accessed and manipulated by using the protocols that are built into the program.

For example, suppose a database includes information on the legislative and executive branches of our government from 1800 through 1980. Imagine also that a student has a question that requires the database to answer. He or she is interested in finding how many presidents during the period 1864–1976 had to work with Congresses in which both the House and the Senate were controlled by the opposing party.

To answer the question, the student will have to translate it into one or more operations or subquestions that fit the protocols used by the software (See Elder & White, 1989). With most databases, this is likely to require that the student first specify in some fashion that all cases be located for the period in question. It may further require the condition to be specified where the President was a Republican and the House and the Senate were Democratic or where the President was a Democrat, while the two houses were Republican.

Database programs, such as the one in our preceding example, also often permit students to enter new data to increase the scope of the base. In the example just provided, a class might be able to enlarge the database beyond 1980 by including current information for the categories established within the database. Once that update is completed, the system would entertain queries that extend beyond the original endpoint of 1980 until the date of the most recent entries.

Other database software, such as *Filing System*, *ClarisWorks*, and *Bank Street Filer*, are generic; that is, they contain no data and are "shells" that will organize and synthesize any type of data. They allow students to create their own information systems on any topic with any categories of information (see Mernit, 1991).

For example, suppose a class research project involves collecting some basic data concerning the nature, scope, and seriousness of the problem of the homeless in America. The teacher has divided the class into 10 groups, each responsible for five states.

After some discussion, the teacher and the groups identify the basic questions they would like to have answered from the research.

- Who are the homeless (e.g., gender, number of children)?
- How extensive is the problem of the homeless (e.g., number)?
- Where is the problem of the homeless the greatest in the United States (e.g., states with highest percentage)?
- How much are local and state governments doing to solve the problem of the homeless (e.g., state expenditures, type of shelters provided)?

One group lists on a large sheet of paper the categories of data that it recommends the class collect and enter into the database according to the procedures specified in the software manual. The categories the students initially include in the database are shown in Figure 11.3.

**Figure 11.3**
**Categories to Include in Sample Database**

Name of state (abbr): ________ Total population of state: ________

Estimated number of homeless: ________

Homeless as % of total population: ________

Percentage of homeless who are males: ________ Females: ________

Percentage of homeless who are children (17 yrs. or less): ________

Annual state and local governmental expenditures for the homeless: ________

Types of shelters provided (select type from the list): ________________________

________________________________________________________________

Other groups make further recommendations, and the teacher points out some changes in the categories that are required by the protocols of the database, for example, not using commas in recording numerical data. The class as a whole then finally adopts a common list of categories.

As a next step, students proceed to do research and mathematical calculations to identify the required information. Then they enter the data under each category. Once this is accomplished, students can use the database to answer their questions and test hypotheses.

Spreadsheet software engages students in social mathematics (Hannah, 1985–86). It enables them to make numerical tabulations quickly, make predictions from extrapolations, and show the impact of one variable on another (e.g., effects of increased cigarette taxes on federal budget).

Within spreadsheets, numerical data are entered in columns and rows (see Figure 11.4), and results may be represented as tabular data or in the form of graphs and charts. For example, the table of data in Figure 7.6 could be entered in the spreadsheet. The data would appear under three columns (a, b, c), which represent states, males, and females) and 51 rows, which represent all of the states and the District of Columbia.

Although many spreadsheets appear foreboding and complex to use, some, such as *ClarisWorks* and *The Cruncher* by Davidson are suitable for students in the middle and secondary grades. *The Cruncher*, for example, is designed for use by those ages 10 to adult.

**Figure 11.4**
**A Typical Spreadsheet**

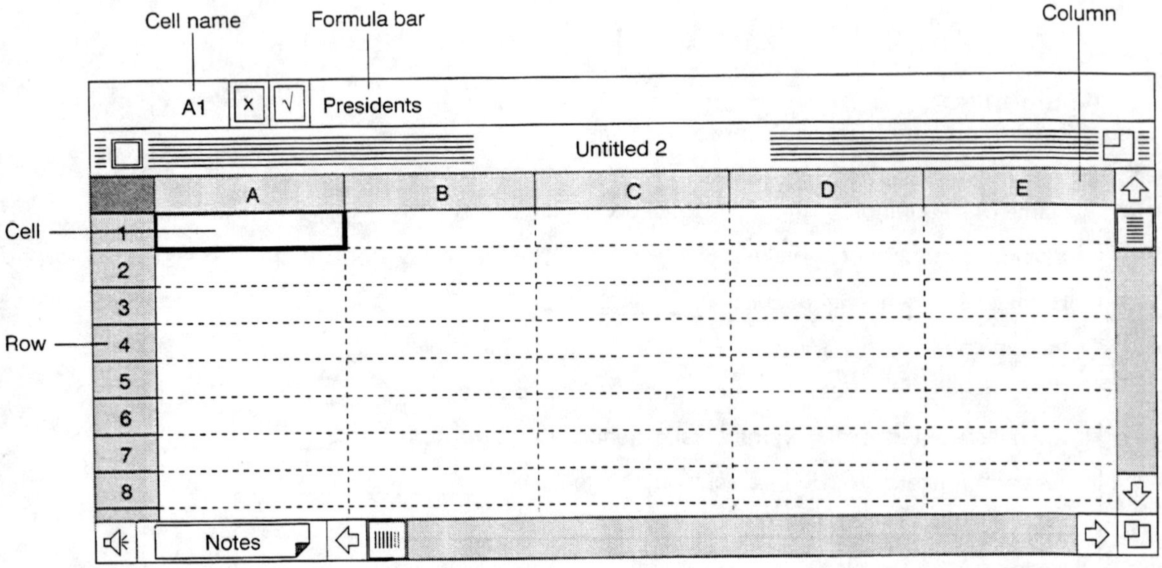

## Using Groups with Computer-Based Instruction

Often teachers have a small group of students work together with a single computer and software program. This may be due to an instructional decision (i.e., objective is best achieved through a group) or a resource constraint (i.e., are not enough computers for whole class). Some programs also are designed specifically to have students work cooperatively in small groups to solve a problem. This type of software is commonly referred to as **groupware.**

Roberts, Carter, Friel, and Miller (1988) have supplied an excellent example of how students in the middle grades were able to work effectively in groups on a sustained basis with a single computer using software called *Survey Taker.*

> A fifth-grade class studying local town government decided to take a survey of the people's feelings about the quality of town services. Class members created the survey, typing into the computer the questions as they agreed upon them. The class wrote twenty questions and then decided to pilot the instrument with another fifth-grade class to see if the questions were clear and sensible. . . . The pilot suggested there were too many questions. . . . Based on the pilot, the class rewrote some questions, cutting the total number to fifteen. (p. 54)

The students then administered the refined survey to adults during parent's night. In doing do, the children separated the respondents into two categories: town employees and nonemployees. As a follow-up, the students spent several months interviewing town officials responsible for public services.

In all cases, effective group work with computers requires some of the same skills and structures that are discussed in Chapter 5. It also involves establishing procedures to ensure that all students have access to the computer and have an opportunity to alternate roles in using it. Additionally, it demands that students have challenging and significant objectives to address.

## Evaluating Social Studies Software

Teachers should examine software as critically as they do traditional print materials and media. This requires that they become conversant with the capabilities and limitations of existing software through the use of objective evaluation criteria.

Evaluation of instructional software should occur at two levels. One addresses general technical and instructional issues such as whether the software functions flawlessly or gives clear directions. Numerous guidelines have been developed for teachers to conduct objective evaluations at this level (e.g., Roberts, Carter, Friel, & Miller, 1988). A second level of evaluation focuses on the way in which subject matter is represented in the software, for instance, whether it is factually correct and addresses significant objectives.

A set of guidelines for the second type of evaluation has been prepared by the National Council for the Social Studies (NCSS) (Rose, Brandhorst, Glenn, Hodges, & White, 1984). The guidelines have three dimensions—*knowledge, skills,* and *values*—following the structure of the NCSS Curriculum Guidelines. Each of the three dimensions of evaluation is represented by a series of questions that are to be considered in evaluating software. The three sets of questions are shown in Figure 11.5.

## TELECOMMUNICATIONS AND ONLINE INFORMATION

The growth in telecommunications applications in recent years has been phenomenal. **Telecommunications** involve sending and receiving information using some combination of a microcomputer, a modem, communications software, and a telephone line. Through telecommunications, students and teachers can exchange information around the world. They also have online access to gigantic databases at remote locations that once were reserved for the military and researchers. The **online** provision refers to the fact that a user is actually interacting with computers that may be several thousand miles or even continents away. The databases accessed include magazines, newspapers, news wire services, reference works, book reviews, government publications, and consumer information.

Studies indicate that students are enthusiastic about online searching and are able to use it effectively (Callison & Daniels, 1988; Callison, 1989). Collis (1988), in detailing the benefits of online database usage, observed:

> The benefits to teachers and students are enormous. We predict a very different approach to social studies if access to worldwide, up-to-date information is made available to classrooms during current events discussions. Accessing information in this way is consistent with an approach to social studies that emphasizes process skills and critical thinking. . . . The ability to retrieve and examine a diversity of opinions on a newsworthy issue independent of the school library resources available could even help redress the considerable differences in opportunity for students in remote, rural schools compared to those in more affluent suburban schools. (p. 48)

Online searches of large databases for social studies instruction for a fee now is possible through programs established for schools by major commercial information services such as *AT&T Learning Network, eWorld, SCHOLASTIC NETWORK*, and *Online America*.

One commercial program, *WorldClassroom* (Global Learning Corporation), combines computer conferencing with access to an online social studies database. Schools that subscribe to the service pay a fee each semester.

**Figure 11.5**
**NCSS Microcomputer Courseware Evaluation Guide**

**KNOWLEDGE**

**Significant Characteristics**

1.01 Validity
Does the courseware emphasize currently valid knowledge from one or more of the social sciences (including history)?

1.02 Accuracy
Does the courseware present a true and comprehensive body of content, free of distortion by omission?

1.03 Reality Oriented
Does the courseware's content deal with the realities of today's world in terms of its flaws, strengths, dangers, and promises?

1.04 Significance of Past and Present
Does the courseware deal with important concepts, principles, and theories of modern society? Does it present significant ideas that convey the excitement of the past, present, and future?

1.05 Bias
Does the courseware avoid bias and/or stereotyping with regard to gender, ethnicity, racial background, religious application, or cultural group? When unfamiliar customs and institutions or different ethnic groups and cultures are dealt with, are they presented in an unbiased and objective manner?

**Content Emphasis**

1.11 Issue Analysis
Does the courseware engage students in analyzing and attempting to resolve social issues? Is a data base provided and does it contain information of sufficient depth and breadth for students to make realistic decisions? If not, can the data base be expanded by the teacher or student?

1.12 Pervasive and Enduring Issues
Does the courseware focus on problems and/or issues that are socially significant? Do the materials demonstrate the reciprocal relationships among the social sciences, social issues, and action?

1.13 Global Perspectives
Does the courseware help students develop a global perspective? Are the students assisted in recognizing the local, national, and global implications of the problems being examined and their possible solutions?

1.14 Development of Society
Does the courseware develop knowledge and insights into the historical development of human society? Do the facts, concepts, principles, and processes presented offer direction in organizing a study of human behavior? Does it help students understand how modern societies develop, the role of central institutions and values of national societies and those of the world community?

1.15 Multiculturalism
Does the courseware help develop an understanding of the diversity of cultures and institutional arrangements within American society and in other societies within the global community? Does it provide a rational explanation for customs and other distinctive aspects of daily life arrangements that are explored? Does it contribute to the students' acceptance of the legitimacy of their own cultural identity as well as that of others?

1.16 Personal/Social Growth
Does the courseware help students understand their own development and capacities, as influenced by their families, peer groups, ethnic groups, media, and the society at large?

**SKILLS**

Social studies education should provide students with the opportunities to develop, practice, and use a variety of thought processes and skills. Students should have opportunities to probe, to extract knowledge from experience, to think and to communicate their findings and conclusions, both orally and in writing. They should learn how to learn—to develop self-direction in gaining meaningful knowledge and employing

*Note.* From *NCSS Microcomputer Courseware Evaluation* (pp. 1–3) by National Council for the Social Studies, 1983, Washington, DC: Author. © National Council for the Social Studies. Used with permission.

**Figure 11.5 continued**

it effectively. The social studies program should develop the student's ability to make rational decisions. In order to accomplish this, it is essential that students acquire skills in critical thinking, inquiry, information processing, and problem solving.

**Intellectual Skills**

2.01 Inquiry and Problem Solving
Does the courseware pose problems which require students to use the methods of inquiry? Specifically, are students given practice in identifying and defining problems, formulating and testing hypotheses, and arriving at valid generalizations?

2.02 Critical Thinking
Does the courseware foster the development of critical thinking skills of distinguishing between fact and opinion, detecting slant and bias, determining cause and effect, and evaluating the reliability of sources?

2.03 Higher Cognitive Levels
Does the courseware help students develop and/or reinforce the thought processes of analysis, synthesis, and evaluation? Do students encounter material that helps develop their understanding of the relationship between elements and how these elements fit together as a whole? Are students given opportunities to use information to construct a new communication? Are students asked to make judgments based on appropriate criteria?

2.04 Divergent Thinking
Does the courseware encourage divergent thinking which allows students to provide a variety of answers for difficult questions?

2.05 Concept Formation
Does the courseware present a broad range of illustrations, models, and examples which are appropriate for helping students imagine, dissect, conceptualize, define, or recognize relationships between patterns or concepts?

**Decisionmaking Skills**

2.11 Processes
Does the courseware foster the decisionmaking skills of identifying alternatives, establishing criteria to evaluate the alternatives, evaluating the alternatives in light of criteria and making the decisions? Are students given the opportunity to retest, reinterpret, and reorganize their beliefs about facts and values?

2.12 Learning Environment
Do the courseware and its accompanying materials create a social environment populated by believable characters confronting difficult circumstances and choices?

2.13 Choices
Does the courseware require the student to make choices, and are those choices then used as data for reflection?

2.14 Information Base
Does the courseware's data match the kind of data that would be accessible by citizens outside the instructional context? Is the courseware flexible enough to allow the alteration and addition of information, so that students can practice making decisions under a variety of factual and value circumstances?

2.15 Consequences
Does the courseware confront students with realistic consequences (for themselves and for others) of decisions they are required to make in using the courseware?

2.16 Assessment
Do the courseware and its accompanying materials assist the teacher and the student to assess the latter's skills and abilities in decisionmaking?

2.17 Degree of Certainty
Does the courseware provide experiences in making decisions under conditions of uncertainty? Does the courseware help the student recall the basis on which decisions were made and to make revised decisions informed by new understandings?

**Figure 11.5 continued**

**Information Processing Skills**

2.21 Orientation Skills
Does the courseware foster the development of map and globe skills?

2.22 Chronology and Time Skills
Does the courseware provide students practice in interpreting chronology and applying time skills, i.e., sequencing events and trends and identifying and using measures of time correctly?

2.23 Graphic Data Skills
Does the courseware help students develop skills of reading and interpreting, constructing and drawing inferences from graphs, tables, and charts?

2.24 Gathering and Processing Data
Does the courseware provide opportunities for students to develop skills in locating, organizing, interpreting, and presenting data?

2.25 Content Reading Skills
Does the courseware facilitate the development of the student's word attack skills and the ability to read on the literal, interpretive, and applied levels?

2.26 Communication Skills
Does the courseware or its accompanying material foster adequately developed communication skills and provide opportunities for communicating effectively orally and in writing?

**Cooperation and Participation Skills**

2.31 Interaction
Do the courseware and its accompanying materials require groups of students to work together? Do the learning tasks require a division of labor? Does successful completion of the tasks require shared information?

2.32 Cooperation
Do the courseware and its accompanying material reinforce the importance of, and provide support for, cooperation in resolving conflicts over contradictory facts and values?

2.33 Social/Political Participation
Does the interaction with the courseware and its accompanying materials enhance the student's ability to participate effectively in the social and political processes of his/her school and community?

2.34 Follow-up Activities
Does the courseware or its accompanying materials offer suggestions for activities that follow logically from the use of the courseware? Does the courseware allow students to experience vicariously the positive and negative consequences, the costs and benefits, the frustrations and satisfactions of taking action?

**VALUES**

**Societal Orientation**

3.01 Influence of Values on Behavior
Does the courseware help students develop an understanding and appreciation of the influence of beliefs and values on human behavior patterns?

3.02 Procedural Values
Does the courseware help the student identify and develop an appreciation for values that underlie substantive beliefs and procedural guarantees expressed in this nation's fundamental documents?

**Valuing Processes**

3.11 Beliefs
Does the courseware require the student to identify his or her own beliefs, to make choices based on those beliefs, and to understand the consequences of the choices made?

3.12 Conjoint Reflection
Does the courseware require conjoint reflection on feelings, behaviors, and beliefs?

3.13 Defensible Judgments
Does the courseware support a process of value analysis by which learners can make rational, defensible value judgments?

3.14 Feedback
Does the courseware track the process students use in making value judgments and provide useful feedback with respect to its quality and improvement?

Using this program, students around the world have an opportunity to communicate with their peers and contribute to an international student newspaper. In North Carolina, for example, it is possible for anyone at a remote location to search online through the electronic list of holdings of the major universities in the state. Several other states make similar provisions.

## The Internet

Many telecommunications are sent along the **Internet,** a giant electronic data highway that speeds messages and information from networks of linked computers along to their destinations. Those who share access to the Internet may send messages, retrieve information and files from databases, and connect with thousands of other networks around the world. These networks can be connected by a host of individual computers. Currently there are estimated to be between 4 and 15 million stations in over 100 countries, although no one is sure of the actual numbers.

Access to the Internet generally is arranged by a commercial service, university, or an educational institution for a nominal charge. For example, the state of Massachusetts, through the Mass LearnNet, gives an Internet connection to any school within the state that requests it. TENET in Texas, CORE in California, FIRN in Florida, and VaPAN in Virginia have statewide networks for K through 12 teachers.

The Internet was created in 1969 by the Pentagon to help researchers and the military expedite the sharing of information around the world. Increasingly, however, it is being used by teachers and students to access and share information and break down the barriers between school and real-world learning (Pawloski, 1994). The Global School House Project, for example, links students from different states and countries to work on common projects. The Internet also reduces the isolation that many classroom teachers feel and increases the potential for collaborative activities.

The introduction to *Where on the Globe Is Roger?* (see Figure 11.6) illustrates how the Internet may be used in conjunction with the study of countries. Therein, Roger Williams, a retired pilot, offers to have students join him electronically for his jaunts around the world.

Increasingly, journals and newsletters are becoming available in electronic form over the Internet. *The Electronic Newsstand,* sponsored by *Educom,* for instance, offers free access to articles from leading magazines and newsletters (1-800-403-6397). Plans are underway to replace the Internet with a more powerful system known as the **National Research and Education Network (NREN).** Traditional telephone companies, such as BellSouth, also have plans afoot to provide Internet-like services to homes, schools, and businesses.

## Electronic Mail (E-Mail)

One of the primary uses of the Internet is to send **Electronic mail (e-mail).** "Use of electronic mail in education has grown rapidly in recent years, reflecting proliferation of microcomputers, modems, networks, and easier-to-use software" (Updegrove, 1991, p. 37). E-mail is a system of sending and receiving communications across great distances at relatively little cost. Once a school or classroom is set up for telecommunications and access to the Internet, the only direct cost for e-mail often is the price of a local phone call.

E-mail can be sent from individual to individual or from an individual to a group. Each individual or organization on the Internet is assigned an **address.** Addresses can be used to contact organizations as well as individuals. For example, a social studies teacher who needed help with planning a unit on the French Revolution might contact the Educational Resources Information Center (ERIC) Clearinghouse on Information and Technology for help at the address: *askeric@ericir.syr.edu.*

Networks on the Internet can link teachers and students around the world and allow international collaboration. An example is the I*Earn Project (345 Kear Street, Yorktown Heights, NY 10598), which links schools in 20 countries through both e-mail and telephones. The organization assists young people in developing projects that make a meaningful contribution to their societies and the planet. It also arranges international exchanges so that students can work together on site. A recent project was the Nicaragua Water Pump Project to construct village pumps to provide clean water.

Apart from the potential for cross-cultural insights and sharing from regional, national, and international hookups, e-mail affords students in social studies classes opportunities to obtain timely and reality-based information for research projects. As an illustration, a middle-grade class compared its ideas of what made up an ideal community with those of other students in the United States and abroad (Brehm & Waugh, 1993). Similarly, during the height of the Persian Gulf War, students in Tennessee got firsthand accounts from Israeli students about the Scud attacks.

E-mail also can help students hone their communication skills. Since e-mail protocols promote focused writing (i.e., identifying audience and the purpose of the message), revising and editing before sending are important. Because the message will be sent out over a public forum to an unseen audience, students also tend to be motivated to produce an exemplary communication.

## Two-Way Video Conferencing

Besides text messages and files, the Internet can carry graphics, still or animated video data, and sounds, if they exist in digital form. **Two-way video conferencing** (sometimes known as **desk-top video conferencing**) is an application of this capability. Students from around the nation and the world, using their computers, telephone connections, and special software, can link to sites known as **reflectors** and exchange video images in **real time** (that is, as they are created).

It also is possible to include sound and written messages. Images can be provided by a digital camera, regular video cameras that are connected

**Figure 11.6**
**Introduction to *Where on the Globe Is Roger?***

**Introducing... Where on the Globe Is Roger?**

Join Roger Williams, a global adventurer and raconteur, as he leaves South America and travels to South East Asia. Roger is driving around the globe in his 1982 Dodge truck and he wants to take you along on his trip—via your connection to the Internet. You can plot his travels on your global map; read his entertaining dispatches from the exotic places he visits; ask him questions; and make friends with the students in the places he visits.

Global SchoolNet Foundation is pleased to provide you with "free travel passes" to take a most amazing electronic journey with Roger!

Here is an invitation from Roger to all the school children around the globe.

Dear Boys and Girls,

I would like to introduce you to what I think will be a great adventure for us all and a chance to learn about countries around the world, first hand. My name is Roger Williams. I'm a retired Airline Pilot and U.S. Marine Corps Aviator. I was born on a ranch in Texas on October 3, 1936, graduated from High School in Austin, Texas, and then spent one year at the University of Texas.

My dream from the fourth grade on was to become a Marine Pilot. That dream was realized after many years of hard work in April 1962. While in the Marine Corps, I flew off aircraft carriers during the Vietnam War. I have always enjoyed traveling and I think this will be the ultimate trip as I drive my truck across every continent around the globe.

On the first leg of my journey. I departed from Southern California, on January 14, 1994, and drove through Mexico and all of Central America. I then shipped my truck from Panama to Northern Chile. From there I drove the full length of Chile and crossed into Argentina and proceeded to Tierra del Fuego. Upon completing my goal of reaching Tierra del Fuego by mid April 1994, I then proceeded north

to a video capture board, or a special inexpensive miniature video camera (e.g., QuickCam for less than $100). As we go to press, Apple Computer has announced the development of its own program for two-way video conferencing, called QuickTime Conferencing (fax# 1-800-510-2834).

Picture four small groups of students, ages 14 to 15. Two are from rural communities in different areas of the United States; another is from an urban school in Slovakia; and the other is from a suburban area in Germany. Each group is clustered around a computer station facing a camera smaller than a baseball that includes a built-in microphone and sits atop the monitor.

Engaged in a conference over the Internet, the students are comparing the results of interviews they had conducted. Earlier, they had asked selected individuals in their communities to answer the question: "What does it mean to be a 'good' citizen?" On the monitor, in four windows, each group can see and hear each other as they discuss what they learned and the anomalies in their data.

**Figure 11.6**
**continued**

through Argentina to Brazil and shipped my truck from Santos, Brazil, to Brisbane, Australia.

Throughout my travels, I visited local schools and helped the children communicate with kids back in the United States.

I am about to begin the next part of my journey. I am flying to Brisbane on August 1, 1994, to start my trip through Australia, Indonesia, Malaysia, Thailand, and possibly Burma—and, then on to China and Russia. I hope to be able to cross Russia then travel into Europe through Spain and Portugal. I will cross into Africa and finally return home sometime in late 1996 or early 1997.

As you can see, it will be a grand adventure and I hope you can join me through activities being coordinated by the Global SchoolNet Foundation. You see, challenge is an integral part of the human experience. Without it, life becomes very dull. We all have to challenge ourselves if we expect to grow and help make a better world for people to live in. Through participating in this adventure, I would hope you will be able to form life long friendships with other students around the world.

With better global human understanding, the possibility of violent conflicts diminishes. I am hoping all of us can contribute to a lasting World Peace.

I will be sending you summaries of my travels and when possible, digitized photos, using a special device called ComputerEyes that hooks up to my Apple laptop computer. I look forward to answering your questions and will do the best that I can. If my answers sometimes seem short and to the point, that is just the way I am—so just bear with me!

Sincerely,

Roger

Apart from the costs related to the Internet telephone connection and the computer station, the cost for each group would be less than $100 for the camera/microphone. Software that could make the conference a reality exists as freeware called *CUSeeMe* (available from the following e-mail address: CU-SeeMe_L@Cornell.edu).

## Social Studies Resources on the Internet

Once you have access, how do you actually locate resources and display information stored on the Internet? Since the Internet is not owned or controlled by a single source, searching for items and individuals can be complex and frustrating. In addition, movement from one document to another typically is cumbersome.

Most efforts to simplify access and movement have centered around development of protocols to link documents stored along the Internet. The

**World-Wide Web** (WWW) is such a system. In conjunction with the WWW, "friendly" software interfaces that incorporate color, sound, still and motion pictures, and text have been developed to display linked documents. Two popular interfaces are **Mosaic** and **Netscape** (Pike et al., 1994).

*Mosaic* and *Netscape* allow the user to "browse" and "navigate" among documents by clicking on a highlighted piece of text that contains **hyperlinks** to a related document. For example, students using *Netscape* with the WWW might access the Library of Congress at the following address: http://lcweb.loc.gov/homepage/1chp.html. Thereafter, using a mouse, they could click on a highlighted link to obtain information on countries or browse through the library's holdings and then return to their starting place.

Marx (1995, pp. 1–2) has provided a list of WWW resources accessible with *Mosaic* or *Netscape*. A sample of these, along with a description, is shown here:

http://wings.buffalo.edu/world/vt2/City.Net
World Map—a good place to start exploring the world.

http://www.ncsa.uiuc.edu/Edu/Classroom/classroom.html
Good links to educational resources in all subject areas.

http://www.lib.uci.edu/sources/social.html
Internet sources: Social sciences

http://history.cc.ukans.edu/history/WWW_history_main.html
The World-Wide Web Virtual Library: History.

http://www.law.cornell.edu/supct/supct.table.html
Supreme Court decisions.

http://www.ic.gov/94fact/fb94toc/fb94toc.html
*The World Factbook 1994*—information from over 200 countries.

http://www.csulb.edu/gc/libarts/am-indian/to_1600.html
First section of multimedia history of Native Americans.

http://www.csulb.edu/gc/libarts/am-indian/
*American Historical Images on File*

## MULTIMEDIA IN THE AGE OF EMERGING COMPUTER TECHNOLOGIES

Emerging video technologies have resulted in increasingly sophisticated tape and disc players that are designed for use with a computer. A microcomputer can access data from these video media in essentially the same way that it accesses other data from software. In addition, through these technologies it is possible to catalog and view video data in nonlinear ways (see Martorella, 1989). To illustrate, a student could view only those frames of a videodisc on the American Revolution that contained subject matter dealing with the incident at Lexington Green.

Definitions of the term abound, but essentially, the term **interactive multimedia** refers to some combination of video, sound, graphics, and images orchestrated by a computer. "Interactive multimedia—the marriage of text, audio, and visual data within a single information delivery system—represents a potentially powerful tool for teachers and students throughout the curriculum" (White, 1990, p. 68). *Interactivity* refers to the fact that the user controls his or her path through a program.

Interactive multimedia technologies show promise of aiding social studies teachers in motivating students and translating abstract ideas into more concrete examples (Martorella, in press). The effective and full use of these electronic aids, however, will depend on how skilled social studies teachers become in their applications. As Simon (1990) has underscored, "It is increasingly clear that as powerful new technologies and software proliferate, teachers will need to learn more about these new tools on a continuous basis" (p. 8).

Emerging multimedia systems can incorporate sounds and images from CD-ROM discs, video cameras, VCRs, digital cameras, scanned pictures, and videodiscs. Also, software, such as *QuickTime* from Apple, allows teachers and students to create and edit motion images and sounds as digital files that can be pasted into HyperCard stacks. For example, a student report on immigration might include with the text edited clips of film footage on Ellis Island taken from a program on The Discovery Channel. Figure 11.7 describes a high school scenario in which students are studying the Constitutional Convention (Fernlund, 1993).

Multimedia systems increasingly have gained acceptance in many sectors of our society other than schools. They already are widely used by the military and industry for individual employee training by museums such as the Smithsonian Institution to provide general information for visitors. The most common systems employ interactive videodiscs.

Within interactive multimedia systems, microcomputers can access data from any location on videotapes or discs. Video data also may be mixed with expository text. Using special software, teachers also can superimpose prompts on the video material to pose a question or call attention to some special aspect of the subject matter. Further, alternative sound tracks are possible (e.g., instruction accompanying the video in either Spanish or English).

## Interactive Multimedia Systems in Social Studies Instruction

Social studies teachers may employ interactive multimedia systems in either of two basic ways. They can access off-the-shelf, professionally designed kits that include components such as videodiscs, computer software, and related teacher and student materials. Alternately, teachers can create their own multimedia systems (e.g., see Kanning, 1994). Examples of both applications in the social studies curriculum at the elementary, middle, and secondary school levels already exist across the United States.

**Figure 11.7**
**High School Use of *QuickTime* (Apple Computer)**

**High School Classroom: Constitutional Convention**

A U.S. History class of 35 students is working in groups of three or four students, each assigned a multimedia project on the Constitutional Convention. The room has one multimedia work station with a laser printer, video disk player, scanner, and CD player attached to the computer. The remainder of the room has several tables for group meetings, 10 computers with dot-matrix printers and several hand-held scanners. Students are using HyperCard software for their projects. Students at the work station are choosing video segments from a laser disc on American History and selecting historical paintings from a Humanities laser disc. *QuickTime* from Apple Computer allows students to select video clips and sound to incorporate in their project. These students are coordinating graphics with the information they have gathered. Students at one of the individual computers are scanning legal documents and placing them in their HyperCard stack. They are also scanning sketches and other graphics to include with their annotated bibliography. One group is creating a project on the slavery issue and the resulting compromise at the convention. The HyperCard stack will be a resource for other students who can use it to discover more about slavery in American history. Other group multimedia projects are on the Bill of Rights, James Madison, the powers of Congress, the Presidency, and the Supreme Court.

From "Learners, Technology, and Law-related Education," by P.M. Fernlund, 1993, *Law Studies, 28.*

The number of existing professionally designed interactive multimedia programs for the social studies is growing. We will consider briefly two illustrative commercial programs that are appropriate for the middle and secondary grades: *GTV: A Geographic Perspective on American History* and *Martin Luther King, Jr.* Each contains videodiscs and software that can activate the videodiscs. Both IBM and Apple Macintosh versions are available from Optical Data Corporation (1-800-524-2481). These interactive programs have gained wide acceptance in classrooms across the United states where they are helping to enliven social studies instruction.

Picture a class studying American history. A small group of students is huddled in front of a videodisc player, a computer, and a color monitor. In the player is one of the two discs in a program called *GTV: A Geographic Perspective on American History.* Each of the two discs contains one hour of video and audio data on various aspects of American history, including still photographs, graphs, maps, and music. In addition to the video data, students can access additional program information on a range of topics, such as colonization, the Industrial Revolution, immigration, westward expansion, and independence.

As students select a topic from the menu by clicking a mouse, clear, crisp videodisc images appear on the color monitor within three seconds, providing visual data on the topic selected. After viewing the data, students

**Increasingly, schools are using advanced video and computer technologies to enhance instruction.**

may be queried on the computer screen concerning what they have seen. If they have questions, they have an opportunity to link to other related information in the computer program. They also may return to the menu of topics and select a new, related sequence of videodisc images or "browse" through the data. To complete their assignments relating to the era of Theodore Roosevelt, students are consulting a CD-ROM source, "Who Built America?" a multimedia history of America from 1876 to 1914.

Consider further a similar series of activities with another class in which students are studying the life of Martin Luther King, Jr. and his role in American history. As part of their study, the class can use an interactive multimedia program that employs a videodisc, *Martin Luther King, Jr.*, containing visual and audio data that documents his accomplishments, beginning with the Montgomery bus boycott in 1955. Students can access data about key points in his life, view film footage of these events, hear and read complete texts of his "I Have a Dream" speech, and examine important documents by interacting with the system.

Other representative multimedia programs are listed in Figure 11.8.

The demand for these types of instructional materials is likely to continue to grow as states with textbook adoption policies become more flexible in how a "text" is defined in an era of high technology. Utah and Texas, for example, now permit adoptions of resources such as videodiscs in lieu of textbooks.

**Figure 11.8**
**Other Multimedia Programs**

| Title | Publisher | Description |
|---|---|---|
| *Visual Archives of American History* | Scott Foresman | Cross section of still and motion visual data from American history correlated with a basal textbook. |
| *Powers of the President* | Optical Data Corporation | Relates to the role of the President and the powers of the executive branch. |
| *Struggles for Justice: Women, Labor, Immigrants* | Scholastic | Features selected episodes in the history of three groups. |
| *The Video Encyclopedia of the 20th Century* | CEL Educational Resources | Contains 42 videodiscs of assorted national and world events. |

We will examine briefly two cases where social studies teachers created their own multimedia programs. These involved a Macintosh computer and related HyperCard software.

Basic multimedia systems also can be combined easily with data from a CD-ROM unit (discussed later in this chapter) to afford multiple linkages of databases. Fundamental commands are not complex, and sets of instructions (HyperCard scripts), images, and drawings from one program can be easily "borrowed" and copied into another. This latter capability facilitates teacher sharing and thus saves considerable time.

Because of the nonlinear way video data are accessed in an multimedia system, existing videodiscs can be used for a different instructional or informational purpose than the author intended. This is done by referencing selected frames and using the data to address points that were not part of the author's objectives. Such a use is referred to as **repurposing** a disc.

Note the following example of how a team of teachers created their own social studies materials using a Macintosh computer, HyperCard software, and a repurposed videodisc entitled, *The Vancouver Disc.* The videodisc contains a collection of single pictures (still frames) with motion sequences of different places, things, and incidents that occurred over time in one city, Vancouver, British Columbia. Its presumed original purpose was to provide viewers with a varied database concerning Vancouver.

In repurposing the disk, the teachers selectively applied both sound and video data from *The Vancouver Disc* to new uses. The title of their instructional program was *Why Cities Develop Where They Do* (Vest & Bjork, 1989). Its goal was to facilitate students' understanding of the phenomena that caused cities in the United States to develop in particular geographical locations.

One feature of the program was a video quiz that requires a student to choose the reason that a city prospered after viewing a series of video segments. Video music (i.e., music on the video sound track without the video) provided positive reinforcement when the learner selected the correct answer.

Another example of teacher-made materials is the multimedia units developed in *The Refugee Awareness Program* (TRAP). TRAP was created to address significant refugee issues and develop related instructional materials in the social studies curriculum. The project is based at the College of Education and Psychology at North Carolina State University and was supported in part by a grant from the United States Institute of Peace (Martorella, 1993).

TRAP has as its broad long-range goal the infusion into the secondary curriculum of a greater awareness of the origins, nature, scope, and implications of the growing world refugee crisis. Toward this end, TRAP has developed and conducted specialized course and seminar sessions for inservice secondary social studies teachers. It has also assisted teachers in creating related instructional materials, including interactive multimedia units.

The four units developed by TRAP all employ a videodisc, *Refugees: Marginal Living Conditions*, which was originally produced as a videotape by the U.S. General Accounting Office (GAO). Each focuses on different aspects of refugee issues. In addition to general background information, each unit includes a copy of a computer disk containing HyperCard files and Voyager VideoStack software that controls the videodisc player.

**Using Videodiscs.** The video data in an interactive multimedia system can be accessed from tape or disc, but videodiscs are the most common format. Currently, only a relatively small number of commercial videodiscs are available for social studies instruction, but the number is increasing.

## Microcomputers and CD-ROM Technology

In addition to videodiscs, many systems labeled "multimedia" now use **CD-ROM** (Compact Disc-Read Only Memory) units because of their large storage capacity and ease of access and relatively low cost. A CD-ROM, which looks like an audio CD, is 5 inches in diameter and can hold approximately 270,000 pages of information or a mix of text, images, full-motion video, and sounds. This means that entire libraries of print, pictures, and sound can be stored on a few discs. CD-ROM discs are accessed by a computer connected to a special drive that plays the discs.

Callison (1989) saw a promising future for the use of CD-ROM technology in social studies instruction:

> From one CD-ROM station, the student can compare statistics from hundreds of tables to show longevity trends or comparisons from one country to another. The student, working at the one computer terminal, will be able to move from a map of a given country to its capital, to a street map of that city, and then shift to maps that represent the historical development of that country relevant to world history during the past centuries. (pp. 85–86)

CD-ROM applications increasingly are finding their way into middle and secondary schools. For example, now available on CD-ROM discs are sound and video enhanced versions of encyclopedias: *Compton's Multimedia Encyclopedia* and *Encarta Multimedia Encyclopedia.* Also available in CD-ROM format are *Books in Print* and *Reader's Guide to Periodic Literature.*

XIPHIAS has developed *Time Table of History: Business, Politics, and Media,* a collection of key events in history related to wealth, power, and knowledge. Another disc, *How the World Works,* recounts a brief history of civilization.

Also, the National Geographic Society has produced a program for the middle grades, *The Presidents: It All Started with George,* that includes motion-picture footage, period music, animated maps, and time lines. The Society also has created a disc entitled *Picture Atlas of the World.*

*Voices of the 30s* is a product of Sunburst/Wings for Learning. It mixes sights and sounds of the 1930s with classroom activities on a CD-ROM disk.

The Voyager Company has developed *Who Built America?,* mentioned earlier, which covers data from 1876 to 1914 taken from the American Social History Project. Additionally, the company has begun to produce full-feature films, as well as complete texts of books in the CD-ROM format.

Microsoft *Bookshelf* is a collection of seven reference books with full sound and video on a single disk. A search for an entry will include all the works.

The Bureau of Electronic Publishing has produced two history disks: *U.S. History on CD-ROM* and *World History on CD-ROM.* Both include books, documents, photographs, and archive materials.

*Geopedia* by Britannica is a world geography program on CD-ROM that engages students in map-related activities.

Future generations of CD-ROM discs will be accessible at faster rates and hold even more data. When that point is reached, they are likely to replace videodiscs because of their lower costs and ease of use.

## Cable Television and Social Studies Instruction

Approximately, two thirds of all schools now receive some form of cable television for classroom instruction. Within the copyright restrictions, cable networks offer a vast store of contemporary television programming in flexible formats for instructional applications. As we considered in Chapter 9, major cable networks now provide special news and other educational programs that may be taped under certain conditions.

*Assignment Discovery*, produced by The Discovery Channel (1-800-321-1832), is an example of outstanding cable programming. It provides social studies programs via cable that may be taped for classroom use. Social studies and contemporary issues programs are aired on Tuesday and Friday during the school year at 9 A.M. (ET). Examples of recent programs are "Bill of Rights: Power to the People," "How the West Was Lost," and "The New Immigrants."

A sample lesson plan for "The New Immigrants" is given in Figure 11.9.

Since many of the *Assignment Discovery* programs extend over several hours and have broad themes, it is possible to build units around them. For example, a high school teacher, developed a one-week unit relating to the Industrial Revolution around text assignments and four *Assignment Discovery* programs (Discovery Networks' Educator Guide, 1993). She wished to show the effects of industrialization, such as population growth, sanitation problems, pollution, and agribusiness. The four programs she used, all of which illustrated the effects of industrialization on developing nations, were *The Arctic: Nomads of the Ice*, *Indonesia: Pressure of Population*, *Earthfiles: Waste and Fresh Water Management*, and *The Politics of Food*.

## Distance Learning

Imagine a small high school in a poor rural area and an American Government class. The class and several others are being taught by a professor who is located at a university 250 miles away. The teacher and students, who can see and hear each other, communicate via satellite transmission, telephone, and facsimile machines. They are engaged in **distance learning,** a process in which courses are transmitted in "real time" from locations remote to the classroom.

A growing number of states (e.g., Massachusetts, Texas, and Virginia) have established distance learning projects to enrich and broaden classroom instruction. In other cases, distance learning has provided elective courses, such as Economics or Sociology, to schools that lack the resources, teachers, or student population to justify such offerings.

An example of an extensive, diversified distance learning program is Mass LearnPike, which reaches over 200 Massachusetts school systems, as well as those in many other states. Mass LearnPike beams programs taught by experts to these systems from its Cambridge studios. It offers both programs on traditional social studies themes (e.g., *Ancestors: A Multicultural Exploration)* and *electronic fieldtrips* (e.g, *The Lowell Mills)*.

With **electronic fieldtrips,** a museum or historical site, such as Ellis Island, is brought to the students instead of the reverse. Local experts can

**Figure 11.9**
**Sample Lesson Plan for "The New Immigrants"**

**Contemporary Issues**

**Activities**

CULTURAL AWARENESS

**Before viewing:** Investigate and briefly describe the changes in the make-up of the populations that formed the waves of immigration in U.S. history since 1900. Within schools with diverse populations, what strategies are practiced to sensitize students to a multicultural learning environment? Why are they necessary? What do you suspect are the special needs of immigrants who have come from violent homelands? What services are available in your community to help them combat the scars of the past?

**After viewing:** What are the cultural characteristics of the Asian, Hispanic, and Muslim immigrants to the U.S.? Predict why these groups will face different assimilation problems as compared with European immigrants of the past. What evidence was presented in the documentary to suggest that some immigrants are never acculturated? Explain where you stand and why on the issue of requiring immigrants to learn English. What are the intergenerational problems that arise between immigrant parents and their children who are raised predominantly or exclusively in the U.S.?

POLITICAL AWARENESS

**Before viewing:** Research the principles of the Immigration Act of 1990 and how it changed U.S. policies. What has been its significance thus far? Identify the political forces that oppose lenient immigration laws. What are their arguments and solutions to the problems? How do they get their opinions heard by lawmakers?

**After viewing:** How does the film portray the infusion of immigrants into politics? Argue for or against the likelihood that within three decades there will be a U.S. President whose family roots are from a non-European country. As a political leader of an immigrant group, how would you combat the problems of immigrants who fail to become U.S. citizens and exercise their right to vote?

*Source:* The Discovery Channel *Discovery Network's Educator Guide,* Lesson Plan.

focus on special features or artifacts and answer questions, much as they would during a conventional fieldtrip.

## Teacher- and Student-Made Video Materials

Teachers and students who have access to a video camera can collect and analyze their own visual data from field work, trips, interviews, and other activities. Bracey (1989), a teacher of a sixth-grade class described in part how her students created a videotape designed around the five themes of geography (see Chapter 3) that focused on their school.

**Figure 11.9 continued**

ECONOMIC AWARENESS

**Before viewing:** To what degree do immigrants pose a threat to the employment opportunities of U.S. citizens? Poll classmates and chart their beliefs as to whether or not immigrant groups pose a burden to the economy. Poll again after viewing and chart any changes.

**After viewing:** What are the arguments made about the value of immigrant groups to the economy of the U.S.? Explain why you agree or disagree with the argument as it works in your community.

**Interdisciplinary Activities**

1. Math/Technology: Use a computer to chart three different waves of immigration in U.S. history. Reflect the numbers of people, countries of origin, and one other pertinent fact about their demographics, such as where they settled or their occupations.
2. English/Language Arts: Write a first-person description of the adjustments a teenage immigrant could face coming from a foreign country to your school. Vary the country of origin among classmates and research the particular cultural differences and clashes that have been typical for that group.

**Media Literacy**

1. Discuss how well the director was able to represent the issues and problems related to immigration. Rate the effectiveness of scenes showing religious, political, and cultural diversity. If you were to re-shoot one of these topics, which would it be and how would you script the scene?
2. Evaluate the impact of the narrator. What was appealing about his presentation? What could be improved?

> We began our project, *Where in the World is Ashlawn School?*, with shots of a globe and maps showing Ashlawn School's exact location. . . . [A student] interviewed the former owner of the land on which Ashlawn is built. We included some old photographs of the original dairy farm, and footage of the owner's home and the milk house . . . We taped a visit to the Arlington Historical Society . . . and to the Arlington County courthouse. (Bracey, 1989, p. 4)

Video media also can be used effectively in the classroom in other ways. Thomas and Brubaker (1972) have outlined a number of applications, including the following:

1. Demonstrating how a project is to be done by showing an example from the preceding year's class,
2. Evaluating a tape of student presentation as a means of focusing more specifically on certain points,
3. Aiding absentees by providing tapes of key classroom activities that the student missed and which could not be easily recaptured otherwise, and
4. Informing parents about special classroom activities or projects.

Teachers may also use a video camera to monitor their own teaching by taping social studies lessons. One effective technique for analyzing taped class sessions is to turn off the sound and concentrate on certain specific aspects of nonverbal behavior, such as eye contact, on each play of the tape. After a session has been recorded, a teacher might select a 15-minute segment for the analysis.

One suggested procedure for organizing and processing the data is to divide a sheet of paper into two columns. Label the left one "Nonverbal Behaviors" and list the series of distinct behaviors in the order in which they occurred over the time segment selected. In the right column, list and separate the corresponding reactions of the students, verbal and nonverbal, under the heading "Student Responses."

## USING TRADITIONAL MEDIA EFFECTIVELY

As we noted earlier in the chapter, traditional media continue to assume an important role in social studies instruction. Such media include filmstrips, photographs, artifacts, 16mm films, transparencies, slides, records, audiotapes, and, more recently, videotapes. When used effectively, these media provide information in relation to a particular question, hypothesis, issue, or problem. They can either introduce or help resolve some puzzle that a student is to consider in the context of the curriculum.

Media also can furnish primary source materials such as film clips of actual events or oral histories. Additionally, they can help translate the abstractions of symbolic data in the social studies into concrete forms of expression that students can more easily comprehend and appreciate.

Wood (quoted in Onosko, 1992) offered an example of how a film can be used effectively at the outset of a high school unit. She used a brief film segment as a springboard or "grabber" to engage students in a question central to an understanding of the American Revolution: How were the Colonists able to win the Revolutionary War?

The initial lesson in the unit unfolds as follows.

> *Introductory Grabber:* Show a ten-minute excerpt from the film *Revolution*, starring Al Pacino and Natassia Kinski. The excerpt shows one of the first bat-

> tles of the revolution and clearly illustrates the differences between the British army (organized, uniformed, machine-like precision) and the colonists (chaotic, rag-tag, inadequately equipped). After viewing, ask students for their initial impressions. What did they see? What were the differences between the British army and the colonial army? Make a list of observations on the board. What overarching conclusion can we draw from the apparent differences between the two sides? (The students can't fail to note that the British had a much stronger fighting machine than the Americans.)
>
> *Introduce the Central Question (How in the world did the Colonists win?):* If students wish to suggest answers, write their ideas on the board as hypotheses. Continue brainstorming for other ideas that might help explain the American victory and write them on the board (e.g., military power, strategy, leadership; economic resources, supplies; ability to transport supplies; public support, participation, morale; political organization, allies; propaganda efforts; knowledge of geography; moral justification). Once the list is complete, ask the students to categorize their ideas and hypotheses. Limit the number of categories to four or five (e.g., military, public support, resources, political organization). (Wood, quoted in Onosko, 1992, p. 194)

As Wood's example illustrates, it is not the medium itself that necessarily makes it effective as an instructional vehicle. Rather, it is the teacher's understanding of how one form of visual data can serve an important instructional purpose and advance students' thinking.

Often, for example, it may be more effective for instructional purposes if a teacher repurposes the media (i.e., uses it in a way that is different than its author intended). Consider a short film that shows people from a culture quite different from our own engaged in some typical activity. Initially, the film might be shown with the sound track turned *off.* At the conclusion of the viewing, students might be asked a basic question, "What did you see?"

The class' responses could be recorded on a sheet and then covered with another sheet of paper. As a next step, the class could be subdivided into three groups. The first group would be asked to observe how *time* was used by the participants in the film. A second group would be asked to focus on the *people* and what each person did. Group three would be responsible for observing which *things* the people used and how.

The same film clip then would be shown a second time. After this viewing, each of the groups would be asked to summarize its members' individual observations and report its findings to the class. Again, the observations would be recorded on a sheet and then covered. At this point, the teacher could elect to stop or repeat the reviewing of the film, each time recording the latest round of observations of each group.

Typically, each new viewing will reveal additional observations that were missed in earlier sessions. The simple observational framework of *time, people,* and *objects* corresponds to that used by anthropologists in ethnographic field work. In a social studies class, the framework provides an interesting vehicle for systematically processing and analyzing visual data.

Teachers who have access to the ubiquitous VCR and a video camera have powerful technological allies. Increasingly, information that once was provided to schools in the form of filmstrips and 16mm film is being offered on video cassettes. The rapid growth of video rental stores also has presented teachers with a relatively inexpensive video materials. Classic films may be rented that dramatize social issues, value conflicts, or ethical dilemmas (e.g., *The Red Badge of Courage)*. Some rental units also stock tapes of documentaries or special television series.

## EMERGING TECHNOLOGIES AND THE CHALLENGE OF THE FUTURE

What technological developments that can enrich the teaching of social studies loom on the horizon?

We have entered an era in which the lines between elements of technology are becoming blurred. Integrated sound, still and motion images of all types, all regulated by microcomputers with increasing capabilities have become the norm. CD-ROM technology continues to become more sophisticated and less expensive.

Both the memory and storage capacity of computers continue to grow, even as they shrink in size. High-capacity storage devices now are relatively inexpensive and readily available for all major computers, even notebook versions. Computers can recognize our handwriting and voices.

Several further developments that are promising for schools seem likely. Interactive multimedia systems increasingly will be used in many sectors of our lives, including the classroom. Videodisc and CD-ROM units that can *record*, as well as play audio and video data, will increasingly be available in schools as the technology develops and costs per unit drop.

Software such as Apple's *QuickTime* will extend the powers of the teacher to incorporate or create visual information in a multimedia environment. Such software will make it possible to easily compress and store lengthy segments of still and motion video as digital (computer) files, then edit and move them into other files.

Gradually, too, it will be easier for teachers to apply and incorporate into their instruction more and more technological advances. The telephone will become the standard of technological "user friendliness" that newer computer-based tools emulate. Telephone companies, now empowered to challenge cable companies, by the end of the decade will flood our homes with a smorgasbord of video data, from popular films to educational programs. All of these data will be easily stored in the new generation of computers.

Advancing cellular and radio technologies will permit each individual to have a personal telephone number that can be accessed anywhere on the globe. Satellite technologies and distance learning techniques will be refined and made available to all schools to further extend their access to information and reduce isolation.

The Internet or its successor will be easily accessible by all students and teachers, and thereby their reach will extend beyond our borders to other nations of the world, making education truly global. In addition to communicating on the Internet, students and teachers will be able to tap into a expanding repertoire of databases.

Even our concepts of a book will undergo changes. Electronic books that fit in the palm of the hand, have clear resolution, and provide complete texts will inch their way into the schools. These new electronic tools will allow students to do key word searches, experiment with the text, or even create large print to compensate for poor vision.

The challenge for us as teachers of social studies is both exciting and demanding. We must determine which roles technology and the rich informal educational system beyond the school most appropriately can play in the development of reflective, competent, and concerned citizens.

## GROUP ACTIVITIES

1. Visit a middle or secondary school in your community that is reputed to use technology extensively. Make a specific list of the various items of technology that exist there and the ways that they are used in social studies instruction. Discuss those things that surprised or impressed you.
2. Visit a county or regional media center in your area to obtain an overview of the latest media materials for the social studies, including computer-related technologies. Discuss your findings and those things that surprised or impressed you.
3. If one is available, visit a large video rental store. Identify a list of tapes and discs available for rental that might be used in social studies lessons.
4. Contact a local media specialist in a school or a school system and ask the individual to identify a local school that is hooked up to the Internet and uses the resources it provides in the social studies program. Then visit the school to learn how the system works and is being used.

## INDIVIDUAL ACTIVITIES

1. Examine and evaluate two social studies software programs: one for the middle grades and one for the secondary grades. Using the evaluation criteria given in the chapter, assess the strengths and weaknesses of the programs.

2. Contact Optical Data Corporation at 1-800-524-2481 to obtain more information on its interactive multimedia social studies programs.
3. Contact The Discovery Channel at 1-800-321-1832 to obtain more information on the social studies programs.
4. Select one of the newer technological applications discussed in the chapter, such as multimedia or CD-ROM systems, and read a related article that further explains its application to the social studies. Identify the author and source and summarize what you learned.

## REFERENCES

Apple Computer. (n.d.). *The Macintosh advantage.* Cupertino, CA: Author.

Association for Supervision and Curriculum Development. (1995). *Only the best: The annual guide to highest-rated education software/multimedia for preschool–grade 12.* Alexandria, VA: Author.

Bilof, E. G. (1987). How to design and use a culture area database with PFS:FILE and PFS:REPORT. *The Social Studies,* 35–41.

Bracey, B. L. (1989, Fall). Making a geography video—It's elementary. *Geography Education Update,* p. 4.

Brehm, B., & Waugh, M. (1993). The influence of telecommunications and classroom interactions on the problem solving behaviors of middle school students. Annual Meeting of the American Educational Research Association, Atlanta, GA.

Budin, H., Kendall, D. S., & Lengel, J. (1986). *Using computers in the social studies.* New York: Teachers College Press.

Callison, D. (1989). School media programs in the information age. In M. A. Laughlin, H. M. Hartoonian, & N. M. Sanders (Eds.), *From information to decision making.* Bulletin No. 83. Washington, DC: National Council for the Social Studies.

Callison, D., & Daniels, A. (1988). Introducing end-user software for enhancing student on-line searching. *School Library Media Quarterly, 16,* 173–181.

Collis, B. (1988). *Computers, curriculum and whole-class instruction: Issues and ideas.* Belmont, CA: Wadsworth.

Ehman, L. H., & Glenn, A. D. (1987). *Computer-based education in the social studies.* Bloomington, IN: ERIC Clearinghouse for Social Studies/Social Science Education.

Elder, C. L., & White, C. S. (1989, November). A world geography database project: Meeting thinking skills head-on. *The Computing Teacher,* 29–32.

Erickson, R. (no date). *Macintosh educational software correlation guide to the history-social science framework for California public schools.* Cupertino, CA: Apple Computer.

Fernlund, P. M. (1993, Spring). Learners, technology, and law-related education. *Law Studies, 28,* 3–5.

Hannah, L. (1985–86, December/January). Social studies spreadsheets and the quality of life. *The Computing Teacher,* 13–17.

Hunter, B. (1985). Knowledge-creative learning with data bases. *Social Education, 51,* 321–324.

Kanning, R. G. (1994). What multimedia can do in our classrooms. *Educational Leadership, 5*, 40–94.

Martorella, P. H. (1989). *Interactive video and instruction.* Washington, DC: National Educational Association.

Martorella, P. H. (1993). Refugee issues in a globally interdependent world. *Educational HORIZONS*, pp. 157–160.

Martorella, P. H. (Ed.) (in press). *Interactive technologies and the social studies: Issues and applications.* Albany, NY: State University of New York Press.

Marx, S. (1994). Social studies Internet resources. Unpublished paper. New Mexico State University.

Mecklenburger, J. A. (1990). Educational technology is not enough. *Phi Delta Kappan, 72*, 105–108.

Mernit, S. (1991, February). Black history month—Let your database set the stage. *Instructor*, pp. 110–112.

*Multimedia source guide.* (1995–96). Justin, CA: *T.H.E. Journal.*

Onosko, J. J. (1992). An approach to designing thoughtful units. *The Social Studies*, 193–196.

Pawloski, B. (1994). How I found out about the Internet. *Educational Leadership, 51*, 69–73.

Pike, M. A., Kent, P., Husain, K., Kinnamin, D., & Menges, D. E. (1994). *Using Mosaic.* Indianapolis, IN: Que.

Roberts, N., Carter, R. C., Friel, S. N., & Miller, M. S. (1988).*Integrating computers into the elementary and middle school.* Englewood Cliffs, NJ: Prentice Hall.

Rose, S. A., Brandhorst, A. R., Glenn, A. D., Hodges, J. O., & White, C. S. (1984). Social studies microcomputer courseware evaluation guidelines. *Social Education, 48*, 573–576.

Simon, M. (1990). Expanding opportunities for teachers to learn about technology. *Electronic Learning, 9*, 8–9.

Thomas, R. M., & Brubaker, D. (Eds.). (1972). *Teaching elementary social studies: Readings.* Belmont, CA: Wadsworth.

Tyre, T. (1990, May). Hypermedia: Practical platforms emerge. *T. H. E. Journal*, pp. 8, 12, 14.

Updegrove, D. A. (1991). Electronic mail in education. *Educational Technology, 31*, 37–40.

Vest, L. B., & Bjork, B. J. (1989). *Why cities develop where they do.* (Computer Program). Raleigh, NC: North Carolina State University, Department of Curriculum and Instruction.

Vockell, E. L., & Brown, W. (1992). *The computer in the social studies curriculum.* Watsonville, CA: Mitchell McGraw-Hill.

Watson, B. (1990). The wired classroom: American education goes on-line. *Phi Delta Kappan, 72*, 109–112.

White, C. S. (1990). Interactive media for social studies: A review of *In the Holy Land* and *The '88 Vote. Social Education, 54*, 68–70.

CHAPTER 12

# Adapting Social Studies Instruction to Individual Needs

**Matching Social Studies Instruction to Students' Developing Capabilities**

Enactive, Iconic, and Symbolic Social Studies Activities
Social Discourse in the Classroom

**Social Studies for the Middle Years**

Exemplary Middle Grades Schools
Exemplary Social Studies Programs and Teachers

**Individualized Instruction and Individual Differences**

Individual Differences Among Students

**Organizing the Classroom for Individualized Instruction**

Computers
Multilevel Reading Materials
Learning Contracts

**Using Jackdaws and Teacher-Made Materials for Individualizing Instruction**

Instructional Resources for Individualizing Instruction

**Individual Styles of Thinking and Learning**

Thinking and Learning Styles
Matching Thinking Styles to Instruction
Matching Learning Styles to Instruction

**Individualization and Cultural Diversity**

**Equity for Those With Disabilities**

Public Law 94-142
Mainstreaming
Strategies for Mainstreaming Students for Social Studies Instruction

**Equity for the Gifted**

Societal Perspectives on the Gifted
Identifying the Gifted
Approaches to Gifted Education
Gifted Students in Social Studies Classes

*Marty, Sue, Jason, and Hakeem attend an urban high school with 2,200 other students. They all come from the same neighborhood, have identical GPAs, and take many of the same classes together. Each, however, is unique in some important way that determines what impact their education will have on them.*

*In a democracy, a public educational system must be sensitive to this uniqueness and attempt to provide all students with equal opportuni-*

*ties for reaching their full potential. Ideally, this means teachers should capitalize upon students' special strengths and help compensate for their limitations. It also means providing students who are lumped into categories—such as gifted, culturally different, less able, and disabled—with different learning experiences appropriate for their capabilities.*

*In a pluralistic society, students often arrive at the school door more different than alike. Their differences may include languages, religious beliefs, intellectual abilities, physical and psychological impediments, traditions, and customs. Regardless of their race, religion, ethnicity, intellectual capabilities, gender, and other characteristics, all students deserve an equal chance to learn and succeed.*

*Teachers can achieve the equitable treatment of students by suspending judgment initially on what they can expect of each student with respect to classroom performance, learning, behavior, and aspirations. When a teacher's preconceived expectations are that a particular individual will be industrious, bright, well-behaved, and will bring rich experiences and high learning ideals to the classroom, these views are likely to affect positively the teacher's behavior toward the student. By contrast, if the teacher associates negative labels with students, whatever those descriptors may be (e.g., retarded, lower class, failure, or lazy), the teacher's behavior toward the students may be negative (Good & Brophy, 1991).*

## MATCHING SOCIAL STUDIES INSTRUCTION TO STUDENTS' DEVELOPING CAPABILITIES

Treating students as individuals also requires providing them with social studies materials and activities that are appropriate for their growing capabilities. Psychologists and educators frequently use the term **development** to refer to three basic types of changes—physical, social, and cognitive—that individuals continue to undergo.

Examples of marked physical developmental changes over time include variations in height and weight, the size of various parts of the body, and general motor ability. For example, males' motor coordination typically improves through the middle years, enhancing their basketball playing.

Illustrations of differences in social development often are more subtle. As a youngster grows to understand which patterns of behavior in social situations are considered acceptable or valued by others and which are not, social development progresses. This process requires learning to function effectively in social settings both within the peer and the adult cultures. It also includes learning what is considered to be appropriate with respect to dress, language, customs, courtesies, and many other social protocols.

In recent years, educators increasingly have focused on the process of cognitive development. As students advance in years, they typically interpret and respond to intellectual tasks in qualitatively different ways. Their processes of reasoning and problem solving and their understanding of the physical and social world undergo significant changes. Among other things, youngsters alter their views concerning space, time, quantity, morality, and cause-effect relationships.

Bruner (1973), whose theories draw heavily on the work of Piaget, has suggested a three-fold schema as an explanation of how cognitive development occurs. His research indicates that children and adults learn through one of three basic modes: the **enactive mode** (doing), the **iconic mode** (imagery), and the **symbolic mode** (words) (Bruner, 1973).

## Enactive, Iconic, and Symbolic Social Studies Activities

During each of these stages, Bruner argued, learning occurs predominantly through either (a) doing something, (b) viewing images, or (c) interpreting symbols, such as spoken or written words. As an example, students might learn about the Boston Tea Party by role-playing the event (enactive mode). Alternately, they might view a film dramatization (iconic mode). Another way of learning is through reading an account of the event (symbolic mode). Teachers can facilitate students' learning by presenting them with activities that capitalize on their current dominant mode of thinking.

Developmental growth, Bruner argued, involves mastering each of the increasingly more difficult modes of representation, enactive to iconic to symbolic. It also includes development of the ability to translate each form into the other (Bruner, 1973). For instance, translation might occur through a discussion of what had been observed and learned from a picture, such as occurs when a student is shown a painting of the Battle at Lexington Green and is asked to write a paragraph describing the event.

## Social Discourse in the Classroom

Regardless of the mode through which students acquire information, they require opportunities to communicate their findings and raise questions. Social discourse involves students in sharing experiences, taking roles, discussing, disputing, and listening in small- and large-group activities. Strategies for conducting such activities are discussed in detail in Chapters 5 and 8.

As students increasingly interact with others, they begin to internalize the existence and significance of alternative points of view. Social discourse in social studies instruction, whether in small groups or class discussions, also can be instrumental in refining and improving students's thinking. When students engage in verbal give-and-take and defend and explain their ideas, they not only share their thoughts but test them. In short, students's conversations in groups, when they have purpose and guidelines, stimulate both social and cognitive growth.

## SOCIAL STUDIES FOR THE MIDDLE YEARS

Caught in a twilight zone between childhood and young adulthood, the needs and capabilities of middle grades students (typically those in grades 5 through 8) often appear to shift at a dizzying pace. One social studies educator, Brown (1982), has observed:

> In terms of the total life-span, the transition from pre-adolescence to early adolescence is a metamorphic development of monumental proportions, having extraordinary consequences for the individual and widespread implications for social studies educators. Dramatic changes occur at this time in the areas of physical, mental, emotional, and social growth and development. Not only is the overall transition into adolescence highly significant, but the customary uneven rates of change in these areas, either independently or through interaction, often result in complex patterns of development which necessitate important considerations for teaching and learning. (p. 30)

Students in the middle grades are making the transition between Piaget's stages of concrete operations and formal operations. Their thinking is becoming increasingly abstract and complex. They are edging toward the capacity for propositional thinking and are developing a surer grasp of time and a wider range of analytical skills.

Brown (1982) offered an example of a social studies activity involving propositional and hypothetical-deductive thinking that a student at the stage of formal operations is able to complete but that one at the stage of concrete operations could not: "If the United States dollar rose in value to be worth five Canadian dollars . . . how would life (in both countries) be affected?" (p. 39).

Students in the middle years also are undergoing shifts in their social orientation. Chapin and Messick (1989) have noted, for example: "Socially, middle-grade children are entering the age of reciprocity in friendship and human relations. They are able to see that their actions have social consequences. When they are in a group, they are eager to seek fairness. They relish opportunities to make rules, establish consequences for breaking them, and carry out enforcement of the rules" (p. 94).

### Exemplary Middle Grades Schools

In recognition of the special developmental characteristics and needs of middle-grades students (those typically in grades 5 through 8), there has been a surge in the growth of middle schools. The effective middle school differs from the traditional junior high, which was often seen as a miniature high school, in more respects than grade organization (Allen, Splittgerber, & Manning, 1993). Creating an effective middle school involves a transformation in the way that teachers, administrators, support professionals, and staff work with students and one another and allocate instructional time (Allen & Stevens, 1994; "Social Studies and the Middle School," 1991; Stevenson, 1992).

Among their recommendations, George and Alexander (1993) have suggested that middle schools include the following features:

- *Guidance.* Each child should have an adult who is responsible for providing advice on academic, social, and personal matters.
- *Transition/Articulation.* There should be a smooth articulation between elementary and high school, and all learning experiences should be carefully coordinated.
- *Block Time Schedule/Interdisciplinary Teams.* There should be blocks of instructional time in the daily schedule, and students should be taught by interdisciplinary teams of teachers.
- *Appropriate Teaching Strategies.* A variety of effective teaching strategies should be employed.
- *Exploratory.* There should be a variety of elective courses or activities, including intramural athletics, for students.
- *Appropriate Core Curriculum/Learning Experiences.* A core of learning experiences and skills should be required of all students.

An earlier foundation task force report (Carnegie Corporation, 1989) made recommendations similar to those of George and Alexander. It also called for students and teachers to be teamed and stay together through the middle grades.

## Exemplary Social Studies Programs and Teachers

Social studies programs for the middle grades should consider both the often wide differences in the developmental levels and the increasing intellectual capacities of youngsters. The scope and sequence model adopted by the state of California considered in Chapter 3 offered several guidelines for how such programs might be organized. It suggested that programs ground historical analyses in the lives of people and events to capitalize on students' growing interest in other people. Further, it urged that teachers emphasize the use of concrete instructional aids, such as maps and globes, to help students making the transition from the stage of concrete operations.

What type of social studies teacher is needed for the emerging middle school? Buckner (1994) identified two lists of characteristics that he contended excellent middle-level teachers have. One dealt with *personal characteristics* and the other with *professional characteristics.*

Personal characteristics were: "look like they feel good about themselves, demonstrate warmth and kindness, are optimistic, are enthusiastic, are flexible, are easy to talk with, are humorous, are friendly, are respectful toward students (Buckner, 1994, p. 18)."

Professional characteristics were: "are easy to understand, are fair when grading, are available when students need to speak with them, provide extra help for those students who need it when beginning unfamiliar material, are well-organized for class, use a variety of activities and materials in class, ask easy, average, and difficult questions, really know the subjects they teach, are careful to compliment students for doing a good job, are careful to correct students who do not pay attention, let students have some say in homework assignments, do not use the textbook each and every day of class (Buckner, 1994, p. 18)."

Examine the two lists of characteristics, and identify in each the six characteristics *you* regard as the most important. Compare your analyses with the responses of 394 middle school students who completed the survey in 1989–1990.

The 394 middle-level students in the study ranked the following as the top *personal* characteristics: are willing to listen, are respectful toward students, accept students, demonstrate warmth and kindness, are easy to talk with, and are friendly (Buckner, 1994, p. 18).

With regard to the top professional characteristics, students identified the following: really know the subjects they teach, are easy to understand, are fair when grading, and provide extra help for those students who need it (Buckner, 1994, p. 18).

## INDIVIDUALIZED INSTRUCTION AND INDIVIDUAL DIFFERENCES

The rise of middle schools and related curricula is but one manifestation of how educators attempt to individualize instruction for developing students. In its simplest form, **individualized instruction** is that which makes provisions for some set of differences among learners. Since there are many differences among students, it would be impossible for a single teacher to consider all of them for any given learning task. Typically, teachers select some set of differences that they regard as especially significant to recognize in the instructional program. They then consider the resources available and begin to develop strategies and materials for instruction.

### Individual Differences Among Students

Some differences are relatively easy to address and involve only modest adjustments in classroom practices. An illustration is moving a student who has slightly reduced visual acuity to the front center row. Others may require major reorganization of the classroom or even of an educational system.

For example, it is widely accepted that all students enter kindergarten or the first grade at approximately the same chronological age. Recognizing that, developmentally, students differ widely in the ages at which they are ready to begin formal learning would challenge this common practice. It would require fundamental changes in both legal statutes and school admission policies.

Some differences among students that have been used in the past as a basis for individualizing instruction include the following:

| | |
|---|---|
| Prior knowledge | Reading abilities |
| Attention spans | Developmental capabilities |
| Achievements | Learning and thinking styles |
| Vision problems | Motivational levels |
| Hearing problems | Cultural experiences |
| Interests | Physical settings preferred for learning |
| Interpersonal skills | Amounts of time needed to complete a task |

Whenever teachers select some set of these or other differences to address with special instruction, they engage in a form of individualized instruction.

## ORGANIZING THE CLASSROOM FOR INDIVIDUALIZED INSTRUCTION

Among the tools that social studies teachers in the middle and secondary grades have found especially useful for developing instruction that takes account of individual differences are *computers*, *multilevel reading materials*, and *learning contracts*. Each of these tools offers students an opportunity to learn through a medium or environment that is responsive to individual needs or strengths.

### Computers

As we noted at some length in Chapter 11, computers have the capacity to enliven social studies instruction in many ways. Students can work individually or in small groups and at their own pace. For students who have been absent, computers also can be used for reviews of material. Others can use the computer to practice skills or extend their understanding of a topic.

Appropriate software also can accommodate a range of attention spans, motivational levels, and learning paces of students. Increasingly, too, new peripherals and software, such as videodisc players and videodiscs and CD-ROM units and compact discs, offer access to an enormous range of sophisticated data and colorful graphics.

### Multilevel Reading Materials

The individual differences in the levels at which students read in the middle grades are often vast. They become even more pronounced in the secondary grades. This phenomenon is an especially serious obstacle to learning in the area of the social studies where much of the subject matter in schools typically is available in written form.

In Chapter 10, we considered in-depth how providing students with varied reading materials and strategies for comprehension affords them opportunities for success, even though their individual reading abilities may vary considerably. If an interesting mix of different reading materials is available on the same topic, students can seek their own levels of proficiency and challenges, progressing as their comprehension and self-confidence grow. Where multilevel adolescent literature is used, the basal textbook can serve as a basic reference work, consulted as needed.

### Learning Contracts

**Learning contracts** are a simple way to provide students with individualized learning tasks, while clarifying the objectives of an activity. They also help students learn to establish reasonable deadlines and work schedules. Further, contracts can help teachers with managerial tasks, such as keeping track of which students are working on different projects and what their deadlines are.

There is no set format for a learning contract. Typically, it spells out (a) what a student agrees to do, (b) which resources will be used and in what ways (c) how to determine when each phase of the activity has been completed, and (d) when the activities will be completed. An example of a basic learning contract for the middle grades is given in Figure 12.1.

## USING JACKDAWS AND TEACHER-MADE MATERIALS FOR INDIVIDUALIZING INSTRUCTION

Individualizing instruction may require materials that are designed by the teacher for use with a particular class. One example is the use of *jackdaws*

**Figure 12.1**
**A Learning Contract for an Eighth-Grade Class**

**Contract for the "Powers of the President" Assignment**

I, ______________________________, am contracting to complete the activities listed below for the "Powers of the President" assignment.

1. Complete all of the activities in the jackdaw kit.
2. Pick one activity from the Activity Sheet and follow all of the steps.
3. Select one of the software programs in the computer corner and answer the questions on the sheet in the corner.
4. Read two of the books on the reading list.
5. Have a conference with the teacher to discuss what I have learned.

Student's Signature: ______________________________ Date: __________

Teacher's Signature: ______________________________ Date: __________

(Dowd, 1990; Rasinski, 1983). Loosely defined, **jackdaws** are kits of various kinds of materials built around a single theme, with the focus being an individual, a document, an event, an issue, or a place. Some examples of topics are:

Henry V
The Magna Carta
Reconstruction
Abraham Lincoln
Japanese American Internment
The French Revolution
The Struggle for Suffrage

Both teachers and students can contribute items to a jackdaw kit. Typically, jackdaws are housed in an attractive and sturdy container or box that holds all of the relevant materials. These may include some combination of artifacts and three dimensional objects such as clothes, utensils, models, and coins; copies of primary source materials such as historical documents, advertisements, maps, legal documents, birth certificates, and letters; books, magazines, articles, charts; and pictures; teacher-produced items such as dioramas and drawings (Dowd, 1990).

As an illustration, Dowd (1990) noted that a jackdaw created by The Institute of Texan Cultures in San Antonio with the theme "Early Texan Frontier Life" was housed in an old pioneer trunk and contained a washboard, a quilt, a bonnet and dress, a coffee pot, and lye soap. Some excellent commercial jackdaws also are available (see Figure 12.2), but they are limited in the types of materials they contain.

Jackdaws should be designed to be self-instructional and for the use of a single student or a small group of two to three students. They should accommodate individual student needs and allow them to freely explore all of the materials in the kit. Beyond the opportunity for self-exploration, teachers should include structured cues and tasks to help students focus on salient points and issues. To simplify analyses, different colored sheets should be used for different types of information.

In addition to the collection of materials, jackdaws should contain the following:

- A sheet that lists all of the items in the kit (see Figure 12.3),
- Any special instructions on how the materials are to be examined,
- A set of questions designed to stimulate students' thinking as they examine the materials,
- Commentary sheets that provide appropriate background or context for the materials included,
- A set of activities to be done in conjunction with an examination of the materials,
- A list of references and readings for students, and
- Special instructions for how to divide tasks if a small group is to use the kit

**Figure 12.2**
**Commercially Produced Jackdaw**

**The Depression**

On October 29. 1929, the New York stock market crashed and heralded the onset of the great Depression. It has been estimated that between twelve to fifteen million workers were unemployed by 1933. What were conditions really like in the cities? What problems were faced by the farmers? How was the discontent of the nation manifested?

In a format designed for both personal enjoyment and classroom participation, this Jackdaw puts the evidence directly in the reader's hands. Through the use of primary materials—newspapers, pictures, flyers, posters, etc.—the reader can sense the feelings of fear, discouragement, futility and anger as the people attempted to survive the black days of the Depression. Historian: Andrew Bronin.

Primary Source Exhibits:
- Page 1 of *Variety*, Wednesday, October 30, 1929.
- The Depression: A Family Album.
- Sign: "Unemployed—Buy apples 5¢ each."
- Depression Scrip.
- A&P Advertising Flyer, 1933.
- Auction sale poster for farm equipment, North Dakota, 1933.
- Page 1 of The Emporia Gazette, May 11, 1934.
- Photo Sequence: A Texas Dust Storm.
- Page 1 of *The Daily Worker*, Monday, January 27, 1930.
- Broadside: "Veterans March to Washington," 1932.
- Campaign flyer: "Closing-Out Sale of the G.O.P. Party," 1932.
- Poster: "NRA—We do our part."

*Note.* From *Jackdaws: Portfolios of Primary Source Documents* (p. 25), compiled by A. Bronin, 1993, Amawalk, NY: Golden Owl. Copyright 1993 by Golden Owl Publishing Company. Reprinted by permission.

## Instructional Resources for Individualizing Instruction

Effective individualized instruction requires a variety of resources within a classroom. These include technology tools such as the following:

### Technology Tools

- Listening post with multiple sets of headphones
- Filmstrip projector with screen
- Microcomputer and peripherals such as a printer, CD-ROM drive, and modem
- Record player
- Tape player
- Videotape machine
- Slide projector
- Videodisc player
- Compact disc player
- Overhead projector

**Figure 12.3**
**Jackdaw Contents**

1 Outline of Cherokee dates and events. Taken from J. Ed. Sharpe's book *The Cherokees Past and Present.*
2 Map of the boundaries of Cherokee country. Taken from *The Cherokees Past and Present.*
3 Broadsheet on Cherokee origin and history.
4 Broadsheet on Cherokee government.
5 Symbol of the seven clans of the Cherokee. Taken from *The Cherokee Past and Present.*
6 Broadsheet of the Cherokee religion.
7 Cherokee poem "The Corn Maiden." Taken from Mary Newman Fitzgerald's book *The Cherokee and His Smokey Mountain Legends.*
8 Carved wooden figure of the Eagle Dancer. Taken from Rodney Leftwich's book *Arts and Crafts of the Cherokee.*
9 Broadsheet of the Cherokee language.
10 Cherokee alphabet. Taken from Samuel Carter III's book *Cherokee Sunset: A Nation Betrayed.*
11 Cherokee glossary. Taken from *The Cherokees Past and Present.*
12 Clipping from the Cherokee newspaper, the *Cherokee Phoenix*. Taken from *Cherokee Sunset: A Nation Betrayed.*
13 Broadsheet on Cherokee dwellings.
14 Arts and crafts of the Cherokee. Taken from *The Cherokee Past and Present.*
15 Cherokee crafts.
16 Arrowheads.
17 Cherokee Memorial to U.S. Congress, December 29, 1835. Taken from the *American Heritage Book of Indians.*
18 Various photographs dealing with the "Trail of Tears."
19 Map of the "Trail of Tears." Taken from *Cherokee Sunset.*
20 Map of the Cherokee Reservation in Oklahoma. Taken from *Cherokee Sunset.*
21 Photo of John Ross.
22 The story of Tsali, a Cherokee hero. Taken from *The Cherokee and His Smokey Mountain Legends.*
23 Broadsheet on the contributions of the Indians. Taken from *The Cherokee and His Smokey Mountain Legends.*

*Note.* From *The Cherokee Indians* by J. Allen, 1991, Unpublished manuscript.

Students also need a collection of multimedia and print materials similar to the list that follows.

**Multimedia and Print Materials**

- Collections of photographs and pictures
- Globe and maps
- Models
- Dioramas
- Tapes, records, films, filmstrips, videodiscs, slides, compact disks, computer software, and video cassettes
- Study prints
- Simulation games
- Artifacts
- Compasses
- Posters
- Magazines and newspapers
- Historical fiction works
- Nonfiction and biographical informational books
- Textbooks
- Reproductions of historical documents
- Time lines
- Teacher-made materials
- Reference works
- Cartoons
- Charts, graphs, and tables
- Travel folders
- Catalogs
- Yellow pages
- Atlases
- Bulletin boards

## INDIVIDUAL STYLES OF THINKING AND LEARNING

A further element for teachers to consider in individualizing social studies instruction is the dominant pattern or *style* students employ for acquiring new information. Taking into account students' preferred style for acquiring information involves providing alternative ways and learning environments through which to approach an assignment, acquire knowledge, or solve problems. Teachers who are sensitive to students' styles try to find the best match between the learning task and the style of individual students.

### Thinking and Learning Styles

The term **thinking (or cognitive) style** refers to the pattern we typically follow in solving problems, engaging in thinking, and generally processing information. Individuals may vary their thinking style from one task to another, but one style usually is dominant and stable over a period of years (Witkin, Moore, Goodenough, & Cox, 1977). Researchers report that thinking styles develop early in life and influence not only the ways we learn but also our career choices (Witkin et al., 1977).

*Learning styles* are similar to thinking styles in that they also represent patterns that we typically follow in learning. **Learning styles** are the set of preferences we express about the conditions for learning something. Certain learning style differences appear to be biological, while other are developed through experience (Dunn, Beaudry, & Klavas, 1989).

## Matching Thinking Styles to Instruction

Some of the systems for classifying thinking styles are quite complex. One system that has been applied to classroom instruction is based on the work of Witkin and his associates. They identified two basic thinking styles, which they labeled **field-independent** and **field-dependent** (Witkin et al., 1977). Some of the salient comparative characteristics of each type are summarized below.

***Field-Independent Individuals:***

- Can deal effectively with unstructured problems,
- Are task oriented,
- Are relatively unconcerned with social interaction,
- Can deal effectively with abstract thinking, and
- Are intrinsically motivated.

***Field-Dependent Individuals:***

- Are relatively effective in remembering information that has social content,
- Prefer group activities,
- Prefer highly structured tasks and activities, and
- Are extrinsically motivated.

Teachers who wish to adapt their social studies instruction to account for differences in thinking styles among students could offer alternative choices such as structured (dependent) versus unstructured (independent) assignments (Guild & Garger, 1985). Similarly, teachers could offer guidelines for activities that provide open-ended (independent) versus specific and detailed (dependent) instructions.

They also could ensure that alternatives in instructional strategies are available such as discovery (independent) versus expository (dependent) approaches. Further, they could offer students choices between working alone (independent) or in groups (dependent) on tasks.

**Measures of Thinking Style.** More detailed information on the characteristics of the two types of thinking style is available, as well as paper-and-pencil measures that are easy to use and score. A test, available in two forms (group and individual) for middle and secondary school students, is called the *Embedded Figures Test.* It is available from the Consulting Psychologists Press, 577 College Avenue, Palo Alto, CA 94306.

## Matching Learning Styles to Instruction

In contrast to our thinking style, our learning style may vary over time and from task to task. It also may include a host of visual, auditory, or kinesthetic factors that influence how we learn. To illustrate, applying Bruner's theory of the three modes of learning discussed earlier in this chapter, we may prefer to learn something by *observing* two or three dimensional items (iconic mode). Alternately, our preference may be to rely on the *spoken or written word* (symbolic mode). A further preference might be for *hands-on* activities that emphasize learning by doing (enactive mode).

Our learning style also may involve conditions such as the temperature or ambience within a classroom, seating arrangements, our mood and motivations, our physical state, the sounds around us, and the time of day that is optimal for learning (Dunn, Beaudry, & Klavas, 1989). Our learning style may even include the hemisphere of our brain that appears to be the dominant one in processing information (McCarthy, 1990).

A basic approach to adapting instruction by matching learning styles involves an analysis of the conditions in the school environment that the teacher can actually control. The next step is to decide for which of the conditions it is practical or productive to provide students with options in social studies instruction.

Further, the teacher should identify the objectives and activities for which options are to be included. Two additional steps are to survey student preferences concerning the options the teacher is prepared to offer and to develop the actual instructional alternatives for the students.

**The 4MAT System.** Other approaches focus on providing alternative instructional strategies that are responsive to students' dominant preferences. The **4MAT system,** for example, assumes there are four major learning styles, all equally valuable (McCarthy, 1990):

- *Style One.* Learners who are primarily interested in personal meaning,
- *Style Two.* Learners who are primarily interested in understanding facts,
- *Style Three.* Learners who are primarily interested in how things work, and
- *Style Four.* Learners who are primarily interested in self-discovery.

McCarthy contended that students need to learn through all four styles, not just their preferred one. She also stated that they should engage in activities that draw on both hemispheres of the brain.

**Multiple Intelligences.** In a similar vein, Gardner (1991, 1993) has developed a theory of **multiple intelligences (MI).** It postulates that individuals learn through at least seven comprehensive modes or intelligences.

- *Bodily-Kinesthetic Intelligence.* Ability to use our bodies to indicate ideas and emotions,
- *Interpersonal Intelligence.* Capacity to distinguish emotions, feelings, and motives of others,
- *Intrapersonal Intelligence.* Ability to introspect and act flexibly on self-insights,
- *Linguistic Intelligence.* Ability to communicate effectively either orally or in writing,
- *Logical-Mathematical Intelligence.* Capacity to reason clearly and facility with mathematical operations,
- *Musical Intelligence.* Ability to distinguish, manipulate, and communicate musical elements, and
- *Spatial Intelligence.* Capacity to distinguish and manipulate spatial and visual elements.

Gardner (1991) has written: "We all are able to know the world through language, logical mathematical analysis, spatial representation,

**Howard Gardner's theory of multiple intelligences offers a framework for individualizing social studies instruction.**

musical thinking, the use of the body to solve problems or make things, an understanding of other individuals, and an understanding of ourselves" (p. 12). Where individuals differ, he maintains, is in the relative strengths of each type of intelligence and in the ways we use them to accomplish various tasks.

Benson (1995) has provided an illustration of a lesson for middle-years students using an MI approach (see Figure 12.4). The example includes activities that address each of the seven types of intelligence.

Developing special instructional strategies for identifying learning styles, such as in the 4MAT system or the multiple intelligences approach, requires special training and some assistance and practice. On the other hand, all teachers can adapt their instruction in some ways to accommodate differences in students' learning styles.

A number of learning-style inventories already have been developed and are marketed commercially. These employ paper-and-pencil measures that ask students to indicate their preferred conditions for engaging in learning activities.

One measure that is widely used is the *Learning Style Inventory* (Dunn & Dunn, 1992). The authors have organized learning style preferences into five categories: *environmental, sociological, emotional, physiological,* and *psychological.* These include an assortment of specific preferences, such as whether students like sound or quiet when they are learning; whether they like to eat while doing some task; whether they prefer to remain stationery or move about the classroom; and whether they like to work alone or in some way with others (Dunn & Dunn, 1992). The instrument for identifying learning styles of students in grades 3 through 12 is available from Price Systems, Box 1818, Lawrence, KS 66044-1818.

A similar measure that covers 23 categories of conditions, the Learning Style Profile, has been developed by the National Association of Secondary School Principals (NASSP) (Keefe & Monk, 1986). It can be used with middle and secondary school students and is available from the NASSP, 1904 Association Drive, Reston, VA 22091-1598.

## INDIVIDUALIZATION AND CULTURAL DIVERSITY

As we considered in Chapter 9, we are an increasingly pluralistic society and our classrooms reflect this fact. More than 20 million people in our nation have a native language other than English. In California, for example, during 1988, one in six students were foreign born (Olson, 1988). In some areas of that state, it is not uncommon to find over 20 different languages spoken in a single elementary school.

As the two examples in Figure 12.5 demonstrate, classrooms in urban areas across the United States increasingly house a great mix of cultural groups. Represented are immigrants, refugees, and undocumented resi-

**Figure 12.4**
**Sample Lesson for Middle Grades Using a Multiple Intelligence Approach**

| | |
|---|---|
| **Level:** | 7th grade |
| **Subject:** | Social Studies |
| **Objective:** | To understand the importance of loyalty and duty in the Japanese culture. |
| **Monday:** | (Linguistic Intelligence): Students will listen to the importance of philosophy in the Japanese society. Students will listen to some of Confucius' sayings concerning family and duty to that family. Students will listen to the importance the Shinto religion places on the spirits of the dead which are found in all of nature. Students will listen to the Buddhist value of ancestors. |
| **Tuesday:** | (Spatial Intelligence): Students will observe art that demonstrates the importance the Japanese place on family loyalty and duty. Students will watch a film on the history of Japanese culture. |
| **Wednesday:** | (Bodily-Kinesthetic): The students will learn how to do four moves in Judo, one of the martial arts used in Japan. The students will be taught that the proper way to begin any martial art is with great respect. It is considered a duty to do so. |
| **Thursday:** | (Musical Intelligence): Students will listen to a demonstration of Japanese music played by three of the members of a musical group from Japan who attend the University here. |
| **Friday:** | (Logical-Mathematical Intelligence): The students will classify the different philosophies and religions of Japan to see a clear history of cultural belief in duty and loyalty. |
| **Monday:** | (Interpersonal Intelligence): The students will divide into four groups. Each will study and discuss a separate philosophy and/or religion of Japan which has influenced the presence of duty and loyalty in their culture. They will select one student from their group to present the results of their study and discussion to the class. |
| **Tuesday:** | (Intrapersonal Intelligence): The students will write about how they think they would feel when the atomic bomb fell on Hiroshima if they were Japanese and their mother was caught under fallen rafters. They could escape if they left her and possibly not escape if they helped. |

*Note.* From *Planning for Multiple Intelligences* (p. 2) by L. Benson, 1995, Raleigh, NC: Department of Curriculum and Instruction, North Carolina State University. Reprinted with permission.

dents, as well as diverse populations of native born citizens, all speaking in many different tongues and having different individual needs. Further, the cultural expectations of parents within these groups often clash with those of the school, as Figure 12.6 illustrates.

**Figure 12.5**
**Diversity in Two Urban Middle Schools in Wisconsin and California**

| Milwaukee Middle Schools | Oakland Junior High Schools |
|---|---|
| **Kosciuszko** | **Roosevelt** |
| Student enrollment: 741 | Student enrollment: 1,039 |
| 17% African American | 22% African American |
| 3% Asian | 50% Asian |
| 57% Latino | 27% Latino |
| 3% Native American | 1% White and Native American |
| 20% White | 65% Eligible for free lunch |
| 84% Eligible for free lunch | 57% With limited proficiency in English |
| 7% With limited proficiency in English | |

*Note.* Data based on 1992–1993.
*Source: Instructor Middle Years,* February 1994, p. 29.

**Figure 12.6**
**Incongruities Between American Teachers' Expectations and Asian Parents' Expectations**

| American Teachers' Expectations | Asian Parents' Expectations |
|---|---|
| Students need to participate in classroom activities and discussion. | Students are to be quiet and obedient. |
| Students need to be creative. | Students should be told what to do. |
| Students learn through inquiries and debate. | Students learn through memorization and observation. |
| Asian students generally do well on their own. | Teachers need to teach; students need to "study." |
| Critical thinking is important. Analytical thinking is important. | It is important to deal with the real world. |
| Creativity and fantasy are to be encouraged. | Factual information is important; fantasy is not. |
| Problem solving is important. | Students should be taught the steps to solve problems. |
| Students need to ask questions. | Teachers are not to be challenged. |
| Reading is a way of discovering. | Reading is the decoding of new information and facts. |

*Note*. From *Assessing Asian Language Performance* (2d ed) (p. 14) by L. L. R. Cheng, 1991, Rockville, MD: Aspen Systems. Reprinted with permission.

The unprecedented challenges these students present have been overwhelming for many school districts, particularly in urban centers. Teachers have the difficult responsibility of trying to ensure that the diversity students bring to the classroom enriches rather than impedes all students' learning.

## EQUITY FOR THOSE WITH DISABILITIES

Of all the categories of students vying for individualized instruction in our schools, citizens with disabilities have received the most attention in the past decade. The basic issue is how to provide instruction appropriate to their special needs.

In recent years, there has been considerable progress in addressing the needs of special students. Once the level of awareness toward those with disabilities was raised, many organizations and businesses voluntarily changed policies and procedures that created hardships. The passage of federal, state, and local laws also has expanded access to public facilities through requirements for provisions such as ramps at sidewalks and Braille instructions in elevators.

### Public Law 94-142

Schools, like other institutions in our society, have been affected through governmental statutes and regulations concerning those with disabilities. The most significant of these was the **Individuals with Disabilities Education Act,** usually referred to as **PL 94-142.** Passed in 1975 (and renamed in 1990), it stated, in effect, that if any school system in the United States wished to receive special federal funding, it had to make provisions by 1980 for "free, appropriate, public education."

PL 94-142 affected all students with disabilities, regardless of their impairments. Such disabilities include the following:

| | |
|---|---|
| Speech impairment | Orthopedic impairment |
| Hearing impairment | Emotionally disturbed |
| Learning disability | Physical impairment |
| Visual impairment | Behavioral disturbance |
| Mental retardation | |

In practice, however, the vast majority of mainstreamed students with disabilities are classified in just four categories: learning disabled, emotionally disturbed, speech impaired, and mentally retarded.

One of the lingering controversies surrounding special students concerns the labeling or classifying of them. The issues center on the validity of

**Figure 12.7**
**Ten Commandments for Communicating with People with Disabilities**

1. Speak directly rather than through a companion or sign language interpreter who may be present.
2. Offer to shake hands when introduced. People with limited hand use or an artificial limb can usually shake hands and offering the left hand is an acceptable greeting.
3. Always identify yourself and others who may be with you when meeting someone with a visual impairment. When conversing in a group, remember to identify the person to whom you are speaking.
4. If you offer assistance, wait until the offer is accepted. Then listen or ask for instructions.
5. Treat adults as adults. Address people who have disabilities by their first names only when extending that same familiarity to all others. Never patronize people in wheelchairs by patting them on the head or shoulder.
6. Do not lean against or hang on someone's wheelchair. Bear in mind that disabled people treat their chairs as extensions of their bodies.
7. Listen attentively when talking with people who have difficulty speaking and wait for them to finish. If necessary, ask short questions that require short answers, a nod or shake of the head. Never pretend to understand if you are having difficulty doing so. Instead repeat what you have understood and allow the person to respond.
8. Place yourself at eye level when speaking with someone in a wheelchair or on crutches.
9. Tap a hearing-impaired person on the shoulder or wave your hand to get his or her attention. Look directly at the person and speak clearly, slowly and expressively to establish if the person can read your lips. If so, try to face the light source and keep hands, cigarettes and food away from your mouth when speaking.
10. Relax. Don't be embarrassed if you happen to use common expressions such as "See you later," or "Did you hear about this?" that seem to relate to a person's disability.

*Note.* From National Center for Access, Chicago, IL., n.d.

the process, particularly where there is considerable weight given to scores on IQ tests. Critics of current practices contend that, given the normal variance in such tests and their dependence on culturally bound references, it seems likely that many students have been improperly labeled.

The category of "learning disability" is particularly susceptible to misapplication; the actual criteria used to classify students as learning disabled often are difficult to distinguish from those teachers informally use to describe a student as a "slow learner" or "not working up to potential." Many teachers who struggle with entire classes of students with low motivational levels, poor self-concepts, and a variety of educational, social, and economic deficits would argue that labels are less meaningful than specific strategies that attempt to match instructional programs with the needs and abilities of individual students.

**A Least Restrictive Educational Environment.** One of the significant provisions of PL 94-142 for social studies teachers was that students with disabilities had to be educated with nondisabled ones to the maximum extent possible and in the "least restrictive" educational environment. What this last provision means in practice has been the subject of considerable debate and varying interpretations. Many different implementations of the provision exist in schools across the nation.

**Individualized Educational Programs.** In addition to the provisions already mentioned, PL 94-142 contained a section requiring for each student the development of an **individualized educational program (IEP).** An IEP is a written plan with specific details concerning a student's present level of educational performance, the educational program to be provided for the student, and the criteria that will be used to measure progress toward the objectives. The student's parents and the student, where appropriate, are to be involved in the development of an IEP. The teacher also may participate in a conference. An IEP may take any form, but by law it must include the basic components indicated.

Many states and local school districts have developed sample formats for use by local school districts in developing an IEP. Figure 12.8 is an example of one such format.

## Mainstreaming

School practices associated with the provision for a least restrictive educational environment often are referred to as **mainstreaming** those with disabilities. This means bringing them into the mainstream of public education by placing them in regular classrooms for at least part of their education. An assumption of PL 94-142 is that students with disabilities will advance socially, psychologically, and educationally when they are not isolated from other students. Further, the assumption is that they will be better prepared for the realities of the world if they have to function in normal environments. The law also assumes that the experiences of nondisabled students with students with disabilities should help break down stereotypes and negative attitudes.

In many schools, some students with disabilities always have been mainstreamed. Students in wheelchairs and those with poor eyesight, hearing problems, and assorted psychological disorders, for example, have been assimilated into many classrooms long before legislation required it. Among other things, what PL 94-142 attempted was to increase both the scope and

**Figure 12.8**
**Sample Format for Developing an IEP**

**Individualized Education Program/Service Delivery Plan**
(To be completed after Part 1 of the IEP is developed)

Student: ______________________________
School: ______________________________
ID#: ______________________ Grade: ________

Check Purpose
[ ] Initial Entry
[ ] Annual Review
[ ] Reevaluation
[ ] Change in Placement
[ ] Change in Identification
[ ] Other: __________

I. AREA OF IDENTIFICATION (ELIGIBILITY) (mark only primary condition)*
[ ] Academically Gifted
[ ] Autistic
[ ] Behaviorally-Emotionally Handicapped
[ ] Deaf-Blind
[ ] Hearing Impaired
[ ] Mentally Handicapped
  [ ] EMH [ ] S/PMH [ ] TMH
[ ] Multihandicapped
[ ] Orthopedically Impaired
[ ] Other Health Impaired
[ ] Specific Learning Disabled
[ ] Speech-Language Impaired
[ ] Traumatic Brain Injured
[ ] Visually Impaired
Other Needs: ______________________________
______________________________

II. RELATED SERVICES
[ ] None
[ ] Audiology
[ ] Counseling Services
[ ] Occupational Therapy
[ ] Physical Therapy
[ ] Speech-Language
[ ] Transportation
[ ] Other __________
__________

*Child meets the eligibility criteria of the State Board of Education and is in need of special education.

III. LEAST RESTRICTIVE ENVIRONMENT (PLACEMENT)
A. AMOUNT OF TIME IN EXCEPTIONAL EDUCATION:

| Type of Service | Sessions per Wk./Mo./Yr. | Min. Per Session | Hours Per Wk. |
|---|---|---|---|
| Consultation | ______ | ______ | ______ |
| Direct Special Education | ______ | ______ | ______ |
| Related Services | ______ | ______ | ______ |
| ______ | ______ | ______ | ______ |
| ______ | ______ | ______ | ______ |
| Total | ______ | ______ | ______ |

B. CONTINUUM OF SERVICES: Check the services considered by the committee, and circle the decision reached. Give reason(s) for options rejected and the decision reached. A continuum of services must be considered.
[ ] Regular - Less than 21% of day (up to 1 hour 15 min.)
[ ] Resource - 21% - 60% of day (1 hr. 15 min. to 3 hrs. 30 min.)
[ ] Separate - 61% or more of day (excess of 3 hrs. 30 min.)
[ ] Public Separate School - 100%
[ ] Private Separate School - 100%
[ ] Public Residential - 100%
[ ] Private Residential - 100%
[ ] Home/Hospital - 100%

PRESCHOOL
[ ] Regular* - Up to 6 hours per week
[ ] Resource* - 6 to 18 hours per week
[ ] Separate* - more than 18 hours per week
[ ] Public Separate School - 100%
  *Applicable only in a classroom setting
[ ] Private Separate School - 100%
[ ] Public Residential - 100%
[ ] Private Residential - 100%
[ ] Home/Hospital - 100%
[ ] Home/Family - minimum 1 hour per week

AGENCY: Check where the student is receiving special services.
[ ] 1. LEA/School in Attendance Area
[ ] 2. LEA/School Not in Attendance Area
[ ] 3. Another LEA
[ ] 4. Other __________

Reason(s) for options rejected ______________________________
______________________________
______________________________

Reason(s) for decision reached ______________________________
______________________________
______________________________

C. REGULAR PROGRAM PARTICIPATION: Circle the regular class(es) in which the student is enrolled and list the letter(s) for any modification(s) in the blank provided.

| | | | | |
|---|---|---|---|---|
| ____ Reading | ____ Library | ____ History | ____ For. Lang. | ____ Vocational |
| ____ English | ____ Music/Art | ____ Science | ____ Physical Educ. | ____ Recess |
| ____ Spelling | ____ Economics | ____ Health | ____ Chapter 1 | ____ Homeroom |
| ____ Math | ____ Social Studies | ____ Writing | ____ Remediation | ____ Other |
| ____ Language Arts | ____ Lunch | ____ Assemblies | | |

Appropriate classroom modification(s), if any:
a. Grading
b. Peer Tutoring
c. Oral Test
d. Abbreviated Assignments
e. Alternative Materials
f. Extended Test Time (Tchr. Test)
g. Large Print Books
h. Audio Tapes
i. Tape Recorder
j. Interpreter
k. Auditory Trainer
l. Assistive Devices
m. Computer/Typewriter/Word Processor
n. Other __________
__________
__________
__________
__________

*Note.* From Wake County Public School System, Raleigh, NC, 1993.

number of all types of students with disabilities who would be mainstreamed. It also sought to establish the legal right of all students to such education, whether the schools wished to provide it or not.

The basic social intent of PL 94-142 was to bring all individuals with disabilities, as much as is possible, fully into the mainstream of society, including its schools. The "least restrictive environment" provision of PL 94-142 did *not* require that all students with disabilities be placed in regular classrooms or that all aspects of their education occur there. It *did*, however, place on school districts the burden of proof to show that some part of these students' education cannot take place in a regular classroom setting.

## Strategies for Mainstreaming Students for Social Studies Instruction

Glazzard (1980) has developed a list of 44 specific suggestions for what teachers can do to adapt classrooms for mainstreamed students. Her suggestions cover six categories of disabilities.

There also are a number of instructional strategies that can facilitate mainstreaming of special students for subject-matter instruction (see Curtis, 1991; Ochoa & Shuster, 1981). Some of the most successful approaches have involved *cooperative learning* techniques (Margolis, McCabe, & Schwartz, 1990), such as those discussed in Chapter 5.

Examples of how the *physical environment* of the classroom might be adapted to accommodate various disabilities include removing barriers to facilitate easy movement and seating special students near the chalkboard or doors. Other ways to assist students involve tape-recording and providing outlines and notes of lessons and attaching Braille labels on materials (Barnes, 1978). Additional strategies include allowing students to answer test questions orally and allowing those who have orthopedic impairments to be dismissed a few minutes early for their next classes.

Sanford (1980) offered a number of strategies and guidelines that are specific to social studies instruction in a mainstreamed classroom. To aid students with visual problems in geography instruction, for example, he advocated the use of tools such as Braille atlases, relief maps and globes, dissected maps of continents and countries, and landform models featuring three-dimensional tactile maps.

Bender (1985) also has advocated extensive use of visual materials, such as various graphic organizers (see Chapter 10), with special students in social studies classes. He observed that many students with disabilities learn better when subject matter is presented through some visual representation.

For administering social studies tests to mainstreamed students with mild disabilities, Wood, Miederhoff, and Ulschmid (1989) have made a number of suggestions, including the following:

1. Give examples of how students are to respond.
2. Provide directions both orally and in writing.

3. Offer alternative ways to test the same item (e.g., orally or written).
4. To reduce errors, let students circle correct answers rather than use answer sheets.
5. Use only one type of question (e.g., multiple choice) per sheet.
6. If a modified test is required for a mainstreamed student, design it to look like the regular one.

In some cases, materials for students with certain disabilities are available through special agencies. For example, students with visual and hearing disabilities are served by several agencies that loan special media social studies materials such as *captioned* films and filmstrips and audio recordings of texts. Many community agencies offer the use of these materials or they may be secured from the following organizations:

American Foundation for the Blind
15 West 16th Street
New York, NY 10011

American Printing House for the Blind
1839 Frankfurt Avenue
Louisville, KY 40206

Captioned Films for the Deaf
Special Office for Materials Distribution
Indiana University Audiovisual Center
Bloomington, IN 47401

## EQUITY FOR THE GIFTED

Another category of special students in our schools is the **gifted.** As it passed the Gifted and Talented Children's Act, in 1978, the Congress asserted boldly, "The nation's greatest resource for solving national problems in areas of national concern is its gifted and talented children."

The gifted are arguably one of our nation's most valuable natural resources. They enrich and enlighten our world through their contributions to literature and the visual and performing arts. They produce our scientific breakthroughs and new technologies. Our societal problem solvers, national leaders, great artists, and top scientists come from their ranks.

In these and a host of other ways, gifted and talented individuals are an important national resource. Whether we nurture and use wisely this resource in great measure depends on what special provisions our educational systems offer.

## Societal Perspectives on the Gifted

American society historically has existed in a state of tension concerning the gifted student (Delisle, 1991; Laycock, 1979). One school of thought maintains that the gifted are an elite who are well qualified to look out for themselves without any special help. This perspective reasons that schools filled with average students and those with special problems should focus their limited resources on the majority, not the gifted minority.

At the same time, our society promotes the notion of excellence and the ideal that individuals should strive to achieve all that their abilities allow. Schools are alternately chided and prodded when they ignore this societal goal. We exhort our schools to help produce exceptional individuals who will keep our nation in the forefront of the world in areas like technology, industrial productivity, space, the arts, peacekeeping, human rights, and standards of living. When we seem to lag or fall behind, as in the 1950s in the space race with the former Soviet Union, we initiate national crash programs and offer special incentives to stimulate the education of talented individuals.

## Identifying the Gifted

Who are the gifted? Definitions vary considerably, but most gifted individuals possess some combination of the following characteristics (Marland, 1972):

| | |
|---|---|
| Leadership abilities | Special academic aptitudes |
| Creativity | General intellectual abilities |
| Artistic abilities | Psychomotor abilities |

Some states and local school districts have created operational meanings for those characteristics that they use to define gifted students. For example, a school may consider a score of 130 or above on an individual IQ test as an indicator of general intellectual ability. Such procedures, however, have come under attack on the grounds that they are too limiting and favor students reared in the mainstream culture (Baldwin, 1978; Frasier, 1989). The critics favor alternative procedures and instruments to identify giftedness in students whose backgrounds are dissimilar to the majority of students (Sisk, 1987).

## Approaches to Gifted Education

Schools that provide for the special needs of the gifted usually employ some variation of three organizational approaches to their programs (Maker, 1982; Sisk, 1987). One approach is to group students in one or more subjects by *ability*. For example, students judged to be gifted in social studies might be placed together, either by grades or across several grades. A variation of this approach is to place all students designated as gifted together for all subjects.

A second approach is to keep students within a regular classroom setting, but to provide *enriched* learning experiences in one or more subjects. Enrichment may be provided within the regular classroom setting or through so called "pull-out" programs, where gifted students are taken from their classrooms to special programs one or more times a week.

The third basic approach emphasizes *accelerating* students' progress in mastering subject matter. Either through special in-class activities or other types of special programs, students advance as rapidly as they are capable through the study of a subject. When a "grade" of subject matter has been mastered, a student advances to the next grade. Under the accelerated approach, for example, a gifted student might complete three years of the social studies program in a single year.

## Gifted Students in Social Studies Classes

Sisk (1987) has observed that the "social studies, more than other subjects, offers gifted students a chance to deal with real problems in the world, problems that have their roots in the past, direct application to the present, and implications for the future" (p. 171). Several different sets of characteristics that seem to distinguish general giftedness in social studies have been identified (National Education Association, 1960; Plowman, 1980; Sisk, 1987).

Consider a sixth-grade class composed of students who have demonstrated exceptional *cognitive abilities* in the area of social studies. Signs of exceptional cognitive abilities in the area of social studies might include the following:

With respect to *verbal ability*, the student exhibits signs of:

1. A high level of language development,
2. A vast store of information,
3. Advanced comprehension,
4. Facility in speaking and in expressing complex ideas,
5. Asking many and often original questions,
6. Unusual curiosity and originality in questions,
7. Ability to engage in sustained, meaningful, give-and-take discussions,
8. An exceptional memory,
9. Large vocabulary, and
10. Varied interests.

With respect to *written work*, the student exhibits signs of:

1. An unusual capacity for processing information,
2. A special knack for seeing unusual or less obvious relationships among data,
3. A pattern of consistently generating original ideas and solutions,
4. Unusual examples of cause-and-effect relationships, logical predictions, and frequent use of abstractions,
5. An unusual ability to accurately synthesize large bodies of information,
6. The capacity to use with ease a number of different reference materials in solving problems and testing hypotheses,
7. Advanced reading ability,
8. Unusual ability to understand alternative points of view or to place oneself in another's shoes,
9. A large storehouse of information, and
10. Creativity.

Among the ways in which special social studies programs for the gifted have been provided to address the special cognitive abilities described above are:

- *Using Alternative Materials at Advanced Reading Levels.* Example: Using 11th-grade and above materials on American history to supplement or replace normal 8th-grade American history text and program.
- *Using Exclusively Discovery Approaches and Simulations and Role-Playing Techniques.* Example: Substituting the usual narrative expository study of a topic with a series of discovery lessons and simulation and role-playing activities that are open-ended and require consideration of alternatives and problem solving.
- *Using a Special, Alternative Curriculum.* Example: Substituting a year's course of study in geography, economics, or anthropology for the standard basal text in the 12th grade.
- *Employing Mentors Specializing or Working in Areas Related to the Social Studies Curriculum.* Example: Under the guidance of a mentor specialist, having a student conduct a project to obtain data regarding the ethics of seal hunting (see Figure 12.9).
- *Emphasizing Problem-Solving Assignments and Activities.* Example: Reorganize the sixth-grade curriculum around a series of units that involve problem-solving tasks.
- *Focusing on Research as Conducted by Social Scientists.* Example: Organizing several units around the use and analysis of primary and secondary source materials.

**Figure 12.9**
**Plan for a Mentorship Activity**

**Finalized Plan for a Community-Based "Mentor-Directed Enrichment Project"**

Mentor's Name Jeannie G. Pupil's Name Grania M.
Project Topic Sealing: Right or Wrong?
Project Meeting Time Friday Afternoons 1:00-3:00 or longer

| | Week # Learning Activities (Including Resources) | Related Learning Outcomes |
|---|---|---|
| Phase I Planning proposal | 1. (a) Mentor writes up proposed project in his or her area of expertise<br>(b) University instructor and enrichment teacher use proposal to match mentor to an interested pupil | (a) Preparing for first meeting with pupil |
| Phase II Agreeing on finalized project plan | 2. (a) Introduce proposal and topic<br>(b) Find out what Grania knows about seals and sealing, and what her attitudes are (can change project plan if necessary)<br>(c) Prepare questionnaire for next week's interview, and role-play an interview using tape recorder | (a) Increasing intrinsic motivation<br>(b) Planning an enrichment project<br>(c) Posing answerable questions<br>(d) Interviewing skills<br>(e) Practicing courtesy |
| Phase III Carrying out the project plan | 3. (a) Visit Vancouver Aquarium to observe seals<br>(b) Interview (tape record) seal trainer discussing what seals are like<br>(c) Take slides of seals; sketch them | (a) Observation skills<br>(b) Interviewing skills and confidence<br>(c) Background knowledge about seals<br>(d) Artistic skills |
| | 4. (a) At school, Grania decides which sketches, slides, and information are to be used in her presentation<br>(b) Read materials on seals and compare to observations made at aquarium | (a) Decision-making and organization skills<br>(b) Comparing and contrasting |
| | 5. (a) Assess project thus far (review)<br>(b) Prepare and rehearse questions for next week's interview with Gordon Rogers (a "pro-sealer" from Newfoundland) and the following week's interview with someone from the Greenpeace organization (anti-sealing) | (a) Grania has greater voice in preparing questions<br>(b) Brainstorming imaginative questions |
| | 6. (a) Interview Gordon Rogers<br>(b) Obtain leads to other pro-sealing sources | (a) Gain a "pro-sealer's" point of view firsthand<br>(b) Refine interviewing skills |
| | 7. (a) Interview spokesperson from the Greenpeace organization<br>(b) Obtain leads to other anti-sealing resources<br>(c) Obtain materials to be used in presentation (including visuals) | (a) Gain an anti-sealing point of view firsthand<br>(b) Refine interviewing skills |
| Phase IV Completing and presenting the project | 8. (a) Organize the material to be used in the class presentation<br>(b) Mount Grania's sketches<br>(c) Mould clay seals; paint them<br>(d) Prepare posters to display pro and con information | (a) Decision-making and organization skills<br>(b) Lettering posters (neatness) |
| | 9. (a) Role-play the class presentation (mentor demonstrates; pupil practices)<br>(b) Objectively present both pro and con information to allow class members to decide for themselves if sealing is right or wrong | (a) Speaking skills and self-confidence<br>(b) Objective reporting of controversial information |
| | 10. (a) Pupil gives class presentation and answers questions about what she liked best about her project, and so forth. | (a) Public speaking skills<br>(b) Thinking "on one's feet" while answering questions |

*Note.* From "Mentor-Assisted Enrichment Projects for the Gifted and Talented" by W. A. Gray, 1982, *Educational Leadership, 40*, pp. 19–20. Copyright 1982 by Association for Supervision and Curriculum Development. Reprinted by permission.

- *Studying Problems and Cutting-Edge Issues.* Example: Focusing the entire seventh-grade curriculum that deals with world cultures on the problem of world hunger, how different countries have been affected by it, what the projections for the future indicate, and what are some scenarios of how the world of the future could be different if a solution to the problem could be found.
- *Use of Student Projects.* Example: As an alternative to studying about communities in the basal text, students design, carry out, and evaluate with teacher assistance a series of projects to better understand their local community.

## GROUP ACTIVITIES

1. Visit a classroom in either a middle or a secondary school that includes a mix of cultural groups. Identify all of the ways that the classroom is culturally diverse and the procedures the teacher follows to respond to the diversity. Discuss your findings.
2. Select a local school district in your area and determine how it identifies gifted students in the elementary, middle, and secondary schools. Also, determine which of the three approaches to gifted education discussed in the chapter the district employs. Discuss your findings.
3. Write Harvard Project Zero Development Group, Longfellow Hall, Appian Way, Cambridge, MA 02138 for a list of schools that are implementing MI theories. Contact one of the schools to learn about results.
4. Examine Figure 12.5. Then develop your own chart and compare the results.

## INDIVIDUAL ACTIVITIES

1. Select any middle or secondary school social studies basal textbook. Pick a topic or a sample of subject matter that is part of the text narrative (symbolic mode). Develop a sample activity to illustrate how the same material could be taught to a youngster through the iconic mode. Repeat the process for the enactive mode.
2. Construct a jackdaw for either grade 7 or 8 dealing with any social studies topic. Follow the directions and suggestions within the chapter.
3. In addition to the learning style approaches discussed in this chapter, identify some others that could be used with either middle or secondary grades students.

## REFERENCES


Allen, H. A., Splittgerber, F. L., & Manning, M. L. (1993). *Teaching and learning in the middle level school.* (1993). Englewood Cliffs, NJ: Merrill/Prentice Hall.

Allen, J. (1991). *The Cherokee Indians.* Unpublished manuscript, North Carolina State University, Department of Curriculum and Instruction, Raleigh.

Allen, M. G., & Stevens, R. L. (1994). *Middle Grades Social Studies.* Boston, MA: Allyn & Bacon.

Baldwin, A. Y. (1978). *Educational planning for the gifted: Overcoming cultural, geographical, and socioeconomic barriers.* Reston, VA: The Council for Exceptional Children.

Barnes, E. (1978). *What do you do when your wheelchair gets a flat tire? Questions and answers about disabilities.* New York: Scholastic Book Services.

Bender, W. N. (1985). Strategies for helping the mainstreamed student in secondary social studies classes. *The Social Studies, 76,* 269–271.

Benson, L. (1995). *Planning for multiple intelligences.* Raleigh, NC: Department of Curriculum and Instruction, North Carolina State University.

Bronin, A. (1993). *Jackdaws: Portfolios of primary source documents.* Amawalk, NY: Golden Owl.

Brown, J. A. (1982). Developmental transition in the middle school: Designing strategies for the social studies. In L. W. Rosenzweig (Ed.), *Developmental perspectives on the social studies.* Washington, DC: National Council for the Social Studies.

Bruner, J. (1973). *Beyond the information given.* New York: Norton.

Buckner, J. H. (1994, February). What makes a great middle school teacher? *Instructor Middle Years,* 18–19.

Carnegie Corporation. (1989). *Turning points: Preparing American youth for the 21st century.* New York: Carnegie Corporation.

Chapin, J. R., & Messick, R. G. (1989). *Elementary social studies: A practical guide.* New York: Longman.

Cheng, L. (1991). *Assessing Asian language performance* (2nd ed). Rockville, MD: Aspen Systems.

Curtis, C. K. (1991). Social studies for students at-risk and with disabilities. In J. P. Shaver (Ed.), *Handbook of social studies teaching and learning.* New York: Macmillan.

Delisle, J. R. (1991). Gifted students and social studies. In J. P. Shaver (Ed.), *Handbook of social studies teaching and learning.* New York: Macmillan.

Dowd, F. S. (1990). What's a jackdaw doing in our classroom? *Childhood Education,* 228–231.

Dunn, R., Beaudry, J., & Klavas, A. (1989). Survey of research on learning styles. *Educational Leadership, 46,* 50–58.

Dunn, R., & Dunn, K.(1992). *Teaching secondary school students through their individual learning styles.* Boston, MA: Allyn & Bacon—Longwood Division.

Frasier, M. M. (1989, March). Poor and minority students can be gifted, too! *Educational Leadership, 44,* 16–18.

Gardner, H. (1991). *The unschooled mind: How children think and how schools should teach.* New York: Basic Books.

Gardner, H. (1993). *Multiple intelligences: The theory in practice.* New York: Basic Books.

George, P. S., & Alexander, W. M. (1993). *The exemplary middle school* (2nd ed.). Orlando, FL: Harcourt, Brace.

Glazzard, P. (1980). Adaptations for mainstreaming. *Teaching Exceptional Children,* 26–29.

Good, T. L., & Brophy, J. E. (1991). *Looking in classrooms* (5th ed.). New York: Harper & Row.

Gray, W. A. (1982). Mentor-assisted enrichment projects for the gifted and talented. *Educational Leadership, 40,* 19–20.

Guild, P. B., & Garger, S. (1985). *Marching to different drummers.* Alexandria, VA: Association for Supervision and Curriculum Development.

Keefe, J. W., & Monk, J. S. (1986). *Learning style profile: Examiner's manual.* Reston, VA: National Association of Secondary School Principals.

Laycock, F. (1979). *Gifted children.* Glenview, IL: Scott Foresman.

Maker, C. J. (1982). *Teaching models in the education of the gifted.* Rockville, MD: Aspen Systems Corporation.

Margolis, H., McCabe, P. P., & Schwartz, E. (1990). Using cooperative learning to facilitate mainstreaming in the social studies. *Social Education, 54,* 111–114, 120.

Marland, S. (1972). *Education of the gifted and talented.* Washington, DC: U.S. Government Printing Office.

McCarthy, B. (1990). Using the 4MAT system to bring learning styles to schools. *Educational Leadership, 48,* 31–37.

National Education Association (1960). *Project on the academically talented student.* Washington, DC: English for the Academically Talented Student.

Ochoa, A. S., & Shuster, S. K. (1981). Social studies in the mainstreamed classroom. In T. Shaw (Ed.), *Teaching handicapped students social studies: A resource handbook for K–12 teachers.* Washington, DC: National Education Association.

Olson, L. (1988). Crossing the schoolhouse border: Immigrant children in California. *Phi Delta Kappan, 70,* 211–218.

Plowman, P. (1980). *Teaching the gifted and talented in the social classroom.* Washington, DC: National Education Association.

Rasinski, T. (1983). Using jackdaws to build background and interest for reading. Washington, DC: U.S. Department of Education, National Institute of Education. (ERIC Document Reproduction Service No. ED 234351).

Sanford, H. (1980). Organizing and presenting social studies content in a mainstreamed class. In J. G. Herlihy & M. T. Herlihy (Eds.), *Mainstreaming in the social studies.* Bulletin 62. Washington, DC: National Council for the Social Studies.

Sisk, D. (1987). *Creative teaching of the gifted.* New York: McGraw-Hill.

Social studies in the middle school: A report of the task force on social studies in the middle school. *Social Education, 55,* 287–293.

Stevenson, C. (1992). *Teaching the ten to fourteen year old.* White Plains, NY: Longman.

Witkin, H. A., Moore, C. A., Goodenough, D. R., & Cox, P. W. (1977). Field-dependent and field-independent cognitive styles. *Review of Educational Research, 47,* 1–64.

Wood, J. W., Miederhoff, J. W., & Ulschmid, B. (1989). Adapting test construction for mainstreamed social studies students. *Social Education, 53,* 46–49.

CHAPTER 13

# Evaluating and Assessing Student Learning

*Increasingly, schools are being asked to provide specific indicators of student learning and comparisons with their classmates' achievements in social studies. Tests, grades, assessment, and evaluation have become an integral part of the process of schooling. Teachers are expected to provide reasonable and clear answers to basic parent questions such as, "What did my youngster—not the class—learn in social studies this year?"*

## THE DIMENSIONS OF EVALUATION

**Evaluation** can be seen as a way of making a decision about the value of something based on some systematically organized data. Literally, the term means "to determine or judge the value or worth of something or someone." Parents and other societal groups look to educators for evaluations of how successful our schools have been in achieving their objectives. Students, more basically, wish to know simply, "How am I doing?"

Evaluation has many objective and subjective dimensions; it involves much more than "giving tests" and labeling students. The National Council for the Social Studies (NCSS) has stated: "To gauge effectively the efforts of students and teachers in social studies programs, evaluators must augment traditional tests with performance evaluations, portfolios of student papers and projects, and essays focused on higher-level thinking" (1991, p. 285).

We first will consider some of the nuances, issues, and mechanics associated with different dimensions of evaluation. Then we will move beyond them to examine how a teacher develops an evaluation framework. This is what guides teacher decisions about what is important in the curriculum and how best to assess what students have learned.

## Grades, Assessments, and Standards

**Grades** are one of the shorthand ways of communicating the results of an evaluation. "Rodney got an A in social studies" means that the teacher evaluated his performance and decided it was exceptional. In the absence of a grade, a sentence, symbol, or other means could have served the same purpose. Grades, however, often are used because they are easy to record, communicate to others, and compare.

Perhaps most significantly, grades can be reduced to quantifiable terms. This means that separate evaluations from different subjects, each totally unrelated, may be merged and used to form a new, single evaluation; for example, "Reba was a 3.35 student."

In contrast to grades, **assessments** are those systematic ways we use to collect our data. They encompass measures such as simple charts for keeping track of the number of times a student asks questions in a social studies class and comprehensive collections of student work. Assessments also may include paper-and-pencil measures, such as tests that are used to measure how much subject matter a student has learned.

**Standards** are related to both assessment and evaluation. They are the criteria teachers use for making judgments. Standards determine what every student should know, how carefully something should be assessed, and what is satisfactory performance or an acceptable level of learning. Teachers' standards determine whether they are regarded as "easy" or "tough."

The ultimate purpose of grades, assessments, standards, and evaluation should be to validate and improve teaching and learning. Consequently, assessment should be an ongoing part of social studies instruction rather than a culminating activity. In Figure 13.1, an excerpt from a California Assessment Program document (California Assessment Program, 1990) summarizes nicely what an ideal evaluation program might encompass.

# THE USE AND MISUSE OF TESTS

Testing has assumed a large role in our society over the past half-century. Tests and testing probably will dog students throughout at least the early part of their lives and occupational careers. It is safe to say that students who enter a public school in the United States will take countless tests of all types before they graduate. College and the world of work likely will present yet another battery of tests for the student to take.

Although tests can aid the teacher in some aspects of evaluation, they often are inappropriate measures of what a student has learned. Tests, especially paper-and-pencil tests, sometimes are used on occasions where other tools would be more efficient or suitable. It seems obvious, for example, that it would be inappropriate to use a paper-and-pencil test dealing with art to discover whether students were exceptional artists. Rather, we likely would have a qualified artist or panel judge their artwork. So it is with many aspects of achievement in the social studies. If we wish to evaluate how well students can use data to solve a problem or to determine how effectively they apply techniques of research, for example, student productions or projects probably are more appropriate than a test.

Critics of existing testing practices also point to their potential negative consequences (e.g., Darling-Hammond & Lieberman, 1992; Mitchell, 1992). One particularly penetrating criticism of many tests is that they are biased with respect to ethnicity, social class, and gender. In addition, Darling-Hammond and Lieberman (1992) also have charged:

> Because of the way in which the tests are constructed, they place test-takers in a passive, reactive role, rather than a role that engages their capacities to structure tasks, produce ideas, and solve problems. . . . Teaching has been geared to the tests, reducing students opportunities for higher-order learning. . . . Many studies have found that because of test-oriented teaching, American students' classroom activities consist of listening, reading textbook sections, responding briefly to questions, and taking short-answer and multiple-choice quizzes. They rarely plan or initiate anything, create their own products, read or write something substantial, or engage in analytical discussions or in projects requiring research, invention, or problem solving. (p. B1)

## Norm-Referenced Tests

Two basic types of social studies tests that students typically are required to take throughout their school careers and beyond are *norm-referenced* and *criterion-referenced* tests. **Norm-referenced tests** allow teachers to compare their students with the norms or results obtained from the performance of a sample group of other students on the same test (Williams & Moore, 1980). They provide answers to a question such as, "How does the performance of this 10th-grade class compare with that of other 10th graders?"

**Standardized Social Studies Tests.** So called **standardized tests** are those that have standardized sets of instructions for administering the tests to insure uniform test-taking procedures, such as the California Achievement Tests. They have been administered to a given population and contain

**Figure 13.1**
**Summary of an Ideal Evaluation Program**

What if...
A Vision of Educational Assessment in California

**What if** students found assessment to be a lively, active, exciting experience?

**What if** they could see clearly what was expected of them and believed that the assessment provided a fair opportunity to show what they had learned?

**What if** they were challenged to construct responses that conveyed the best of what they had learned—to decide what to present and how to present it—whether through speech, writing, or performance?

**What if** they were educated to assess themselves to become accurate evaluators of the strengths and weaknesses of their own work, and to prescribe for themselves the efforts they must make to improve it—ultimately, the most important form of assessment available to our students?

**What if** the assessment allowed students to use their own backgrounds and indicated ways of building on their strengths for further learning?

**What if** their learning were recognized by the school and the community when they had made outstanding progress—regardless of their initial level of achievement?

**What if** teachers could look at the tests and say, "Now we're talking about a fair assessment of my teaching;

**one that** focuses on the essence of the student outcomes that I am striving for—not one that focuses on the peripheral skills or the isolated facts which are easiest to measure;

**one that** shows they can produce something of value to themselves and to others—an argument, a report, a plan, an answer or solution; a story, a poem, a drawing, a sculpture, or a performance; that they can conduct an experiment, deliver a persuasive oral presentation, participate cooperatively and productively in groups;

*Note.* From *California: The State of Assessment* by California Assessment Program, 1990, Sacramento, CA: California Department of Education. Reprinted by permission.

scores and percentiles. Usually, the items on a standardized test have been refined over time. For example, three types of questions have been eliminated through field tests and trials: (a) those that are poorly worded or ambiguous; (b) those that most students answer correctly; and (c) those that most students answer incorrectly.

Major sources of information on all of the standardized tests currently available, including those in the area of social studies, are the *Mental Measurement Yearbooks* and *Tests in Print*. They are available in most college libraries and contain information such as a description of a test, where it can be purchased, and one or more critiques of its strengths and weaknesses. Some examples of standardized tests for the social studies are *California Achievement Tests, Iowa Tests of Basic Skills,* and *Sequential Tests of Educational Progress.*

**Figure 13.1**
**continued**

**one that** is accessible to all my students, yet stretches the most capable students as well—not one that measures some mythical minimum competency level.

**one that** matches the assessment that I use on a day-to-day basis to guide my teaching and that guides my students in their learning—not one that takes an artificial form and then naively expects students to give a natural response in an artificial situation;

**one that** doesn't take valuable time from the teaching/learning process, but is an integral part of that process;

**one that** doesn't treat me as a "Teller of Facts," providing and prescribing the concepts and the content that students are to study—but rather as a coach and a fellow learner, helping my students to become active learners who are prepared to discover what is important to them now and enthusiastic about learning in the future?"

**What if** the new assessments led parents, taxpayers, legislators, and the business community to exclaim:

"**I can see** that the schools are focusing on the important things—that students are achieving levels of academic excellence which truly prepare them for the future.

**I can see** that students are learning what they need to fulfill themselves as individuals, to become concerned and involved citizens and workers who can adapt to the changing demands of our world—creative people who can think and take initiative, who care about what they do, and who can work with others to solve problems.

**I can see** the results in the newspapers, which give me the information I need in terms I can understand, which show me the progress our schools are making on assessments that really matter, and where they need my help and support"?

Teachers should realize that the subject matter sampled in standardized tests *may not correspond to what is being studied in any individual classroom.* This may occur since the specific subject matter and curriculum for a given grade level may vary from district to district. As a consequence, standardized tests often exclude social studies information and skills that are considered to be important to teachers. Further, as Darling-Hammond and Lieberman (1992) have cautioned, "They are inappropriate tools for many of the purposes that they are expected to serve, including tracking students, determining promotions, and allocating rewards and sanctions to students, teachers, and schools" (p. B1).

In sum, as they use and interpret the results of standardized tests, teachers should consider carefully whether what they measure matches the objectives of the classroom social studies program. Unless a clear match exists, the standardized test is useful only as a general diagnostic measure of what students know.

## Criterion-Referenced Tests

In comparison to norm-referenced tests, **criterion-referenced tests** allow teachers to compare the performance of their students against some standard of what they should know (Popham, 1988). To develop large-scale criterion-referenced tests, school districts contract with test publishers to develop suitable materials for the school's curriculum. These tests provide answers to questions such as, "How does the performance of our students compare with the criterion of what we expected them to know or demonstrate." An example of a criterion would be: Given an unlabeled globe of the world, a student will be able to correctly identify 80% of the world's major waterways.

## The National Assessment of Education Progress

In 1969, after six years of gestation, a consortium of states embarked on a national project known as the **National Assessment of Educational Progress (NAEP),** which is still in existence. The NAEP was an attempt by states to begin collecting evaluation data across the various participating states. It attempts to measure student growth in various areas of the school curriculum, including areas of the social studies.

Samples of students from across the United States have been included in the ongoing NAEP project. Findings have been reported for age groups 9, 13, and 17. Tests are repeated on a cyclical basis, and results are published and made available to the general public, as well as participating school districts.

## National Standards and National Testing

In recent years, some groups both separate from and within NAEP also have called for the establishment of **national standards** for subjects within the curriculum. For example, the 1994 Goals 2000: Educate America Act called for the development of voluntary national standards by the year 2000. These standards would establish what all students in the United States should know and when they should know it.

To date, five professional organizations have worked on standards related to the social studies curriculum. Their efforts are represented in the History Standards Project, addressing the area of history; the Geography Standards Project, dealing with geography; the National Council on Economic Education Standards, focusing on the discipline of economics; National Standards for Civics and Government, working with civics and government; and the NCSS Curriculum Standards for the Social Studies, addressing the social studies as a whole.

As we go to press, the final recommendations of the organizations concerning standards are still emerging. For an update on the progress of the various projects and more information, write the organizations at the following addresses:

Center for Civic Education
5146 Douglas Fir Road
Calabasas, CA 91302-1467

National Council on Economic Education
432 Park Avenue
New York, NY 10016

National Center for History in the Schools
University of California at Los Angeles
10880 Wilshire Boulevard
Suite 1610
Los Angeles, CA 90024

National Council for Geographic Education
1600 M Street, NW
Suite 4200
Washington, DC 20036

National Task Force on Standards
National Council for the Social Studies
3501 Newark Street, NW
Washington, DC 20016-3167

Examples of standards that appear in the draft versions of the recommendations are offered here. As Figure 13.2 shows, the National Geography Standards identify 18 basic standards to be used across the grades (Geography for Life, 1994).

Each basic standard, in turn, is accompanied by a set of more detailed **performance standards.** For example, Figure 13.3 displays part of the Grade 12 performance standards for Standard 10: The geographically informed person knows and understands the characteristics, distribution, and complexity of Earth's cultural mosaics. Student proficiency in the use of the content and performance standards is to be assessed at the end of grades 4, 8, and 12.

On the other hand, the Civics Standards are framed around five basic questions (Center for Civic Education, 1994). Under each question, in turn, are grouped 3 to 5 related questions as shown in the Figure 13.4, which relates to the middle grades.

Each question, in turn, is associated with a specific set of standards students are to achieve. An example related to the question, "What are the distinctive characteristics of American society?" (question IIB) is provided in Figure 13.5.

**Figure 13.2**
**Proposed National Geography Education Standards**

**The World in Spatial Terms**

1. The geographically informed person knows and understands how to use maps and other graphic representations, tools, and technologies to acquire, process, and report information from a spatial perspective.
2. The geographically informed person knows and understands how to use mental maps to organize people, places, and environments in a spatial context.
3. The geographically informed person knows and understands how to analyze the spatial organization of people, places, and environments on Earth's surface.

**Places and Regions**

4. The geographically informed person knows and understands the physical and human characteristics of places.
5. The geographically informed person knows and understands that people create regions to interpret Earth's complexity.
6. The geographically informed person knows and understands how culture and experience influence people's perception of places and regions.

**Physical Systems**

7. The geographically informed person knows and understands the physical processes that shape patterns on Earth's surface.
8. The geographically informed person knows and understands the characteristics and distribution of ecosystems of Earth's surface.

*Source:* From *Geography for Life* (pp. 34–35) by National Geographic Society, 1994, Washington, DC. Reprinted by permission.

The NCSS also has developed a set of standards to guide teachers. As shown in Figure 13.6, the NCSS standards consist of 10 thematic strands that are to be included at every grade level (NCSS, 1994). Attached to each strand is a set of specific performance expectations. For example, Figure 13.7 illustrates the relationship of Standard 9, Global Connections, to performance expectations across the grades.

The NCSS also encouraged educators to combine its standards with those proposed by other projects. Following this suggestion, educators could construct "customized" curricula to meet local needs.

Apart from a push for national standards, a related but separate movement is afoot to establish a **national test** in each subject area at various grade levels. Who would administer such a test is uncertain, since, as

**Figure 13.2 continued**

**Fundamental Human Systems**

9. The geographically informed person knows and understands the characteristics, distribution, and migration of human populations on Earth's surface.
10. The geographically informed person knows and understands the characteristics, distribution and complexity of Earth's cultural mosaics.
11. The geographically informed person knows and understands the patterns and networks of economic interdependence on Earth's surface.
12. The geographically informed person knows and understands the processes, patterns, and functions of human settlement.
13. The geographically informed person knows and understands how the forces of cooperation and conflict among people influence the division and control of Earth's surface.
14. The geographically informed person knows and understands how human actions modify the physical environment.
15. The geographically informed person knows and understands physical systems affect human systems.
16. The geographically informed person knows and understands the changes that occur in the meaning, use, distribution, and importance of resources.

**Environment and Society**

17. The geographically informed person knows and understands how to apply geography to interpret the past.
18. The geographically informed person knows and understands how to apply geography to interpret the present and plan for the future.

we discussed in Chapter 1, the federal government plays only a limited role in the regulation of local schools. A national test would require national standards, but the reverse is not necessarily true. Various educational agencies could be involved in developing and sharing assessment procedures based on a set of national standards.

Proponents argue that both proposals would improve education by establishing common goals for all schools. They point to the fact that many other nations of the world already employ such approaches. Critics, on the other hand, maintain that the proposals would work to the disadvantage of poor and minority students, who have special curricular needs. They argue further that national standards or testing would tear at the fiber of local school curricular autonomy and destroy diversity and creativity.

**Figure 13.3**
**Part of the Grade 12 Performance Standards for Standard #10**

**The Characteristics, Distribution, and Complexity of Earth's Cultural Mosaics**

*By the end of the twelfth grade, the student knows and understands:*

1. **The impact of culture on ways of life in different regions**
2. **How cultures shape the character of a region**
3. **The spatial characteristics of the processes of cultural convergence and divergence**

*Therefore, the student is able to:*

A. **Compare the role that culture plays in incidents of cooperation and conflict in the present-day world, as exemplified by being able to**

   Identify the cultural factors that have promoted political conflict (e.g., the national, ethnic, and religious differences that led to conflict in sub-Saharan Africa in the 1960s, central Europe in the 1980s and 1990s, countries within the former Soviet Union in the 1990s)

   Identify the cultural characteristics that link regions (e.g., the religious and linguistic ties between Spain and parts of Latin America; the linguistic ties between Great Britain and Australia; the ethnic ties among the Kurds living in Iran, Iraq, and Turkey)

*Source:* From *Geography for Life* (pp. 203–204) by National Geographic Society, 1994, Washington, DC. Reprinted by permission.

## PERFORMANCE ASSESSMENTS

As we have seen, proposals for national standards and testing frequently also embrace the use of **performance (or authentic) assessments** as part of an overall program of evaluation. These assessments are a way of measuring student learning that requires the active construction of responses in the context of performing real (sometimes called "authentic") tasks (Perrone, 1991). Among other features, performance assessment approaches typically tap multiple sources of information to determine what students have learned in every phase of the social studies program.

Although performance assessments may employ paper-and-pencil tests, these have a limited role in the total evaluation process. Tests that assess only knowledge of social studies subject matter cannot provide thorough and comprehensive measures of social studies learning. They typically pass over knowledge of processes and skills.

**Figure 13.3 continued**

Explain how members of the U.S. Peace Corps have to adjust to living and working in countries with cultural traditions that differ significantly from their own (e.g., how they learn and are taught to adapt themselves to non-American dietary habits, social customs, lifestyles, and family and community values)

**B. Analyze how cultures influence the characteristics of regions, as exemplified by being able to**

Analyze demographic data (e.g. birthrates, literacy rates, infant mortality) to describe a region's cultural characteristics (e.g., level of technological achievement, cultural traditions, social institutions)

Compare the economic opportunities for women in selected regions of the world using culture to explain the differences (e.g., the lives of Bedouin women within the Islamic tradition versus those of women in Scandinavian countries)

Describe the relationship between patterns of in-migration and cultural change in large urban and manufacturing centers, especially those near international borders (e.g., how the presence of large numbers of guest workers or undocumented aliens results in modification of an urban center's cultural characteristics)

Among those types of learning that paper-and-pencil tests of knowledge typically ignore in the social studies are the ability to:

- Identify, clarify, and solve an open-ended problem,
- Use spatial tools such as maps, globes, and compasses to locate objects,
- Identify cause-effect relationships among social data,
- Develop, execute, and critique an oral presentation to argue on behalf of a position or valued principle,
- Generate and test hypotheses and generalizations,
- Apply and relate concepts,
- Take and defend an ethical position,
- Organize a body of related information into a graph, chart, or table,

**Figure 13.4**
**Grades 5 Through 8 Content Standards**

I. What are civic life, politics, and government?
   A. What is civic life? What is politics? What is government? Why are government and politics necessary? What purposes should government serve?
   B. What are the essential characteristics of limited and unlimited government?
   C. What are the nature and purposes of constitutions?
   D. What are alternative ways of organizing constitutional governments?

II. What are the foundations of the American political system?
   A. What is the American idea of constitutional government?
   B. What are the distinctive characteristics of American society?
   C. What is American political culture?
   D. What values and principles are basic to American constitutional democracy?

III. How are the values and principles of American constitutional democracy embodied in the government established by the Constitution?
   A. How are power and responsibility distributed, shared, and limited in the government established by the United States Constitution?
   B. What does the national government do?
   C. How are state and local governments organized and what do they do?
   D. Who represents you in local, state, and national governments?
   E. What is the place of law in the American constitutional system?
   F. How does the American political system provide for choice and opportunities for participation?

IV. What is the relationship of American politics and government to world affairs?
   A. How is the world organized politically?
   B. How has the United States influenced other nations and how have other nations influenced American politics and society?

V. What are the roles of the citizen in American democracy?
   A. What is citizenship?
   B. What are the rights of citizens?
   C. What are the responsibilities of citizens?
   D. What dispositions or traits of character are important to the preservation and improvement of American constitutional democracy?
   E. How can citizens take part in civic life?

*Note.* From *National Standards for Civics and Government* (pp. 31–32) by Center for Civic Education, Calabasas, CA. Reprinted by permission.

- Conduct an interview to gather social data,
- Write a report summarizing important similarities and differences among issues, events, and individuals, and
- Evaluate the evidence presented in competing arguments.

## Social Studies Performance Assessments and Portfolios

To redress the limitations of paper-and-pencil tests, teachers frequently employ *portfolios* of performance (or authentic) assessments (See Armstrong, 1994). A **portfolio** consists of samples of a student's work accumulated in a folder over a period of time. Additionally, it may include observations and comments regarding a student's activities by parents and teachers.

Portfolios are intended to provide a holistic view of a student's capabilities in social studies. Optimally, the student and the teacher should review portfolios periodically throughout the year to chart progress. Student productions for a portfolio might include the following types of items:

- Written essays, papers, projects, and exercises;
- Skits, debates, oral reports, panels, and role playing;
- Cooperative learning group outcomes;
- Skill demonstrations (e.g., using reference materials and interviewing techniques);
- Creations of products (e.g., dioramas, oral history collections, exhibits, videotapes, audiotapes, artifacts, photographs; bulletin boards, posters, card sorts, and time lines);
- Rating forms, checklists, and observation forms;
- Diaries, journals, and logs;
- Experiments;
- Teacher anecdotal records; and
- Teacher interviews.

Some key differences between standardized testing and authentic assessment are displayed in Figure 13.8.

Two sample authentic assessments of social studies instruction follow. The first example shows how a basic *rating form* was used with a middle-grades class to assess the quality of students' oral reports. Each student was judged using the following questions:

Did the student
speak so everyone could hear?

**Figure 13.5**
**Content Standards for a Middle Grades Question About the Characteristics of American Society**

1. **Distinctive Characteristics of American Society.** Students should be able to identify and explain the importance of historical experiences and geographic, social, and economic factors which have helped to shape American society.

   To achieve this standard, students should be able to

   - Explain important factors that have helped shape American society
     - Absence of a nobility or an inherited caste system,
     - Religious freedom and the Judeo-Christian ethic,
     - A history of slavery,
     - Relative geographic isolation,
     - Abundance of land and widespread ownership of property,
     - Social, economic, and geographic mobility,
     - Effects of a frontier,
     - Large scale immigration,
     - Diversity of the population,
     - Individualism,
     - Work ethic,
     - Market economy,
     - Relative social equality, and
     - Universal public education.
2. **The Role of Voluntarism in American Life.** Students should be able to evaluate, take, and defend positions on the importance of voluntarism in American society.

*Note.* From *National Standards for Civics and Government* (pp. 43–44) by Center for Civic Education, Calabasas, CA. Reprinted by permission.

finish sentences?
seem comfortable in front of a group?
give a good introduction?
seem well informed about the topic?
explain ideas clearly?
stay on the topic?
give a good conclusion?
use effective costumes, pictures, or other materials to make the presentation interesting?
give good answers to questions from the audience? (Maeroff, 1991, p. 279)

Note how instruction and assessment are *interrelated* in this example. That is, the results of the assessment would give students relatively clear directions for what they need to do to improve their work.

**Figure 13.5**
**continued**

To achieve this standard students should be able to

- Explain factors that have inclined Americans toward voluntarism, e.g., colonial conditions, frontier traditions, religious beliefs;
- Identify services that religious, charitable, service, and civic groups provide in their own community, e.g., health, child, and elderly care; disaster relief; counseling; tutoring; basic needs such as food, clothing, shelter; and
- Identify opportunities for individuals to volunteer in their own schools and communities.

3. **Diversity in American Society.** Students should be able to evaluate, take, and defend positions on the value and challenges of diversity in American life.

   To achieve this standard, students should be able to

   - Identify the many forms of diversity in American society, e.g., regional, linguistic, racial, religious, ethnic, socioeconomic, familial;
   - Explain why diversity is desirable and beneficial, e.g., increases choice, fosters a variety of viewpoints, encourages cultural creativity, increases understanding of one's self;
   - Explain why conflicts have arisen from diversity, using historical and contemporary examples, e.g., North/South conflict; conflict about land, suffrage, and other rights of Native Americans; Catholic/Protestant conflicts in the nineteenth century; conflict about civil rights of minorities and women; present day ethnic conflict in urban settings; and
   - Evaluate ways conflicts about diversity can be resolved in a peaceful manner that respects individual rights and promotes the common good.

**Figure 13.6**
**Curriculum Standards for the Social Studies**
*Note.* From *Curriculum Standards for the Social Studies* by National Council for the Social Studies, 1994, Washington, DC.

I. Culture
II. Time, Continuity, and Change
III. Peoples, Places, and Environments
IV. Individual Development and Identity
V. Individuals, Groups, and Institutions
VI. Power, Authority, and Governance
VII. Production, Distribution, and Consumption
VIII. Science, Technology, and Society
IX. Global Connections
X. Civic Ideals and Practice

**Figure 13.7**
**Specific Performance Expectations for Standard 9, Global Connections**

Social studies programs should include experiences that provide for the study *of global connections and interdependence,* so that the learner can:

| Early Grades | Middle Grades | High School |
|---|---|---|
| a. Explore ways that language, art, music, belief systems, and other cultural elements may facilitate global understanding or lead to misunderstanding; | a. Describe instances in which language, art, music, belief systems, and other cultural elements can facilitate global understanding or cause misunderstanding; | a. Explain how languages, art, music, belief systems, and other cultural elements can facilitate global understanding or cause misunderstanding; |
| b. Give examples of conflict, cooperation, and interdependence among individuals, groups, and nations; | b. Analyze examples of conflict, cooperation, and interdependence among groups, societies, and nations; | b. Explain conditions and motivations that contribute to conflict, cooperation, and interdependence among groups, societies, and nations; |
| c. Examine the effects of changing technologies on the global community; | c. Describe and analyze the effects of changing technologies on the global community; | c. Analyze and evaluate the effects of changing technologies on the global community; |
| d. Explore causes, consequences, and possible solutions to persistent, contemporary, and emerging global issues, such as pollution and endangered species; | d. Explore the causes, consequences, and possible solutions to persistent, contemporary, and emerging global issues, such as health, security, resource allocation, economic development, and environmental quality; | d. Analyze the causes, consequences, and possible solutions to persistent, contemporary, and emerging global issues, such as health, security, resource allocation, economic development, and environmental quality; |

*Note.* From *Curriculum Standards for the Social Studies* (p. 44) by National Council for the Social Studies, 1994, Washington, DC.

In the second case, a 12th-grade class demonstrated understanding of how world views are influenced by the map projections we employ (Geography for Life, 1994). Students were asked to write a 500-word editorial about the cultural biases reflected in map projections. References to two specific projections were required.

## TEACHER-MADE PAPER-AND-PENCIL TESTS

Some of the most frequently used evaluation devices in the middle and secondary grades are **teacher-made paper-and-pencil tests.** These often

**Figure 13.7 continued**

| Early Grades | Middle Grades | High School |
|---|---|---|
| e. Examine the relationships and tensions between personal wants and needs and various global-concerns, such as use of imported oil, land use, and environmental protection; | e. Describe and explain the relationships and tensions between national sovereignty and global interests, in such matters as territory, natural resources, trade, use of technology, and welfare of people; | e. Analyze the relationships and tensions between national sovereignty and global interests, in such matters as territory, economic development, nuclear and other weapons, use of natural resources, and human rights concerns; |
| f. Investigate concerns, issues, standards, and conflicts related to universal human rights, such as the treatment of children, religious groups, and effects of war. | f. Demonstrate understanding of concerns, standards, issues, and conflicts related to universal human rights; | f. Analyze or formulate policy statements demonstrating an understanding of concerns, standards, issues, and conflicts related to universal human rights; |
| | g. Identify and describe the roles of international and multinational organizations. | g. Describe and evaluate the role of international and multinational organizations in the global arena; |
| | | h. Illustrate how individual behaviors and decisions connect with global systems. |

include features and items that resemble those found in norm-referenced and criterion-referenced tests. They differ from commercially prepared tests largely in the uses to which they are put and in the procedures used to develop them.

## Posttests and Pretests

As one dimension of evaluation, teachers typically give tests *after* students have studied a subject. These are often referred to as **posttests.** Tests also can be used as diagnostic measures to determine what students know *before* they begin study of a topic. Used in this fashion, such measures are called **pretests.**

Pretests can provide direction for the shape of a unit by identifying students' interests and gaps or misconceptions in their knowledge. Compari-

**These students are editing videotape for a social studies project.**

**Figure 13.8**
**Standardized Testing Versus Authentic Assessment**

| Standardized Testing | Authentic Assessment |
|---|---|
| • Creates a mythical standard or norm which requires that a certain percentage of children fail. | • Establishes an environment where every child has the opportunity to succeed. |
| • Pressures teachers to narrow their curriculum to only what is tested on an exam. | • Allows teachers to develop meaningful curricula and assess within the context of that program. |
| • Emphasizes one-shot exams that assess knowledge residing in a single mind at a single moment in time. | • Assesses on an *ongoing* basis in a way that provides a more accurate picture of a student's achievement. |
| • Focuses too much importance on single sets of data (i.e., test scores) in making educational decisions. | • Provides *multiple* sources of evaluation that give a more accurate view of a student's progress. |
| • Treats all students in a uniform way. | • Treats each student as a unique human being. |
| • Discriminates against some students because of cultural background and learning style. | • Provides a *culture-fair* assessment of a student's performance; gives everyone an equal chance to succeed. |
| • Regards testing and instruction as separate activities. | • Regards assessment and teaching as two sides of the same coin. |
| • Produces scoring materials that students often never see again. | • Results in products that have *value* to students and others. |
| • Focuses on "the right answer." | • Deals with *processes* as much as final products. |

*Note.* From *Multiple Intelligences in the Classroom* (p. 116) by T. Armstrong, 1994, Alexandria, VA: Association for Supervision and Curriculum Development.

son of scores with those on the posttest also can indicate how much students actually have achieved as a result of instruction. The **K-W-L technique,** described in Chapter 10, is an illustration of how this can be done.

A number of specialized books, materials, and guidelines exist to help teachers construct their own tests (e.g., Airasian, 1991; Popham, 1988; TenBrink, 1994). Once a teacher has determined that student achievement can best be measured through a teacher-made test, several basic choices exist. These generally consist of identifying or creating *essay* and *objective test* items.

## Constructing Essay Test Items

**Essay questions** are an especially effective way to measure students' ability to organize, analyze, apply, synthesize, and evaluate in their own words information they have learned. Such questions provide students with the freedom to think broadly and to express themselves in different ways. Student essays, however, often are difficult to assess with objectivity. Further, of necessity, they can cover only a narrow range of objectives in a short period of time. They also are time consuming to score and allow students to digress.

In some cases, essay questions also penalize students who have in reality learned a great deal but have trouble expressing themselves in standard English. Translating concrete objects and ideas into abstractions represented by essay answers is a cognitive task that is related both to development and to language facility. Those for whom English is a second language, for example, often have more difficulty in stating something in their own words than in demonstrating learning by selecting, identifying, applying, or demonstrating among alternatives.

**General Guidelines.** Two basic guidelines for constructing well-designed essay questions are to:

1. Use clear, specific, and simple language.
   a. Yes: Describe three major ways in which the economic systems of the United States and China differ.
   b. No: Elaborate briefly on the distinctions between the economic systems of the United States and China.
2. Limit the scope of the question and the expected answer as much as possible.
   a. Yes: Identify two significant presidential characteristics that Kennedy and Theodore Roosevelt shared.
   b. No: How was Kennedy like Theodore Roosevelt?

*Before* teachers present essay questions to students, they should construct a model answer for each question. The model should list the major points, items, or type of discussion the teacher will accept as correct, partially correct, or satisfactory (Tenbrink, 1994). It also should indicate the relative weights that will be assigned to each element in the answer.

For example, note the short-answer essay question given in Figure 13.9 (Scott Foresman, 1983). Let us assume the question is worth a total of 7 points and that there are seven elements in a correct answer, each worth 1 point. The teacher will accept the following three elements as correct for the middle area: both were important men; both wanted to govern wisely; and both led political parties.

Under *Jefferson's Views*, the teacher will consider as correct any two of the following three items: as little government as possible is best; common people should have power; and farming should be major industry. For *Hamilton's Views*, the teacher will accept any two of these: strong federal government is best; wealthy should have power; and strong businesses are necessary.

**Figure 13.9**
**Assessment Item: Short-Answer Essay**
*Note.* From *American Past and Present*, Teacher's Edition Workbook, by Joan Schreiber et al. Copyright © 1983 by Scott, Foresman and Company. Reprinted by permission.

**Diagramming Two Different Views**

Thomas Jefferson and Alexander Hamilton were both very important men during the beginning of the United States. Both men wanted the country to be governed wisely, but each had views that were very different.

While Hamilton felt that the federal government should be strong, Jefferson believed that as little government as possible would be best for the people. Hamilton felt that the wealthy should run this government. Jefferson believed that common people should have the power.

Jefferson wanted farming to be the country's main industry. Hamilton felt that strong businesses that provided many jobs were necessary. Both men led political parties that supported their own beliefs. Jefferson and his followers became known as Republicans. Hamilton and his followers became known as Federalists.

Complete this Venn diagram. In the middle area, summarize three things that Jefferson and Hamilton shared in common. Then summarize each man's differing views below his name.

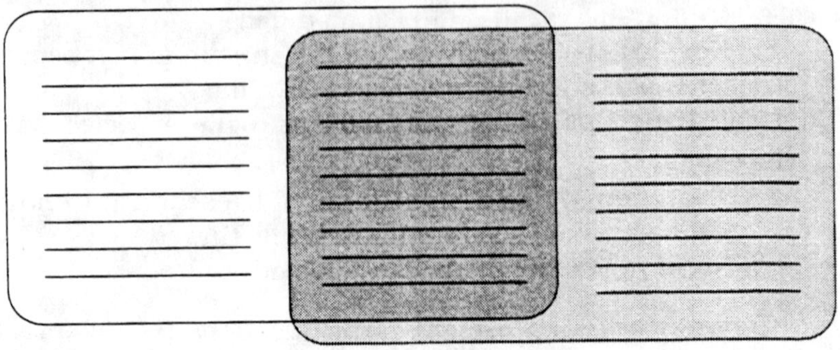

An alternate approach to scoring an essay question is to use a **holistic scoring** approach. Using this technique, the teacher reads the answer quickly and scores it as a whole without analyzing the components of the answer. Each essay is given a rating that reflects the teacher's assessment of its overall quality.

## Constructing Objective Test Items

The term *objective* in the context of testing refers to the way in which responses to a question will be graded, not to the nature of question itself. Deciding to include one item instead of another on a test to represent learning is a *subjective* judgment of the teacher.

**Objective test** items are relatively easy to grade quickly and are not susceptible to teacher bias in scoring. They also permit many objectives to be addressed in a short period of time and do not penalize students who lack verbal skills. On the other hand, objective items encourage guessing and are often more difficult and time consuming to construct than essay questions. They also afford students no opportunity to demonstrate divergent thinking.

**Types of Objective Test Items.** Types of objective test items most appropriate for use in the social studies are *multiple-choice, alternative response,* and *matching* questions. There are many variations of each form possible, as well. Several of the texts cited in the References provide comprehensive instructions on constructing each of these types.

A fourth form of objective test item, *completion* or *fill-in-the-blank* also exists, and is used by some social studies teachers. Typically, however, its use in social studies is fraught with problems. Clear and unambiguous items are difficult to construct. Also, students often can respond with many reasonable completion items, besides the correct one.

Consider, for example, this poorly constructed completion question: "__________ __________ was the author of the __________ of __________." The correct answer expected is the set of four words, "Thomas," "Jefferson," "Declaration," and "Independence." In reality, however, myriad plausible alternative sets of answers are equally correct (e.g., "John," "Steinbeck," "Grapes," and "Wrath").

An example of each of the three types of objective items recommended—*multiple-choice, alternative response,* and *matching* questions—follows, accompanied by some guidelines on the writing of the item.

*Multiple-Choice Questions.* The largest of the 50 states in terms of population is which of the following?

a. Wyoming
b. Delaware

c. West Virginia
d. Rhode Island

Some basic guidelines for writing multiple-choice questions include the following:

- The stem (the first part) should state the question or issue.
- All choices should be plausible, related, and ideally, approximately the same length.
- Use four options and avoid use of the options, "All of the above" and "None of the above," which often confuse students.
- Preferably the stem should be stated in a positive form, avoiding the use of terms such as *not* and *never.*
- Organize the stem around one idea only.

*Alternative Response Questions.* All of the following statements deal with the newspaper article you have been given. If the statement is true according to the article, circle the *T* next to it. If it is false, circle the *F.*

T F The country has been experiencing economic problems.
T F Agriculture is a major part of the economy.
T F The percentage of the population under age 20 has increased.

Some basic guidelines for writing alternative response questions include the following:

- Each statement should include a *single* point or issue.
- Statements designed to "trick" or mislead students if they do not read carefully should be avoided.
- Avoid terms such as *always, never, all, generally, occasionally,* and *every,* which signal the correct answer.

*Matching Questions.* Look at the two sets of items that follow. The set on the left lists cities, and the one on the right gives states. In front of the set of cities is a blank space. Write in each space the letter of the state that belongs with the city.

| | |
|---|---|
| ___ Denver | a. North Carolina |
| ___ Philadelphia | b. California |
| ___ Camden | c. South Carolina |
| ___ Raleigh | d. Pennsylvania |
| ___ Tampa | e. Colorado |
| ___ Los Angeles | f. Rhode Island |

___ Providence
g. Wyoming
h. New Jersey
i. Virginia
j. Florida

Some basic guidelines for writing matching items questions include the following:

- The items in each column should be related.
- The directions should state clearly what the student is to do and any special limitations on the use of choices (e.g., whether items can be used more than once).
- Generally, there should be more choices than can be matched.
- The order of the items in each set of choices should be either alphabetical or random.
- The number of items in the shorter column should be less than 10 to avoid students wasting time by searching through long lists.

### Test Software

Publishers of basal textbook programs now include computer software with banks of test items that are correlated with the subject matter of the text. This type of software allows easy modifications of tests and sharing of items with other teachers. A number of commercially developed software programs also make it possible for teachers to create an entire test. Examples are *Test Generator, Test Quest,* and *QuickTests.*

## EVALUATING REFLECTION, COMPETENCE, AND CONCERN

Effective, meaningful evaluation is transacted for some significant purpose. We conduct evaluations to determine the relative effectiveness of significant components of our instructional program and to validate student achievement.

We have suggested throughout this text that in social studies our ultimate goal should be the development of reflective, competent, and concerned citizens. Correspondingly, the evaluation system and the assessments we devise should tap each of these three dimensions of the effective citizen. Moreover, our objectives and our curricular programs should guide the character of our evaluation and assessment system, rather than the reverse.

In the preceding sections, we have considered some issues associated with evaluation and a repertoire of assessment strategies that can aid in the evaluation process. We now will examine some sample assessment items specifically related to measuring the dimensions of reflection, competence, and concern that we considered in earlier chapters. The items illustrated will include a mix of the following types of performance assessments:

test items
research sheets
teacher interviews
rating scales
cooperative learning outcomes
creation of products
checklists

Results from each of these forms of assessment may be accumulated in individual student folders. These products, or illustrative samples of them, can be reviewed periodically to evaluate student progress.

## Assessing Reflection

We have characterized reflective citizens as those who have knowledge of a body of facts, concepts, and generalizations. Reflective citizens also are capable of channeling that knowledge into action in the form of problem solving and decision making. The achievement of instructional objectives related to the development of these characteristics can be measured in a variety of ways.

Let us consider some different sample items, which are arranged by the type of assessment used. For each type, the dimension of reflection it attempts to assess is listed and an example is given.

***Using an Essay Test Question to Assess Reflection***

*Dimension:* Identification of critical attributes of a concept.

*Example:* List the criterial attributes of the concept of revolution.

***Using a Multiple-Choice Test Question to Assess Reflection***

*Dimension:* Developing a generalization from facts.

*Example:* Examine the graphs shown in Figure 13.10 and answer the questions that follow them.

*Dimension:* Forming a hypothesis.

*Example:* Look carefully at the cartoon on the overhead projector to answer this question. Circle the sentence that explains why the man is crying in the cartoon.

a. He can't find a place to sleep.
b. The people around him won't help him.
c. It is an act to generate a handout.
d. He has no inner strength.

***Using a Research Sheet to Assess Reflection***

*Dimension:* Identifying cause-effect relationships.

**Figure 13.10**
**Multiple-Choice Test Question**

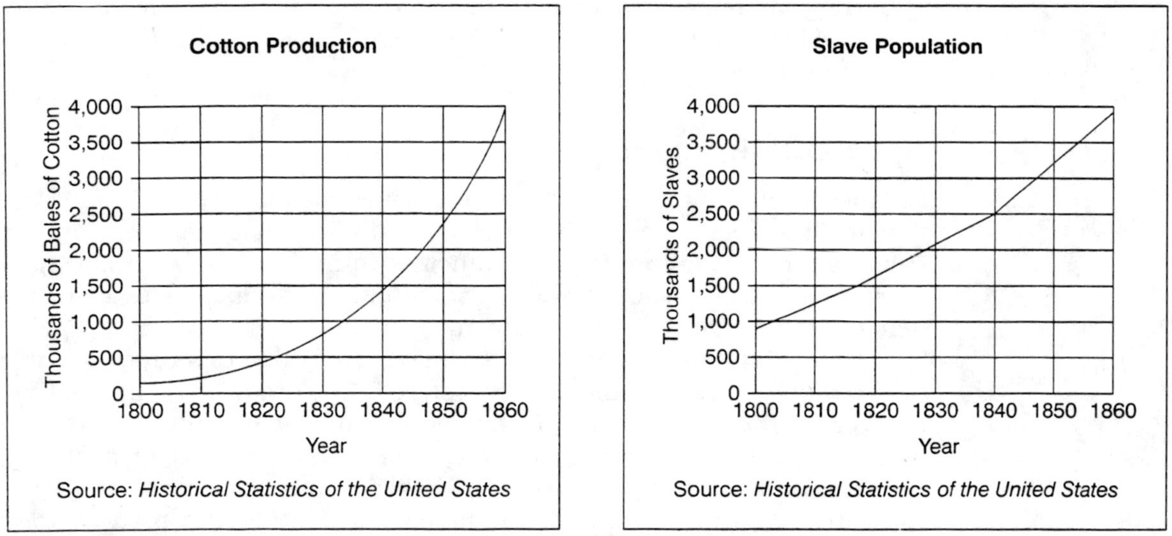


What might be concluded about the relationship between cotton production and slaves?

a. To produce more cotton, fewer slaves were needed.
b. To produce more cotton, more slaves were needed.
c. Cotton production was not related to slavery.
d. An increase in slaves caused a decrease in cotton production.

*Note.* From *Teacher's Resource Guide: The American Nation* (p. 145), 1976, Englewood Cliffs, NJ: Prentice Hall.

*Example:*

The statements below refer to events discussed on pages 686–691 of your text. Read each statement carefully. Then, for each statement write the *cause* of the event.

a. Thousands of Cubans fled their island and came to the United States.
*Cause:*
b. In the 1960s some women's groups called for "equivalent pay."
*Cause:*
c. In recent years many Hispanics have been elected to public office.
*Cause:*
d. Migrant farm workers had little chance to get an education.
*Cause:*
(*Teacher's Resource Guide*, 1986, p. D127)

*Dimension:* Relating facts and generalizations.

*Example:* Consider the following generalization: "The end of World War II caused major economic problems for the world." Identify five sets of facts that support this generalization. Record each set of facts using the Procedure Sheet that you were given for this report.

For your references, consult the books that have been set aside in the library. When you have completed the research sheet, place it in your social studies portfolio.

## Assessing Competence

Competent citizens were described earlier as having a repertoire of talents that include social, research and analysis, chronology, and spatial skills. Paper-and-pencil tests often are sufficient to measure such skills. As with many other skills in life, however, some citizen competencies can best be demonstrated through actual performance.

**Checklists** are inventories that show, from demonstrations with real tasks, which skills students have mastered. They may be completed by the teacher or the student and are especially useful for objectives that are either-or types (i.e., either the student achieved the objective or not).

**Rating scales** appear in many different forms (e.g., attitude inventories introduced in Chapter 8). Unlike checklists, they can be used to measure the *degree of progress* students have made. For example, a teacher may assess whether a student has demonstrated considerable or minimal growth in an area, rather than merely check "has made progress" or "has not made progress."

Let us examine some different sample assessment items that include checklists and rating scales. For each item, the dimension of competence it attempts to measure is listed, followed by an example.

### *Using the Creation of a Product to Assess Competence*

*Dimension:* Demonstrating map-making skills.

*Example:* Create a map that shows someone who is traveling by car from our school how to get to the Crossroads Shopping Mall. In your map, include the features listed on the attached sheet. Also, consult your compass and use it in constructing the map.

When you have completed the map, ask two people who can drive if they could locate the mall using your map. Based on their answers, make any final changes that are needed. Then place the map in your social studies portfolio.

### *Using a Checklist to Assess Competence*

*Dimension:* Use of reference materials.

*Example:* A checklist similar to the one in Figure 13.11 could be constructed to assess students' use of simple reference materials. When a student has demonstrated the skill satisfactorily, a check is made next to the student's name.

**Figure 13.11**
**Sample Checklist for Reference Sources**

**Reference Sources Checklist**

| | Mary | Bill | Tara | Fred | Jo |
|---|---|---|---|---|---|
| 1. Uses picture captions and titles to organize information | ___ | ___ | ___ | ___ | ___ |
| 2. Uses glossaries and dictionaries to identify word meaning | ___ | ___ | ___ | ___ | ___ |
| 3. Uses dictionaries as aids to pronunciation | ___ | ___ | ___ | ___ | ___ |
| 4. Uses a variety of reference works | ___ | ___ | ___ | ___ | ___ |
| 5. Uses an atlas | ___ | ___ | ___ | ___ | ___ |
| 6. Uses the telephone directory and the Yellow Pages as sources of information | ___ | ___ | ___ | ___ | ___ |
| 7. Uses an index to locate information | ___ | ___ | ___ | ___ | ___ |
| 8. Uses newspapers and magazines as sources of information | ___ | ___ | ___ | ___ | ___ |
| 9. Writes letters to obtain information | ___ | ___ | ___ | ___ | ___ |
| 10. Constructs computer databases | ___ | ___ | ___ | ___ | ___ |

***Using Rating Scales to Assess Competence***

*Dimension:* Group skills.

*Example:* Each student working within a group would be rated on each of the characteristics in Figure 13.12.

***Using the Creation of a Product and Teacher Interview to Assess Competence***

*Dimension:* Construct a time line organizing major events.

*Example:* Make a time line that shows what you think are the major events that occurred during 1929 and 1942 in the United States. Then, be prepared to explain to the teacher in a conference why you felt these events should be included.

***Using Cooperative Learning and the Creation of a Product to Assess Competence***

*Dimension:* Establishing factual claims.

*Example:* Students are assigned to a Jigsaw II cooperative learning group (see Chapter 5). Each expert is given a different sheet of factual claims that

**Figure 13.12**
**Group Participation Rating Sheet**

Student's Name ______________________ Date ____________

Group Members ____________________________________

Date Group Formed ___________

Each of the characteristics of group participation will be rated as follows:

5 = Consistently Exhibited
4 = Frequently Exhibited
3 = Occasionally Exhibited
2 = Seldom Exhibited
1 = Not Exhibited

| *Characteristics* | *Rating* |
|---|---|
| 1. Accepts ideas of others | ___ |
| 2. Initiates ideas | ___ |
| 3. Gives opinions | ___ |
| 4. Is task oriented | ___ |
| 5. Helps others | ___ |
| 6. Seeks information | ___ |
| 7. Encourages others to contribute | ___ |
| 8. Works well with all members | ___ |
| 9. Raises provocative questions | |
| 10. Listens to others | ___ |
| 11. Disagrees in a constructive fashion | ___ |
| 12. Makes an overall positive contribution to the group | ___ |
| Total Rating | ___ |

Additional Comments:

have been made concerning the Columbus voyages and their impact. Each expert is required to research the information on his or her sheet and determine what the best evidence suggests. Following the Jigsaw II procedures, each expert briefs the other members on the findings. Each group then creates a poster that lists "claims" and "facts."

## Assessing Concern

We have characterized concerned citizens as those who are aware of and exercise fully and effectively their rights and responsibilities as members of our society. They also are aware of and responsive to the larger social world around them. In addition, they are willing to make commitments and act on social issues at the local, regional, national, and international levels. Concerned citizens also establish personal priorities and make ethical decisions with respect to significant values and issues of greatest concern to them.

In assessing students' progress toward developing dimensions of concern, teachers may find tools such as checklists, research sheets, anecdotal records, and rating scales especially helpful. These instruments can be equally valuable as pretests or posttests.

Let us consider some different sample items. For the item, the dimension of concern it attempts to measure is listed, followed by an example.

### *Using a Research Sheet to Assess Concern*

*Dimension:* Perspective taking.

*Example:* From our study and discussion of the colonial period, what can you say were the attitudes of these different groups toward their experiences? List as many things as you can for each group. Then try to put yourself in the shoes of the English, the Africans, and the Indians, and offer some reasons for *why* they might have felt this way (see Figure 13.13) (Adapted from Wallen, 1974, p. 37).

### *Using an Essay Test Question to Assess Concern*

*Dimension:* Taking a stand on ethical dilemmas.

*Example:* Examine the dilemma presented in pages 110–111 of your textbook. State your position on what course of action should be taken. Then, suppose that you had taken the opposite position. What are some reasons you might have given for your stand?

When everyone is finished, we will break into groups to discuss your answers.

### *Using a Checklist to Assess Concern*

*Dimension:* Developing sensitivity to alternative points of view.

*Example:* A checklist similar to the one in Figure 13.14 could be constructed by individuals working in a group. If a student has demonstrated the behavior, a check is made next to his or her name.

## A FRAMEWORK FOR EVALUATING THE OUTCOMES OF SOCIAL STUDIES INSTRUCTION

To this point, we have been examining assessment techniques associated with evaluation. Let us now consider a scenario in which a teacher, Ms.

**Figure 13.13**
**Sample Research Sheet**

| *How the English Felt* | *Why They Felt This Way* |
|---|---|
| ____________ | ____________ |
| ____________ | ____________ |
| ____________ | ____________ |
| *How the Africans Felt* | *Why They Felt This Way* |
| ____________ | ____________ |
| ____________ | ____________ |
| ____________ | ____________ |
| *How the Native Americans Felt* | *Why They Felt This Way* |
| ____________ | ____________ |
| ____________ | ____________ |
| ____________ | ____________ |

**Figure 13.14**
**Checklist of Student Behaviors Related to Sensitivity for Alternate Points of View**

| | Tod | Abe | Jean | Rea |
|---|---|---|---|---|
| 1. Is open to new ideas | ___ | ___ | ___ | ___ |
| 2. Listens while others speak | ___ | ___ | ___ | ___ |
| 3. Is willing to change his or her mind | ___ | ___ | ___ | ___ |
| 4. Does not ridicule others' ideas | ___ | ___ | ___ | ___ |
| 5. Does not engage in name calling | ___ | ___ | ___ | ___ |
| 6. Does not reject those who disagree | ___ | ___ | ___ | ___ |
| 7. Supports others' rights to speak | ___ | ___ | ___ | ___ |
| 8. Is curious about ideas different from his or her own | ___ | ___ | ___ | ___ |

Schwartz, armed with these techniques, develops an evaluation plan from the ground up. Suppose at the beginning of the year, she is engaged in designing an evaluation framework for the first report card period.

After some reflection about her students, she decides the following assessment procedures will be appropriate and adequate as measures of their learning in social studies.

- Scores from teacher-made tests,
- Anecdotal records of class interaction,
- Checklists of group participation skills,
- Ratings on individual projects,
- Ratings on oral reports,
- Scores from a standardized test, and
- Checklists of written assignments.

The further decision she makes is related to the percentage of the total evaluation that should be assigned to each of the seven measures. Again, Ms. Schwartz made a subjective judgment. That is, she decided which indicators would be more important than others in determining student progress.

Ms. Schwartz decided that ratings of individual projects should receive the greatest weight. Her rationale was that a great deal of class time during the evaluation period would be spent on project activities. Correspondingly, she assigned the smallest percentage to a standardized test, since only one would be given, and it would cover only a small set of subject-matter objectives addressed by the course.

The sizes of the remaining five pieces were determined on a similar basis. (If Ms. Schwartz had deemed it appropriate, all of the pieces could have been of an equal size or of some other proportion.) Once she had made her decisions about the relative importance of the different components of the course, her evaluation framework, as shown in Figure 13.15, was established.

## Matching Evaluation and Instructional Goals and Objectives

In making her evaluation decisions, Ms. Schwartz looked to the goals and specific instructional objectives she had established for the social studies program. The seven elements of her evaluation framework addressed all aspects of the program considered to be important for the time period considered. These elements also encompassed those areas in which the class would spend most of its time during the evaluation period.

In addition to an evaluation pie chart, an **evaluation grid** sometimes is useful for determining whether all the teacher's goals or objectives have

**Figure 13.15**
**A Sample Evaluation Framework**

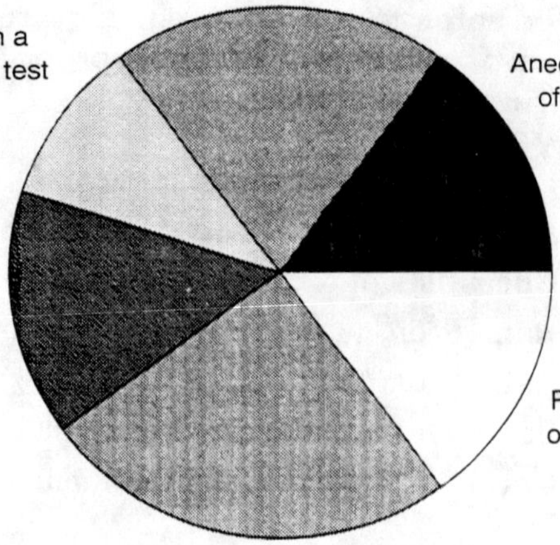


been reflected in the evaluation framework and in which ways. It involves listing all of the instructional goals or objectives that the teacher considers to have been important in one column. In the next column are matched those ways in which student achievement of the goals or objectives are to be measured (e.g., through ratings on an oral report). A portion of a sample evaluation grid is shown in Figure 13.16.

**Figure 13.16**
**Evaluation Grid**

| Important Goals | How Achievement of the Goals Will Be Assessed |
|---|---|
| Identify major ethnic groups within the United States and some of the traditions associated with each of them. | Ratings on an oral report<br>Individual projects<br>A teacher-made test |
| Learn research techniques associated with locating information from written materials. | Skill demonstrations<br>Samples of individual student papers<br>Anecdotal record |

## GROUP ACTIVITIES

1. Identify several teachers in grades 5 through 12. Show them the example of an evaluation framework in the chapter and ask them to share their own framework. Also, ask them to discuss the rationale for their decisions. Compare your findings.
2. Examine one of the standardized tests available for social studies. Note its name, the publisher, the copyright date, and the grade level at which it is used. Also identify the different forms of questions that are included (e.g., multiple choice) and the topics or subjects that it covers. Discuss your findings and reactions.
3. Locate samples of report cards or report statements that are used by local schools. Determine how well they assess the dimensions of the schools' social studies programs. Discuss your findings and conclusions.

## INDIVIDUAL ACTIVITIES

1. Consult the section in the chapter on essay tests and design an essay question for any aspect of an eighth-grade American history course. Also construct a model answer with weights for each portion of the answer.
2. Covering the same topical area as in question 2 in the group activities above, construct a multiple-choice, alternative response, and matching question. If you need further assistance, consult one of the reference works cited or a similar source from your school library.
3. Develop either a checklist or a rating scale to assess whether students have acquired some set of research and analysis, spatial, or chronology skills that you have identified as appropriate for secondary school students. Refer to Chapter 7 for a list of skills keyed to grade levels.
4. Pick any grade and a unit from a corresponding social studies basal text. Develop three performance assessments that would be appropriate for assessing how well students had learned the information in the text.

## REFERENCES

Airasian, P. (1991). *Classroom assessment.* New York: McGraw-Hill.

Armstrong, T. (1994). *Multiple intelligences in the classroom.* Alexandria, VA: Association for Supervision and Curriculum Development.

California Assessment Program. (1990). *California: The state of assessment.* Sacramento, CA: California Department of Education.

Center for Civic Education. (1994). *National standards for civics and government.* Calabasas, CA: The author.

Darling-Hammond, L., & Lieberman, A. (1992, January 29). The shortcomings of standardized tests. *The Chronicle of Higher Education,* pp. B1–B2.

Maeroff, G. I. (1991). Assessing alternative assessment. *Phi Delta Kappan, 73,* 272–281.

Mitchell, R. (1992). *Testing for learning: How new approaches to evaluation can improve America's schools.* New York: Free Press.

National Council for Geographic Education. (1994). *National geography education standards.* Washington, DC: The author.

National Council for the Social Studies. (1991). *Testing and evaluation of social studies students.* Washington, DC: Author.

National Council for the Social Studies. (1994). *Curriculum standards for the social studies.* Washington, DC: Author.

National Geographic Society (1994). *Geography for life: National Geography Standards.* Washington, DC: Author.

Perrone, V. (Ed.). (1991). *Expanding student assessment.* Alexandria, VA: Association for Supervision and Curriculum Development.

Popham, W. J. (1988). *Educational evaluation* (2nd ed.). Englewood Cliffs, NJ: Prentice Hall.

Scott, Foresman Social Studies. (1983). *America past and present: Teacher's edition workbook.* Glenview, IL: Author.

*Teacher's resource guide: The American nation.* (1986). Englewood Cliffs, NJ: Prentice Hall.

TenBrink, T. D. (1994). Evaluation. In J. Cooper et al., *Classroom teaching skills* (5th ed.). Lexington, MA: D. C. Heath.

Wallen, N. E. (1974). *Getting together with people.* Reading, MA: Addison-Wesley.

Williams, P. L., & Moore, J. R. (Eds.). (1980). *Criterion- referenced testing for the social studies.* Bulletin No. 64. Washington, DC: National Council for the Social Studies.

# Index